PHILIPPINES

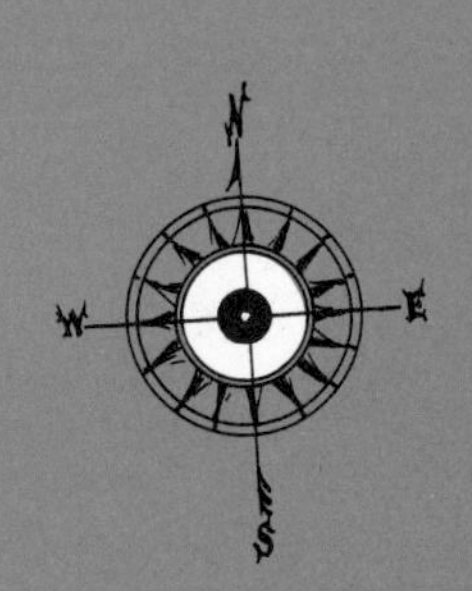

PACIFIC OCEAN

es Sea

Molucca Is.

Manado

EQUATOR

Australian New Guinea

Sukarnapura

West Irian

Wamena

INDONESIA

Banda Sea

Arafura Sea

Indonesian (Port.) Timor

AUSTRALIA

FIVE JOURNEYS FROM JAKARTA

Inside Sukarno's Indonesia

President Sukarno with No. 2 wife Madam Hartini and entourage visit the Javanese village of Sukabumi (see page 340).

MASLYN WILLIAMS

FIVE JOURNEYS FROM JAKARTA

Inside Sukarno's Indonesia

WILLIAM MORROW & COMPANY
New York, 1965

By the same author

THE STONE AGE ISLAND: New Guinea Today

 Published simultaneously in Canada by George J. McLeod Limited, Toronto. Printed in the United States of America. Library of Congress Catalog Card Number 66-11592.

For Cooney

"I feel somewhat troubled because I am conscious of the size of the responsibility I hold. I know that in your hearts you ask 'What is the President going to enjoin upon us . . . what will the Great Leader counsel?' I know that this is awaited with beating hearts filled with hope. I know, too, that this address is heard by the whole world. Is pried upon and spied upon by a part of the world. I wrote the speech with a pounding heart. Frankly I tell you here that several times I had to change the paper since from time to time I could not stay my tears."

Sukarno
Independence Day, 1962

"I will quote again the Blessing–Message of the President–Great Leader of Our Revolution: 'Do not sell thy soul for a plate of nuts.' "

General Sutjipto
Secretary–General to the
Conference of Supporters
to the Revolution Leadership

Contents

List of Maps

Foreword

Indonesia is a muddled country, but this is a muddled age and a state of confusion is no disgrace. It is a lovely country, rich in colorful accretions of Eastern culture, and prolific (its women are a paradigm of fecundity). The men are pleasant, generous, easy to get along with.

The president of Indonesia, Sukarno, is something new in modern politics: an Asian folk hero, a father figure, a warrior-prophet, and a nuisance. There is, I think, a tendency among Westerners, which I share, to overrate his present importance to Indonesia and his significance as a key figure in world politics. He is human and mortal, and the busiest people in Jakarta today are those who prepare for his death and the subsequent scramble for the fragments of his authority.

Yet neither he nor his people can be written off as of no account: the confrontation of Malaysia, alone, makes for danger on a world scale and should be understood. And (let us face it) if we cling to a dream of One World, our vision must include Asia and even admit that Asia may have something essential to contribute which we ourselves are lacking.

Sukarno believes this and he may be right. To Afro-Asian leaders at Bandung he said, "We can make exchange with the advanced countries . . . can extend to them our ideas for their material things." The thought is more than fanciful, and when opportunity came, with publisher's money and Indonesian agreement, for me to travel four months freely in this country and to range yet more widely than I had done before, it seemed both sensible and neighborly for an Australian to profit by the offer.

The Indonesian departments of Foreign Affairs and Information both gave more assistance than I had a right to expect, and my conscience is not altogether easy in that this book is no courteous *quid pro quo*. But I found it not easy to fit into the Indonesian scene or to accept Asian ways and levels of subsistence, although I was willing enough, God knows, to try and was given every easement by the people, equally in the capital and in provincial towns and villages. So if this book pays no compliment to the state of Indonesia it is at least written with good intent and much affection for its people.

I have taken the liberty, at the risk of irritating readers, of interposing extracts from a few letters written, during my five journeys, to a lady of my acquaintance; not that they uncover any additional dimension of analysis, but because they may serve to point up the sense of isolation and perplexity that often possessed me and so give focus and perspective to opinions written sometimes under stress.

M. W.

PART I

Prologue

Flight Q/F 733, out of Sydney
Destination Jakarta
Distance 3,086 nautical miles
Flying time 7½ hours
E.T.A. Jakarta 1800 hours

We fly at 31,000 feet with an air speed of 580 miles an hour. The flight is so smooth that we seem motionless, suspended in an empty sky. Down below, in contradiction, like a fly crawling across a soiled winding sheet, the minute shadow of our aircraft slides swiftly over the lifeless landscape of Australia's empty center. The temperature on the ground at this time of the day will be around 120 degrees fahrenheit; it is seven years since it rained down there.

Here in the comfort and security of the aircraft, two and one half hours out from Sydney and five hours yet from Jakarta, luncheon is being cleared away.

In the seat across the aisle, just ahead of me, there is an Australian—a big, red-faced fellow with yellow hair. Already at the airport bar, he has told me about himself. He is a mechanic, specializing in the maintenance of heavy earth-moving equipment. He is going to Indonesia on contract to look after the machinery being used to clear large areas of Borneo jungle where the Indonesian government plans to settle thousands of landless peasants from the overcrowded islands of Bali and Java. The machinery that he will look after is a gift from the Australian people to the people of Indonesia. I said to him in the bar, joking, "Are you sure that you are not going to build airstrips for the Crush Malaysia program?"

He suddenly turned livid and primitive. "Don't say things like that to me, mate. I'm an Australian. If these bastards want to start a war with Britain they'll get their arses kicked well and truly, and I'll be one of those who'll do the kicking." He picked up his beer and moved away from me, along the bar, muttering and looking very angry.

The ferocity of his reaction made me feel numb and empty inside, and I cursed my stupid sense of humor and taking my drink went and sat against the glass wall of the waiting room, overlooking the tarmac. And when we were called to board the aircraft I let him get well ahead, not wishing to tangle with him again.

Since take-off he has been drinking with earnest diligence, as is the Australian practice, introspectively without thought of enjoyment. There is nothing of the Middle-European element of levity in Australian drinking, nor of the American neuro-psychic approach to the use of alcohol. With us it is a serious business, almost a religion.

But the beer has done him good. For the past hour he has been making simple, unproductive efforts to establish an intimacy with the hostesses. Being accustomed to Australian men they take no notice, knowing that so long as he has a drink in his hand he will stay tractable and content like a baby sucking a comforter. One of them leans across him to take away his luncheon tray and his eyes, a little dimmed with alcohol, try to focus on the line of her bust. But when a second girl passes with a tray of liquors (free to first-class passengers) his gaze shifts automatically and swiftly, and he puts out a hand to prevent her passing.

She has been avoiding him for the past fifteen minutes but the aircraft is half-empty and she cannot pretend to be continuously busy. She proffers the tray without smiling but he is not discouraged and makes great play of choosing and appeals to her to help him. She hands him cherry brandy. The young Indonesian sitting beside me watches this air-borne Western grotesquerie with wide eyes. In Asia there is decorum and a strict division between a man's public and private attitudes toward women. There is no overlapping.

The young man's name is Nissen. He is slim, neat, brown, and twenty-three years old, a student librarian going home after a year of postgraduate study in New Zealand. He is an enthusiastic and visionary young man who speaks eagerly, in capital letters, of The Indonesian People—Our Revolution—and The Nation's Great Leader. Already, in the short time we have been in this airplane, I have come to know him quite well although my interest in him is carefully tentative and devoid of real feeling. I find that I get too easily caught up in other people's dreams and delusions.

He has invited me to spend some time with his family at their summer home at Bogor, in the hills beyond Jakarta. He says that his father, a government official, has a guest pavilion and that I will be most welcome. We will get up each morning before dawn and go fishing. It is a five-mile bicycle ride to the river, through the hillside tea plantations and terraced rice fields; and the road is steep. We agree that as I am no longer young I might find this exhausting, but Nissen thinks that he will be able to borrow a car for these excursions. Many of his friends are students and will want to take the opportunity of practicing their English. One of them will no doubt be able to borrow a car. Already, for Nissen, the idea has become a reality.

We discuss the project in detail though I know that the moment the aircraft touches down at Jakarta this present intimacy will cease, and if by chance I meet him in the street tomorrow I shall find it difficult to recognize his face or remember his name: like many white people I find it difficult to distinguish one casual colored acquaintance from another. Indonesian friends tell me that they have the same problem of identifying casual white acquaintances.

But I have become interested in the girl whose photograph he carries in his wallet. She and Nissen are engaged to be married. The picture is a colored postcard with serrulated edges and it shows a thin, white, fair girl, slightly round-shouldered, dressed as a bridesmaid. She wears a short-sleeved, ballerina-length blue frock trimmed with black ribbons, and holds a bouquet of pink carnations to her breast. The pose is rather affected and old-fashioned. She is without a hat but has a small floral arrangement on top of her head which gives her an odd, elongated look.

I hold the picture in my hand, and she stares steadfastly at me with the fragile defiance of an unsophisticated middle-class girl who has been taught from infancy that women are born to sorrow.

Looking at the photograph I am reminded of the sentimental greeting cards which were popular in Europe at the turn of the century and which can still be bought second or third hand at many of the bookstalls on the banks of the Seine. I have a friend in New York who collects them.

The girl's name is Angela and her father is a small-town storekeeper, a deacon and a lay preacher of the Fundamental and Evangelical Church of New Zealand, that little land of apples and fat lambs. Nissen is a Moslem, and ever since he showed me the photograph I have been wondering how so simple and inexperienced a girl will fit, without discomfort to herself or embarrassment to Nissen and his relatives, into the context of Indonesian Islamic family life with its tight-knit and intricate complex of genealogical relationships, obligations, and responsibilities. I feel sorry for her, perhaps irrationally, and can find nothing sensible to say while looking at the picture and am glad when the hostess interrupts to take away our trays. Nissen replaces it carefully in his wallet, then excuses himself and goes off to sit for a while with an Indonesian friend further back in the aircraft, leaving me with an irritating sense of failure and guilt.

I am annoyed with myself. It would have been easy enough to have been a little enthusiastic, to have simulated happy surprise, or at least to have made some simple congratulatory sound to cover up my doubts. There is little merit in this niggling negative honesty, determinedly worn like a discipline.

But in a while my mind quiets.

Flying at this height and sitting alone, with no external stimuli to activate the imagination, one becomes detached and acquiescent—achieves a sense of remoteness and psychical isolation which is part of the phenomenon of modern air travel. One has left one place behind without reaching another and what lies between is timeless and irrelevant, nor is there any real connection with the environment (the inside of an airplane is totally unemotional).

I am relaxed—no longer split by a multiplicity of compulsive and conflicting urgencies, limbs and fingers no longer animated into trivial reflex activities—but because of this passivity the voice of the Englishman in the seat behind me has assumed a stereophonic quality.

He is saying, "There is still money to be made in Southeast Asia but we must realize that as we no longer pay the piper we cannot call the tune. The Asian people have felt the excitement of independence. They are enjoying the novelty of being able to shop around in the international super-markets spending their own money, even if much of it is borrowed. They no longer have to buy British or Dutch or French as they did when they were colonies. But nations are still people and consequently creatures of habit, and when they have shopped around and are ready to spend their money they mostly go back to the tradesmen they know. But still we have to understand that their independence has bought a new relationship, and that now we must meet the customer half way."

This Englishman lives in a two-storied, red brick house in Kent with a clean, green-fingered wife who wears tweeds and grows roses, winning the prize year after year at Saint Swithin's Harvest Festival with a Mixed Bowl or Any Other Variety. They have two children, a boy and a girl, who go to good schools and are no trouble except that the girl gets chilblains in winter. A nice family, to whom two hundred million Southeast Asians are simply "Daddy's customers." His order book, together with market reports and foreign exchange tables, is in the briefcase under his seat. In three days he will be home again.

And the yellow-headed mechanic from Australia, asleep now with his head thrown back and softly whiffling through wet lips, will soon settle without trouble into his job in the jungle. Quite soon he will develop a patronal affection for the Indonesian people (Australians, like Americans, are desperately sentimental) although sometimes, feeling unaccountably restless and a little lonely, he will complain that the country is barbarous and uncivilized and that the beer has no flavor. Then he will go off to Balikpapan and find a girl to take to bed and next day will feel better.

Six days a week he will work hard, stripped down to a pair of greasy shorts and rubber scuffs, teaching young men by eager example the ways of his trade, and he will boast openly and loudly to other white men that his lads are the best in the business and equal to any at home. But let him hear one of these same lads speak, even in jest, against Malaysia or disparage Britain, and his sentimentality, outraged and inadequate to deal with reality, will turn to violence. His plain, pink face will become ugly and his voice harsh, and he will curse all Indonesians vulgarly and blindly without quite knowing why. And for a while, full of resentment and self-protective anger, he will treat the young men brusquely and will stubbornly stay away from Balikpapan, not able to share his anger with any Indonesian, male or female.

And what about myself, instinctively worried for the white girl who is going to marry Nissen? What is the justification for my concern, what logic in the undefined assumption that she is making some shocking, elemental sacrifice in marrying an Asian man? Always this feeling that there are two kinds of human beings, we and they—white people and others—and that in some preordained way we are superior: the Englishman, the yellow-haired mechanist, and me.

Why?

Extract from a letter
Written in flight
Sydney to Jakarta

I don't seem to have made a very good start to this journey, having already upset one man, disappointed another, and become impatient of a third. I am obviously setting out under the wrong astral conjunction and am out of tune with the universe; or perhaps simply disjointed in spirit, not sure that I want to make this journey at all or, if I do want to make it, why? To be truthful, I feel faintly ridiculous and entirely inadequate in the role of Diogenes and already lonely without you.

So, as usual, I turn back to you in spirit, knowing that as I talk and you listen the uncertainties will diminish and that even if the answers still fail to project themselves sharply, the conviction will return that there *are* answers and that, in time, they will be found. This, surely, is what keeps us all going—the certainty that there is a sensible pattern somewhere and an ultimate resolution. It is what makes our stupidities seem no more than passing stupid and our shame endurable.

So I am going to Indonesia to look for a truth which will satisfy me; for I do not believe that the wars and mass murders and blundering destruction of the past fifty years have no more meaning than a collection of newspaper headlines and commentaries. Nor do I believe that bland, official handouts are an adequate explanation of what is happening to us or where we are going. If the travail of the past half-century has produced nothing more than a magnification and rearrangement of old hates and extravagant nationalistic ambitions, then we must all accept that the bomb is the logical and proper climax to human evolution: the inevitable self-destruction of a civilization that has outlived its relevance.

It seems to me that in many countries leadership has become simply a public profession, like shop-keeping or prostitution, and that its attributes are no longer faith, hope, conviction, and courage but caution and equivocation. And the churches have failed us, too, making of our living religion a part-time, ritualistic fill-in for peasants (although in both fields of faith, secular and religious, two notable exceptions of this century spring to mind in John the President and John the Pope). But, you ask me, what has this to do with my journey? Simply this:

I do not wish to accept any more ready-made judgments thrust upon me by professional politicians and glib commentators. I should like to choose my own hates and resentments, to pick my own goals and the means of reaching them. For I begin to feel certain that our only hope of dodging the bomb (I use the word figuratively) is for the people of the whole world to enter into a dialogue of faith and friendship and protestation so insistent and so loud that it will drown out the tatty catch-cries bellowed into microphones, the appeals to cupidity or fear, the loud-mouthed promises made by thimble-and-pea politicians who line up to recite their lines whenever the party masters give the command.

I am going to Indonesia because it could be true that in the Afro-Asian countries the original impetus, the dynamic of human continuity, has been kept alive through the past three centuries of suppression; that in their "backwardness" they are nearer to the original truths than we are; that the violence and seeming anarchy and confusion (a pale reflection of our own atrocities) are the natural and inevitable extravagances of people suddenly released from a long and debasing bondage.

We of the West lost the track at the time of the Industrial Revolution. It is possible that if we go back a way and join our "emerging" neighbors on some common ground we may pick it up again and go on together, stronger, safer, and surer than we are now. And while the leaders on both sides build protective fences around their areas of disagreement, let the people find among themselves other areas of common need, understanding, and affection.

I am going, then, on a pilgrimage to meet my neighbor. It may do good to nobody but myself but I am a person, a created thing with the right to be me: not a guinea pig, dumb and expendable. I do not look forward to these many months without seeing you. The country is fidgety and suspicious and full of tensions, especially in Jakarta since the burning of the British embassy. Western opinion is impatient of Indonesian policies, and the Indonesian people are resentful and on the defensive with foreigners, complaining that we have a completely negative attitude toward their problems. It would be easier to respect this resentment if President Sukarno could be persuaded to drop his policy of confrontation against Malaysia.

The Indonesian government has promised to smooth my way as much as it can but admits that communications are inadequate and run down, so that it may all be physically difficult and discouraging; inevitably, then, I will miss you more than usually.

M.

Sometime tomorrow, if he is on duty, I will see Soejono. He is a Clerk at the Hotel Indonesia (everything at the Hotel Indonesia is in capital letters, including the prices). Soejono and I have been friends since the night two years ago he took off his uniform and took me to a football game played between Jakarta and Sourabaya in the Sukarno Stadium. It was a strange and unsettling experience for me, being the only white person in a crowd of forty or fifty thousand. I felt vaguely afraid (being timid by nature) and could not concentrate on the play; but after the game, Soejono took me to the room where he lives with his wife—two other families share the little house—and they gave me my first real Indonesian meal. Afterward they introduced me to a man who had a spare room in his house, and the next day I left the hotel. Since then I have stayed with this man whenever I have been in Jakarta.

Besides being a booking clerk, Soejono writes verses, some of which I have helped him translate and paraphrase. It is pretty elementary stuff, but it indicates the lines along which many Indonesian people are thinking (especially the younger generation) since they freed themselves from the Dutch. There is a piece he calls, "Before the Time of the Coming of the Barbarians." This is it:

> Many stories of my country
> Are found in the lontar leaves[1]

[1] Lontar leaves are strips of palm, shaped like rulers, generally an inch or so wide and something over a foot long. Much Indonesian literature and history has been inscribed over the years on these leaves, in Sanskrit, Arabic, and old local languages, especially Javanese and Balinese. The leaves are threaded together on string to make volumes.

(The books of our ancestors)
Written many centuries ago in Sanskrit,
The language of scholars, priests, and poets,
When the people of the West
Were still primitive.

The lontar leaves tell of our ancestors,
How they traded with the people of China,
Of Malaccar and Madagascar.
Rich merchants from India and Arabia
Came in big ships to do business with us,
While the people of Europe
Were riding in coracles.

The masts of a thousand foreign ships
Made a forest of sticks
In the Musi River at Palembang,
Where they lay among their reflections.
And in that city there were many monasteries,
And a university, famous from China to Sailan[2]
For the teaching of religion and linguistics
When white people
Had little learning.

Have you seen our temple at Borobodour,
A wonder to the whole world,
Built by architects and craftsmen of Java
More than a thousand years ago
In honor of the Lord Buddha?
The writing on the lontar leaves
Tells how it was built:
But afterward, when the barbarians[3] came,
There was no more writing.

It is not unusual for truth to become fractured under the impact of patriotism, and God knows there is little enough fact in much that passes as history, let alone in a young man's occasional verses; yet it was through Soejono the reception clerk, and not through politicians or administrators (although they were all kind

2 Sailan equals Ceylon (Indonesian).

3 The barbarians referred to by Soejono are, of course, the Portuguese, Spanish, Dutch, and English explorers and adventurers who came to the Indonesian islands in the fifteenth century.

to me), that I first began to perceive, in part, the historical validity of the Indonesian attitude toward the Western world. And it was sitting with him in his little room, working over his verses while his wife cooked the meal on a charcoal brazier in the passageway, that I glimpsed in the young man's lines persuasive flashes of fact and forgotten truth that had long been lost under the lumber of three hundred years of foreign occupation. I became aware, too, of a depth and delicacy of pride that had been long suppressed and had become so sensitive that it flinched under any rough touch of thoughtlessness or flamed out in quick and bitter resentment against ill-considered arrogance or even misunderstanding. And I felt the anxious desire for complete recognition and total friendship (not charity or politically motivated philanthropy), unspoken in the dignity and the sweetness of his lovely young wife and his friends and neighbors.

Like many of his generation, first fruits of the revolution, Soejono had looked back into the past to find his own beginnings, to fix a point from which he and his friends could begin again, with dignity, to live equally with all others in this world. So it was easy to overlook the brash comparisons in the tag lines of his verses, remembering that up until the fifteenth century the patterns of international trade had made the islands of Indonesia one of the busiest mercantile centers the world has known, principal staging place in the commerce which flowed with the trade winds, back and forth, between the countries ruled by the Abyssinian kings and the sultans of Zanzibar and Madagascar and those of the great emperors of China. So that Soejono's vision of a thousand ships swinging in the river at Palembang, although having the fragility of make believe, came closer to historical accuracy than his simple rhetoric would suggest.

Great fleets of merchant ships did indeed lie there in the wide, yellow-black river at Palembang and in other Indonesian ports, for weeks and sometimes months on end waiting for the wind to change or the doldrums to end—ships from China, the Philippines, India, Ceylon, and Africa, bigger ships, some of them, than any that sailed at that time out of European ports. Some of these vessels, designed especially to withstand typhoons and tornadoes in the China seas, were solidly built of Siberian fir, with hulls three and four planks thick. The biggest had private cabin accommodations for a hundred passengers, with auxiliary rooms for wives, children, and servants. They grew vegetables on board and carried dried meat, fish, and preserved eggs for provender.

While waiting for the winds to change, the foreign merchants built themselves warehouses, offices, and shops, and some set up homes with local women so that many respectable men had one family in their own country and another in some Indonesian port (a Moslem being allowed four legal wives and the Chinese traditionally considerate about concubines). Each port town had its foreign colonies, consulates, banking houses, mosques, shrines, and temples, besides Indonesians from other parts of the archipelago—Javanese, Sumatrans, Buginese, Balinese, Moluccans, and Achinese. So it would be true that many Indonesians of that time were much-traveled, learned, steeped in a mixture of many cultures, and sophisticated while the arts and crafts of the Indies were then richer, more various and elegant that those of northern Europe.

Nevertheless, I matched Soejono's touchy pride, protesting at his making crude barbarians of my own ancestors (we already had an admiral in the family, that far back, or so my mother claimed), but it was true enough that the people of the North Atlantic seaboard, stretching from Scotland down to Spain, were then among the most isolated, insular, and unsophisticated of all the people of the civilized world, remote from the main centers of international trade and politics, and furthest from the chief seats of learning and knowledge; and like most isolated people, they were tight-minded, bigoted, ignorant, continuously at war with each other and, in consequence, chronically impoverished.

Their nearest centers of international commerce were those which lay at the end of the great trade routes spanning Asia and Eastern Europe—the mercantile cities of Venice, Alexandria, Aleppo, and the rest. In these markets the rich or their agents could buy intricate ornaments of gold and silver set with pearls or precious stones from India, Siam, and Ceylon. Traders from far-eastern parts of Asia and the sea-kingdoms of the Malayan archipelago brought silks, sable, and ermine furs, ebony, teak, and sandalwood, spices, ivory, tiger's teeth, and the skins of tigers, leopards, and bears. Apothecaries in these ports sold strange, expensive medicines—crocodile gall to make child-bearing easy, and powdered rhinoceros horn as a specific against impotency in aging males (the English refused to believe in any such creature as the rhinoceros and stubbornly insisted that only the unicorn grew a single horn possessing such cogent powers). European gentlemen of fashion could buy live monkeys to amuse the ladies, and sailors sold for curiosity little dead griffins made to look like mummified human midgets. In side alleys and along the quays parrots, hornbills, macaws, and other gaudy birds could be bought, and little black boys who made sweet-natured slaves and body servants.

This rich and sophisticated trade came from the East by two routes. One was the southern seaway which passed among the islands of Indonesia, crossed the Indian Ocean to Ceylon, then went up into the Persian Gulf or the Red Sea (where its traffic ran the gauntlet of Saracen pirates), and afterward by camel train across Arabia and into the Mediterranean. The other main stream came overland by caravan from China, skirting the northern border of Tibet to pass through southern Russia, so into Asia Minor and the Levant.

The land routes were long, with banditry (a "respectable" profession) adding its own tolls to the tally of official imposts, duties, levies, bribes, and tributes, so that prices were multiplied many times over; and with Moslems in control of most of the Mediterranean, Western traders at the best of times could only nibble at the fringes of this rich international commerce (although the Venetian merchants Maffeo, Niccolo, and Marco Polo were notable exceptions, being more than friendly with the great Mongol Emperor Kublai Khan, and free to come and go as they pleased).

I should have known all this long before Soejono taught me; I should at least have learned something of Asia and its history at school in Australia, along with the names and dates of European kings and queens, and the calendar of Christian saints and the voyages of Columbus, Cook, Magellan, and the rest. But I knew little or nothing of it—only that Christian crusaders, returning home over the years from campaigns against Islam, told fabulous tales full of the wealth and wonder of lands lying far over on the eastern coasts of the world and of legendary islands where spices grew almost wild; tales that set covetousness and money-hunger running in the blood of the frequently impecunious European kings, made merchants impatient and itchy-fingered, and plagued the imagination of priests eager to gather all sinners, known or unknown, into the fold of Christendom. So that eventually they cried out together, "Let us find a new way, a safe way, into Asia and the coasts of Cathay, that we may become rich and powerful, and that sinners may be saved."

Together they studied the maps, sought out philosophers, geographers, and seafarers who might give advice and enlighten them in this undertaking. They built new ships and sailed from the ports of Portugal, Spain, England, and Holland, and found not only a new westward sea route to Asia (discovering the Americas on the way) but, braving the southern cape of Africa, found yet a second seaway into Asia.

The whole world now lay open and exposed to Europe's quarrelsome monarchs and mercantile adventurers (to say nothing of the priests), and their rivalries swiftly followed through the new sea routes into southern and southeastern Asia. Under the guise of trading posts they established forts and strongholds. By bribery, violent treacheries, and ruthless cheating they broke up the old trading arrangements, the liaisons and loyalties of many centuries, reduced and divided a dignified civilization, and in its place created a number of abject vassal states—India, Ceylon, Burma, Malaya, the Philippines, and Indonesia.

That is the story as Soejono sees it, not in those words, but deeply and with that meaning. It is the story that is being written into the history of a hundred million Indonesians. But to me it seems a shade too facile, too one-sided, not taking into account much that was weak and unequal in the old civilization. I am not so sure that I go along with this story the whole way even if the "historical facts" are technically correct (and admitting the ruthlessness of the Imperialists). It could be that the old civilization of Asia was rotten underneath, unjust, inefficient in every way and due for extinction in the normal course of mankind's development. It could even be that the white superiority is still not only a fact but a demonstrable fact.

Soon we will be over the coast of Java and in a little while will reach Jakarta. Australia is a long way behind. We have passed over the Timor Sea. Underneath us now the Indian Ocean reflects the late-slanting sun like smoothly burnished pewter. The passengers stretch and stir and look at their watches to check the time (we have advanced two hours). The Australian wakes, yawns, and looks around for the hostess to bring him another beer. Nissen comes back to his seat and begins to gather up the last-minute shopping that he brought on board, gifts for his family.

Fasten seat belts.

The aircraft turns in over the coast, slants across the ships in the outer harbor, and drops down over the city. Roof-tile red and the brilliant living green of tropical grass, and palm trees crowding the edge of the airport. It is like coming in low over a village. Boxlike huts with palm-mat walls and dirt floors huddled together at the end of the landing field, leaning one against the other for support. Branchless papaya trees with clusters of green and yellow fruit hanging at the top under a few sparse leaves. Bananas. Chickens scrabbling in the dust and brown dogs with lean ribs foraging without enthusiasm. Naked babies sitting on the bare ground scratching patterns with pieces of stick. Alongside the runway, as we roar along with flaps standing upright and quivering in the slipstream, two men sickle the long grass and hang it upon sticks. They have paid some official for the right to do this and will sell the grass to men in the villages who have oxen or ponies to feed.

Near some tin sheds there is a nest of slender antiaircraft guns, pointing like pencils into the sky. Each gun has a low wall of sandbags round it. Nissen cranes forward to watch through the window as we touch down but makes no comment as the guns flash past. But we can hear the Englishman behind us. "They come from Czechoslovakia, not paid for, of course, and they don't work. No spare parts. It's the same with everything in this country." There is no malice in his voice, no ill will, not even condescension. Just complacency and the certainty that everything here is inferior and of no consequence.

Outside is a hot, gusty wind full of dry dust. It tugs at the row of flags flying on high staffs in front of the airport. There are more than fifty of these flags, half of them Indonesian (red and white) and the other half Russian. Nissen says that Mikoyan has come from Moscow to visit the president. It is, he says, a matter of armaments. Walking across the tarmac we pass aircraft belonging to the Indonesian air force. Some of them come from Russia, others from the United States, and some from Britain.

Young men in uniform are at every gateway and entrance and walk about in the foyer. All of them carry automatic rifles and look serious, but there is no trouble. One wonders why this charade of armed watchfulness should be necessary and suspects that it is a matter of keeping the young men employed. But the girls at the currency control tables are friendly and smiling, and the customs clerk marks my bags without asking me to open them. Outside in the foyer a gesticulating taxi driver aims his way at me through the crowd.

"You go where?"

"Kebajoran."

"Five thousand rupiah."

"Don't be silly."

"How much?"

"One thousand."

"Okay."

He takes up my bags and pushes back through the crowd. His car is very old and painted a vivid green with plain house paint. None of the windows can be adjusted. One of the back doors is tied shut with rope. He is clearly not a licensed driver, and this is not a registered cab. But people must eat. This is the first rule of the Republic. The West can afford to insist on standards of administrative order and efficiency, can even make a fetish of it, but here the first need is to survive, and after that to try to catch up with a technological civilization which was developed while generation after generation of Indonesians was held to a level of a medieval peasantry.

It is easy for us of the West to criticize. It is also, of course, just as easy to make too many excuses. And it is going to be difficult to recognize the truth that I am seeking.

PART II

Jakarta

CHAPTER

1

I lay in the dark on a narrow bed covered only with a sheet, listening, while my senses slowly explored their whereabouts. The air was heavy with the scent of frangipani, and somewhere quite close by there was a dull thumping sound, muffled and without echo or resonance. Then the soft, stupid cooing of a dove, and after that a slow, strained, creaking sound of a heavy wooden door being slowly opened.

I recognized the instrumentation; the creaking sound was made by a strange purple and green lizard (about eight inches long) which lives in the ceiling of this house. The thumping was Nah, the servant, pounding maize to mix with the breakfast rice—an economic measure advocated by the president. The dove hangs in a wicker cage above her head, complaining, in the narrow passageway that runs between the family portion of the house and the domestic area.

Memories of other mornings came into place as I waited for the Muezzin to call from the great mosque at Kebajoran (his voice is recorded on tape and played through loudspeakers fixed in the minaret). Then the sun would rise and it would be daylight again in Jakarta.

Last night, when I arrived, Nah gave me a message from my host, a minor government official, to say that he had gone to a conference in the provinces, that he would be back in a day or two, but meanwhile would I make myself comfortable. So I had unpacked and given Nah some things to put in the store cupboard: canned cheese, powdered milk, meat concentrates—things difficult to come by in Jakarta and in any case too expensive for the ordinary wage-earner. For my host I had brought razor blades and shaving cream, toilet paper, and a shirt. For Nah and the niece who helps with the laundry and the housework (a pretty and provocative girl from a village in West Java) I had some cotton stuffs with which they could make clothes for themselves. They had taken them with wide eyes and, having gone into the tiny room beside the kitchen where they live, had stood fingering the material and stroking it. When I went to sleep they were still whispering.

Now I heard Nah put aside the mortar and pestle with which she had been pounding the maize and begin to move about between the little kitchen and the dining room, setting breakfast although it was still not properly daylight. She called softly to her niece and soon afterward I heard water splashing somewhere out in the backyard. The girl would be bathing, using an old saucepan with which to dip water from a concrete tank in the bathhouses and pour it over herself. The water would be running down like thin silk over her tea-colored skin.

I got up and hung the mosquito net over the wires that run across the room, then pushed open the wooden window shutters to look at the morning. A ginger cat stepped past me into the room and dropped onto the floor, a thin-flanked, lean-hipped animal with no tail and tight, protuberant testicles. It stalked stiffly on tiptoe across the room, crying harshly for food. It loves nobody but itself, this arrogant, ill-mannered cat. It makes me shudder. I hate it.

I have stayed in this house often since Soejono introduced me to my host, the government official, with whom he had some casual business acquaintance. My host is a dignified and quiet man. I find it difficult to believe that he has spent much of his life in prison or concentration camps. Here in Java, when he was still a young man, not long out of school, the Dutch put him into solitary confinement for activities connected with his position on the committee of an Indonesian national mass education movement; after that he spent ten years of exile as a political prisoner in the swamp lands of West Irian (then Netherlands New Guinea) where among his fellow-prisoners were Hatta, later first vice-president of the Republic, Sjahrir, the first prime minister, and Lukman, at that time a small child exiled with his parents and now first deputy secretary-general of the Indonesian Communist Party, the PKI.

Eventually, when the Pacific war made it necessary for the Dutch to remove their political prisoners from New Guinea, my host spent some time in a prisoner-of-war camp in Australia (Lukman's mother died in this camp); but I have never heard him speak against the Dutch, or against anybody for that matter, except that now and again he mutters, almost apologetically, that some of today's Nationalists seem more concerned with their own security and advancement than with the problems of the nation. But elderly men talk this way anywhere, especially if they have not been successful.

The Dutch, having done penance for a period, seem to have been forgiven, their sins remitted and filed away under the heading of history, to give place to a continuous niggling criticism of America and Britain and, of course, an obsessive condemnation of Malaysia.

It begins early in the morning on the radio. First the national anthem, "Indonesia Raja Merdeka," then the hate song, "Crush Malaysia" ("Ganjang Malaysia"). It goes on all through the day, and each day every newspaper runs a statement or speech which praises the President, attacks Malaysia, condemns or ridicules the Tunku Abdul Rahman, and glorifies the young volunteers who are training to liberate Malaya from the Imperialists.

It is part of a calculated campaign of indoctrination—textbook stuff, childishly elementary but infective, especially among these politically inexperienced people. One wonders if Indonesian leaders realize what they are achieving with this methodical mutilation of the minds of their people.

I heard someone softly slipper across the tiled floor of the living room and speak quietly to Nah. Then the radio was switched on. I guessed it to be one of my host's many relatives visiting Jakarta for a few days, since all Indonesians, rich and poor, have dozens of peripatetic relatives who come and go without announcement like nomad Arabs, and camp in the house or grounds of any family with whom they have ties by blood or marriage.

Whoever was in the next room pulled up a chair and the national anthem blared out suddenly and was turned down quickly to listening level. Then came "Ganjang Malaysia" and a statement from Dr. Roeslan Abdulgani, whose disquieting title is Information Mental Guidance and Psywar Minister-Coodinator of the Musjawarah [Deliberative Elders] Working Body of the Supreme Operation Command. His morning message said that the President had accepted a new life-title making him Supreme Leader of the National Association of Football Clubs.

There was a report that the chairman of the Union of University Students had condemned "America's provocative and war aggressive activities against the People's Democracy of North Vietnam," warning the people of Indonesia that "our vigilance must be increased." (Yesterday the students demonstrated outside the offices of the Stanvac Oil Company demanding that American industrial interests be confiscated.) Then came the usual references to the British Imperialism, the Malayan subversion, Abdul Rahman being a tool of the reactionaries, etc.

I found it depressing and went out into the garden to look for Nah, and asked if she and her niece would come to the German circus with me in the evening. She was horrified and held up her hands and said that the tickets were six hundred rupiahs each, more than she was paid each week, and that if I had that much money to throw away there were many things that she needed for herself and the girl. The niece, watching from the kitchen, made faces at me so I told Nah that we would all go anyway, at which she turned and, catching sight of the girl giving encouragement, stormed at her and sent her to buy bread from a street vendor. The girl ran off, laughing.

The street vendors of Jakarta are busy before the sun gets up, jog-trotting through the streets, calling their wares with snatches of descant or short, sharp, barking sounds (all that is left of phrases worn down with constant repetition). Most of them strike gongs as they go, or blocks of wood or bamboo nodes, in rhythm with the swinging of the carrying poles that bend and sway across their shoulders under the weight of baskets still full from market; others, ringing bells, add tinkle and tintinnabulation to the early morning orchestration. Later the continuous ground bass of traffic on the highway will almost drown it.

Nah and the other servants in the street (no white-collar family is so poor that it doesn't keep at least one servant) know each sound, can separate one from another and hurry to the front of the house to intercept a vendor, bring him to the back door, and buy vegetables, fruit, fish, meat (mainly for the rich), bread in flat cakes or loaves, milk for the children if they can afford it, rice in various cooked forms, soya bean flour, nuts, spiced eggs, hot or cold soups. Other men will come later with household goods—brooms, baskets, oil for lamps, charcoal for cooking, clothes pegs, coat-hangers, ladles made from coconut husks, flowers both fresh and false (plastic is the height of middle-class fashion), sandals and sun glasses, and balloons for the children. And there are street stalls on every corner for the sale of cigarettes, drinks, lottery tickets, and sweetmeats. This is a city of three million people with the habits and manners of a village.

But six lanes of traffic speed along the highway between Kebajoran, where the middle classes live, and Jakarta, where they work. I sat beside the driver of a spacious, light-gray Mercedes sent by the Foreign Office. Two other passengers were in the back seat, one of them a young diplomat recently returned from Egypt, sent to fetch me for an interview with his chief, the other a Traffic Department official who watched out of the window with a look of studied concentration.

We were hemmed in tightly, going with the fast flow of early morning traffic like a stick in a swift stream. On one side a bare-framed vintage jeep kept pace, swaying alternately toward and away from us as though dancing a *pas de deux,* while the driver talked over his shoulder to passengers bulging out of the back; on the other side a Cadillac, all shine and sheen of newness, smoothly carrying two Asian men, expressionless with the impassive, protected look of those who have no worries about money, sex, or heaven; and in front of us a rattling, sagging, asthmatical bus breathing black smoke like a story-book dragon.

The traffic is mostly raffish, unruly, and without discipline—cannibalized vehicles of every make and age mixed in with horse-drawn drays and wagons, bicycles, bemos, and a stream of *betjaks* (the tricycle rickshaw of Indonesia). They all go with no regard for rules, pass each other on either side indiscriminately, compete for loopholes and openings in the flow, cut in, swerve, swoop, and stop suddenly; it seems disorderly, irresponsible, and dangerous although there are few collisions and seemingly little ill temper.

Every few minutes we pass a breakdown being rushed to the

side, opened up for examination, or abandoned. It is not a matter of mechanical ineptitude but of economics; the shortage of foreign funds. Parts wear out and cars break down like worn-out horses. Nothing can be done. Riding into town, one begins to wonder if, after all, the critics are not justified, wagging their heads and saying that the country is running down, cannot go on much longer, must collapse economically. What then? Civil war and victory for the Communists.

"In many countries," said the man from the Traffic Department, "they use television to observe and control the traffic. I have studied this subject. It is very interesting." He looked out of the window again.

A young man riding a motorcycle swung past us, weaving a mazy way through the traffic. He sat arrogantly upright, hands in the pockets of a black leather jacket, guiding the machine by the swaying of his shoulders and the pressure of his thighs. It seemed suicidal.

The driver beside me scowled and muttered, "Cross Boy" (the local synonym for far-out fellows), adding that he should be in Borneo with the volunteers, exercising his recklessness on the British. The man from the Foreign Office laughed; but the Traffic man agreed with the driver, adding that the youth ought to be arrested and dealt with. "In any Western country where the traffic is properly organized, that boy would be in prison." But he spoke without conviction, as though the notion of putting anyone in prison was fundamentally foreign and repugnant.

Further on the traffic stopped, coagulated into a question mark. We speculated: a breakdown, an accident, a police search? There were rifle shots, the sound of mortar shells exploding, of whistles being blown. Word came back, passed from car to car, that it was an army exercise.

We sat, hemmed in for half an hour with the car windows shut to close out the smoke coming from the bus shuddering in front of us. We took off our jackets and fanned ourselves with papers. Apart from the discomfort nobody seemed concerned that a military maneuver should be timed to coincide with peak hour traffic on the only city expressway.

Soldiers suddenly appeared among us, using the cars as cover: young men in jungle uniforms sprouting stiff sprigs of camouflage, twigs and leaves in their helmets or poked into their clothing to break the shape and form of figure. Their faces were daubed with dirt, and all stared ahead with fixed and seemingly deadly intent.

Most of the people sitting in cars looked bored although in no hurry, but our man from the Foreign Office rolled down the window and spoke to a young soldier crouching alongside, asking him about the exercise. The soldier answered over his shoulder, urgently, making the situation seem almost real, "We are attacking the telephone exchange."

Whistles blew and the young soldier scuttled on, hunched over his rifle, threading a swift, twisting way among the stationary cars until he came, with many others, to the edge of the expressway. Here they threw themselves down on the grass, pretending to enfilade a block of square, white buildings a hundred yards away. Between them and their objective imitation shell bursts threw up little fountains of smoke and earth. The man from the Foreign Office shook his head. "They are crazy. This telephone exchange is a very inefficient installation. Whoever holds it will be handicapped and lose the battle. Better to destroy it than to capture it. Better still, leave it in the hands of the enemy."

The bus in front of us clattered, jerked forward, and threw out a jet of thick fumes. We slipped past and opened the car windows. Already, although it was not yet eight o'clock, heat lay like a hot poultice on the city, and any breath of air seemed a reprieve from continuous discomfort that would last, now, until sundown. We surged on under a ceiling of white sky, and banners slung at even intervals across the streets like slats in a ladder—slogans, exhortations, announcements, and invocations:

> In the Name of Allah Ever Onward No Retreat
> Hail Bung Karno—Father of the Revolution
> Cement Afro-Asian Friendship
> Crush Every Form of Imperialism
> Boycott United States Films
> Praise God for the Thomas Cup

The banners, sponsored by government departments and recognized national organizations, together give a potted commentary on the Indonesian ideology and political creed. On one hand a devotion to God, the Republic, the President and the cause of Afro-Asian freedom; on the other, a blanket denunciation of Western culture and colonialism in all forms and manifestations.

References to Communist countries were guarded and noncommittal, giving acknowledgment where it seemed merited, as in return for armaments and gestures of solidarity—polite rather than effusive.

Some of the slogans were touching. The simple declaration "Thank God for the Thomas Cup" was official comment on Indonesia's victory over Denmark in the world badminton championships. When it was gained, Sukarno made a public statement affirming his belief that victory had clearly been arranged by God Himself as a sign of sympathy with the Indonesian people. But elsewhere there were complaints that the Indonesian embassy in Tokyo (where the match was played) had arranged that a thousand Indonesian students should attend and systematically upset the Danish players with comment and distractions. There was also, inevitably, talk of bribery.

It is a subject that seems somewhat overstressed. Most foreigners speak with unctious disgust of corruption in Jakarta: the bribery, black-marketing, thievery, cheating, unashamed prostitution. The talk seems to me to be tinged with hypocrisy since most foreigners live pretty well and with easy consciences on the profits of black-market currency transactions, claiming that there is no other way to make ends meet. The sickness is familiar to Westerners, common to most countries recovering from war or revolution and suffering concurrently from poverty and disrupted government. Many centers of European culture have had similar days of shame.

The man from the Traffic Department, watching me jot down the slogans said, "These banners make the streets into classrooms for the masses. The people can learn about the revolution as they go about their business. They can see how Our Leader is making us into a nation. This is as much a matter of education as the teaching of children in our schools. The rich have their newspapers, radios, even the TV, but what of those who live in the streets? They, too, are Indonesians. They need to feel proud of what we are doing, to have the right to share in the spirit of freedom and to identify themselves with the rest of us, members of one family." It was said sincerely, without embarrassment, but the Foreign Office man seemed sceptical and kept silent.

Until we came to the great sports complex beside the expressway, built for the Asian Games. Then he waved his hand. "See, there is the people's food. When they have no money to buy rice they can come here and listen to the president tell them stories from the Ramayama and learn how we delivered ourselves from the wicked Dutch and so discovered the way to freedom and empty bellies."

He leaned over from the back seat to speak directly to me.

"The stadium was paid for by the Russians; this expressway, by the United States. The clover-leaf cross-over we are now approaching (a greater work of creation than the temple of Borobodour) was built by the French. China paid for the Asian Games and the Hotel Indonesia was constructed with money from Japan and is managed by an American airline. So I buy black-market rice to feed my children. What kind of revolution is this?"

I was surprised that he spoke so openly, and he seemed to sense this and said without prompting, "It's all right, Achmed is my brother-in-law and will not report me. And the driver cannot afford to make trouble." They grinned at each other. "In any case we are speaking privately and not stirring up strife and discontent among the people; and I would like you to understand that it is our custom to solve problems by open discussion.

"Also it is necessary to speak out loud sometimes, even to oneself. It is bad to pretend all the time that everything is wonderful. We should sometimes criticize ourselves and not leave it to foreigners."

Achmed said, "These people at the Foreign Office read the American magazines and listen to Radio Malaya and so they get bad-tempered. The President is right to ban them. There is no sense in letting other people make you angry with yourself and lose faith in your nation."

"I do not lose faith." The Foreign Office man began to get animated. "I believe as much as anybody in the future of my country. We have the people and the resources. But I have been in other countries and know that it takes more than faith to build a nation, and miracles are not achieved by making fine speeches, although they are sometimes necessary to keep the people keyed up.

"But we must not let the mystique of The Revolutionary Hero dazzle our eyes and blind us to the deficiencies of some of our leaders. There are too many incompetents still in government jobs just because they are old revolutionaries. Too many selfish, greedy people, who are making fortunes out of our troubles. If you can get a good government job you can get rich in a few years." He suddenly smiled and pointed to himself and then at Achmed. "Not as a member of the Foreign Office or the Traffic Department, nor as a school teacher. There's no money in such jobs. Only wages and an issue of rice. But be a judge, or a senior police official or a customs officer or get a job issuing import and export permits. Very good. Some of these people do very well. They have television and two cars and there are some who can afford to take their friends to dinner at the Hotel Indonesia."

CHAPTER

2

When we came to the hotel we stopped, briefly, so that I could speak to Soejono the clerk, and arrange to spend a little time with him and his wife before leaving Jakarta. He told me that he was working on another poem, this time about the hotel itself, taking it as a theme. He called it "The Concrete Cash Register" and presented the hotel as a symbol of Western civilization. His wife, he said, was studying economics now and they had in mind going into business later on. No, they were not expecting a child but were planning a family in due course. Catching my look of surprise he said, smiling, that one could learn many things working for the Americans.

The Hotel Indonesia is air-conditioned and shady. As you leave it and step out into the street the heat flings itself at you and a fierce light strikes at your eyes, making them flinch and shut tight with pain and resentment. Across the way, in a roundabout in the middle of the wide highway, a great concrete pylon rises high into the sky, holding aloft a romanticized statue-group of a man and a woman who stand with outstretched hands to embrace the whole wide world in simple and affectionate welcome, offering flowers; on the other side of the highway workmen have begun to tidy the burned-out British embassy. And further along the road is the British Council library, now closed down by order of the Indonesian government.

I spoke to one of its officers not so long ago; he was a fair young

Englishman married to a Javanese girl and very happy in Jakarta although afraid of the mounting atmosphere of violence being built up by the government's official hate-makers. Now he has gone back to England with his Javanese wife, or perhaps to India or some other Asian country; and the friends he had in Jakarta and the dozens of students he helped with his lectures and books and English-language lessons on the radio will have one less point of contact with the outside world, one less avenue of access to the knowledge they crave and need if they are to do something to help their country make progress, and they retire still further into discouraged and reluctant isolation while the extremists busy themselves with other mischief.

There was more war-play in progress as we passed Freedom Field, with young men and women from nearby government offices busy at the drill and exercises that all must do each week whatever their normal occupations: clerks, typists, office cleaners, messengers, supervisors, schoolteachers, administrators. Once a week they parade outside their offices before work for a recitation of the national pledge of loyalty, the raising of the flag, and an inspirational talk given by the head of the section or department on some aspect of government policy or ideology.

To anyone who has seen all this happen before in Europe it is disturbing. One tries hard to understand and would like to believe that it is a necessary part of creating a native Indonesian consciousness and identity; but behind the speeches one hears the sad sighs of many million war dead who listen for the loud-speakers, the bugles, the bombs, and the lamentations to begin again.

They say that Indonesia's official attitude toward the United States and Britain is impersonal, that differences are a matter of political ideology, devoid of malice or emotional antagonism; but it seems more realistic to believe, and to fear, that whatever the intention of the government and however genuine the national sentiment of friendship for all, violence is begotten and hatred is hatched under the government blanket.

And I felt sad and a little sick to see the young men and girls marching along the edges of this great open area called Freedom Field (the girls seeming unsexed and ugly in men's trousers and ill-fitting khaki shirts that make them look more like badly stuffed scarecrows than fecund women), while in the background long convoys of trucks bring soil to level off the area and to take away the rubble of buildings that had been demolished to make room for the Freedom Monument.

"No trucks available for road-making work," said the Foreign Office man, "no benzine to be had for business purposes. Only for the monuments. History repeats itself. Our ancient rulers ruined the country building temples and burial places for themselves, leaving the people too poor to fight the Dutch; and now, having regained our freedom after three hundred years, we start the process once more. We are childlike, we Javanese; people love us for our simplicities. Perhaps we should be satisfied to be loved for these reasons and not expect to be admired for our cleverness."

The monument that is being built in the middle of Freedom Field rises in layers to a central column which soars higher than any other piece of architecture in the city. It is to be the sign and symbol of the new Indonesia, born out of revolution and the suffering of the people. It will house, underground, a library and museum to contain the evidences and relics of Indonesia's existence back to Pithecanthropus erectus, the Java man who walked upright half a million years ago when the islands of Indonesia were part of the landmass of Malaya. People from the villages, visiting the capital, will be able to trace their racial and national history through thousands of years of growth and achievement, encompassing times of wonder and periods of wisdom when their country seemed to be the center of the known world and the cradle of great civilizations—until the Europeans came. In the chief place they will see the sacred relics of the revolution and, crowning all at the top of the column, an effigy of the President, the Architect and Supreme Commander, the Great Leader, Bung Karno.

"It will not be finished until after the President is dead," said the driver. "His fortune-teller has told him that he will die when his statue is set on top of the column, so he will not let them finish it." It is difficult in Indonesia to know where reality ends and the make-believe begins.

At the bottom of the Djalan Mahommed Husni Thamrin (named after the revolutionary leader of Jakarta) the traffic stopped again. This time police kept the street clear and soon the wailing of sirens made a passageway of sound through which outriders came thundering on motorcycles, then jeeps with armed police, soldiers in weapon carriers, more outriders, then black limousines followed by other men on motorcycles. The cavalcade flashed past us fast as a dream, and like a dream was lost as the traffic closed in again over the track that it had taken.

The driver said, "It is Mikoyan, he is going home."

When we came to the Foreign Office there was a crowd outside watching a dozen painters at work on a great mural covering the outside wall for eighty feet or more. Designed by Hendra, one of the leaders of the "New Awakening" era of Indonesian art, it is a crude, multicolored cartoon idealizing the revolution and the aspirations of the Indonesian people. In its central motif a cluster of vigorous, square-jawed Indonesians (physiological caricatures of the slender, graceful reality of the race) charge down in battle dress with rifles and fixed bayonets upon decrepit, abject parodies of a fat Uncle Sam, an aged John Bull, and a dandified Adbul Rahman, with a ridiculous little Australian capering in the background. Dominating the design is President Sukarno, larger than life, a stern but benevolent father-figure standing behind his people, pointing the way to a glorious dawn.

It is a simple, childlike thing, but for a people who hold courtesy and good manners to be among their chief characteristics it seemed strangely located in a place where foreign diplomats and journalists pass back and forth daily, most of them, I suppose, wanting to be fair and to properly understand the problems and difficulties of Indonesia and its leaders. But these are the continuous contradictions, confusing at first, that soon become exasperating and make it difficult to admit the sincerity of a people who fervently protest their peaceableness while busily stirring up strife.

So I went into the Foreign Office feeling impatient.

"You must not look for the differences between our way of life and yours," said the kindly man who received me. "You must look for the similarities, the points where our two cultures meet and our hopes and national aspirations coincide. You must discover that we are human beings as you are, with the same sensitive pride, the same desires for friendship and the same fears of war and conflict. We are people, like your people, with the same capacity to be happy or to suffer."

I wanted to tell him that his words were empty and a demonstrable hypocrisy, meaningless, being contradicted every minute of the day by the actions of the government. But it seemed better to wait. Capital cities are not always a true compendium of a country. In the provinces and other islands I might find a cleaner, clearer picture of the Republic. Outside Jakarta, I hoped and believed, the image would be less clouded and confused by politics or newspaper talk and the corrosive effects of three million sets of city-bound frustrations chafing one against the other. I thought, also, that in the more isolated places I would be treated simply as a visitor, not as a professional "observer" to be watched, indoctrinated, and lectured at. So I said that I had not come to criticize but to look at Indonesia with a particularly sympathetic eye; for, as I admitted in the end, "I am of Irish blood and my father's country was occupied by foreigners for three hundred years, as yours was, and my Great-Uncle Michael was hung by the British for a rebel; and I have an understanding of the Indonesian ethos." At which his face broke into a wide smile and he hit me heartily upon the back and we parted, loving each other.

Later in the day I was taken to the Blueprint Hall, a beautifully designed modern building of six stories standing on the spot where President Sukarno proclaimed the independence of Indonesia on August 17, 1945. Each story is seventeen meters (approximately fifty-six feet) high. A column in front of the building is shaped like a crowbar, signifying that independence must be followed by hard work and national development, and on top of the column is a symbolic shaft of lightning, implying that the declaration of Indonesian independence struck the world with electrifying force.

Inside this building is the vision of the Indonesia that is to be, all set out on the six floors—hundreds of fine, well-made models of hydroelectric water supply and irrigation schemes, mines and steelworks, schools, universities, hospitals, laboratories, railway and road systems, docks, harbors, shipyards, bridges, factories, tourist centers with huge hotels; telecommunication systems, television stations, air-radio and navigational aids; giant tanks, guns, rockets, huge flights of warplanes, battleships, nuclear reactors; and as a background to all this, maps, charts, graphs, photographs, lists of statistics, slogans, and excerpts from the President's speeches.

It is an astonishing sight, this huge, beautiful building filled with something that doesn't exist. As I stood there wondering where to start, a line from a poem I had long forgotten came back into my mind. "Tread softly because you tread on my dreams."

Usually the building is busy and filled with the murmur and continuous movement of people being guided about in groups, or parties of school children with their teachers, but it was closed now for a period of rearrangement, and empty of people, so that I stood alone in the first great gallery waiting for a guide (the director was anxious that I should be shown everything and have it clearly explained in English).

He came with four girls, shy but excited to have a foreign writer to escort. The director said, "They can all speak English," and the girls giggled and twittered and said that their English was poor but that among them they would manage. I felt the better for having them there, believing that I could manage girls so young and bend them to my own inclination in the matter of what to see and what not to waste time over, but I was much mistaken for as soon as I started off to look at something in the middle of the gallery they all cried out in surprise and alarm and jostled me back to the starting point like shepherd dogs retrieving a recalcitrant old ram. I made gentle attempts to break away, smiling at them and pretending not to understand what they were at, but they would not meet me on this and steered me back to start the tour properly, from the beginning.

It took three hours in all and I was exhausted and for the last hour took nothing in, although they continued to be gaily relentless and inflexible and never for a second let me rest or gloss over any part of the display. Much of it was above their heads and I soon ceased to ask questions, even out of politeness, because they had no considered answers, only statistics and official explanations learned by rote, recited guidebook fashion and interlarded with caption-quotes. "To build a Just and Prosperous Society." "Listen to the Message of the People's Suffering." "Our Struggle." "Our Plan." "Our Great Leader." In a while the words became irritating coming from the lips of these pretty children, and I began to think of other things.

I stood at last in front of models of a spaceship and an orbiting satellite set against a huge photo-mural of the night sky with a caption reading, "The People of Indonesia Must Be Space Conscious." Out in the fields the farmers plough with wooden ploughs and oxen, and the women reap the rice ears by hand. And in

Jakarta there are no water closets or shower baths or footpaths to the streets, and one cannot buy toilet paper. So "The People of Indonesia Must Be Space Conscious!"

We of the West have more subtle idiocies. Such elemental self-deception as this is too much for our kind of mind to encompass. I could understand these girls being in some juvenile, unthinking way inspired by all this and proud to belong to a newly emerging nation vital with humanitarian ideas and ambitions, but that national leaders and trained experts should solemnly sponsor this make-believe, this shadow-play, seemed to me an exaggerated way of escaping from reality; a form of dreaming that might end in disaster. But the same was said of the Russians fifty years ago!

Before I left the building the girls gave me coffee and cakes, served on a balcony overlooking the spot where the president had proclaimed the Republic, and they made me promise to send them my book when it was written, but first to come back in a month, when the whole exhibition would have been changed and brought up-to-date with new models of other projects and objectives.

Late in the afternoon, when the hours of siesta were over, I called upon Dr. Abdulgani, who received me in his house sitting bare-footed and cross-legged on a sofa. He spoke for an hour and thirty minutes, separating the subjects of his discourse with irregular yet graceful movements of his mutilated hand (torn in half by a bullet during the revolution against the Dutch). He is a practiced and adept interpreter of the Indonesian attitude, beginning with the five principles of the constitution—belief in God, humanity, Indonesia, representational government, and social justice—then moving on fluently to discourse upon the need for a national identity, the problems left by the Dutch, the British-Malayan threat, United States interference in Southeast Asian affairs, non-alignment, the logic of the president's theory of Guided Democracy, and the bogey of Communism.

"You people in the West fear and hate Communism for what it might do if it gains power in Asia, but we Indonesians fear and hate the Western colonial powers for what they have already done in Asia over the past four hundred years. When the Russians armed Cuba, the Americans cried Assassin, but when the British put their troops into North Borneo we are supposed to keep quiet. It is time for the West to think with its whole mind and not with the bit that faces inward." There was no malice or hysteria in his manner of speaking. He was as courteous as the matter allowed.

Two male secretaries sat in the corner of the room with notebooks open, ready to write down anything he wished done or remembered, and a maid-servant brought sirops and continuous cups of coffee. Guards, car drivers, servants, and casual visitors were sitting about in the pavilion near the entrance to the house. Dr. Abdulgani went on talking.

"The Dutch developed this country to support a quarter of a million Europeans in luxury and eighty million Indonesians on a level of bare subsistence, and when they went they left us destitute and broken down, with a legacy of rebellions and uprisings all over the archipelago. Now we are a hundred million people and increasing by two million every year, and we are trying to raise the standard of living for everybody, starting with nothing. We are spread over three thousand islands and have few ships. We have practically no heavy industries. We must find foreign exchange to import every piece of machinery. You should keep these historical difficulties in mind and not expect to see miracles wherever you look."

I drew breath, ready to speak, but his words came on in waves, preventing me. "Europe committed suicide with its two great civil wars, and America, the inheritor of its authority, signaled the final failure of Western civilization and morality when it dropped the atom bomb. The people of Asia and Africa knew then that they could no longer leave their destiny in the hands of the European powers. The time had come for them to choose their own way. And now you ask why we reject your Liberal-Capitalist politics. We reject them because they begot colonialism, and it is against colonialism that we revolted and against which we continue to struggle in Malaysia."

The telephone rang in an outside room and a servant came to say that it was a call from the Minister for Foreign Affairs, Dr. Subandrio. Dr. Abdulgani excused himself. When he came back he made a signal to his secretaries and they went out for a moment. One came back with a photographer who took pictures of the minister and me sitting together. The other brought a parcel of books and pamphlets neatly tied with tape; the collected speeches and writings of Dr. Roeslan Abdulgani. He gave them to me and led me to the door with his arm across my shoulder. "Ask for anything you need and go wherever you wish. We have nothing to hide. Be fair with us—that is all we ask."

Extract from a letter
Jakarta
Midnight

I have just come from a circus, surprised to have found in the contrived excitement and calculated defiance of danger a sense of tranquility and assurance, an escape from confusion into order and reality. After a day of ideology, indoctrination, and make-believe the simple extravagances of clowns seemed almost stately: their mad music, for instance, much less manic than "Ganjang Malaysia" or any other chauvinistic jingle. Even the sight of wild lions and tigers slinking in a ring around their trainer seemed less sinister than the intrigues of Jakarta's politicians and only mildly likely to turn into a sudden nightmare of disaster. And acrobats on the high trapeze, flinging themselves through space, tempted death with a flippancy so meticulous that their safety appeared unassailable. A giant cyclist riding a miniature velocipede made eminent sense, while the sight of four graceful ladies maintaining their balance on huge spheres which they spun with their feet without falling off had a logic that was almost soporific.

The performers were all foreigners, all white, and no word was spoken during the entire performance, yet we all enjoyed ourselves tremendously. I suppose the inference is oversimple. Real life has not the innocent anarchy of a circus performance, and once speech is involved the avenues of misunderstanding and damage open wide, letting in confusion.

Earlier in the evening I had an interview with the chief of the combined information services of Indonesia, a master of the technique of being interviewed without allowing the interviewer to ask a question. He addressed me for an hour and a half and had I been able to get a word in edgewise I would have disagreed with much that he said; but he was too practiced and fluent for me. It was a fascinating experience. The man himself is so frank, open, and easy in his manner, almost humorous, and seems free from fanaticism. Yet he directs this continuous barrage of indoctrination propaganda that appears to be leading Indonesia inexorably into a war in which the suffering of its people will be greater than any they have ever known. I liked him, but when I left him I felt discouraged.

No one on our side seems to know how to deal with the situation. Diplomatically the Americans are giving way, with a great deal of honest patience; in any case, they have their hands more than full in Vietnam. The British are playing for time, hoping that Sukarno's overextravagant handling of the Malaysia matter will gradually alienate his foreign friends (except in Peking) and lose support at home. The Australians here are said to be working well and sympathetically as go-betweens, but they are up against the nineteenth-century attitudes of the government in Canberra, and the almost complete lack of channels of public information and discussion in Australia.

We ought not to expect Indonesians to fit neatly into familiar Western patterns of thought and behavior. They approach us from an opposite historical position, and their mental and spiritual points of view differ from ours in a fundamental way. The more they try, or are urged, to copy us the less they are themselves, and one of their major problems is to decide just how much of the West they can imitate and absorb without destroying what is best in their own character. For us, the obligation is to make some real effort to understand their difficulties.

At the moment I am sitting like a Moslem in the middle of my bed, under a net, with dozens of frustrated mosquitoes clamoring to get at me. It is just after midnight, and quiet. I must sleep and get up again in four hours to go to the airport and catch the plane for Makassar. A car is waiting outside the house now, with the driver sleeping in it. He says he wants to be sure that I do not miss the plane. The courtesy is typical of these people.

Makassar is the capital of Southern Sulawesi. Look at the map and go northwest across the Java sea to the island which looks like a limp starfish. It is the biggest of the outer islands, and in its central mountains bands of rebels still hold out against the Jakarta government.

This morning, waiting to pick up my tickets at the airways office, I saw a white man arguing with one of the clerks. He seemed angry (he had obviously lost his seat on the plane—a common occurrence here). When he had gone off muttering and red-faced, my guide said, "You white people eat too much meat and it makes you angry." He was quite serious about it.

I will be away several weeks. Please keep writing so that there will be letters when I return to Jakarta.

M.

PART III

Sulawesi

CHAPTER 3

At Makassar there was a reception committee on the tarmac, and as we taxied in the hostess asked us to stay seated while a party of official guests disembarked. Through the porthole I could see a group of about a hundred men and women formed roughly into three sides of a square, and an harassed man, wearing the ribbons of the Indonesian Islamic Party in his lapel, was putting them into position and forming two lines of women into a corridor through which the visitor should pass. The women stood swaying and nodding like twin borders of gay flowers. The arriving guests were obviously important, for the central group of the reception committee included the provincial governor and his staff, the chiefs of the armed services, and police. The latter were in dress uniforms, while most of the civilian men wore tropical suits, or at least clean white shirts and ties. Only the news photographers were dirty, a hallmark of professionalism copied from Italian films.

The harassed man hurried between the two lines of women and stood looking up at the door of the aircraft with his head on one side, like a bird. When the door opened a very big African stood framed in the opening, smiling. He wore an ankle-length coat of fine wool and underneath it a white abba and a small white cap on his head. A banner hanging across the entrance to the passenger lounge read "Africa Loves Peace But Will Defend Herself," and one of the group waiting to receive the guest held up a placard inscribed "Afro-Asian Solidarity Is Essential for the Future of

Mankind." He nodded in approval and stepped forward while the people clapped.

Everybody watched as he walked toward the reception committee and began to move along the lines shaking hands and smiling. I felt detached and irrelevant. No one took any notice of me and nobody came to meet me although telegrams had gone from Jakarta advising of my arrival. But I took a car into town and enjoyed being alone for a little while and away from Jakarta in a green landscape of rice fields and copses of coconut palms and little rivers of clean, clear water. We were stopped by military police at a checkpoint where the road to the airport joins the main road into town, but my letter of accreditation from the Foreign Office carried me through with a salute and a smile in a matter of minutes.

The checkpoint is there to screen out agents and spies operating for Kahar Muzakkar, the Islamic zealot, who still holds out against the government in the central mountains of the island. He waits there with his band of fanatics until the death of President Sukarno, or some other national calamity or crisis, loosens the ties between the outer islands and Jakarta. When that time comes he and his men will emerge from hiding and try once more to convert Sulawesi, and then all of Indonesia, into a Moslem State. Occasionally, Kahar's men come down from the mountains to make mischief or do business (or both) or to slip out through Makassar into the Philippines or Malaya to contact outside backers. Three weeks ago, says my driver, a gang of them tried to shoot their way past the checkpost, and two of them, and a policeman, were killed in the melee.

As tropical sea ports go, Makassar is clean and for the past two years has taken second place in the President's contest for the neatest city in Indonesia (Bandung always wins); its main streets are wide and tree-lined, and the parks and strips of grass along the pavements are cropped short by white-flecked deer tethered under the trees. The biggest buildings—the government block and barracks, the mosque, church and hotel—are painted white. A breeze blows straight into town from the sea so that there is mostly a fresh feel about the streets, even at midday. But still it is shabby.

Especially the hotel.

We must face this matter of the hotels of Indonesia from the beginning. They are, practically without exception, squalid by

Western standards, and there is no point in railing against each one separately as we come to it in the course of these journeys, although some are so bad that additional involuntary comment might be inescapable. The main thing to realize is that Indonesians themselves have little use for hotels. They were built in Dutch days for the use of Europeans, visiting government officials, commercial travelers, business men, foreign visitors, tourists, and white holiday-makers from the other islands of what was the Netherlands East Indies (it seems so long ago).

When the Dutch went home the government of the Republic took over the hotels and they have been occupied ever since by the families of officers of the armed forces, posted for duty away from their own districts. Only a few rooms in each hotel are kept for casual travelers, for although Indonesians travel as much as other people their custom is to stay with relatives or friends wherever they go. So no money has been spent on these hotels. They are run down and decrepit.

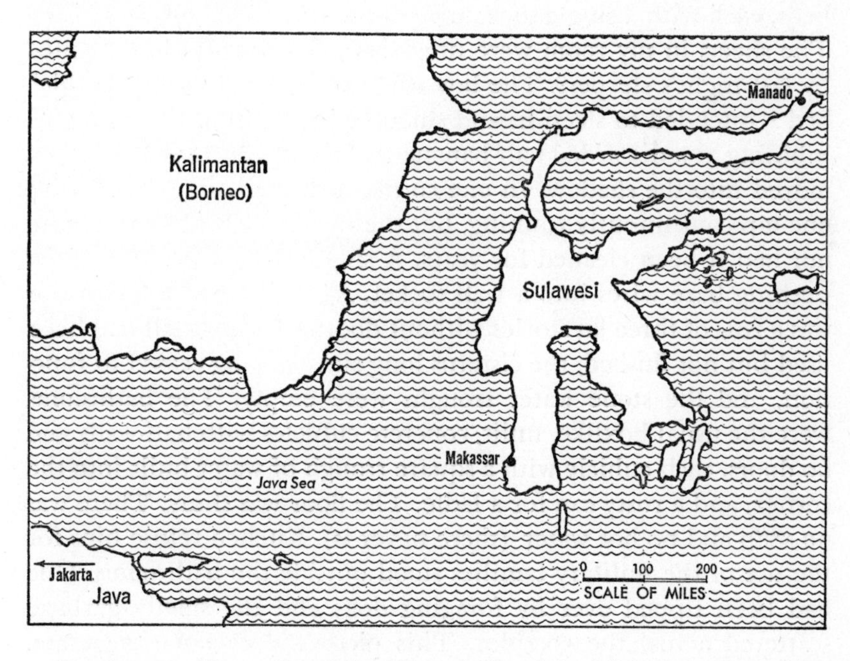

On the outside walls of the Grand Hotel in Makassar the white paint is flaked and stained. Inside, the carpets are threadbare and the chairs have broken springs. Where dozens of bright lights once lit the foyer and dining room a single fly-specked globe now throws a dismal token glow. Threads of cobweb hang from the broken ceiling fans and float with each breath of breeze. The cocktail bar has high stools and advertisements for beer and schnapps, but its shelves are bare, although in a glass case on the counter a bottle of Japanese whisky is displayed with five bottles of Chinese wine made from essences. The labels show red dragons breathing flame. Two men sit at the bar drinking sweetened lemonade. It is a brave attempt on the part of the management to stay Western and up-to-date.

I checked in and left passport, air tickets, and registration fee to be taken to the police station. The clerk said that he would notify the governor's office across the road that I had arrived. I went to my room. These hotel rooms are the same everywhere in Indonesia. They are built around an open courtyard, and each has a little private patio with saloon-type swinging half-doors leading back into the room. Then there are louvered wooden doors that can be locked. And inside the room a gauzed-in cage with two beds, each with a single sheet and pillow and a Dutch-wife bolster. The sheets in my room were unwashed, and both pillows dented by last night's sleepers. The boy who carried my bag asked which bed I intended to sleep in and smoothed the pillow. A cockroach nibbling at a discarded half banana looked up from the floor, then moved into the shadow. In one corner a hand basin gurgled with one tap continuously running, but there was no plug for the basin nor had it been cleaned for years. A single light was operated by pushing bare wires into a wall socket. At the end of the corridor was a row of three lavatories without door fastenings. All had been used but not flushed, the cisterns long since having ceased to function, and the stone water troughs were empty. The bathrooms were the usual boxlike, unlit, concrete cubicles with half-walls and no doors, each cubicle with a square trough of water built into the corner, and a rusty can for a ladle. The floor was slimy. There was no soap and no hot water (there never is). Kitchen refuse bins for the use of the military families stood outside the bathrooms. One had been tipped over by foraging dogs and the smelly garbage scattered across the corridor. This picture does not exaggerate. Later, in Java, I stayed in hotels that were cleaner, but in other places they were worse than here in Makassar at the Grand Hotel.

The President is unhappy about these hotels. He knows that Western visitors are revolted by them, and their replacement is high on the list of priorities in his national development plan. I had seen models of several great, modern, luxury hotels when the four girls had guided me around the Blueprint Hall in Jakarta and had felt that to build them while people were sleeping in the streets of Jakarta and other cities was unrealistic and irrational. But one day they will be built. It is a matter of national dignity, and the Indonesians are a proud people.

When I came back to the foyer an old clerk from the governor's office sat waiting with a note. He sat still, the patient Asian, not seeing my approach, a little, thin, quiet figure in khaki drill, the uniform of the civil administration. He is from the island of Ambon and has five children and twelve grandchildren and speaks proudly of his eldest son who is a meteorologist (he releases the balloons and reads the wind and rain gauges at the weather station). Another son is a civilian employee of the army, a clerk. They are a fairly secure family.

The old man has been a government clerk for forty-one years, first with the Dutch, then under the Japanese, and now with the Republic. Clearly the change came too late for him. He speaks only when spoken to. In respose his face wears a worried, anxious look, and when wakened out of whatever fearful reverie he lives in he looks around anxiously for help, finding any kind of responsibility intolerable. If the problem can be passed on to someone even less important than himself he quickly shifts the burden, and when the matter in hand is resolved he smiles. The smile is magical. His thin, disciplined lips stretch sideways until they touch the tips of his down-pointed ears and he becomes, suddenly, a leprechaun and no longer an uncertain, scared old man.

When I came to him he stood up swiftly and held out the letter, anxious in case he might have to explain its content. But when I read it and put it in my pocket without comment, the smile came and we sat and chatted over a sirop. When he smiled again I felt a great love fill me and a sense of oneness with this old man and all the people 'round about—the hotel clerk busy in his office, the barman with nothing to do but wipe the counter and swish flies away from his little alcove, and the crippled shoe-cleaner sitting outside on the step in the fierce white sunlight. He told me that he would retire within the year and would get a pension. When I asked what he would do then, he said that he would rest and sometimes would go for walks with his grandchildren. "It will be good," he said, "to no longer have to carry so much responsibility." I understood him—knew the strain and pain that pressed upon his mind and body as he tried to deal with problems which to him had no meaning, no substance in reality, no point of reference in his understanding of history and of being.

Being an office messenger for Dutch officials, this he could understand—fetching cups of coffee, bottles of cold beer, filling ink pots, carrying papers from one official to another. It was a proper job for a poor man. And bowing to Japanese soldiers had not been much more degrading than shuffling on one's knees in the presence of those local sultans who ruled by courtesy of the Dutch until the Republic deposed them. But to be in the vanguard of a new civilization was too much. What could he know of hydroelectric schemes, steelworks, cement factories, of the president's Political Manifesto with its references to the five principles of Pantja Sila and Usdek, and the evils of neocolonialism? There was no ritual to make meaning of these things, no legends, plays, dances, poems or paintings to give expression to them, to link back to anything real. Only memoranda from Jakarta, jargon and speeches, and an unending procession of official visitors and dignitaries.

Soon he would retire and become absorbed again into the realities of a ritual of living that bound everything together: God, the universe, plants and animals, and all people. He sat there close by me, in the foyer of the hotel, across the road from the governor's office, thin hands resting on lean thighs, eyes fixed on paradise.

The letter from the governor's aide, Andi Bahruddin, apologized that I had not been met (the telegram from Jakarta had not come) but invited me immediately to a wedding, and when the old man had gone back to his office I took a bath and changed into a suit and sat waiting in the foyer until fetched.

Bahruddin came and took me, hurrying, to a suburban street to the house of the bridegroom, where we found him sitting in the best bedroom at a dressing-table, like a woman, watching himself in long mirrors while an old man fussed over him. I had seen the young man before, under ordinary circumstances and wearing Western clothes, and failed now to recognize him immediately for he wore the traditional wedding costume of his race and religion, and the expression on his face was serious and devotional. The room was small and much of its space filled by a double bed spread with purple covers, but standing all around against the walls or squatting on the floor were men and boys, and others sitting on the edges of the bed, every one of them dressed in such magnificence of colored silks and satins patterned with gold and silver thread and wearing krisses and ornaments so jeweled that the scene seemed like the dressing room of a theater in which some Eastern extravaganza was about to be played. I checked the thought, however, reminding myself that this was Makassar and not Sydney or New York or Manchester, and that I was seeing the normal preparation for an Eastern wedding, the essential ritual, centuries old, designed to stress the significance of marriage in the whole creative scheme of human existence, not merely an off-hand, formal, conformist gesture made to satisfy a disinterested society.

I pressed through the doorway of the bedroom to pay my respects and murmur good wishes, and although the young man smiled acknowledgment he did not speak or hold out his hand but went back to watching himself in the mirror with soft, meditative eyes, while the old man who was dressing him placed little metal flowers of gold and silver in the folds of a scarlet scarf which he wore turbanlike round his head. His tunic was of black silk decorated with busts of Nefertiti worked in silver thread; and his sarong, rich blue and crimson, was caught up at the waist in a ruche and weighted at the hem with tablets of gold. In his waistband he wore a kris, the handle and scabbard of which were overlaid with gold filigree.

The best man, a slender youth, and two younger aides were yet more gorgeous than the bridegroom, wearing the same kind of garments but in delicate pastel shades: the best man in pale pink and gold, the two lads in tunics of young green and silver, with gold and mauve sarongs. One of them stood patiently and expressionless while an aged, white-robed tailor, sitting cross-legged on the floor, stitched at the hem of his sarong. Four other lads, still younger, helped the dresser, handing him ornaments, pins, and clips. These lads were in white also, and one of them carried a silver staff. Another held a silver water pitcher, and the third a silver bowl, while the smallest carried a silver box containing sweetmeats, betel nut, and other comfits.

There was a single female in the room—a young girl superbly dressed, her arms encased in sleeves of gold. She was of the bride's family and attended the dressing of the bridegroom and his retinue to give approval. In the corner of the room, a very old man, bent and toothless, squatted on the floor leaning forward with his arms around a great bundle wrapped in a blue and gold shawl: wedding presents for the bride.

Friends of the bridegroom, mostly age-mates, squeezed in and out of the room to congratulate or cheer him or to offer a blessing or alternatively to make the kind of jest made at weddings everywhere. All spoke without inhibition, as though he were not there, some saying loudly that he was lucky to find so rich a wife who needed a husband badly, and others making male jokes about marriage and the honeymoon, to all of which he responded with a slow, soft smile and a sigh and a lowering of his womanish eyes.

In the front room of the house the married female friends and relatives of the bridegroom's family sat in rows sipping pink lemonade and nibbling at cakes and biscuits. They sat with heads together, bobbing and nodding, such color and grace of shape and draperies like a riot of cymbidiums, brilliant and beautiful. Their shoulders bare and bosoms discreet yet accentuated, with golden ornaments in high-coifed jet black hair, these Eastern women seem the essence of all femininity, acquiescent, ready at any time to be got with child, accepting without question their procreative role—not with zest (one suspects) but as naturally as flowers bloom. They sat side by side generating a gentle ripple and hum of marriage conversation, no face showing signs of strain or even the tiredness of age, no worry or urgency, no indications of tenseness, impatience, or emotional confusion. There must be, of course, other women, strong-minded, intellectual, twentieth-century zealots who seek some active role in the new revolutionary society, but these are more surely to be found in the keyed-up political climate of Jakarta than in this medieval atmosphere of a provincial city.

And in a side room some twenty girls, unwed, sisters and cousins for the most part, were making ready to take the bridegroom's private gifts in procession to the bride. Each had the care of a decorated tray and on it carried some intimate article such as might be given by husband to wife: a pair of slippers, a handbag, a reticule, cosmetics, scents, hair-brushes, underclothing (even a brassiere displayed nakedly, points upward on a tray), and such personal things.

I went outside and sat among the men of the family and their friends, under a palm bower hung with colored lights and set with small café tables where servants came continuously with tea, coffee, sirop, or lemonade, cakes and little delicacies of rice.

Then messengers, dressed as brilliantly as the bridegroom's men, came from the house of the bride to say that she was ready to receive the groom, at which the girls who were to take the gifts became flustered, until their fathers and brothers took charge and ushered them into family cars, which then formed up behind a shoddy open truck on which a jazz band was settling itself. It seemed incongruous, this band: an unwashed, ill-dressed, unkempt group of youths who would have fitted with more dignity into a fourth-rate Western night club and looked as out of place among these Eastern wedding guests as moulting magpies among birds of paradise.

When all was ready and the last girl's swirls of silk tucked safely away, the cavalcade moved off, watched discreetly by the neighbors. The band played military marches and when it reached the end of the street the remaining men piled into cars and followed after, leaving only the bridegroom to come with his retinue.

My friend Bahruddin, a young man of consequence in Makassar not only because of his influence as the governor's aide, but on account of princely connections and riches on his wife's side, took me then by back streets to the bride's house, where I saw her sitting on a divan, serious and unsmiling, being fanned. She, too, was richly dressed, and sat motionless, more like a doll than a woman. She acknowledged my compliments with a shy but dignified inclination of her head but otherwise took no notice of me, or of others who came and went quickly to whisper a blessing, to enquire if all were ready, or to announce with excitement that the family of the bridegroom was approaching.

The room in which she sat was full of young women whispering. She and her two attendants, sitting side-by-side on the divan, alone were silent. She wore crimson silks and golden slippers, and on her fingers and arms dozens of gold rings and bracelets, and a long necklace of gold medallions as big as dollars. The two attendants wore green and purple. Artificial fringes of black curls were painted on their foreheads and cheekbones, and their eyes were heavily outlined. I found myself thinking that scenes similar in almost each detail must have been familiar to poets and writers whose love songs and stories were written into the Bible and other holy books—the *Song of Solomon,* the *Story of the Foolish Virgins,* the *Rubaiyat.* I could hear the mounting excitement in the outer rooms and knew that the old women were saying among themselves, "Behold, the bridegroom cometh."

When he came into the house he was taken to greet the bride formally, staying only a few moments before retiring to the best bedroom, where the priest waited to perform the ceremony (the bride having no part in the religious ritual). Had the girl been of lesser social status and the man higher she would perhaps have followed the old custom of washing his feet at the entrance to the house as a sign of submission, for this is still usual.

The room in which the religious ceremony took place was filled with flowers and flickering candelabra, and the smell of incense and spices. The bridegroom sat cross-legged in the center of the bed, which was covered with a purple spread. The girl of the bride's family sat behind him with a fan. Old men crouched all around to guide and prompt him through the ritual interrogation and to witness the signing of the marriage bond. The Iman came and climbed up onto the bed to sit cross-legged, facing the groom. They leaned toward each other, their heads almost touching. A cross-eyed photographer darted here and there like a dragonfly zigzagging above a pond. All the other men looked tense and concenrated.

The Iman took the bridegroom's clasped finger tightly in his own right hand, and with the other kept his place in the Koran, while he whispered the Prophet's holy words. The bridegroom's eyes were shut. The girl with the fan leaned back so that she could not overhear the words. The photographer let off a flash. There were swift, sibilant questions from the Iman, and nervous almost inaudible replies from the bridegroom, prompted anxiously by the old men clustered on the bed. Questions and replies followed one after the other for a long time; then suddenly all of the old men sat back and, lifting their hands to their ears, cried out "Amen." A relative produced the marriage bond and it was signed. Then each man in the room came to the bridegroom and, taking his hand between their palms, one by one, gave a double shake, then touched themselves lightly on the breast. When every man had given this blessing the bridegroom was led to the bride and put beside her on the divan, no word being spoken. When they had arranged themselves the old man, his chief attendant, whispered to him and the bridegroom shyly put out his hand and laid it on the girl's thigh. So he had touched her publicly. Put his mark upon her. Possessed her. They were now married in the eyes of God and the law and man, in the manner of their ancestors.

None of the guests had taken part in this ceremony, only the two sets of attendants and the Iman. The women sat gossiping inside the house while the men drank tea and coffee outside, talking politics and business. Now the bridegroom's old attendant put his head round the door of the bridal chamber and hissed, and when the women looked up he nodded with satisfaction. The knowledge ran through the house and out into the garden, and to the men under the arbor. The band began to play Western swing.

Later, during the evening, the bride's parents would give a more public reception in one of the public buildings of the town; and tomorrow there would be still another reception, arranged by the bridegroom's family. At each of these receptions there would be perhaps a thousand guests to be entertained, fed generously and kept supplied with cigarettes and drinks. Some city dignitary and the provincial head of the Department of Religious Affairs would make formal speeches, and a humorous encomium full of advice and private jests would be delivered by an old family friend. Then everybody would file past the bridal party, posed on a small stage, to offer congratulations and leave gifts of money in a basket. Meanwhile the jazz band would play again and little teenage girls with thin, unformed voices would sing sentimental prewar Western songs—"Ramona," "Over the Rainbow," "When the Red, Red Robin" and others of that time and type—instead of the gamelan music and Eastern singing of their own national idiom. And listening to the inadequate, unkempt band playing in the garden of the bride's house I felt a little disappointed and found myself sympathizing with President Sukarno, who hates this substitution of imitation Western ways for the traditionally rich pattern of Indonesian life and culture.

Bahruddin, with business to do for the governor before the two o'clock siesta, excused himself, saying that he would collect me from the hotel in the evening and take me to dine with the rector of the university, Professor Mononutu, a close friend of the president and a man of importance in the province. Meanwhile a guide was waiting to show me around the town.

The guide's name was Karim and he was as miserable a young man as I have ever known. His mother, long dead, had been a native of Makassar, and his father had been an Indian pedlar who, when alive, had traveled back and forth between Makassar and Madras dealing in silks and semiprecious stones. He had kept two wives, one here in Sulawesi and the other in India, and was good to them both within the limits of his means, until he died of cholera. Karim was then less than a year old.

When his mother had finished mourning she married a local farmer who needed money to pay a money-lender who held a mortgage on his land. This farmer had grown-up sons of his own who were able to help work the land, and it seemed sensible to sell Karim (who could contribute nothing) and use the money thus obtained to pay off the money-lender. So his mother went to the market place and sold her child to a widow of reasonable means whose own sons had grown up, married, and left home.

Karim's mother received three thousand rupiahs for her baby, an amount sufficient at that time to keep a peasant family for a year or more although not enough now to pay for two ham sandwiches at the Hotel Indonesia in Jakarta; and the transaction was without doubt satisfactory to everybody, including Karim, who was too young to understand. It allowed his mother to bring a dowry to her new husband with which he could pay the money-lender and redeem his land and so support her adequately for the rest of her life. The widow was happy with a child to care for, and Karim was assured of a good start in life.

But before long the widow married a man from the Moluccas who took her away, and because this man did not want Karim the boy was left behind with an old schoolteacher who received a sum of money for which he undertook to bring up Karim as his own son. And this he did until he himself reached retiring age and returned to his own village to eke out his days, leaving the boy in Makassar to make his own way as best he could. Karim was then thirteen years old, a thin, introspective boy, who smiled rarely, but he was a reasonable scholar. His ambition was to be a surgeon.

The influence of the old teacher was sufficient to get him work as a messenger boy in the Department of Education so that he could keep himself; and because his guardian had taught him to speak and read English he made progress in the service and was now, at the age of twenty-one, a government translater and interpreter. But he still aimed to become a surgeon and spent three afternoons a week working as an honorary orderly at the hospital for the sake of experience and four nights attending lectures at the university medical school.

We talked about this as we went around the town. He said that his job paid him seven thousand rupiahs a month (worth a dollar at black-market rates but equivalent in purchasing power to about ten dollars) and that he sometimes got food at the hospital and one regular meal each day with the family with whom he stayed. His biggest problem was to get access to textbooks so that he could study. At the university there was an average of one book to each five students, each student holding the book for a few days and then passing it on.

There had been, until recently, a United States Information Service library in the town, with a membership of seven thousand, mostly students from the university and the high school. It had provided books for study and for entertainment, and a record library and player, with a room in which young people could meet and amuse themselves with music. But pressure from the Communists had caused the government to close it down, and study was now that much more difficult. At his present rate of progress he thought that he might get through his final examinations in ten years' time, unless he could get an overseas scholarship. He had been offered such a scholarship, he said, to study in Moscow, but this would have meant first spending a full year studying Russian, which would be difficult; in any case, being a devout Moslem, he did not want to go to Russia.

As we had talked we had driven through the city, coming eventually onto a wide corso that runs along the waterfront. Local fishermen had nets spread to dry along the sea wall, and deep-sea men were laying sails upon the beach for mending while others paddled back and forth to their praus anchored offshore: big, twin-masted wooden ships with yards hung slantwise to take lateen sails. Ships have been built here to the same pattern for hundreds of years and still trade out as far as the Philippines, Cambodia, Burma, and Java.

These Makassar people were a great naval power in the sixteenth century, well known in all the Eastern seas from China to India, trading in times of peace and fighting battles in times of war. Torres saw them doing business in West New Guinea in

1603, and Matthew Flinders met them on the northern coasts of Australia two hundreds years later, trading with the Aboriginals, although by then their fighting days had ended and the Dutch were their overlords.

The conquest had been no walkover for the Hollanders in spite of their big ships and cannon and the bribing of allies among jealous and disgruntled sultans on other islands. They had started out to take Makassar in 1634 and twenty years later, having not yet succeeded, were keeping a blockade which the Makassarese opposed with such vigor that the Dutch sued for a truce; for there was an oath that the sailors of Makassar swore at that time which went along these lines:

> As a strong wind makes dry leaves fly from the trees,
> As a stream bears driftwood swiftly,
> As a needle pulls thread through a cloth,
> So shall we go, O Lord, at your command,
> To meet the enemy.
> Speak and we shall obey!
> And if at your word we do not go, let it be known
> to generations yet unborn,
> That our bodies were not worth burying.

It was thirty-five years before Makassar fell; and although an arrogant Dutch historian later said that the Indonesians were "a nation of coolies and a coolie among nations," this and other islands never did capitulate completely, nor did the bitter memory of Dutch aggression and treachery diminish during the ensuing centuries (the parallel with Ireland persists) so that today there is a problem in Makassar over the future of the old fort which overlooks, and once guarded, the harbor.

Nobody knows how long it has been there—and this is the quandary. Some say that it was originally built by the Malays, who were first to make the city great, and that it was one of a chain which extended through the archipelago right out into the Bay of Bengal; and if this is so, the fortress is an ancient national monument which should be restored and preserved and made much of. Others say that the Portuguese built it as a trading post, before the Dutch came, for they were the first Europeans to settle in these islands; and if this is true then it could, in decency, be left standing but adapted to some useful purpose. But there are those who say that it is Dutch, built upon the site of the original native fortress after the city first fell to the white invaders, in which case the local patriots would have it pulled down, stone by stone, and so built over it that not the slightest reminder of past shame would be left standing.

I asked Karim what he thought of the matter and he said, "I cannot afford to have an opinion because I live here, along with hundreds of other people who have nowhere else to go, and for me it is better if the argument continues so that we may all have somewhere to sleep."

We went in through a long tunnel in the wall, wide enough for an ox cart to enter, and came into a spacious quadrangle big enough to hold companies of soldiers but bare now except for a few banana plants and some poultry scratching in the thick gray dust. High, two-storied stone barracks buildings lined each side, the lower levels having been originally planned as stables, sheds, workshops, and storehouses with living quarters above them, some still with wooden shutters, but now the whole complex, including other big buildings further back, was honeycombed and subdivided and partitioned with bits of cloth or hessian hung on rattan and squares of woven palm leaf or wooden chests and ancient pieces of furniture arranged to make alcoves where people could sleep or work or cook. Some of these apartments had been turned into tiny shops, and one long storeroom was a school and another a mosque or meeting place for the people living in the fort.

It was cramped but not squalid, and the scores of children following us, although poorly dressed, were not dirty. Whenever I turned to speak to them they ran away shrieking *belanda* (Dutchman) in simulated terror, then stood at a safe distance and stared until a message came to say that one of Karim's neighbors had made coffee for us. We walked across the courtyard and into the back parts of the fort, where people had their laundry hung out on oleander bushes and women were drawing water from two ancient wells, their earthenware pitchers standing on the stone rim while they waited their turns. Men nodded to Karim and looked curiously at me, but they smiled when I smiled and asked if I were American. When I said that I came from Australia they came forward and shook hands saying, "Good, good."

We finished the coffee and I asked Karim if he would show me his room. He led me without speaking into one of the barrack buildings, through a great stone kitchen and so into a tiny room with ring bolts in the wall which might have been, in olden times, a cell or small stable for sheep or goats. It had no bed in it, only a small round table, two chairs, a small chest, a curtain across one corner to form a sort of wardrobe, a Chinese store calendar, and a lamp. There was a single medical book on the table—*Scott's Year Book of Urology*—and embossed upon the cover was "The Benjamin Franklin Library USIS. Karim looked embarrassed and said, "The USIS library was closed down before I could take the book back, but when I have finished with it I will put it in the library at the university." To change the subject I asked if he slept in this room, but he said no, it was too small to contain a bed and he used it only for studying and slept in the next room, sharing a bed with the children of the family who provided his daily meal.

I left Karim at the fort, for it was siesta time, and went back to the hotel. Later in the afternoon when people began to appear on the streets again I went out and found the house of the bishop of Makassar next door to his cathedral church.

The bishop's servant let me in and closed the door, shutting out the persistent sun, then he led me across the wide, tiled room out into a cloistered courtyard where a little cast-iron fountain dribbled and pigeons played along the gutterings of the roof and a few thin, garden-trained trees made shade. He left me there and went into an inner room.

An Indonesian, wearing a white soutane, crossed the courtyard, passing through an archway that led into the church. Soon afterward a bell rang from the tower, tolling the angelus. *Hail Mary, full of grace*: the familiar words seemed strange and out of place, like the cry of an exile, and suddenly I was lonely for my own kind. As the last attenuated echo of the church bell fell away the call of a muezzin from the city mosque overlaid it.

A young Dutch priest came toward me through the cloisters, crossing himself, and reaching me put out his hand, smiling frankly. Then having told me his name he explained apologetically that the bishop had gone, only two days ago, into the interior and would not be back for some weeks. I asked when, and he looked uncertain. "We cannot say. He is going into villages that have not seen a priest for fourteen years. We do not even know that he will reach them or what he will find when he gets there." He was being cautious, and I knew that I should be patient, that when he was sure that I was not looking for sensational stories he would speak more freely about the bishop's journey.

A lad brought lemonade and we sat down together in the gathering dusk. The fountain splashed and the pigeons strutted and muttered anxiously at each other and clouds of mosquitoes came out of the garden to feed on us.

I explained my visit, and the young priest seemed pleased to see a stranger who was interested in the mission and what he himself was doing. He sent for some papers and, looking at his watch, said that he was expecting a call from a sea captain who had undertaken to give him passage to an island lying to the southeast of Makassar where he had much to do. When the servant brought the papers he spread them out on a table—a map of the island and many plans and sketches of land subdivisions and buildings of various kinds. Then he told me his story: a story that I heard repeated in different forms many times afterward in other parts of Indonesia.

There is this island. It lies off the coast of Sulawesi some two or three days' sailing from Makassar, depending on the weather. Much of it is arid and parts are covered with forests of teak planted by Dutch companies many years ago and now owned by the government and therefore sacrosanct. But there are large fertile areas on the island which, properly farmed and freed from malaria, could give the population of 150,000 a reasonable standard of living. Yet practically all of them live at the lowest tolerable level of subsistence in high-walled villages on the barren hilltops and farm only the arid land along the ridges, leaving the fertile lower slopes uncultivated.

On the face of it the problem seems simply one of education, but of course there is more to it than that. First there is history. For centuries this island has been raided by mainland gangs from Sulawesi who come to plunder crops or take slaves or even heads for ritual reasons (we must remember, however reluctantly, that the white man came here to make money and not to civilize) so that the people of the island have become accustomed to living defensively and in a state of siege.

Then there are the predatory animals: herds of wild pigs live on the island, long-snouted, saber-toothed, and vicious; and swarms of black-faced baboons. Between them these animals devastate crops, decimate livestock and occasionally take and devour little children. If the islanders had guns they could wage war against them, but because Sulawesi is still an active rebel stronghold, and gunrunning is rife and a major crime, the villagers are forbidden firearms and must defend themselves with bamboo spears.

So they have made custom of necessity and live timidly in their hilltop villages behind stone walls six feet-high, leaving the slopes and lowlands to the government teak trees, wild animals, and mosquitoes. Their farming on the ridges is primitive, limited to burning off village areas of bush and cultivating the exposed land for a year or two before moving to another patch. If the single crop fails in any one year the people of that village must depend on others to keep them.

The young priest showed me his plans (the island and its 150,000 people are part of his parish and his special care). He has formed thirty families into a pioneer group and moved them down onto fertile ground. They have dug two deep wells for permanent water and have built a church and a school besides the village houses—an awareness of God and knowledge separates man from the animals, said the young priest, and underlies his superiority to them. They have also built a high wooden fence round the new village and set up an antimalarial clinic.

It is, he admits, a very minor essay in rehabilitation—an experiment which depends more on faith than on material resources, involving only thirty families out of the millions of Indonesians who need this kind of help (he said that the school was made possible by the gift of a thousand slates from a friend in Spain—there is no paper available for these children to write on). The central government has hundreds of problems more urgent, and few funds, and the people of the small outer islands are remote from Jakarta and their voices do not carry.

"Here in Indonesia the Christian missions have found a new apostolate; we work with a new emphasis and a wider view of the work of the church in the world." He rolled up his maps and diagrams and slipped a band round them. "We still run our schools and hospitals, but more and more we preach with our hands and with our labor, not totting up converts and first communions, and making graphs of baptisms and Christian marriages (although these have their own importance) but, seeking out those who most need help, we show them how they might lighten the load of poverty that weighs upon them. We try to give a little substance to the new dignity that their independence has brought them."

We talked on for a little while about the work of the foreign churches all over Indonesia: the training of young men to organize and manage new projects in the villages, to form cooperatives among poor farmers and fishermen, to give a lead in isolated places where there is no one else to do this, and to offer an alternative to Communist methods of local organization and ideology.

The young priest was keen and spoke and moved quickly, as if fearful of the passing of time not spent usefully. He pointed at a photograph of President Sukarno that hung on the main wall of the inner room facing a colored picture of Pope Paul. "There is the protector of the church in Indonesia. So long as he remains in authority we can go on safely with this work, but if anything happens to him the Communists will close in on us and our work will come to an end. I tell you, if we did not have him to protect us we would not last long in Indonesia." He held up his hands in a gesture of finality and looked at me. "And here, in Sulawesi, we have Kahar and his Islamite fanatics against us. They held one of our priests a prisoner in the mountains for nine years and never once let him say mass or read his office. He became ill and when there was a truce they let him come to Makassar for treatment on the understanding that he would go back again. But the President intervened and sent him out of the country.

"People who stay in Jakarta hear only of the confrontation in Malaya and the fighting between Indonesian and British soldiers in Kalimantan, forgetting that we have had a confrontation here in Sulawesi right from the beginning of the revolution, and that there are Christian villages in the interior that haven't seen a priest for fourteen years." He pointed out places on the map which the bishop hoped to visit, escorted by a convoy of soldiers, some of them no more than fifty or sixty miles from Makassar but cut off because the roads to them have been controlled all the time by rebel bands and bandits. "The government is getting the upper hand and driving the rebels back into the mountains. Soon, please God, they will be trapped there and starved into submission, and the people of the villages will have peace for the first time since the Pacific war began and the Japanese came to Indonesia. If only the Western people would realize the truth of Indonesia's sufferings they might be more patient and understanding of her weaknesses."

The servant came and announced the sea captain who, when he had been brought into the cloisters, said that he would be leaving for the priest's island on the early morning tide and would be obliged if his passenger could sleep aboard that night, to which the priest agreed. So I left and walked with the sea captain to the waterfront where he pointed out his prau riding at anchor, a curved white ship on a silver sea, it being late evening and the sun almost below the horizon. At the water's edge a boy waited with a dinghy to take him aboard. But he called to him and the boy came and was introduced to me as the captain's nephew, son of his sister who was married to a Christian of the Toradja people, who live in the mountains, and the three of us went together to a small café nearby. There the two of them ate rice and vegetables and I had a tasty bowl of soup containing cubes of buffalo liver and strips of tripe.

The captain was a garrulous man and told me much about Kahar Muzzakar and the rebels and the sufferings of the inland people, while the boy said nothing but kept eating. How much of what he told me was true and how much made up for the occasion, to impress a foreigner, I have no way of telling. Nor will I argue these matters but will simply paraphrase what he said to me and leave the reader to derive conclusions according to his sympathies or credulity.

"First," he said, "you must understand our past—the early battles against the Dutch hundreds of years ago and then the years of occupation when there were many uprisings and rebellions and it became part of our nature to be always against the government. In all these years we had no help from the Sultans of Java, who had been our rivals, anyway, in matters of trade and commerce, and we expected nothing of the Javanese people but fought our own battles against the Dutch and dreamed of our own freedom.

"But when, after so long a time this freedom came, many of us were prepared to try Sukarno's plan for a united Indonesia, taking in all the territory formerly held by Holland, while others saw neither sense nor glory in the idea of exchanging Dutch masters for Javanese and were against it from the beginning. Then there were those who thought that Dutch missionaries might be allowed to stay to help run schools and hospitals until we got settled, but others said they could see little difference between colonialism and Christianity and that all foreigners should go."

The captain shook his head and sent back his bowl for more rice. "These Dutch are clever and cunning. They took advantage of our differences and our years of inexperience and stirred up rebellion here in Sulawesi between us and the Jakarta government, and not only rebellion but civil war, which is worse, between Moslem and Christian, and between those who agreed with Sukarno and those who wanted local independence, so that brothers were fighting against each other and families split in two, and bloodshed was linked with great bitterness. Then when the Dutch went the fighting was kept going by men who were making big profit out of our troubles—local headmen, army commanders, smugglers, bandits here in our own islands, and foreign merchants in Borneo and Singapore. I tell you, they were years of horrible dishonesty and confusion here in Sulawesi, both in the north and in the south. Menado and Makassar were like besieged cities, and the country people lived in fear and trembling. Whole villages were abandoned and their populations, sometimes running into two, three, or four thousand people, made long marches across the mountains to find peace and quiet; and thousands more came here to Makassar and lived in the streets. Believe me, I have seen the roads thick with them, men, women, and children, and have had my ship loaded down with sick people who couldn't walk and couldn't be left to die in the villages, bringing them here to Makassar. These are things that you Western people have forgotten, or didn't know about."

He turned now to his nephew, a good-looking, dark-skinned boy with an incipient black moustache and serious eyes. "Look at this boy, my nephew. His father is a Christian and his mother a Moslem. He was born to the sound of rifle fire and was a guerrilla when he was ten. He is troubled because he is a good boy and he has killed a man, struggling with him for a rifle left hidden on the beach by smugglers. His spirit is sick and he has come to find quietness with me on my ship. Maybe he will go with the priest to the island and stay there a while to help the people instead of to be always fighting and hiding.

"Many boys have known no other way of life. Ever since they were children they have carried rifles to defend their villages or to guard the family crops and animals. Some have gone away to join the rebels or bandit gangs or smugglers [these are all "acceptable" trades under such circumstances]. Others have made their way to Makassar to join the army so that they could go back and train the other village children to fight Kahar. The things that some of these boys have seen would make a grown man vomit. Village elders circumcised and made to recite Moslem prayers or have their throats cut slowly with a piece of jagged tin—which many of them did. Men crucified by Kahar's fanatics as a sign that they would wipe out Christianity in Sulawesi."

We finished our food and paid for it (a few pence) then went and sat for a while on the sea wall, in the shadow of the old fort, near an open market place: a cluster of small stalls, stands, and makeshift tables, some no more than a sheet of paper spread upon the unpaved ground and goods laid on this. By the fitful light of petrol lamps, flares, and candles, we could see people moving like shadows on a dimly lit stage, stopping to look, to feel, to weigh in the hand doubtfully, to put down and pass slowly on to something else: green oranges in deep baskets, bunches of bananas, papaya, fish, shrimps, shoes, cotton shirts, batiks, books. Somewhere in the fort a radio was playing, and a woman's voice, plaintive with the strain and ache of love, hung high above the dusk-colored street, engaged in shameless conversation with the deep booming gongs of the gamelan, the sharp, demanding clash and clang of metallophones, masculine and angry. I grasped about again inside my mind for some sense of order, some understanding of the pattern of Asia, the calm and the passion, the poverty and riches, the courtesy and cruelty, the long slow tempo of its gentleness, and the quick indiscipline of its sudden, startling barbarisms.

Out in the harbor lights were coming to life on fishing towers—scaffolds set securely on the shallow sea bed and built up to form a platform from which the fishermen work at high tide. The towers are family and clan property, and fishing for the most part a family affair, father and young sons (or the wife when there are no children old enough) going out at sundown with the nets and food enough to last the night. They let the nets down through an opening in the platform, and a bright light is hung just above the water to attract the fish and trap them. Sitting on the sea wall we watched, and listened to the lazy lapping of the tide, the jangle of the gamelan, and the woman's wavering voice.

"There was a man here," said the captain, continuing with his stories of the rebels and their fighting, "named Andi Selle, a prince and local army commander, who had a battalion of troops at his disposal, stationed in the foothills between the Christian Toradja country and the lowland villages of the Moslem Buginese. He took advantage of the confusion caused by the rebellion to declare a state of emergency in his area and to impose military law, which he himself administered. He put a tithe upon the villagers and made them bring part of their food and all of their exportable produce to him, which they did without much question for the man was a prince and the people have been long accustomed to this kind of local rule. But if they refused he came with his soldiers and took everything, and burned down their villages. If a man owned a prau he made a smuggler of him, sending some of them to collect copra, rosin, and rattan from coastal villages and the nearby islands, and others to run the stuff through the Makassar Straits up to British North Borneo or the Philippines, for which activity they could be hung by the central government, for this kind of thing is considered traitorous and treasonable in Jakarta—although they are so busy down there with their Malaysian games they seem to have neither men nor money to spare to help us with our troubles.

"Payment for these illegal exports was made partly in cash and partly in arms and ammunition and military equipment such as radios and explosives, and these were passed on to Kahar to keep him in business and so justify the continuance of martial law as administered by the prince. I tell you, it was good business, such as an American would have been proud of; and nobody suffered, for the local officials were looked after, and no one who played the game according to the rules came to harm. But, before long the Chinese merchants in Java, missing their commission, complained that no goods were coming from Sulawesi and that the government was losing duties and taxes and such, so the commander at Makassar was instructed to move in on Prince Andi Selle and put a stop to his activities.

"The commander of the government forces, Colonel Yusef, a good man, set out from Makassar taking as guides several men who had at one time been in Selle's army, but the force was ambushed and some of these men, who were leading the way, were killed in the skirmish. Yusef withdrew, then came again with reinforcements and this time claimed to have shot Selle himself although no corpse was produced and the people in the hill village say that Selle is still alive and hiding in the mountains with Kahar."

It was dark now and time for me to meet Bahruddin, so I thanked the captain for his stories and shook hands gravely with his nephew, wishing them both a pleasant voyage; then I went by *betjak* to the hotel, jolting and bumping through rough, unlit, streets. And having shaved in the dirty basin, and bathed by pouring water over myself from a rusty can, I dressed and went to the little bar in the foyer and drank pink lemonade, for that is all they had. In a little while Bahruddin came and took me to see Professor Mononutu, the oracle of Makassar.

CHAPTER
4

The divan on which he sat was covered with a rug of golden-red cat skins, a present, he said, from the Chinese staff at the embassy in Peking. He made a vague, offhand gesture with his ivory cigarette holder. "I was our ambassador there, you know, for three years."

I did know, because Bahruddin had briefed me thoroughly on the life and times of Doctor Professor Arnold Mononutu, baccalaureate in the faculty of political science at the University of the Sorbonne, one-time Minister of Information for the Republic of Indonesia, ex-Ambassador to the Chinese People's Republic, presently a member of the President's Supreme Advisory Council and Rector of the University of Makassar.

He seemed a man of seventy or thereabouts and wore his clothes (an embroidered white shirt and blue sarong) with the neatness of a bachelor who has been long cosseted by servants and female relatives. He was a man of middle height, with sparse gray hair, chain-smoking with delicate gestures and speaking continuously with practiced courtesy.

I said that it was gracious of him to invite me to dinner, and he replied with urbanity that he was honored to be host to a foreign visitor who wished to be objective about Indonesia, its problems, and its point of view.

There was a small, silver-framed photograph standing on a table near the divan. It showed the President with his Number One

Wife, Fatmawati, and two of her children and was signed affectionately "Sukarno" in the President's sprawling hand. "We are old friends," said the professor, "right from the early days of the Nationalist Party. Whenever I go to Jakarta I visit him. He likes to talk about the early days of the revolution." The President also has a younger wife, Hartini, who lives with him at the summer palace. She is beautiful and intelligent. As though making excuses the professor said, "Miss Hartini is very good for the President: she helps him to relax."

He led me through the house, stopping to fondle the head of an eleventh-century Sita, in marble, cut (apparently) from a temple group. "My Javanese Mona Lisa," he said. "She is less enigmatic than the lady in the Louvre, having been forcibly seduced, subsequently tried by fire, acquitted and in consequence entitled to look self-satisfied.

"A gift from the artist." He nodded toward a Huang-kei horse picture hanging in an alcove. "And that is by the Javanese painter Srihadi—the influence of Picasso and Braque is evident." We were standing in front of an excellent portrait of an Indonesian woman in formal dress. "The lady is an old friend of mine." A vivid Pan-American Airlines calendar hung alongside the portrait, showing Fujiyama framed in cherry blossom. The juxtaposition did not seem incongruous.

He held back a black tapestry in which Buddhas were interwoven in gold thread, and we passed into a cloistered courtyard, one side of which was furnished richly as a dining and lounge room, shaded on the open side by a giant mango tree. The table was set with white linen, silverware, porcelain dishes, and crystal finger bowls.

The food was Indonesian and first class, the cooking supervised by the professor's sister (who did not appear), and the courses served by three shy boys who nudged each other and hissed whenever there seemed to be a minor hiatus. We drank Vichy water with each course, but the English plum pudding, served at the end of the meal as a compliment to the guest, came in a haze of cognac.

As we ate, the professor talked smoothly of his days in Peking, scattering his conversation with French words and phrases when suitable English escaped him. If he hesitated, Bahruddin prompted him deferentially and with great tact—it was clear that he had taken many guests to listen to the old oracle of Makassar.

The professor seemed to approve of the Chinese culturally and spoke with respect of his friend Chou En Lai, of Chinese performances of *Hamlet* and *Othello,* of the excellence of Chinese servants and their honesty (there were no government spies among them), and of the vast breadth and depth of Chinese cultural history, "immeasurably greater in spiritual and intellectual values than anything originating in the West."

But there were secondary loyalties, also, to the Paris of his student days, and a suggestion that General De Gaulle (*le Gloire de France*) alone of Europe's philosopher-statesmen had understood and striven to acquit the white man's sins, and now stood like a desolate and mighty monument amid the spiritual ruins of Europe.

We moved from the table for coffee, and the tone of the conversation changed. He spoke now without looking directly at me and the words were well rehearsed. "At this moment in history the West has a credit of good will with us. We do not, by instinct or history, lean toward the political East. For example, the students who go away to study first choose America, then Western Europe, and after that Australia and New Zealand. Russia and China come last. There are other than instinctive reasons for this, of course. The Americans give more scholarships and all of our students speak English, whereas they must spend a year or more learning Russian or Chinese if they wish to study in those countries. Also, most of the students follow one of the three religions of Indonesia and do not like to live in antireligious countries.

"But this situation will not last. The reservoir of good will which we Indonesians have for you will run dry. We cannot go on forever being bullied and threatened into following the Western political line. This is precisely why we had a revolution—to rid ourselves of foreign domination."

I ventured a hesitant interruption. "I am sorry, Om No"—I used a respectfully affectionate diminutive of his name and status—"but it does not seem logical to me that you should threaten the West with the loss of your affections because, with all respect, I feel that Indonesia needs Western friendship and help more than the West needs friendship with Indonesia."

There was resignation on his face, and he shook his head slowly. "My good friend, you seem to overlook the basic element in this whole situation, the main historic fact, the truth which has overtaken time." The tone was sympathetic. "We are at the historic stage of the final decline of the West and the ascendancy of the nations of the East, particularly of China." He paused and lit one cigarette from another. "The Americans may not admit to the decline but they are aware of rising China, and what they see frightens them—nothing else could explain the embarrassed involvement in Vietnam, for which there is no moral justification and barely adequate political excuse for the utterly defenseless refusal to admit China to membership of the United Nations.

"Why will you not admit the one truth which is clear to all of us Eastern people: the truth that the West is spiritually bankrupt, has run out of visions, has fulfilled the destiny set down for it in its own mythology and religion—the selling of its soul for money: the betrayal of its own prophets, from Christ to John Kennedy? The Americans can see this and are still young enough to love life and humanity. They may yet have the strength and courage to save themselves: but not Europe, which is too old, and has only a senile lust left to remind it of the virility it once had."

I was about to protest and to say that the West still led in almost everything that man of himself could achieve or create. That for the young people of Asia and Africa the attainment of Western ways and Western standards was the goal of revolution. That the attitude of people like himself and many other Eastern leaders was unctious and unreal, rather like eunuchs advocating continence. But he went on.

"You Australians are simply stupid."

He had played the part of host to perfection from the moment of my arrival, through dinner, until this moment. But now, like Dr. Abdulgani in Jakarta and all other politicians with whom I spoke in Indonesia, he made a hostile audience of me and went on without stop, spinning words as a spider spins a web, to a fixed, inherent pattern.

"With your British veneer you Australians may feel superior to Indonesians. You may even feel big-brotherly while lacking any real respect for us. But these attitudes are not realistic. They are taken from an imaginary position of continuing security behind the skirts of America and Britain. Yet within a generation you may be looking to our millions to protect you from the 'yellow hordes from the north' of which your poets wrote fifty years ago.

"Indonesia and Australia face the same danger—China—and

they should face it together. Your Prime Minister's sentimental devotion to the English Royal family, although touching, is unrealistic and against the interests of Australia, because Britain's paper Malaysia will not be able to protect you from the Chinese dragon when it breathes its fire on you. You will turn to America, as you did before, and if America is still trying to contain Asian Communism, your country will become another United States garrison. But perhaps that is the kind of security and freedom you want for Australia. We Indonesians have different ideas."

He filled in his picture of China with fluent verbal arabesques. "They will force admittance for themselves to the United Nations, when they are ready. Chou En Lai has told me, 'We shall not come in over the wall but through the front door, to our own music.' You must remember that Britain is China's most important trading partner . . . that Hong Kong and Singapore are Chinese cities and China's gateway to world trade . . . that when she is ready she will take them over. And the bomb. A hundred million dead in Europe . . . a hundred million dead in the United States . . . two hundred million eliminated in Russia . . . three hundred million in China. But when the atomic dust settles there will still be six hundred million Chinese."

I said, "What you prophesy may come to pass but the trigger might as easily be pressed in Jakarta as in New York, Moscow, or Peking. The danger does not lie only with the man who has the bomb in his keeping, but in the vanity and recklessness of other national leaders who contrive situations to provoke its use: like the confrontation in Malaysia."

He seemed surprised, as though my comment was more stupid than rude. "The British are entirely to blame for Malaysia. They created it. A weak and contrived piece of political cheating that threatens our security. We have no alternative but to oppose it." I was about to interrupt but he held up his hand and said, "Wait!

"The continuation of Malaysia as a stable political unit in Southeast Asia depends on the loyalty of Britain's ex-colonies in North Borneo, which were brought into the Malaysian Federation to keep a racial balance between the Malays and the Singapore Chinese, who despise the Tunku Abdul Rahman and would like to get rid of him. The British still control these North Borneo ex-colonies with their soldiers and puppet sultans and Chinese merchants whose pay and profits came from England. But the peasant people of these colonies want their independence, and when they get it, as they surely will, Malaysia must collapse; and the pieces will be gathered in by Red China, who will then be looking over our fence.*

"If Malaysia will only honor her agreement to join with us and the Philippines in a Maphilindo Federation, she will have a chance of honorable survival as an unaligned Asian democracy; but as a defenseless appendage of Britain she will fall, and that very soon, leaving us all exposed. Sukarno understands this and is prepared to sacrifice himself and Indonesia as a matter of principle as well as practical politics. In this light our opposition to Britain's fabricated Malaysia is necessary and inevitable, and confrontation has been forced upon us, not only in self-defense, but in defense of democratic freedom everywhere. In siding with the British against Indonesia the Americans are buying even more trouble than they have already in Southeast Asia, and Australia is blindly signing its own death warrant."

I thought that Bahruddin might have thrown me a lifeline, but when I looked at him he only smiled and clearly was not intending to become involved; so having come thus far I said, "Forgetting for a moment the possible collapse of Malaysia from within, it would seem to the noncommitted outsider that Indonesia is playing a dangerous and dishonest game in sending bands of infiltrating guerrillas into Malaysian territory, while at the same time declaring that she is not at war with anybody."

The answer came sharply. "We are sending nobody. The people of Indonesia, having achieved freedom after centuries of struggle, cannot stand by idly and see their neighbors still oppressed by European Imperialists. They have an emotional need to share the freedom they have won, and the government must acknowledge and encourage this humanitarian instinct in its people. Tens of thousands of young men and women have volunteered to give up everything to help the people of North Borneo and Malaya throw off colonialism and find true national dignity. Those who volunteered to go to West Irian and didn't get there are given first chance to go to Borneo or Malaya. Our government believes passionately in peace. It is at war with nobody. But it would be failing in its spiritual duty if it did not help train volunteers

* This conversation took place before the withdrawal of Singapore from the Malaysian Federation.

who generously wish to help their Malayan brothers gain freedom."

Once again, as in Jakarta, I found myself wondering if some essential piece of mechanism had slipped out of place in the machinery of my mind, or if underneath the mask of apparent sincerity and earnestness these Indonesian intellectuals were being wilfully cynical or obtuse; but neither explanation seemed adequate. (I was to find later that most senior Western diplomats have this same feeling of being drawn, against their wills, into an unmapped area of Alice-in-Wonderland abstraction and new-speak when discussing what to them seem straightforward political and diplomatic situations. A top foreign diplomat says that an essential part of the briefing of a Westerner newly posted to Jakarta is a course of Lewis Carroll, George Orwell, and Kafka.)

It seemed, now, too late to turn back from this line of conversation so I said, "From the Indonesian point of view the President may be right in his assessment of the Malaysian issue; but surely the danger is that if you push confrontation too far your country will become an international battleground as Vietnam is now and as Spain was in the thirties; your people will suffer even more than they did previously, and the freedom you have gained will be lost again."

He looked at the photograph of the President and Fatmawati. "Time is running out for Bung Karno, and it is necessary that Indonesia's major problems be resolved before he goes. Our country has not yet solidified into a smoothly functioning political and economic unity. The Communists want to go one way and the army another, and there are still suspicious and unsettled tensions between powerful outer island groups and the central government in Jakarta. The Republic was created and is held together by the power of this man's genius and personality, but this is not enough. Bung Karno will not always be here. We must learn to stand on our own feet as a nation. We must crush Malaysia"—he made a phrase of it, like a battlecry—"not only to guarantee our security but to give us a sense of collective achievement and identity, strong enough to contain and withstand the ferment of our internal differences."

There was much more said before he would let me go, but none of it added clarity or substance to the picture he had outlined of the Indonesian scene, a picture that, to me, was painted in an unfamiliar idiom difficult to interpret. I was tired, wearied with the argument and a rag-bag of impressions gathered during the day; so for my part I could only add that there were, in America and in my own country, many who had affection and sympathy for Indonesia, but if the Republic sought genuine foreign friendships without strings it must offer more and threaten less.

I said, too, that there is little logic in the processes of international politics; that the practice of politics is a matter of expediencies and power pressures; that theories pursued too ruthlessly invite interference which leads to violence, and the chips fall upon the people. It seemed to me, I said, paraphrasing Burke, that Sukarno and his advisors, though having a duty to gratify their people's needs and aspirations, had an equal duty not to inflame and mislead them.

On the Western side, because we have had more experience, there is the responsibility to understand the problems and the attitudes of Indonesia. Its leaders and people are full of reforming zeal. Sukarno says of himself, "I am in love with the romanticism of revolution." They want to create an inspired and inspiring Indonesia, a true God-guided democracy that will be an example to the decadent West. But their own political and economic problems, inexpertly tackled, make them behave in anything but an inspired manner in Western eyes. Still, the West must accept that Indonesia is adolescent, and should not take sides inflexibly against her or make of her a permanent enemy.

Before I left the professor's house I had agreed to speak to students at the university—"Here, in Makassar, we have few opportunities to meet and speak with foreigners and are grateful for a chance to sharpen our wits and try our lances." And at the hotel, in the dingy room, I listened to the news from Radio Malaya (a criminal offense) and heard that Australia has sent more troops to strengthen the defences of Malaysia. A stranger came and stood in the shadows near my door, and I wondered if he were spying on me or merely curious. When the news was finished he asked me if I wanted a woman, and when I thanked him and said no he inclined his head courteously and went away.

Bahruddin came again in the morning (I could not have asked for better attention or a more amiable arrangement of my timetable) and said that he was going out into the country to look at some irrigation work being done by villagers and afterward would be going to a small town whose people were ship-builders. Would I like to go with him?

We set out soon after a breakfast of cold rice, cold tea, and bananas and were chased through the wide white streets by a fresh breeze coming off the sea, and so went inland toward the hills by a road running through rice fields. We passed school children with hoes over their shoulders, singing as they went to work their own school plots, and long files of men on bicycles riding along the margin of the road toward Makassar with sheaves of yellow rice to sell. Each man carried eight or ten sheaves on his bicycle, some hung in panniers over the back wheel and some were slung from the handle bars, each sheaf weighing twenty pounds or thereabouts so that a load on a bicycle might be two hundred pounds.

The season's harvest was nearly over, with most of the fields dry and the stubble pale yellow. But in some there were women still reaping, waist deep in seas of rippling rice, strung out in bowed lines in a blue haze like fishermen leaning against the tide as they draw their nets toward the shore. The women wore wide mushroom hats to shade their shoulders, and scarves about their faces to keep out the light and heat thrown back by the grain: fine, lithe little women as slender and graceful as the rice stalks swaying with the wind; they reaped with up-sweeping, circular strokes cutting the heads of grain with a comblike blade hidden in the hollow of the hand. In the dry paddies men were ploughing with great clumsy wooden ploughs, and boys rode oxen to pasture or to bathe in ditches, disturbing white egrets (elegant as English ladies) and making them rise and tuck their long legs under and flap disdainfully away to adjacent fields.

When we had gone twenty kilometers (twelve miles) we stopped and waited a while under some palm trees to rendezvous with a guide, the Bupati of the area (equivalent, perhaps, to a district commissioner or a county chairman) who came in a clean-painted jeep; he was a square-set, vigorous little man of sixty or so, who took us off the main road into farm tracks and byways until we came to a place where two hundred men were working with hoes and spades and digging sticks in a deep ditch.

Most of them were men of middle age, although there were youths among them flaunting their young powers and working faster than the rest, and a few old men with skinny ribs who dug with careful, neat precision; but all worked well and with spirit, cheerfully, with a flag flying over them (a rough square of black rag on a long stick). The ditch where they were digging was narrow and overgrown and seemed no more than a green, irregular fissure in the ground; but where they had finished it had become a canal, neat and clean-cut, fifteen feet wide at the top and about as deep, with sloping sides.

Bahruddin and the Bupati talked to the leaders of the group, pointing here and there across the landscape, estimating and measuring distance with the eye, nodding at each other with assurance and satisfaction. Afterward they told me that the men of this area, ten gangs of two hundred each (all voluntary workers) had been set a target of thirty kilometers for the month but had cleaned and re-cut a hundred kilometers instead, as a challenge to the men of other areas. We left them and drove through fields and villages to visit other groups, and as we went Bahruddin, representing the governor, and the Bupati, representing the local people, spoke of their plans, hopes, and ambitions.

Irrigation is an ancient art, no more new in Indonesia than it is elsewhere in Asia. In the tenth century the Javanese ruler Mpu Sendok made a hobby of reclaiming swamplands, and when the Dutch came their archaeologists found evidence in plenty of irrigation schemes that were in operation long before agriculture was a science in the West. What seems like new work and the introduction of up-to-date ideas in Indonesia today is simply a reconstruction, a new beginning after a quarter of a century of neglect and deterioration which began when the Japanese came, after Pearl Harbor. Until then these clogged-up, disused ditches were canals carrying water from reservoirs and rivers to the rice fields.

The Japanese stayed three years, disrupting the normal cycle of farming life with the demands and impositions of a military occupation. Then, in 1945, the Western allies attacked the Japanese on Sulawesi, as on the other Indonesian islands, and there were bitter battles before the way was made safe for Dutchmen to come back and rule again in Indonesia (many Allied soldiers still lie in the cemetery outside Makassar). But during the three years of Japanese occupation the Indonesians had resolved that when the war was ended they would not stand patiently like oxen while Dutchmen clamped the yoke of colonialism back upon their necks. Before the Japanese had signed their capitulation, Sukarno had read his proclamation in Jakarta and had drafted the preamble to the constitution of the new Indonesian state: "Thanks to the blessing of Almighty God, and impelled by the noble desire to lead their own free national life, the People of Indonesia hereby declare their independence."

But the Dutch came back just the same, determined to stamp out these heresies and to keep control of the islands which, they said, supplied the life-blood of their nation. "We have ruled here with whip and club for three hundred years," said Governor-General Jonkheer de Jongh, according to Sutan Sjahrir, first prime minister of the Republic, "and we shall remain here for another three hundred years."

The determination of the Dutch was not in doubt. They hung on for nearly five more years, and here in Sulawesi committed crimes of intimidation almost as brutal as any perpetrated during the worst years of the Great World War, butchering 40,000 simple but stubborn village people in a single period of two months. This was not the climate in which to plod ahead with the restoration of irrigation systems, however simple. Men were fighting or fleeing with their families to quieter parts or patiently going on with the minimal processes of staying alive, content to grow a single rice crop each year, in the rainy season, leaving the canals choked with weeds and rubbish.

Four years and more after the war had ended the Dutch were forced to see and accept what everybody else had seen already—that the wheel of history had completed a revolution and the world they knew in 1942 no longer existed. Grudgingly they bowed to international pressure and opinion and went home, back to Holland; but the antagonisms and enmities they had sown and cultivated carefully over the centuries kept local feuds and uprisings alive for more years yet. Here in Sulawesi, in 1950, they inspired uprisings against the central government during which a third of the buildings in Makassar were destroyed and hundreds of civilians killed in street fighting (although the Dutch had nothing to gain).

So it went on; and today, fifty miles further inland from where I stood watching the village men at work, the last of the Dutch-encouraged rebels, Kahar, still holds out. "Less than two years ago," said the Bupati, "he and his fanatics still controlled this area. Now they have been driven back into the hills and for the first time in more than twenty years we are free to live as we want to. To use the land for our own purposes, to grow more food and crops to sell, more livestock to take to market or to eat ourselves.*

"Sometimes in these past twenty years we talked of cleaning out the reservoirs and canals so that we might grow more rice, but sooner of later someone would say, 'What for? To feed the Japanese, the Dutch, the bandits, the rebels?' So we did nothing and grew only enough to keep ourselves alive and waited for better times, while the canals stayed dry and overgrown."

Andi Bahruddin is the prophet of the new era in South Sulawesi. He is young and handsome, a man of good family with a lovely coquettish wife and six fine children. His zeal is tempered with humor and a genuine affection and sympathy for the people of the villages, so that he can sit with them in their houses or in the little roadside eating huts (for they are no more than this), and talk crops and weather and politics with men coming from the fields or passing along the road to and from the market towns. He will drink rough palm wine with them from an old tin cup, praise the cook for his soup, and cunningly conjure up visions of good times ahead while making no promises; so the people of the villages trust him, assured that he will not let the politicians and clerks in Jakarta play tricks with them.

He says to the villagers, "We don't need their aid or experts for a while. We have the manpower and the ability to restore our basic agricultural economy here in South Sulawesi before we start on any of these new industrial projects planned by the central government. Within two years we will have a million hectares of land under irrigation, and each farmer here will grow enough rice to feed his own family and two families in Jakarta. We will become the storehouse of Indonesia."

Here, around Makassar, he has organized the villagers into five major working groups, each group taking in the men of twenty-five villages, and with them he has worked out a plan of restoration based on voluntary labor coordinated toward a common end. It is in line with tradition—an old Indonesian custom which they

* An Army communique issued some months later announced the death of the rebel leader in the following terms:

> God's promise, that the leader of the rebels, Kahar Muzzakar shall be killed in the morning of the 3rd of February 1965, coincided with the Idul Fitri, The Day of Victory. This victory was stated in the Holy Bible as follows; "Glory be to God in the Highest. And on earth peace to men of good will."

The communique is illustrated with photographs of the corpse.

call *Gotong Royong*—mutual self-help, a kind of spontaneous collectivism. Each of these five groups of villages provides two thousand men a day, ten thousand all told, whose first objective is to get the old irrigation systems working again, then the roads reopened and extended, and central barns and storehouses built to hold the exportable surplus of rice which will result from the new irrigation. At the same time he has picked out men with mechanical aptitudes and experience and has them working to put every available piece of motor transport back into operation: of the twelve hundred vehicles owned in this district only one hundred and twenty have the spark of life left in them after so many years of neglect.

We came upon another group working in the main feeder canal which comes from the reservoir, a channel forty feet wide and twenty deep. The two thousand men allotted to this project had reconstructed six kilometers (three and a half miles) of canal in a single week. Their children made a game of gathering stones from the river bed and helped to load the trucks that carry these stones to roadworks, being paid well enough for their trouble by exciting rides to and from the river.

But Bahruddin has his troubles. For example, if farmers had insecticides and fertilizers they could treble the rice crop: but Indonesia does not produce insecticides and has no foreign currency to spare for this purpose at present. As for fertilizer, there is a government plant at Palembang in Sumatra, but production there is not enough to supply a fraction of the needs of the Republic, and the urgency is greater elsewhere than in Sulawesi. In time, when all the plans in Jakarta's Blueprint Hall become facts, there will be many more factories and fertilizer enough to go around. There may even be one in Makassar, for there are already plans for a cement factory, a paper mill, shipyards, and plants for producing power from residual oil and coal dust, for oxygen and for plywood. Nickel and copper mining are on the list and a sugar factory and a dockyard. There is a maize-production plan worked out with a Japanese company by which Indonesia provides land and labor and the Japanese bring machinery which is paid for with a proportion of the crop (which goes to Japan to feed pigs). This is the Indonesian way of doing business and developing the country. I am no economist. I have no idea if this kind of thing will work. But in Sulawesi alone many foreign countries have plans for production-sharing with Indonesia on such projects—

Poland, West Germany, Japan, the United States, Yugoslavia, Czechoslovakia, and Hungary. "It's mostly on paper at the moment," said Bahruddin, "but if we have two or three years of peace we can get all of these things going and make our contribution to the development and security of greater Indonesia."

There was a man of this district named Yusef, born in 1626 (so the legend on his shrine says) who preached bitter hate against the Dutch, and when he died he was made a saint. From youth to old age he fulminated, cried down curses, and urged murder (and why not, when his country was infested with avaricious foreigners?). Many a mother in those days blamed him for a meddling rabble-rouser when burying a son or husband killed in uprisings or reprisals.

We went to the shrine where he lies buried with his wife beside him although she, poor woman, saw little of him in life for he was in and out of prison, exiled to Ceylon in 1683 where he continued to be a nuisance to the Dutch, preaching the jihad to pilgrims going back to Makassar from Mecca, and so was taken further out of mischief's way to South Africa, where he died in 1694. Friends brought his body back home for burying ten years later. Had he lived today and behaved in the same way he would have been a Kahar man, and subject to hanging if caught by Sukarno's soldiers; but being dead he is a holy man and we take off our shoes to walk around his grave. Newly married women, high and low, come in hundreds to his burying place to pray that they will quickly bear sons to their husbands and that the boys will grow to be great patriots. Such things seem strange, and the complexity of man amazing. What is a hero—what is a saint? How fine a line divides inspired patriotism from criminal vanity? When does principle become stubborn stupidity, or right become wrong?

The shrine is a simple little white-washed mausoleum with a rounded roof, set back a bit from the dusty road. (The shop beside it, selling holy trinkets and such, is much bigger.) We came to it through a clutter of ox carts and bicycles, a few cars, and many people on foot, but strangely enough, no beggars were there although small boys were badgering devotees to buy little boxes of flower petals, grass clippings, and pretty leaves with which to decorate the graves of the holy man and his wife.

Inside the shrine there are a dozen graves as well as those of Yusef and his wife (perhaps they are his children or relatives;

nobody could tell me) with room between them for, maybe, twenty people to meditate. The saint's grave is in a corner under a canopy and is strewn with the flower petals, grass clippings, and leaves bought from the small boys outside. An old man, dust-colored and blind, squats by the grave saying prayers continuously for those who leave money in his tin.

I stood barefoot beside him on the tiled floor, with a young soldier and his wife and small child on the other side of me, and watched a peasant woman put her hand upon the headstone, close her eyes, and begin to whisper some supplication. When she had done so she took her hand from the headstone and touched her breast and forehead, then lit a candle and put it to rest on a ledge above the grave, and stood again for a moment in reflection before moving away. The candle flickered against the smoke-stained white walls. So I have seen, a thousand times, some woman in a Christian chapel lay her hand on the statue of a saint, and pray and light a candle and go away strengthened in faith.

Outside in the bright sunlight a rich lady was throwing coins from her car, into the roadway, for the children to scramble after, and for such charity she will receive her reward in due course. The coins are, in fact, tokens purchased from the shop, which when collected by the children are redeemed for a few rupiahs and used again, the shop-keeper making a small commission each time. He also hires out young goats to those who wish to make a ritual dismissal of their sins. For a moderate price you may lay hands on the animal and transmit your iniquities to it, after which a lad will drive it for you out into the wastelands where, theoretically, it will wander alone until the sins are requited; but in fact the goat gets bored and finds its way back to the shop-keeper after a while and is hired out again to some other sinner.

Bahruddin said that his wife came here often when they were first married and laid her simple peccadilloes on a kid and turned it loose so that she should be clean of heart when she conceived. When she knew herself pregnant she made a visit of thanksgiving to old Yusef and went away content. Now, eight years married, she has six children and is still very beautiful, a lively testimony to faith.

As we were getting into the car an army sergeant came to Bahruddin asking for a ride, our driver having told him that we were on our way to Pallengo, the ship-building town; and seeing that the sergeant was stationed there in charge of the defense contingent and was well known to Bahruddin, we were glad to make room for him.

He was a dark-skinned, lithe man, a Toradja from the mountains, and he had been home, he said, to attend the burying of an uncle. He wore his jet black hair in medieval fashion, swept back over his ears and falling almost to his shoulders. His face was wide across the eyes and sloped sharply to a small, effeminate chin set off with a thin beard. He had a narrow line of moustache and a mouthful of shining silver teeth.

There are, at a guess, two million of these Toradja people (recent statistics are incomplete), long known as slavers and head-takers but now nominally Christian, although their practices are animist and their rituals brazenly pagan. From as far back as tribal recollection goes they have held the buffalo sacred and have made its image their symbol of fertility and strength and a protection from evil. The roofs of their houses, built high on stilts, have the high upsweep of its horns (always pointing north and south) and the inside walls and ceilings are inlaid with the same motif, while the social standing of a family is shown by the number of sets of buffalo horns hanging at the entrance to the house.

On the way to Pallengo, prompted by Bahruddin, the sergeant told me of his uncle's funeral: how, when he died, messages were sent to relatives and to notables of neighboring villages, asking them to come for the ceremonies. And while men of his family built guest houses to hold the visitors, others made a mortuary house where the body was to rest until everyone assembled.

The dead man was washed, wrapped in cloth, and placed in a cylindrical wooden coffin. Then, when the mortuary house was ready, he was taken from his own home and carried there by a winding, devious way on the shoulders of several men who danced and jigged and tossed the coffin about violently, intending thereby to confuse the dead man's spirit so thoroughly that it would not be able to find its way back to the house. Before reaching the mortuary the corpse was met by other men who formed into a hollow square and stood around him, chanting the death songs of the Toradja people. (The sergeant sang me part of it, a high-pitched and seemingly formless descant, sometimes in the pentatonic then slipping into microtones and tremolos, so that although I would have liked to take it down I could not, nor was there any way of telling whether the sergeant was a competent or poor singer or how much the jolting of the car contributed to the shakiness of his voice).

While these preliminaries were going on other men, experts in stone work, were carving a niche high up in a rock face on the mountain to make him a tomb overlooking the village. They worked from bamboo scaffolds and ladders lashed together, busy for many days, during which time the guests came. Meanwhile the body rested on a litter inside the mortuary house, visited each day by members of the family, who brought small offerings of flowers and food.

When the grave was ready and all the guests present, the body was brought out on its litter, a palanquin hung with curtains, and the widow and the dead man's daughters climbed in beside it and drew the curtains close. Then the litter was lifted onto the shoulders of many strong men and carried in procession across the fields to a meadow beneath the mountain face. There were buffaloes at the head of the procession, decorated with garlands of palm leaves and led by boys, and all the people of the village followed after, the men wearing white and the women black, some leading pigs or carrying them slung on poles.

When they came to the meadow the litter was set down and the people disposed themselves as at a fair or picnic to watch while groups performed the mourning dances. Then the buffaloes, still garlanded, were paired off and incited to fight; and when the excitement of this had diminished, and the beasts were weary, their throats were cut with scimitars, men hacking away at them barbarously until they fell helplessly onto their knees and could be finally despatched. Then the pigs were pierced to the heart with sharp-pointed sticks, and together with the buffaloes were cut up and the meat distributed for the funeral feast.

Toward evening the dead man was taken from his litter and carried without ceremony to the cliff face, passed roughly from hand to hand up the scaffolding and ladders, and pushed into his sepulcher; a wall of stones was laid across the entrance to keep him from hungry beasts. Then the people went home, back across the fields in the colorless evening light, to the village. A primitive ritual, but perhaps more real than the impersonal, secular, professionally mock-solemn burial services of the West.

CHAPTER

5

The little ship-building town of Pallengo spreads like a dull stain, back from the river, over the drab estuary flats, a brown patch of single-storied wooden houses set on tall stilts to overtop the highest tides. Its few streets are wide and end abruptly in gardens of banana and coconut plants. Two thousand people live here and build ships as their forefathers built them long before there was any contact with the Western world.

We left the sergeant at his house and drove straight to the slipways on the river's edge, where eight ships lay in cradles of scaffolding, some sparsely skeletal, others full-planked and round-bottomed, soon ready to slip into the river and be masted. They were wooden ships, big, broad-beamed, fashioned plank by plank from solid logs of teak. I clambered about one, ribbed like a whale, thirty meters (roughly, 98 feet) from stem to stern and fifteen meters at the waist: not a single nail anywhere, only thumb-thick wooden pins, and the timbers cut, chipped and fitted by hand at every stage, measured by eye or with a piece of knotted string. No machinery of any kind is used. Men's hands and fingers fashion the raw wood with strange, ancient tools in which the only concession to the twentieth century lies in the use of metal augers and in steel blades instead of bronze and iron.

There is a naturalness about the activity, an integration in this ancient relationship between the man and his materials, a collaboration that makes of the man a craftsman or artist and of the material a work of art or craftsmanship, a living thing with character, being, and lifelong purpose. There is no violence, no mechanical brutality as in a factory where machines rend metal, stamp, bend, flatten, and force it into impersonal shapes, making it merely servile, not related in any way to nature.

For centuries, ships like these built here at Pallengo, and in other towns along the coast, have carried the island trade. Back in the days, long before the Dutch, when local sultans had their own trading arrangements with rulers in China, Siam, Malaya, and the Philippines, these ships sailed continuously in and out of a thousand Asian ports and harbors with the simple, stately grace of village-born beauties carrying goods to the market place; and so they sail today. Sometimes, for all their simplicity, they look truly and beautifully breath-taking, set against glorious sundowns or violet night skies, or coming into sight quietly, sadly veiled in soft scarves of gray monsoonal rain. But for all their grace they are sturdy ships, built to withstand the strong green seas beyond the reefs, and the shock of hurricanes and typhoons in the China Sea. In the old days they were warships also, when sultans fought each other over some slight or some dispute about trade or slave-taking or women.

Today's ships are built the same as those that engaged the navy of Genghis Khan and drove it back to China, and the making and sailing of them keeps whole communities occupied as it has done for centuries: timber-getters, carpenters, shipwrights and sailors.

Bahruddin said, "The President understands that we cannot easily and immediatcly graft a twentieth-century civilization onto a sixteenth-century technology and economic system. Foreign experts tell us that we should have a fleet of modern ships for the island trade but to do this we would have to borrow overseas money, and then within two years the ships would be laid up for lack of expert maintenance and spare parts, while the local shipbuilding trade would have been disrupted and the people's livelihood taken away.

"It is better to go slowly. We have our plans for a modern shipyard here in Sulawesi, and in a few years young men from here and other towns along the coast will be learning the new ways and trades. Maybe in ten years or more we will have trained men to build, maintain, and sail sufficient modern ships to take over the island trade. But this won't happen in a day and meanwhile we prefer to do things in our own way."

A dozen of us went, then, to the sergeant's house and had small cakes and fried bananas to eat, and the milk of young coconuts to drink. Then a neighbor brought along a bucketful of fresh palm wine and some dusty bottles of an earlier tapping, all of which we sampled with great seriousness as though sitting in the wine cellars of the Haute Medoc instead of in the house of a young man whose recent ancestors drank buffalo blood on great occasions. Some of the wine was raw and sharp, and some was sweetened with sugar cane. All of it was milky, crude, and unstrained, contaminated with bits of palm-pith and debris, and with insects dead in it. The others watched with curiousity while I tasted each sample with as much courtesy as I could muster, but I could not honestly be enthusiastic, even to please them, although I did my best not to make faces, for I found the taste and flavor of the stuff reminiscent of sheep dip. Also, it lay harshly on the tongue and stomach and would, I am sure, have given me a headache had we stayed much longer.

The front room of the house served also as an office for the sergeant and had a table in it with ink pot, pen, ruler, and a rubber stamp grouped together neatly and a book of army regulations set squarely to one side. There was a map of the district on the wall and, over the table, looking down on whoever would sit there, a colored picture of a man who might have been the sergeant's ancestor—a stern man in his young prime, with long dark hair, a heart-shaped face, and flashing eyes, wearing a white turban and burnoose, and a wide sash with a sword stuck in it, his hand grasping the hilt as though he were about to unsheath and slash at some adversary. The sergeant said, "That is the Sultan Hasanuddin, who fought against the Dutch when they first came to Sulawesi. He is our hero."

Driving back to Makassar we went by way of the Sultan Hasanuddin's tomb, which, since the founding of the Republic, has become the chief national monument in South Sulawesi, and the sultan himself, the district's official hero. Each province has such a hero, always a man who fought against the Dutch, and a shrine, tomb, or monument at which ceremonies and parades are held and patriotic speeches are made on August 17, Proclamation Day, the day of Indonesia's declaration of independence.

There is another hero buried here, near Makassar, the greatest of them all—Prince Diponegoro, who fought the Dutch in Java, where they were thickest and most solidly entrenched, and kept the best part of their army fully occupied for many years. Eventually, he was taken by treachery and exiled here, in Makassar, where he died. But being a Javanese he takes second place to the local hero, and few people know where to look for his grave.

But the Sultan Hasanuddin is hero enough, and Sukarno himself has been here to eulogize the man and establish his local precedence. Being Makassarese he was a famous sea captain and led a thousand ships against the Dutch fleet and scattered it. He also sent a letter to the enemy, saying:

> Allah, who made the whole world, set each people in their appointed place, that they might enjoy and make use of it without giving offence to others. But you Dutch seem to think that you have some special understanding with Him who has thus ordered all things, by which these islands in the Eastern Seas have been set aside especially for the benefit of your people, who live on the far side of the earth. And this we cannot believe, nor will we give in to your impudence; and as often as you attack us we will resist, nor will we retreat, but will go forward against you in the name of Mahomet, the Prophet.

But the Dutch commander sent to Java for more ships and men and bribed the neighboring sultans to abandon and deny Hasanuddin, leaving him to fight alone, without help or friendship, so that he was driven back and Makassar was taken (although the Dutch never held the whole of Sulawesi in subjection). The sultan died in sorrow and lies buried beside the spot where he was proudly crowned: and, as the villagers say, "He sleeps here in magnificence."

We left the sultan's tomb, and driving back to Makassar I laid out in my mind all I had seen and heard since my arrival and, sorting it out, began to trace, in part, the pattern of the Indonesian schizophrenia: on the one hand a gracious, unaffected courtesy, friendliness and generosity toward white people; and on the other a fixed, inflexible, inherent hatred of colonialism—a hatred more profound, more nightmarish, even more deeply ingrained than the American hate of Communism.

For three hundred years the Indonesians stayed frozen in a frame like a film that has stopped in motion. Their customs remained the same; their culture unchanged; their hates stable, concentrated generation after generation against the foreign invaders who became their overlords. Through these centuries their hopes, dreams, and visions were of independence and freedom from foreign interference. Their saints and heroes have always been men who have preached rebellion and have led them time and again in passionate but ineffectual protest against the unimaginative servitude imposed upon them by the Dutch. Their heroes have always been larger than life—mystical beings with the qualities of minor gods. They descended in line from men like Yusef and the Sultan Hasanuddin, through scores of similar heroes, to Sukarno, who brought them finally to the top of the mountain and showed them the promised land.

With these thoughts in the back of my mind I sat that night in the great hall of the university waiting for Professor Mononutu to introduce me to the gathering of students and staff who had come, so I thought, to hear me speak.

The professor stood on the dais, humped over a lectern, searching the sea of faces that looked up at him, creating for himself a silence into which, at any moment, he would flick smooth pebbles of wisdom. There was a final cough at the back of the hall, the scraping of a chair, then quiet. I looked up at the old man from my seat in the front row, beside the registrar of the university, and thought that he looked frail and aged, although he hid it well with dapper dressing (white silk shirt, tan trousers neatly creased, tie to match, and cream shoes). He lifted his hands, almost in blessing, then paused. His mannerisms were professional, almost too perfect, making him seem as much an actor as a savant.

He began modestly, speaking with diffidence of his own long and close association with President Sukarno, of his service as an ambassador and minister of the Republic, of his responsibility to the young minds entrusted to his care. It seemed to me irrelevant and after five minutes I was becoming impatient, wondering when he was going to introduce me. But in a while he said, "We have with us this evening a foreign writer who has come here to see for himself how the Indonesian people are withstanding the attempts of the neocolonialists and their friends to deliver us once again back into the bondage of Imperialism. This man is one of the few Western writers who has troubled himself to come to look for the truth and we are grateful to him for having made this effort." He bowed in my direction and there was a rustling in the hall as people tried to see whom he was speaking of. He waited for quiet and went on. "Others, having no concern for the truth, invent lies, are servile, lick the boots of those who pay them, and write whatever their masters want to read." It was mildly embarrassing, and to anyone familiar with the processes of workaday journalism it sounded naïve. In any case I had hoped to escape the clap-trap and play-acting of second-rate political repertory here at the university and was irritated by what seemed to me an improper and deliberate attempt at intimidation. Also I had developed an affection for the professor and felt disappointed in him and let down.

"A university," he said, "is a storehouse of knowledge and a forum for the discussion of ideas and opinions. Therefore, we welcome our foreign visitor and wait with keen anticipation to hear what he has to say, hoping that he will help us to see our problems in a clearer light. We hope, too, that he will feel free to criticize where there is room for criticism, but that he will not fail to praise where there is occasion for praise."

"Our Great Leader, Doctor President Sukarno, is a man of wisdom. One of the great minds of the age." He looked around, inviting contradiction, playing the game like an expert. "He has not only said that a university is a storehouse of knowledge but that for us in Indonesia it is the schoolroom of the revolution. Its purpose is to shape the minds which will guide and direct the future of the Republic, and to create in its lecture rooms and laboratories the flesh and the spirit of an Indonesian identity. Those who leave these halls of learning to teach others will not only teach what they know or what they think and believe but they will teach what they are. A theorist cannot teach men and women to be patriots. A man must be a patriot himself before he can teach others what is meant by love of country."

I began to fidget, wondering how long he was going on and to what extent he would cut across what I had planned to say. He talked on for a while about the role of the university as an instrument of continuing revolution; then, with a glance in my direction he said, "But while we are creating an Indonesian identity and ethos, our national integrity must be protected. Slowly we are being hemmed in by those who want the world to stand still, who would like to destroy us before we become too powerful for them, so that they may restore colonialism in Asia and bring us again under the yoke." He lifted a finger rhetorically. "The Seventh Fleet of the United States Navy patrols Asian waterways, intimidating us, threatening, trying to bully us with battleship diplomacy into acting according to a script written in Washington. And in Singapore the British have atomic rockets pointing at Jakarta, with Malayan servants standing ready to press the button when London gives the command."

Then, to my astonishment, he turned and looked down and stabbed his finger directly at me. "You may tell your friends that we will not flinch—that we are not afraid of your encirclement or of your rockets." He paused and turned to look again across the rows of silent students, his hands now gripping the sides of the lectern and his neck stretched forward so that he looked like an irritated old turkey. "This is the age of the Afro-Asian people, the age of the true democracy of all of the people of the world, not a democracy of the few, based on race, color, and privilege, but a democracy of all races and nations, in which we of Afro-Asia have by far the biggest part." He looked down at me again. "If you of the West wish to join us in true friendship we will welcome you. If you ignore us you may go to hell."

I was startled, and looked to the man beside me for some explanation. He smiled and patted my knee. "Take no notice—this is for the newspapers and the Communist students. If the professor doesn't take this opportunity to lecture you they will accuse him of failing in leadership and national consciousness."

I thought back on stories told to me in Jakarta. One came from a United Nations official, making a study of the economic situation in Indonesia. He had said, "There are plenty of first-rate economists in this country, especially in the universities, but they are afraid to speak in case they find themselves labeled 'disloyal.' " And when I looked doubtful he named a man who had been dean of his faculty and was dismissed and forbidden to teach elsewhere, because he had said in a lecture that although the president was a political genius he was also an economic illiterate. A group of loyal students had demonstrated against this man and petitioned for his removal.

I had heard also of another economist, an anti-Communist Christian, chosen by the President himself to take the chair at a conference on national economic planning, who was arrested as he stepped out of his house in Jogjakarta to take the train to the capital to attend these meetings, and was held in jail on a charge of corruption laid against him by Communists. No doubt there was something in the charges. Indonesia is not a police state and a man cannot be put in jail for nothing. The man had probably borrowed money or accepted a gift and was vulnerable, although no more so than many other officials and academics who are trying to live decently on laborer's wages. The significant fact is that the arrest was planned simply to prevent a professed anti-Communist from taking the chair at a major national conference; he was released after the meetings and no one was prepared to challenge the action.

So I realized now, listening to the old professor, that although hundreds of students and faculty members sat in the great hall, I alone was his audience; that he was using me as a mark to shoot at, to demonstrate his own irreproachable loyalties, and that the others were there only to witness and approve. It was as though he were making, for his own protection, a public reaffirmation of faith in the doctrine of the state. I felt sorry for this nice old man who had been, last night, so excellent a host.

But now, having fulfilled his political obligations and cleared himself with the Communists among the students, he seemed easier and went on to speak for another thirty minutes, falling naturally into the manner and idiom of a lecturer in political philosophy, taking no further notice of me.

I found his argument interesting. Reduced to essentials it maintained that the emergence of the Indonesian Republic, under its Great Leader, was a major turning point in world history, although he admitted, in passing, that countries like the Congo and Vietnam are at present providing more dramatic action than Indonesia in this current episode of the serial drama of mankind's evolution. But, he said, it will be clear before long that Indonesia's peaceful struggle to assert itself is more significant and far-reaching than all the other international power-play going on around the world today. I registered the word *peaceful* and made a note to query it later.

He went on:

Alone of all the nations of consequence (with one hundred million people and untold resources, it rates fifth among the countries of the world), Indonesia has formulated a social and political ideology which will open the way to the ultimate goal of mankind's long striving—material justice and spiritual fulfilment for everyone; and the unique character of the Indonesian people, which combines the imaginative mysticism of Hinduism with the practicality and disciplines of Islam, while remaining sufficiently flexible to absorb the best of Western intellectualism, fits them to develop this way to salvation and to lead the world along it.

There was more along these lines, all of it sincere and much of it plausible. He pointed out that the Communists deny God altogether (except in Indonesia, where all political parties must officially believe) and that the Western democracies have excluded Him from law, politics, finance, public administration, and high society, so that neither East nor West provides the spiritual means or the incentive for men to achieve an adjusted completeness.

It is the emerging nations, said the professor, especially those like Indonesia whose first political principle is a belief in God and who are aligned with neither East nor West and so uncommitted to ways already laid down, who can most easily make a new beginning in this age and lead humanity back onto the path from which it has so blindly strayed.

When, eventually, he invited me to step up and address the students I was tired and confused and felt that the notes I had prepared would mix awkwardly into the pattern of his dissertation. In any case it was getting late and the audience was already bored.

So I said that I had listened with great interest to the professor and had learned a lot from him and from others during my stay in Makassar, and felt that I understood more clearly the heart and mind of the Indonesian people. But, I said, it seemed to me that the effort to understand must be made by both sides; that we of the West are as new to the present situation as are the emerging nations; that we both need to show good will and a great deal of patience, and to give each other time to get the changing world well into focus.

I said that is it right to fight against colonialism and other major inhumanities that undermine the dignity of millions of people, but that it is not possible to build a worthwhile nation on a foundation of cultivated hate. More than anything we need a climate of trust so that the "haves" can divert their surplus goods and capacities to the "have-nots" without finding it necessary to take sides or discriminate or make self-protective conditions. And in this regard there was a danger that emerging nations, like Indonesia, were as much to blame for creating tensions as the older powers—and as open to charges of hypocrisy.

There seems to be a tendency, I said, among some of these newly emerging nations to take a "holier-than-thou" attitude toward the West, and for the ordinary people of these nations to be regimented by propaganda and a controlled press into thinking negatively about the outside world. There was a stirring among the students when I said this, for their main criticism of the Western press is that its attitude toward Indonesia is entirely and blindly negative. So I smiled and said that it was easy, when trying to emulate other people's achievements and capacities, to pick up their bad habits also, and that they should avoid this.

I waited for silence and then went on. The West is aware of its many sins and knows that the worst of them are ugly, vulgar, and dangerous; but we have consciously chosen the active rather than the contemplative life and in order to achieve great things for humanity we have exposed ourselves to great temptations. The East, with its traditional leaning toward mysticism and its acceptance of material inequality within its own society, might well be horrified by the single-mindedness with which the West pursues its material goals. Yet the West does not condemn the East for its poverty, its diseases, its backwardness in practical things; it is sympathetic and would like to help and share its knowledge and skill and to accept from the East, in exchange, some of its spiritual surplus.

As for believing in God, I said, we agree with President Sukarno that a civilization which disregards God is unlikely to achieve completeness in itself or peace for its people, but faith alone is not sufficient to feed the hungry or clothe the poor. The West has acquired the habit of work, not simply to exist but to progress and create and to try to meet God halfway, even at the risk of losing sight of Him from time to time.

When I had done there were questions first from the representative of the student newspaper, who returned to the standard attack. "Why is your press and radio continuously against us? Why does it pick out and isolate incidentals and put them under a microscope, ignoring the whole body of Indonesia? Why does it accuse us of being a Communist country? Why does the West threaten us all the time? Why don't you leave us alone?"

One cannot stand, tired, before a hostile, foreign audience and answer such questions glibly. I said that it was the job of newsmen to report the things that happen in the world and what important people say about important matters; and that if every day Indonesian statesmen cry out "Crush Malaysia," then they must expect to be reported saying just that. Furthermore, if Communists are allowed to organize and carry out violent and destructive demonstrations against United States and British institutions in Indonesia, then it might be reasonably assumed that the government is pro-Communist or susceptible to Communist pressures. As for the negative reporting, it seemed to me that with its flogging of the Malaysia issue the Indonesian government had set up its own smoke screen, obscuring any general view of its positive and progressive activities. And on the question of threats one could only say that the whole world faces the single, collective threat of extinction; that people everywhere, for their own protection, should keep their leaders in order and tell them that their one job is to solve the world's problems without recourse to aggressive threats; and that this applies as much to Indonesia as to any other country.

There were other, inevitable questions of the type for which there were no simple answers. Then a young man stood up and said quickly and passionately, as though he had been working himself up to it, "You despise us because we burn your libraries and smash windows in your embassies and are horrified when we act without dignity. But you forget that it was the white people who took our dignity away from us in the first place."

I stood there wondering how long it would take to clear away the debris of the past and start again and feeling entirely inadequate to answer for the sins and the mistakes of the whole white world for the past three hundred years. It seemed to me that so much more must be done to adjust the image of the Western man in the eyes of the hundreds of millions of people in Southeast Asia; that name-calling at each other over the fence would get us nowhere. If ever democratic Christianity needed to prove itself by works instead of words, now is the time.

Then a girl got up, neat and pretty, a student. I felt beaten before she spoke—in no state of mind to argue abstractions with an intense young woman. She walked down the center aisle and stood halfway between me and the back of the hall, and in the silence she began: "We thank you for coming to speak to us, for being frank and telling us what you think about our country." There was a smattering of applause. "I am a girl and not so clever, but I understand that each person is two people, an individual and a patriot, and being two people sometimes makes difficulties. When I listen to our leaders I know that they are right, that we must crush Malaysia and free our neighbors from British Imperialism." Expressionless, I tried to hide exasperation at the worn-out phrases forming and falling from her pretty lips, and I wished for an hysterical second that someone would kiss her and stop the flow of words, words, words that had no meaning, give her a baby, make her a mother, turn her back into a pretty girl instead of a robot with a tape-recorder for a brain. She stood there, looking serious. "But when I am at home watching my father talking with his friends, or listening to my brothers make plans for a feast-day dance, I wonder why they should die in Malaysia, and who will gain. And I say to myself, perhaps there is another way." She stopped and looked down as if she had run out of words, and there was quiet. Then she looked up and said, "Thank you for coming," and turned and went back quickly to her seat.

Three men came out of the shadows near the steps of the hall where I had been speaking and invited me to take coffee with them. I was tired and would rather have gone to the hotel but they stood quietly, like men who need a kindness but are too proud to ask for it. Bahruddin seemed keen to leave me with them, so I agreed and went to the house of one of them. He was a lecturer. His wife was away, and we could speak freely. A servant girl made coffee for us.

I said that I had enjoyed being in Makassar much better than in Jakarta. It was good to see men working and achieving practical things, like increasing the rice crop and building ships instead of wading about in words. They listened politely, with other things in mind. Then one of them, a government official, asked me what I had thought of Mononutu's speech, and in reply I said that I had found it interesting but had not expected it to be so long or so belligerently political.

The third man, a technician from the antimalarial section of the Health Department, said, "That's the trouble with Indonesia, too much politics, too much talk. We are run by a lot of enthusiastic revolutionaries who seem to think that material progress is a matter of ideology—that the word *democracy* automatically raises the standard of living without anybody doing any work. Politics is not productive; only work and learning will get us anywhere." The other two watched him as though he might drop dead with the uttering of such heresy; then they looked at me to see if I were shocked.

I said, "It's probably a matter of history moving too quickly. Things don't get time to settle nowadays. You people have jumped several centuries in a matter of a decade or so and you don't have the administrative machinery to handle the transition smoothly. Your leaders are heroes who fought your battles for you and won them, but running a country the size of this, without money and enough trained people to handle the technology and management, is more than they are able to do efficiently. You need a whole new generation that has been taught to fix automobiles and keep buses running, that has its proper proportion of doctors, lawyers, teachers, bookkeepers, and economists to run big business and a banking system. Meanwhile your leaders need to lay down and fix a solid political and administrative foundation for you all to build upon. In today's world, with its tough and ruthless pressures from inside and outside, this is not so easy."

It seemed an impertinence for me to be lecturing these intelligent men from my own position of ignorance but they listened like children hearing music for the first time, and I realized that it was precisely to hear such simple things spoken, which they could not openly speak themselves, that I had been asked to come with them to take coffee. I continued: "Democracy, as a social principle and political system, might help make the majority of the world's people tolerably comfortable and domestically secure, but it does not hold the whole or only answer to the problems of this age. It cannot make bad people good or silly people sensible. We need to go beyond politics of any kind to find the answers to the big questions and to make the great decisions that have to be made if we are to survive.

"In the West," I went on, "we have been able to develop democratic systems of government that are reasonably efficient and allow a fair measure of freedom and justice to most of the people, although by no means all. These democratic parliamentary systems are not ideal and are democratic only inasmuch as they permit ordinarily simple people to share with rogues, idiots, visionaries, and idealists the responsibility of law-making and government. The people still have no real say in the selection of their representatives, but at least they have the right to criticize and the power to get rid of them when their blunders are too ridiculous or criminal. It is a fairly negative kind of democracy and we have no right to be overproud of it, but it has carried mankind several long steps forward from feudalism toward individual freedom, and its possibilities are by no means exhausted."

Theoretically, the constitutional structure of Indonesian democracy is ahead of almost anything the West can show. Every section of the community is represented in the governmental system and no proposals can become law unless they are agreed to by the three major political groups—the President's nationalists, the religious parties, and the Communists—so that no single power group or political party has an unassailable majority in the parliament. But in practical fact the President runs the country. It is he who says, "Crush Malaysia," "Abandon the United Nations," "To Hell with America." This is *guided* democracy. It ranks with the democracy of some New Guinea tribes, the members of which occasionally eat one another, deciding by general consent who shall go into the pot.

The lecturer said, "It is very difficult here for us academicians. We have to teach only one brand of political science and patriotism, and must not say anything that will make our students think for themselves or critically examine the official ideology, even if we feel that some things are wrong and should be discussed openly. Such secrecy plays into the hands of the Communists because it makes people afraid, and fear and hunger are the mainstays of communism. A country in which people may say what they wish, and can get plenty to eat, is not likely to go red."

There was a silence as though things dreadful and very dangerous had been said, and I realized that these were people who had been conditioned through generations to be discreet and to keep their opinions to themselves. Old Yusef the exile, whose shrine I had visited, came to my mind again, and the thousands of Indonesians who had spent the best part of their lives in the swamps of West New Guinea, when it was Dutch, because they talked too much. I was then all the more surprised when the public official said, "Professor Mononutu believes that before anything else we must create an Indonesian identity. It is essential, he says. It must be done at any price. At the price of my own personal identity and pride. At the price of mutilating the minds of our students, like that girl who spoke up at the end of your talk. We must act tough and talk tough to the outside world just to prove that Indonesia has an identity, that it exists.

"But I don't believe this. I don't believe that we have to crush Malaysia to prove that we have an identity. I don't believe that we have to crush anybody. I don't believe that this stupid, impossible campaign has anything to do with identity, or the principles of freedom, or the sufferings of the Indonesian people. I believe that it is a political idiocy, not worth the death of one illiterate soldier. The politicians have lost touch with the true poetry of life and the reality of living and have set up policy in the place of God. Everything is sacrificed to policy—truth, honor, gentleness, justice. What are they doing to us?"

He was trembling. Coffee slopped from his cup into the saucer and in trying to set the cup down he spilled it onto the table and began nervously to mop it up, muttering apologies. The other two stared at him as though he were a ghost.

PART IV

Jakarta-Bali

CHAPTER 6

When I came back to Jakarta and the house at Kebajoran, Nah clapped her hands, laughed with pleasure, and took hold of my bags and carried them into the bedroom, chattering like a parrot. There were flowers on the table, hibiscus and frangipani, put there, said Nah, by her niece. Suddenly I felt as though I had come home, and thought how strange it was to feel so fondly of Jakarta.

My host, who had been away when I last came, was back from his meetings in the provinces and was pleased to see me. I had brought him a few slim cigars from Makassar, it being the custom for returning travelers always to bring gifts. When I had bathed and was cool again we sat in the garden while he smoked one with relish, and we talked.

He had been away to a series of seminars, organized by the Department of Labor to plan and set up teaching systems in areas where industry is feeling the lack of skilled process workers and properly trained mechanics and operators. There is also, he said, the problem of standardizing basic techniques for factory management and administration in the state-owned industries and people's cooperatives.

Then there is the matter of holidays, aggravated by the official recognition of three main religions, Moslem, Buddhist, and Christian, with three separate festival periods to celebrate the births of Mahomet, Buddha, and Christ, not to mention the daily siesta, the Moslem half-day break on Friday, the Christian Sunday, and most people having Saturday afternoon off as well. "We have great respect for religion," said my host. "It is the basis of our national philosophy and the political constitution. Belief in God is the foundation of all other beliefs including belief in the state. Western people may feel that this is a weakness in our economic structure; but we Indonesians realize that the real things of life, like belief in God, are the most important, and if we have to accept some disruption of industry on this account, and a lower standard of living, we will do so. Simple poverty is not a sin or a shameful thing—certainly not as shameful as greed and the exploitation of one's fellows." I thought he sounded a little defensive so I steered the conversation into broader waters, saying that I had not seen a newspaper for some days but had heard rumors that Indonesia was to leave the United Nations.

He shrugged and waved the cigar vaguely. "Why not? It is dominated by the Western power group and cannot deal objectively with the problems of Asia. Sooner or later the Afro-Asian block will have to start its own organization to get justice for the majority of the world's people. The West has to face the fact that it cannot run an international organization simply to keep intact what it has gained by centuries of exploiting the colored people. Its attitudes are conditioned by the desire to stay on top, to give nothing away, and its fear of war is the fear of being destroyed."

Nah came into the garden to say that food was on the table, so we went in and ate cold rice with vegetable soup and papaya, with a little cheese to celebrate my home-coming. We ate without much talk and as soon as we were finished I excused myself and went to my room to read mail and make notes. In my mind, while I worked, I could see a line creeping around the earth, dividing it, with China, Asia, and Africa on one side, and the United States, Russia, and Europe on the other. A final line-up taking shape, based on color and race, with Australia, India, South Africa, and Japan all vulnerable and involved as bases and battlegrounds. But remembering Professor Mononutu in Makassar and his insistence that China is the common enemy of all democracies and Indonesia's greatest danger, there seemed but one conclusion: that Sukarno believes he is able to win any gamble, that there is no card in the pack he will not play, no risk he will not take to shake the faith and muddle the judgment of those who oppose him.

What does he see as he sits under the banyan tree in the garden of his summer palace, pondering on his destiny, conjuring up images and visions of a greatness not yet achieved by any other man in history? What goes on in this strange mind nurtured on fables and shaped by years of striving for an idealized identity? This mind that goes on creating dream after dream, each more exciting and more dangerous than the last, while the substance diminishes? Does he ever feel uncertain or afraid?

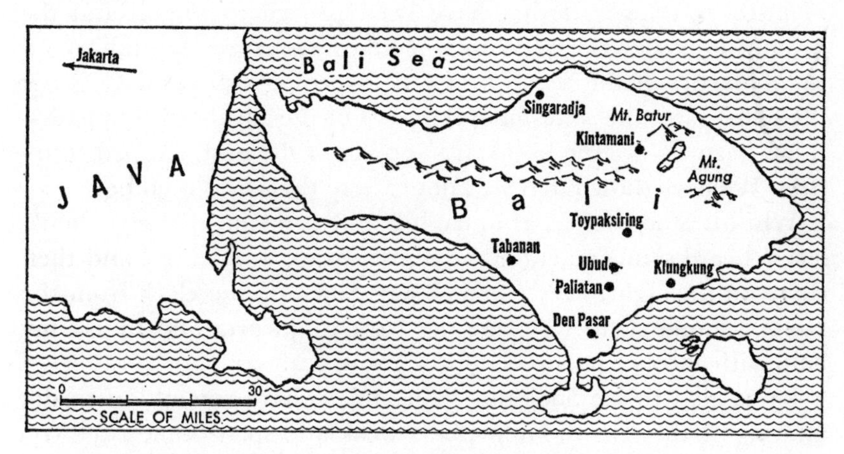

I looked through the heap of pamphlets and books of speeches, accumulated after only a few weeks in Indonesia and already overfilling a suitcase, and leafing through them I found phrases that illuminated the mind and manner of this man as summer lightning illuminates for a fleeting moment the mysterious outlines of a city at night, showing as one stuff and color the grand and the drab, the marvelous and the meretricious.

He speaks of God:

"I came out of my palace and looked up at the sky and saw the sparkling of the stars. I was affected. I was moved. I said, 'O God, my Lord, these stars are Thine own creation and each gives worship to Thee. Thou art the God of these stars. Thou, O God, art the Lord of all human beings, of the animals, the trees, of this grass which I step on. Thou art the God of the sand and of the atoms which can only be seen through a microscope. Thou art the Lord of the whole world, O God, my Lord, creator of the universe, of the sun, the moon and the uncountable stars. And what am I? I am a small thing.' "

He speaks of himself:

"It is because of my unconventional thinking that I am so reviled and so belittled by a section of the world press. But I am quite unrepentant about taking this line. I am proud to make humble contribution to the building of a new world and the creating of a new society for men."

And he sees himself, the prophet of a new age, leading his people toward a new dawn:

"Who is it that have shown themselves to have seen the course of history? Who is it that have been proved to understand the dynamism of our times? Who is it that have correctly understood the dialectics of the revolution now sweeping mankind? It is not the politicians, the statesmen, the press of the advanced countries—it has been *us*—we the backward peoples of the undeveloped countries. We have shown that we know where the world is going!"

While I stood there, rummaging and browsing through booklets, I heard someone enter the house, speak to my host, and then come on through to my room. It was Soejono, the clerk from the Hotel Indonesia, to welcome me back to Jakarta and to ask my help with another poem. Nah brought us tea.

I was glad to see Soejono again and to have something to do, although I thought the new poem weak and spent some time trying to tighten it up, but without much satisfaction. Yet it seemed worthwhile and important that a clerk should want to speak out, however lamely, against the big people, even if what he had to say was no more than the protest of a fretful child rebelling against reality. So we tapped away on the typewriter like conspirators until, almost at midnight, Soejono at least was satisfied with what we had achieved:

My Wife, the Faceless Men, and Me!

My wife crouches by the fire
Her fan flickering;
She is cooking a little fish for my dinner.
My wife is very beautiful—
Beneath her clothing she is like a goddess.
When we have eaten
She will lie beside me
And we will make love.

On the other side of the city,
At his desk,

A secretary of state is writing a speech
For his minister.
Tomorrow it will be on the front page
Of every newspaper (by order);
Foreign correspondents will send it round the world;
It will be on the radio.

In his speech the minister will say,
"We, the People,
"Will resist Imperialism to the last drop of Indonesian blood.
Ever onward, no retreat."
Tell me, please, who are these faceless men
Who speak for me,
Not knowing my name, calling me "The People,"
Spilling my blood for me?

Who will save me from them,
The statesmen,
The public officials, and security men?
Supposing I am the last Indonesian,
Lying with my wife
Who has a body like a goddess:
Do they think I will want to get up and resist Imperialism?
They should ask me first.

When Soejono had gone I listened to the late news and heard a transcription of the President's statement on the withdrawal from United Nations:

"Brothers and sisters, pressmen, note this down correctly—where are the correspondents?—note this down correctly. Don't get any words wrong regarding Malaysia and the United Nations Security Council. Write this down. 'If, in spite of our explanation, Malaysia is made into a member of the Security Council we will leave the United Nations.' Write that down. Are you finished, pressmen?" And so on, with rhetorical repetitions.

Another news item said that by a unanimous vote of the women's organizations President Sukarno had been proclaimed Supreme Shepherd of the Women's Revolutionary Movement.

One of the biggest buildings in Jakarta, a huge square office block on the main thoroughfare, is occupied entirely by the Department of Religious Affairs. Just along the road is another building, almost as big, occupied by the United States AID offices, so that the fountain heads of spiritual and material consolation are close by each other. The AID building has elevators and is air conditioned. The Americans who work there always look neat and clean, and worried. The other building has neither elevators nor air conditioning. The Indonesians who work there, although not dressed as expensively as the Americans, are also neat and clean. But they do not look particularly worried, probably because being free and having a job is still a novelty, and they are not put out of countenance by what, to businesslike Americans, looks like monumental inefficiency and impending economic disaster in the running of the country.

The spokesman for the Department of Religious Affairs put on his necktie to receive me (he is a large, heavy man, and it is hot in his office). Like every other official I met in Indonesia he was friendly, smiling, and extremely courteous, anxious to be as frank as possible and hoping that I would not ask ill-mannered questions. White people are bores. They do not understand that efficiency and forthrightness and apparent truth are very minor virtues. He sent for coffee and we sat down to a low table with two of his assistants, young men, one without socks. The big man put his hand on my knee, smiled, and said, "Now, what do you want to know?" One cannot help loving Indonesians.

We began cautiously. I said, "Your national constitution expressly states that belief in God is a necessary part of the political system in Indonesia." The spokesman responded promptly, "Article 29 of the constitution says that the state is founded upon the belief that there is one God. This has been confirmed by a decision of the People's Consultative Assembly Number 2/1960, Chapter 2, Article 2." He delivered the answer with a finality that brooked no argument, adding, "We Indonesians are a very religious people. We accept that religion is necessary to the survival of the state and that only through religion can there be a development of moral and spiritual strength among the people. The Western countries have forgotten this and their civilization must consequently perish."

I did not follow this hare but asked him to tell me something about the routine functions of the Department of Religious Affairs, for I was curious to know how so much office space could be usefully occupied by a nonproducing department devoted more to matters of faith than to good works and acts of charity.

He explained, then, that religious instruction is compulsory in all educational establishments from kindergarten to university, and that the department is responsible for teacher-training and placement, for syllabuses and examinations, and for supervision and inspection. Additionally, all religious officials and dignitaries are registered with the department, and their activities and working conditions are codified. Then, of course, and he now spoke proudly, there is the fact that there are official "religious" members of the People's Assembly and other governmental and legislative bodies, so that the activities and influence of the department reaches deeply into the political structure of the country as well as into the educational and purely religious aspects of national life.

Elementary schools have six hours of religious instruction each week, and universities have four hours. I asked what happens if a student does not believe in God and he sighed, "This is a problem. Technically, attendance at religious instruction and practice is compulsory but so far no action has been taken against students who don't conform—it is a delicate matter of politics." The two assistants looked sadly down at the table, but looked up again when their chief rallied and said, "But nonbelievers are subversive, and all who disregard the law in this matter of religious instruction are undermining the foundations of the state."

I said, doubtfully, wondering if it was a foolish question, "Is it then laid down in law that the president, or for that matter any minister of the Republic or high official, must admit to a belief in God?"

He replied with genuine surprise, "Of course not. This is a free and democratic country in which people are at liberty to worship according to the promptings of their own consciences." Then he added firmly, "But, by law, it is not possible to be an Indonesian and not believe in God."

I confess that this kind of thing confuses me. I become muddled and lose confidence, wondering if there is some dimension of understanding that I do not comprehend, although I have been warned time and again on these travels not to compare or draw parallels between this Asian world and the West, nor to judge Indonesian attitudes and behavior from a Western point of view. But I think it true to say that when an Indonesian does not wish to admit of a situation he simply says, and believes, that it does not exist, and that this would seem to apply to the President as much as to any other Indonesian.

I took my problem to a Californian who has spent ten years in Indonesia trying to help that country to get going (I do not care for anonymity but it would embarrass him and his superiors to name him).

He said, "The President does not admit that there is any fundamental incompatibility between organized religion and Communism. This matches his refusal to admit that one nation cannot invade another without creating a state of war between them. That without a sound economic system there can be no material progress. That unlimited inflation will send a nation bankrupt. It all tallies, and we must face this. Whether or not we can do anything about it is a question that needs deep consideration. It seems certain that no outside efforts, however genuine or generous, will be able to change the direction in which Indonesia is being led. We have no experience and no mathematics that will help us to plot the probable course of Indonesia's immediate progression. The drama being enacted is pure Javanese. We do not understand the characters nor the plot nor the pay-off. Only one thing seems even partially clear. We cannot change the course of events, but we can prepare for two possible eventualities: one, that this apparently crazy way of running a nation is going to succeed by the kind of miracle that we don't understand (remember that we have been prophesying economic disaster for the past ten years); and, two, that it will collapse in a most terrible shambles and will start a fire that may envelop us all. Our problem is not to try to change the immediate course of events but, on the one hand, to help on a simple level of Peace Corps and AID, without any politics involved, making friends and extending our influence; and on the other hand, to have a policy to put into action if and when some kind of drastic measures are called for. Vietnam is a one-act curtain-raiser compared to what could happen here, and we ought to be sure before it happens what part we intend to play in it, if any."

I will not claim that these were the exact words spoken but the sense is all there and I will go along with the judgment as though it were my own; and for the rest of my journeying through Indonesia, I looked at what I saw from that standpoint, not inflexibly, but at least from a posited point of view.

The big white mosque at Kebajoran sits on a green slope well back from the highway and the busy rush of traffic, serene, neat, and square of structure like a great wedding cake, with two minarets and a big Arabian dome decorated at the top with a blue fluorescent star and crescent. (A bigger mosque is being built in Jakarta at the President's instruction, as a national monument to God, but it is not yet completed. It will, of course, be the biggest in Southeast Asia.)

Every Friday, a little before midday, crowds of men make their way to the top of the rise (the goats cropping the lawn grass disregard them) and many, coming straight from places where they have been unable to perform the statutory purification, stop at the public ablution block and wash themselves before going in to pray. Traditionally, a man should first wash his face, arms, elbows, feet, and a fourth part of his head, then mouth, nostrils, ears, and teeth, cleansing the left side of the body first and then the right, and the toes and fingers before the feet and palms of the hand; but this is for strict ritualists and few go to such lengths, at least in public. But all remove their shoes and wash their feet before entering the mosque and leave their shoes on the steps outside or park them with an attendant together with any parcels, briefcases, umbrellas, or other encumbrances. Some men bring their own praying mats, others hire them or share.

Inside it is spacious, clean, white, and cool, with room for three thousand men to pray, almost elbow to elbow, in long unbroken rows. I stood at the back, near an arched window-opening where fresh little winds seemed to be scampering in and out, watching the men take their places as they came inside.

First they shake out their mats, facing toward a niche in the far wall which marks the direction of Mecca. Then they bow from the waist and, straightening up again, raise their hands to their faces. They kneel, then, and touch the floor with their foreheads and whisper the prayers, each invocation preceded by the bowing and bending low, the uprising, and the prayer: "There is no God but God, and Mahomet is his Prophet." The prayers are mostly formulas; it is not the custom to improvise and make special requests at regular praying times. Always a statement, God is great, God is powerful, God is all-powerful. One of the young men from the Department of Religious Affairs, who has come with me, whispers, "We believe in Him, only He is God, we must worship Him." Absent-mindedly I make the sign of the cross, but nobody takes any notice.

Good Moslems say their prayers five times a day: first before sunrise, then at noon, again before sunset, between sunset and dark, and finally between twilight and the first night watch (the vesper prayer). There is a verse spoken after each prayer: "God! There is no other God but He, the living, the ever living! He sleeps not nor does He slumber. He made the heavens and the earth and all that they contain." The sentiment and the ejaculations stem straight from ancient Hebrew and early Christian liturgies, for Mahomet believed that both religions, in their pure form, were true and that his own was not a new faith but a return to the old simple and severe belief of the desert people, free of ritualistic encrustation and idolatry. He felt himself another Moses, another Jesus, begging the people to repent of their misdeeds, to atone for their falling away from the true faith of their fathers.

As a boy Mahomet traveled in his uncle's caravan from Mecca to Syria (part of the trade route from China and the Indies into the Mediterranean) and they sometimes camped close to a settlement of Nestorian monks, exiled from the main Christian communities because they ascribed to Christ two separate natures, human and divine, and denied Mary's immaculate motherhood. A religious lad, he spent much time in discussion with them, creating, it has been said, as much astonishment by his precosity as the child Jesus did in the temple at Jerusalem. So he was no ignoramus (no common camel driver) but knowledgeable even at an early age and concerned about man's relationship with God.

When eventually he was ready he went into the wilderness, to emerge in due time a prophet, to begin to teach and to write down the revelations vouchsafed to him by God. These became the Koran. He made Friday the holy day of worship so as to distinguish his society from that of the Jews and the Christians. And like all other prophets, he was denied and persecuted by those in authority.

Today as always, Moslems are taught that the great Semitic prophets are equally holy if not of equal rank—Abraham, Moses, Isaac and Jacob, Joseph, and John the Baptist (whose head is in the great mosque at Damascus), and Jesus. Even Miriam or Mary is sanctified. It is not basically an aversion to the Jewish or Christian faiths that has made Islam war with Jew and Christian for more than a thousand years, but territorial disputes and politics.

Thus, I stood among the three thousand men in the mosque at Kebajoran, a single Christian, child of the same basic faith. I felt no different from the others in this matter, the praying clerks, soldiers, businessmen, street vendors, bus drivers, row upon row, bowing, bending low to touch the ground with their foreheads; men in touch for a few moments with the one reality of which they were all certain. Each man, as he came in, retired into a world of his own, alone with God, going about his prayers in his own way until an Iman came and addressed them, speaking with a microphone, although few seemed to take notice but went on with their praying. My guide said that he was reading notices and making general announcements of holy days, fasts, meetings, and such. But when a second Iman came in, dressed in white, and turned his back upon the congregation and began to chant toward Mecca, each man straightened up. Then there was a concerted praying with all bowing and bending like rice in the wind, and the voice of the Iman rising and climbing until it seemed to find a place to rest and cry out across the space that separates men from heaven, "God is great. There is no God but God. He who lives forever." And the three thousand men bowed, and a low moaning went up as they answered, "Only He is God and Mahomet is His prophet."

A little man, a peasant or a workman, came late and stood beside me (the only clear space on the floor of the mosque) and spread his mat; but before kneeling he noticed that I hadn't one and beckoned me to share with him. I hesitated, not wishing to mislead him, but only for a moment, then knelt alongside him and said my own prayers, reflecting that in this ecumenical age it is proper to meet people of any faith halfway.

Going out, when the public prayer was finished, my guide met a friend on the steps, a young Malayan, studying political science at the university. He was a smiling youth who said that he was one of two thousand Malayan students in Indonesia and that he would not go back until the British had been driven out. I did not want to talk politics any more so I made no comment, but took my guide to eat in the Chinese quarter, where we had frog's legs and shark fin soup.

We spoke of a number of things: how, for instance, the President showed political courage and impartiality in dealing firmly with troublesome elements of the three most politically significant sections of the nation—the army, the Communist party, and the Moslems. In areas where local army commanders had rebelled he had ordered government troops against them at the risk of civil war. When the Communists staged a coup in West Java he sent the army to crush them.

The young man said with confidence that Indonesia would never go Communist because sixty percent of the people are practicing Moslems and would not tolerate an atheistic government—that in any case Communism is strong only in Java. But the thought in my mind was that a comparative handful of Dutch had held the millions of Indonesians in thrall for three centuries, and that the Moslem faith had in that time become a comfort rather than a driving force among the village people. Nor is there evidence that Moslems are in any way organized on a national scale or have dynamic leadership.

Later, making my way by *betjak* across town to keep other appointments, I wondered what, in the end, we might expect from God and his churches. In the mosque, being caught up for a little while in the simple ecstasy of prayer and public worship, I had felt secure, and sure somehow that He would not let go of us, would not abandon us to the evils that, with the help of the devil we have devised with such monumental cleverness for our own downfall and destruction.

But now, in the streets, I was not so certain and wondered if it were possible that in this day and age another great prophet could arise to lay bare the grand delusions and deceit we wear so elegantly, and pierce with a bright light the pomposity and confused conceit that keeps us from doing simply what is right. Will another ever come out of some desert or slum and draw to the surface again the deep-down longing for goodness and truth that is in the heart of almost every man, and blaze a new way for it to flow out and over-run the earth? Or had God finally deserted us? I thought of Soejono, crying out with simple indignation in his verses, "Who will save me from the faceless men who wish to spill my blood?"

It is no longer fashionable to believe in the devil. The cloven-footed stranger with a barbed tail and embryonic horns is passé, even as a comedian. Evil is more subtle today, wears respectable faces, keeps files and top-secret documents, uses the mass media. Yet the churches make progress too, and concede that it is now no longer proper to call into question another man's way of praying. Perhaps there is hope yet.

I paid off the *betjak* and walked into a quiet street of respectable houses. A bachelor woman, living alone, is unusual in Java, even in Jakarta, and for a woman who has no husband to be the head of a national institution is stranger still. But Miss Paramita Abdoerachman is an unusual woman. She cuffed the dog across the head, sharply but affectionately, and asked me to come in.

She is about five feet high and around 150 pounds. As a girl she wanted to be a concert pianist. Then a sculptor. Even now, as Secretary-General of the Indonesian Red Cross, she has sudden, fleeting visions of sitting, beautifully gowned, at a grand piano playing Chopin to a spellbound audience. Such dreams attenuate reluctantly.

Under the Dutch, her father was regent of the south part of Jakarta and an area beyond, which meant that he was an aristocrat and a man of consequence among his own people, although a "native" to the Dutch. Miss Abdoerachman was one of seven children, four of whom were boys. The boys all died in infancy and the girls were brought up to be sons so that their early training had overtones of tomboyism. Paramita Abdoerachman became known to her intimates as Jo.

During the Dutch times her mother did social work among the poor of Jakarta, then known as Batavia. She established food kitchens and slum schools and visited the sick. Jo went with her, worked part-time in a hospital, learned first aid at the Red Cross (in those days a privilege for a native girl, even the daughter of a regent), and attended university lectures in ancient history and archaeology.

When the Pacific War began British troops and civilians, escaping from Malaya, came to Java. She nursed many of them at a government hospital until the Japanese arrived and made prisoners of them. The hospital was at Bandung, about 150 kilometers (90 miles) from Jakarta. When the Japanese took it over Jo Abdoerachman walked home. She was young and strong and patriotic.

With the coming of the Japanese, the leaders of the Indonesian revolutionary movement, Dr. Hatta and Dr. Sukarno, began to plan actively for a postwar takeover. Jo joined their clandestine staff and worked as a researcher, part of her job being to check and tabulate Japanese atrocities. For a time she lived among the coal miners of East Java to report on forced labor. Another assignment was to collect evidence of mass executions.

At war's end, still on Dr. Hatta's staff, she became liaison officer between the revolutionary leaders and the Allied occupation forces, it being easier for a woman than a man to move back and forth through the street fighting in Jakarta. She was also secretary to the Revolutionary Cabinet and typed the draft declarations of independence. At night she worked with the Red Cross, picking up wounded in the streets. She is a pleasant woman but uncommunicative. One has to drag information from her. The only experience of which she spoke without reserve was the part she played in preparing the declaration of independence, and for a brief moment I thought I saw a fleeting gleam of pride in her dark, penetrating eyes. (She sat cross-legged on a settee, facing me across a low table, like a female Buddha in Western dress.)

The Allied occupation troops pulled out of Indonesia leaving the Dutch in charge, and life for Indonesian revolutionaries became more complex. Hatta and Sukarno moved to Jogjakarta in Central Java (birthplace of the earlier hero, Prince Diponegoro) and set up government there. The revolutionary army was split into guerrilla units and Miss Jo took a new job, moving all over Java among these units to organize their medical supplies and services.

Inevitably she was captured. The Dutch brought her back to Jakarta and treated her decently, offering her a noncombatant job with their own Red Cross unit, which she refused, preferring to rest a while in prison. But she was difficult to live with, and prison accommodation was needed for more desperate characters, so they released her with a plea to keep out of mischief. She walked back, then, to Jogjakarta and with the blessing of Hatta and Sukarno took charge of the Indonesian Red Cross unit set up to distribute international relief, establish refugee camps, and trace missing people.

Eventually, the Dutch withdrew and Miss Abdoerachman now felt free to settle down to play the piano and to learn to sculpt. But the United Nations sent her to America for a year's sociological study, and when she came home the President asked her to accept a ten-year term as Secretary-General of the Indonesian Red Cross.

It is a big job, full of frustrations, in a territory that includes three thousand islands and is undersupplied with transportation of any kind except horse- and ox-drawn carts, that has inadequate postal and telecommunication services, and that is desperately short of basic medicines, medical personnel, and money (a nurse stopped me in the street yesterday and asked me to help her get penicillin through my embassy, or give her money to buy some on the black market).

In addition to the normal Red Cross work done in most other countries the Indonesian branch trains government workers and schoolchildren in First Aid—part of the Crush Malaysia cacophony; it has been busy in collaboration with United Nations agencies concerned with malaria eradication and the health of children, although withdrawal from United Nations puts these activities in doubt; and its biggest test came with the 1963 eruptions of the holy mountains of Agung and Batur in Bali, and the subsequent earthquakes, which continued for three months.

The number of people killed is not known, although the figure is assumed to be nearly two thousand. The injured were uncounted but those displaced and made homeless came to seventy-five thousand, while a quarter of a million people had their land covered with volcanic ash and made useless for some time. Rivers were dammed with detritus, villages destroyed by fire or flood, and the great temple at Besakih on the slopes of Agung was overrun with molten lava.

The President sent for Jo Abdoerachman and told her to deal with the emergency and to organize relief work. When I said that I was going soon to Bali she lent me copies of letters and reports which she had written about the eruption and the drama of it. She said, too, that when in Bali I should see something of the Red Cross camps she had set up to cope with the homeless and with those who were to be transmigrated for good to settle in Sumatra and Kalimantan. She was concerned with all these things, this quiet, rocklike, solitary woman who had wanted so much to be a concert pianist or a sculptor.

CHAPTER 7

Extract from a letter
Bali Hotel
Den Pasar
Isle of Bali

I left Jakarta again this morning and after a flight of three hours have come to Bali, aware of the incongruity of arriving unaccompanied and without assignation on this, the most romantic of all the islands of Asia. I am enveloped in unreality, having lunched in solitary splendor in the main dining room of this once-famous hotel where the most curious and inquisitive of tourists were used to congregate in the easy days between the two great wars—I feel "like one who treads alone some banquet hall deserted" or a character from "Last Year at Marienbad."

Twenty years ago it would have been difficult to have reserved a table in this hotel without influence, but today I had the place to myself and was attended at lunch by four waiters with another seven standing by in case my requirements exceeded the single dish offered on the menu. When I ordered a small bottle of beer they were all pleased because it engaged two of them for ten minutes fetching, pouring, and waiting to refill my glass while the others watched, smiling.

The only occupied rooms in the hotel are those being used, inevitably, by army officers and their families, waiting for postings to other parts of the island or for proper accommodation to be found for them in this town of Den Pasar, the capital of Bali. Already I have made friends with some of their children, stalking them, tigerlike, along empty corridors through which they run shrieking when I come into sight.

There are advantages in this absence of tourist atmosphere and activity and even in the loneliness which forces me to find companionship among the people who belong here, denying me the lazy status of a mere nonparticipating spectator. And the fact that famous dance troupes are no longer engaged by tourist agencies to dance in the hotel pavilion means that I must go out into the villages to look for Balinese culture, where it properly belongs, in its domestic state. Yet I confess that being continuously alone in a country where nothing is familiar, and where the only constant companions are uncertainty and suspense, is taking toll of my self-sufficiency.

Yesterday, in Jakarta, riding in a *betjak* through narrow back streets to the bank, I passed a small store which displayed a hanging sign reading, with simple dignity, "Goldberg for Spectacles," and seeing it I wanted to stop the *betjack* and go inside this store to see if there really was a Mr. Goldberg in Jakarta. In a single flash of supersensory perception I created an image of him for myself: a man of slightly less than middle height, with a large, proud stomach and thick cheeks, a number of chins, and gray hair, short but thick. He would speak slow, heavily accented English, softly and with sympathy, and would look at me over a pair of his own spectacles with kind, understanding eyes, and I would be comforted and would feel no longer alone. But I was not brave enough to look for him in case there was no Mr. Goldberg.

Instead of Mr. Goldberg I have made friends here in Den Pasar with a young man whose name is Wideh, which, he says, is Balinese for *wisdom,* and he is to be my companion while I am in Bali. He is an official of the Indonesian Department of Information, has a marked cast in one eye, favors a thin, villainous moustache, and has six very long spirals of black hair growing from a mole under his chin which give him a theatrically Oriental appearance. The combined effect is sinister. He also seems to be impatient of foreign writers and much preoccupied with thoughts of his own. But he is polite and appears to do his best to be helpful and efficient. I feel that we will get along well together once we establish rapport.

One of the hotel waiters, a globular youth with the approach of a confidence man, has also attached himself to me as a guide, interpreter, and general procurer and I feel that sooner or later there will be a clash between him and Wideh. The waiter will undoubtedly have regular commission arrangements with car owners and curio sellers, painters and wood carvers, while Wideh will consider it his function to protect me. Already the waiter has arranged for somebody to rent me a car for a few hours tonight, and later in the evening we are to visit a village some twenty or thirty kilometers from here to see a classical Legong dance, the approximate equivalent, in the programatic sense, of our classical ballets.

The hotel is near the corner of the main street of the town and is set back in lawns which are shaded by great flame trees. There are two large and ornate pavilions out in front, the smaller serving as an outdoor lounge for guests and the other as a stage for the performance of the famous Bali dances which were the central feature of the tourist program whenever a ship arrived.

They were fine performances, presented with great pride by dance groups from neighboring villages in the days when the hotel was the hub of the tourist trade, the starting place for tours of the island, a point of contact for artists, carvers, curio sellers, and a meeting place for celebrities—fashionable, alive with music of both East and West, and laughter, and the chatter of gay and uninhibited Europeans and Americans.

It must have been a good hotel by prewar colonial standards. The room that I am using has two large ceiling fans, a dozen light fixtures, a bathtub and a shower with hot and cold water taps, and a heated towel rack. But only a single light is working now and the fans have stopped and there is no hot water. But the place is clean enough and the servants are anxious to please although they have little to do but sit on the steps once the morning cleaning is done.

I have a letter of introduction to the governor, whose official residence is across the square where the Dutch resident used to live, and many messages have been passing back and forth between Wideh and the protocol officer. Apparently the governor is playing tennis, it being a religious holiday, and the protocol officer cannot decide how best to be polite with me without interrupting the governor's game. I have told them not to worry—that I understand perfectly that only an insensitive foreigner would think of arriving on an official visit during the ten-day period of Buddha's birthday celebrations, when all government offices are working at half pressure or not at all.

While I am waiting for word of an appointment with the governor, Wideh has taken me to the university library to show me the collection of the lontar-leaf manuscripts of which my friend Soejono wrote in one of his poems. Some of these books are masterpieces of calligraphy and illustration, the texts and pictures being engraved with an iron stylus on the inch-wide strips of palm leaf and filled in with a mixture of soot and oil—the same mixture as is used for tattooing among the South Sea islanders, who combine the soot from burning coconut fronds and husks with coconut oil to make their tattooing ink.

The books are kept in narrow wooden boxes, ornately carved and decorated with animal heads or sometimes made completely in the shape of animals in the same way as the Balinese cremation coffins are designed, with the backs hinged to form a lid and the whole richly decorated and inlaid with red and gold. The books, an inch wide and about a foot long, fit neatly into these boxes, each of which holds several books, some of them many centuries old. Apart from these lontar manuscripts there is scarcely any domestic record of Indonesian culture, literature, or history.

When I asked Wideh if I could buy a lontar-leaf book he spoke to a small boy who went away; and when we returned to the hotel there was a young man waiting who offered me one for the equivalent of a few shillings, saying that it had belonged to his grandfather but that he needed the money badly and had nothing else to sell. He seemed a pleasant, shy person and clean, although wearing only a frayed white shirt, patched trousers, shoes without laces in them, and no socks. Wideh said that the young man was a village schoolteacher, that he had four children to feed, and was studying to pass examinations which would qualify him for a higher position in the Education Department. Whenever there were tourists he offered his services as a guide so that he could practice his English and maybe make a little commission by introducing them to curio and souvenir sellers. I had not the heart to take his lontar-leaf book for the price he asked so told him to keep it, and engaged him instead to find me another and some village paintings.

Although Wideh has been helpful in all that I have required of him he seems morose and diffident about this transaction. We have only been together a few hours but already I get the impression that he has some major preoccupation. He lacks enthusiasms and behaves like a man who has been let down and sees no hope for the future. I begin to recognize the type—young men who grew through childhood to youth with the revolution, whose eyes and lively minds were fixed on and filled with the vision of an exciting new world, who followed the mystic music and found themselves at the end of their march in an empty field cluttered with unfinished foundations which day by day become more overgrown and neglected. He says, "Bali is still a museum as it has always been—you will find nothing of the new Indonesia here—only souvenirs and curios gathering dust because there are no tourists.

In a few moments the fat young waiter will come with his friend who has the car and we will go to the village where the dancing is to take place. You will be with me to share whatever I see, and so give it meaning.

M.

The waiter sat in the front seat of the car, beside the driver, while Wideh sat behind with me; and when we were a little way from Den Pasar we passed a boy driving ducks along the edge of the roadway, bringing them back from the rice fields where they had been feeding all day. The boy, hurrying behind the ducks, carried a long thin stick with a ragged pennant tied to its tip, and coming to their owner's home he turned them with the stick and sent them scurrying in through a gateway in the wall, quacking and twitching their stern feathers indignantly.

Wideh, smiling wistfully, watched the boy and, catching my eye, said, "When I was young I used to mind my grandmother's ducks and took them every morning to the rice fields beside the main road. When I came to the field I put up my pennant so that the ducks could see it waving above the rice stalks and so would not wander too far away. Then I would go kite-flying with my friends."

I, too, smiled at this reminiscence, pleased that Wideh seemed to have relaxed and let down his defenses, but he added, "This was during the time of the fighting against the Dutch." And I knew then that even here in beautiful Bali the same ghosts walk all day, that history has no perspective, that to all Indonesians the realities of today are less real than the old tyrannies and ancient myths. They are habituated to oppression. They need villains, someone or something to fear and hate.

"I was a spy," said Wideh boastfully, "one of the best in this district although only a small boy. All of us village boys, minding buffaloes by the roadside or ducks in the rice fields, were spies for the guerrilla and student army groups. It was our duty to watch the roads from Den Pasar and the other Dutch garrisons, and when we saw their soldiers setting out to attack our troops one of us would haul down the kite as a sign to our soldiers to take care, while a second boy would run to the advanced post and tell our men which way the Dutch were coming. It was I who usually ran because I was fast, although I was caught once because the Dutch had used a trick and occupied the village from another direction, so that I ran into a trap.

"The Dutch commander made me stand all day in the sun with other prisoners from the village, and I knew that my grandmother would worry when I did not come home with the ducks in the evening, so I pretended to be sick and fell down, and a Dutch soldier pulled me into the shade on the edge of the village. But when he went away I jumped up and ran back to the rice field and found the ducks all gathered around my flag waiting for somebody to take them home."

I asked him then to tell me more about himself and he said that he was a man of the people (he used the phrase proudly), that his father was a peasant who had become a tailor, that his father and mother were divorced when he was six months old, and that he had been brought up in the home of his grandparents. He was the first of his family to go to school and was still studying in the evenings for a master's degree, which would qualify him for a senior teaching position at the university.

In everything he said there seemed a note of sadness, and in the days that followed I noticed that when he was not required by his job of guiding me to concentrate or make conversation, he would lapse into a reverie and sometimes break suddenly into singing sad nostalgic songs. His favorite was a Western song set to the tune of "O Sole Mio" which he said he had learned from Radio Australia under the title, "My Heart Is Calling," and which was "very classical."

Later I learned that he sang it for a young girl who was a student at the university in Den Pasar, and whose ring and wrist watch he wore continuously. He would have married her, he said, except that her family were well-to-do and he must first complete his studies and so gain status and position for himself. But he admitted to kissing her on occasions and when I seemed surprised he said, quite seriously, "Kissing is a part of the revolution—the ancient customs are no longer observed in this regard."

He wrote a few autobiographical notes for me and, reading them now, I see not only Wideh but a whole generation of young Asians, in Indonesia, India, and Pakistan, and in all the lands of Southeast Asia from Burma to the borders of China, breaking through the ancient barriers of illiteracy and ranging over the landscape of this age freely, eager to see, to discover, to know and acquire all that the new world has to offer. These millions of Asian students have faced and refused the humilities that their parents accepted, have thrown off the inhibitions of history and now seek for themselves a new dignity, and for their countries an equal place among the nations.

Four years after leaving high school Wideh became a Bachelor of Arts at the University of Den Pasar, and besides holding his present job with the Department of Information is now assistant lecturer in English at the University of Singaradja on the north side of the island, to which he travels twice weekly by bus. His lectures take the form of readings from nineteenth-century English books on social anthropology, so that his conversation is punctuated with references to "kinship responsibility" and "classificatory siblings." In his spare time, such as it is, he studies old Arabic, medieval Javanese, and Sanskrit so that he can interpret the lontar-palm books, and he aims to take his master's degree in linguistics.

His total possessions are his school books, one pair of dark trousers, a sarong, an old cotton jacket, two shirts, one pair of shoes, and two sets of underwear. He says, "When I get my master's I will become 'social' and must have a black jacket to wear on celebration days, but it will be difficult to get the money for this because I have no land and must buy food for myself and also help my grandparents. I have no money left for clothing."

I learned these things about Wideh over a number of days, during which time we gained a respectful affection for each other: but this evening, at Paliatan, out of Den Pasar, we were still strangers and it was the fat young waiter who played the part of guide, gave names to things, and explained them as we drove by the road which runs through the rice fields toward the great volcano of Agung (the navel of creation) and clips through villages like scissors, separating one walled half from another.

It was getting toward evening, and the men and women had already left the fields. We passed one serious small boy perched on a bufflalo, heading homeward, and a man with a plough on his back, then came to a stream where women were washing themselves. I watched one wade in the water until it reached her thighs, then stopped and with a swift movement whipped off her sarong and sat down so that the water lapped at her breasts. I had not meant to stare (in any case we were moving quickly and she was more than a stone's throw away) but was held by the simplicity of the scene and the beauty of the woman; but the waiter, turning in his seat and seeing where my gaze lay, leered and said, "The women of Bali are beautiful." To which I replied that all women are beautiful because that was God's intention when He made them, so that men might be stimulated and made to feel brave and strong, yet gentle and protective. At which the waiter said, "I see that you are a good man but this is not true of all tourists, many of whom cause great offense by staring at the women when they bathe, which is something we Balinese never do." But his look betrayed him and I thought him lecherous, although pleasant enough and good company.

We came to a crossroads and saw a man and a woman, very old and gray, kneeling at the feet of a stone statue. The waiter said they were making placatory offerings to the devils who frequent such places of danger to make mischief, and that their offering would be a few blossoms and grains of rice spread upon a pad of banana leaf and laid at the idol's feet. Looking back I saw the old lady light a small lamp, and the frail old man, hands on thin thighs, sway forward and pray while a little child watched.

On the outskirts of the town we overtook a procession of children following behind a creature whose legs were those of two men wearing trousers, striped horizontally red and white, but whose face was a fantastical and ferocious wooden mask with long white fangs and bulbous eyes set in a huge and grotesque head, with a long saddle-backed body hung with hair like a yak and glittering with hundreds of little mirrors. It had a stiff, upstanding tail decorated with feathers and hung at the tip with a cluster of jingling bells; huge elephantine ears of gold-coated leather; and a high, gilt crown set upon its head.

"The Barong Matjan," said the waiter, "the tiger spirit."

Two men walked before it, one beating a drum and the other clashing finger cymbals, and two more men carried torches which flickered in the mirrors as the creature danced and pranced along the margin of the roadway, turning its head from side to side as though seeking something to chase, snapping and clacking its wooden jaws, tossing a blood-red tongue and a long black beard of human hair interwoven with red and white flowers.

The Barong is a principal image-symbol of all the magic and mysticism of Bali-Hindu belief and ritual. This strange, imaginary creature contains and displays all the elements of man's understanding—the physical and mystical, spiritual, and animal. It is droll and comical yet mysterious and strangely fearful. It is an object of fun and tomfoolery, of reverence, awe, and veneration.

Each village has a set of Barong trappings, the rich villages keeping costumes for a variety of such creatures—the Pig Barong, the Tiger, the Lion, the Elephant, the Cow—and the poorer villages making do with one. The costumes and head gear, the masks and decorations are kept in a special stable in the Temple of Death, revered as holy, being a representation of the mystical animal spirit which sides with mankind against the evil power of witches from the nether world.

Every Balinese knows that this earth is thick with spirits good and bad: with witches, imps, devils, gods, and disembodied souls seeking sanctuary. They follow him everywhere, hover over and about him, waiting to catch him out, to trap and entice him into risky situations. His life is a continuous dialogue with the invisible, an intercession, a penance, a ritualistic conversation of gesture, offering, prayer, and compromise with the unknown, made complete in a cycle of temple festivals and spectacular dance ceremonies which are offerings to the gods and for which the island was, in more accessible times, world famous.

The Barong plays its part in all important festivals, has its own feasts, takes part in others, receives offerings, is invoked in times of pestilence and community misfortune. It is the central character in some of the great plays of the Balinese stage and a supervising spirit in trance dances. Great magic abides in its beard which, dipped into a dish of water held by a priest, makes it holy and a remedy for all kinds of sickness. Men and women possessed by devils are restored to normal understanding if sprinkled with this holy water. Young men who stab themselves viciously with their krisses while in a trance do not harm themselves if first washed in the water that the Barong has blessed with its beard.

This is no affected make believe, no highly contrived way of life designed to attract tourists. To the Balinese people, God, the great spirit, is a real presence with many manifestations, male and female, all of whom are themselves gods and goddesses with special attributes, powers, and functions derived from the one supreme God. Each merits and requires veneration. To neglect or show them disrespect brings inevitable retribution. Ancestors, too, are deified and so must receive regular ceremonial attention. Consequently, life on Bali has become an almost continuous spiritual and ritualistic discourse between the people and the supernatural powers that surround them.

The famous dances, dramatic ballets, and temple ceremonies,

then, are not primarily a stylized diversion or highly developed folk art, but acts of piety, dramatic declarations of faith, rich propitiatory offerings.

If sickness comes upon a village, rice crops fail, or domestic animals are stricken with disease, the reason is uncovered by a priest or priestess who, having gone to the temple, sits before a shrine in a state of induced trance and there receives a message from the gods pointing out some failure or neglect to honor an anniversary properly, to give thanks for some occasion of satisfaction, or to celebrate a feast with suitable ceremony.

When the omission is made clear the villagers combine to repair neglected shrines and temples, to refurnish (or redeem from the Chinese pawn shop) the instruments of the gamelan orchestra, to mend the costumes of the dance and drama troupes, to rehearse appropriate dances, and to prepare a temple feast.

To call Bali the island of a thousand temples is no euphemistic extravagance. Each house has its own temple, each community should have at least three: the original temple around which the community grew (the navel temple), the town temple where official ceremonies are held, and a temple of the dead, built in the cemetery or cremation ground. Some families have temples of origin; some villages have temples to honor the god of a local landmark—a hill, lake, or sea temple, a temple for the god of the rice-fields, the river, the market place; and every temple has an anniversary day, to be celebrated with a feast, followed by a dance or drama.

We came to Paliatan a little after dark when the first stars were already riding high above the palms, and the flickering of tiny oil lamps showed where women were setting up food stalls in a little open court by the temple entrance. A young man was clambering up the carved sides of the great gateway setting lanterns into its niches, and from somewhere inside came the fitful, intermittent sound of someone practicing on a metallophone.[1]

Across the roadway men were coming to their *bandjar* (club-

[1] Balinese and Javanese orchestras are called gamelans and consist of metal percussion instruments of the xylophone (or metallophone) family, gongs, cymbals, and drums. The metallophone is a xylophone with heavy metal keys. In Bali the principal instrument of this kind is called a gender; this instrument generally carries the melody.

house) to sit and talk and drink palm wine or coffee, some still fondling their fighting cocks although they should have been put to roost soon after dusk, while other cocks, under wicker cages on the edge of the verandah, watched thin, timorous dogs scavenge in the shadows.

The waiter said that we would have an hour or more to wait and that we should go to a café for something to eat and he would tell me the story of the Legong. Wideh, impatient of the waiter's chatter and intrusiveness, said that he had friends in the *bandjar* and would sit with them until the dance started.

Of all the dances of Bali the Legong is the most famous and perhaps the greatest and most beautiful—a distillation of the incomparably varied and rich drama of the Balinese dance repertory, a refinement of all the grace, shape, form, and flow of human movement. It is abstract, simple, mystical, and, being danced by young girls rarely more than twelve years old, is stripped of any sensual excesses. Yet it is lyrical and vitally alive, and the dancers are so distinctive that no two performances are alike.

Simply as spectacle the Legong and most other Bali dances are memorable. A temple, or the courtyard of a nobleman's house, is the stage, flickering torches or a single petrol lamp is the usual illumination, and the vividly rippling, rich music of the gamelan orchestra is a continuously sounding background. The dancers are dressed from top to toe in cloth of gold and upon their heads wear great golden helmets dressed with fresh flowers. Silken scarves, a silver belt, mirrors, and colored stones complete the ornamentation. The gamelan players, too, dress in colored tunics, and the village crowd creates a living framework of vitality. But to come to this untutored in the simplest outline or meaning of the dance is to be wasteful of time and opportunity, for without some elementary understanding of what is being expressed, and some knowledge of the choreographic idiom, however flimsy, the dances of Bali can seem meaningless and become quickly boring.

Seeing us standing by the car, undecided, a man came from the direction of the temple and, after speaking to the waiter, touched my arm lightly, inviting me to follow him. We passed through the temple gateway and came into a walled courtyard in which were several pavilions. One, dimly lit with high-glassed oil lamps, was being used as a dressing room by the dancers, three small girls, one so young that her breasts had barely begun to form, and the other two not much older. They seemed dull and docile, submitting silently and without expression to those who were dressing them and painting their faces, while a priest sitting to one side prayed over them.

In a while we went back to the forecourt and found that a crowd had begun to gather and that the best places were taken. I stood at the back and, being taller than the average Balinese, would have been able to see without difficulty; but within a few minutes a man came from the *bandjar* across the road bringing a chair, and took me closer to the front, where people made a place for me.

The gamelan players settled down now, sitting cross-legged on the ground. The drummers (who lead the gamelan) tuned their drums, fingering out tentative rhythms which the others picked up and followed for a few phrases to get the swing and pitch. They sat with their backs to the temple entrance, under the shadow of the great gateway towering into the blackness behind them like two huge book ends built of red brick, edged and inlaid with gray volcanic stone dug from river beds and carved and fretted, decorated with points and pinnacles and niches in which the lanterns flickered. Stone steps led up to the temple entrance, with monstrous stone animals guarding the approaches, watching the villages who sat waiting for the dance to begin.

Then men came drifting across from the *bandjar,* moving quietly, like shadows, with no edges or angularities. Children whispered behind their hands excitedly, enticing each other to clamber and creep into closer places. A man in the gamelan lit a cigarette, and the match in his cupped hands lighting up his face made it seem a piece of statuary, with the sheen and patina of polished copper.

We had been waiting, perhaps, an hour when the three girls entered casually, without grace, looking simply like children dressed up for an occasion, and came down the temple steps into the forecourt, through the gamelan. The two Legong dancers stopped at the foot of the steps and sat behind the musicians, but the third girl (the attendant, called the Tjondong) came forward and stood before the audience, first putting down two fans upon the ground, one at each corner of the stage. The crowd fidgeted for a moment and settled.

The gamelan played a few vague notes of introduction, then

gathered into a sudden *sforzando* that burst and let loose a cataract of shining sound which spread swiftly among the instruments. The Tjondong stiffened, quivering like moonlight on a lake. Her body moved slowly and her arms opened like a water lily coming into bloom (she was no longer an untutored village child). She went through the motions of opening the curtains which divide the infinitesimal and temporal now from eternity. "Went through the motions!" How inadequate it sounds. Each movement was a deliberate, simultaneous articulation of joint, limb, and feature: finger, wrist, neck, eye, hip, knee, foot, and ankle.

She went, then, in wide curves, gliding swiftly, knees bent and arms outstretched, fingers flicking like the wings of a humming bird, short, sharp, angular movements of her neck accenting the rhythm and beat. The clashing of the gamelan pursued her as she returned in sweeping circles to the center of the stage to sit submissively while the reciter began to tell the story of a princess who was beautiful, and a king whose love, passion, and anger brought him to death because he could not seduce her.

When the reciter had finished she took up the two fans, and the Legongs rose up out of the shadows behind the gamelan and came to meet her as she moved toward them. They joined, then, in a coy, seductive, playful, undulating dance which ended when the Legongs finally took the fans, and the Tjondong swooped back up the temple steps to disappear into the darkness.

The Legong dancers now became a continuously shifting vortex of sound and spectacle, making at times a glittering arabesque of movement, then a mime, mimicking the lineaments of each character: the king, his sad wife, the princess, her servant. Each gesture made some clear, grammatical contribution to the narrative, its mood and meaning. There were moments when the dancers were little priestesses performing ritualistic acts of mystical withdrawal, others in which, together, they showed two sides of the same character; at other times their innocence underlined the primal passions—fear, hate, and anger. There is a love dance, a shimmering agitato, knee to knee, cheek softly brushing cheek, with sudden little accents of gesture full of pleasure or tender pain; flutterings as of butterflies about to mate, then swift retreat in wide circling curves. One can understand that noblemen frequently make wives of these little girls even before they reach puberty.

The Legong story and the structure of the dance are always the same, lasting about an hour or a little longer, during which time the dancers never leave the stage and are seldom still. There are minor local variations in the narrative and differences of choreographic emphasis deriving from different teachers and outstanding dancers. But no performance could be dull: not to a child or to a tired old man, nor to a person of great intellect and refinement, nor to a lunatic. It is too real, too magic a thing, done almost without understanding, by children.

Whether or not the performance I saw in the village of Paliatan was a great one, typical, above or below average, I have no way of telling for I only saw one other. All I know is that it opened my mind to a new dimension of experience and expression; that for one moment during the performance I was reminded that a few weeks earlier, in New York, I had seen a *pas de deux* danced by two of the greatest artists in Western ballet and now, watching these village girls, I was vaguely ashamed that I had thought the others graceful.

When the dance was over I was ready to return to Den Pasar and the relaxing familiarity of a hotel bedroom (the single whisky bottle in my suitcase a tenuous lifeline to the West); but Wideh, having rejoined us, said that his friends in the *bandjar* had spoken of a Ketjak dance being performed in the village of Bedulu, about ten kilometers away, and that we should go because it might not be possible to see this dance again during my stay in Bali; people came across the world to watch it, especially in this village where it originated. I was reluctant but Wideh seemed to wish that we should go, and asked that we might take two of his friends from the *bandjar,* who stood there with the waiter and the driver, all watching me make up my mind.

We drove between sleeping fields and through walled villages, lit only by stars and the tiny shrine lights, while one of the men, a scholar, talked of the Ketjak. "The story," he said "is based upon an episode from the Hindu legends of the Ramayana and centers on events that take place after Sita, the wife of Rama (an incarnation of the god Vishnu) has been ravished by Ravana, king of all the evil demons. Rama enlists the help of the monkey kingdom to revenge himself on Ravana, and in the battles which follow the demon king's prime minister is killed by the monkey chief. When this happens the rage of Ravana is so great that the heavens roar, the earth groans, and volcanoes erupt; a great raven spits blood and the sky turns red. In his anger Ravana wakes his brother, a great fighter, and sends him with a mighty army of demons and drives the monkey into exile."

The Ketjak is not a dance in the sense that the Legong is a dance. The story is recited and the action mimed but there is no involved choreography. The dynamic and dramatic effect is created almost entirely by a great chorus of men who represent the monkey army and provide a continuously running accompaniment of onomatopoeic comment and sound effect—so much so that the Ketjak is more commonly known to tourists as the Monkey Dance, the word *ketjak* itself being a simplification of the simian sound "k'tjak k'tjak."

We came then to Bedulu and entered a courtyard of the dwelling of the local prince (himself on a visit to America) where several hundred people were already assembled, the elderly among them sitting along the edge of a pavilion which made one border of the stage space, the younger adults standing up behind them inside the pavilion, and the children sitting on the ground. We moved in among them and took our places behind the children.

As in Paliatan where we had seen the Legong, a great gateway made a backdrop although here the gamelan was not prominent but set aside in an adjacent pavilion, where it seemed to play aimlessly, while the middle of the courtyard was busy with men settling themselves into a dense circle, forming tight rings one inside the other and leaving a space in the center for the actors. In this space was a tall wooden candelabrum holding half a dozen flares, which gave the only light.

There were, perhaps, one hundred and twenty men or more, skins gleaming, naked but for white sarongs pulled tightly between their legs. Each man wore a red hibiscus behind his ear and had daubs of white pigment on his cheeks. They moved crouching, quickly making places for themselves, and as soon as they settled there was silence.

They became tense and leaned forward, looking at the ground as if praying. They began to chant in unison, a muted barking sound on a single note, rising to a chilling crescendo, and then they swayed back, became upright, and together fell forward again, hissing their breath outward. Their bodies swayed like a tree top in a high wind, and with their breath they simulated the swishing sound of branches rising and falling. A naked baby pressed back against my legs and gripped me fearfully with his little fingers.

Somewhere out of the forest of bodies climbed a weird, whining dithyramb as of an ancient crone complaining to all creation. The men swayed faster and the sounds they made became swift and rhythmic until suddenly their arms flew up, reaching, and they leaned back and lifted their faces so that the flare light shone on them, and their fingers, splayed and extended, fluttered frantically. Then they bowed down again into a dark, shut, mumbling, whispering secrecy out of which the weird voice came again as if seeking some escape.

But the monkey-man sounds began once more to mount and to pursue the voice and overtake it as a wave overtakes debris, catches it up and carries it, curls across and enfolds it, then falls itself and fragments into a myriad whispering mysteries. Four times the voice rose and four times the concerted sound of the monkey-men came chasing after it, escalading in short, sharp, barking phrases while the men swayed, reached up and stretched with fingers twitching and flickering in the torch light. Each time the cycle was repeated the men created strange new sounds and cadences, inhuman, simulating coarse animal cries, then marvelously imitating gongs and drums and cymbals.

As the dance developed other characters entered by the great gate and came into the torchlit ring to play the parts of godlike lovers, the demon king, monkey chief, and mythical raven. The chorus of monkey-men split in two, became opposing forces of good and evil, took sides, rose up against each other like great threatening waves, alternating, creating at one moment a punctuation in the drama, at another a symbolism of antagonism, a curtain to conclude an action, a background, a chorus (with the lone voice threading through it all the tragic pattern of the narrative); and finally, at the finish of the dance, with the remaining character players prostrate beneath the torches, the monkey-men dropped down, subsided sighing, to cover them.

One might simply say that these villagers produced a clever pantomine, imitating monkeys and recreating the sounds and conversation of the gamelan; that the weird whining voice retelling the Ramayana story was quaint and queer, and the setting and staging strange; that together they created a unique, sensational tension. But it seemed to me, as in the Legong, that in the centuries of isolation these village people, working primitive material over and over again with few, if any, outside interpolations—shaping, editing, extending—had refined the pure elements of expression without shedding anything of the essential, primal strength. In the primitive arts of drama, dance, and storytelling they had stayed closer to the realities of the tragedy of man; to the basic drama of his life of love and suffering; to an understanding of his essential but ineffectual collaboration with destiny.[2]

[2] Some of the best authorities have said that the Ketjak derives from another dance called the Sanghyang in which a choir replaces the gamelan and a trance state is induced in the dancers, mainly by the chanting. In this trance state the dancers receive the complaints and commands of their ancestral spirits which, seemingly, have been offended and have sent sickness or misfortune to the village. When these messages are received, the dancers, still in their trance, make offerings at the ancestral shrines while the chorus chants invocations and exorcisms. These dances are still performed regularly but the idea of the choral element has been borrowed and used as a starting point from which to develop this separate form of drama and dance, the Ketjak.

CHAPTER

8

Because it was late when the Ketjak finished, and I was tired from having seen so much that was new to me, we stayed the night in Bedulu and in the morning drove back to Den Pasar in leisurely fashion, stopping to see such things as seemed interesting.

Near Ubud, the home of many painters and musicians, we saw a young woman from the Bronx being taught how to play the gender. How marvelously do Americans make the strangest dreams real. She sat with her teacher, the leader of the village gamelan, in the courtyard of the house of an elder, among the chickens, watched by a little boy eating rice out of a banana leaf with his fingers. Two fat white pigeons sidled to and fro along the ridge of the rice barn, fluttering down now and then to pick up grains shaken loose from sheaves by women of the household who came to take the daily ration. A beautiful young woman, mother of the boy, spread bedding upon the ground to air. As a girl, said the waiter, she was a Legong dancer. Her father, a famous musician in his day, now gray and portly, sat in the shade of the guest pavilion and listened. He, in his heyday, had led a gamelan at exhibitions in Paris and New York.

Each village home in Bali is enclosed within a high wall which keeps out wandering spirits and marauders. If the family is rich the wall is built of brick and has ornamental gates; if it is ordinarily poor the wall is made of mud and thatched with rice straw or coconut palm fibers, and the gateway is simply a gap in the wall framed with wooden posts. Whatever the gateway, it has a shrine or niche on either side for offerings, and behind it is a screen to hide the home from demons who might pause to take the offerings at the gate.

Inside each enclosure is a temple court containing family shrines: one for the household ancestors, one each for the holy mountains Agung and Batur (where all the great gods of Bali live), one, as a rule, for the deity who rules the ground upon which the house stands, and others for gods to whom the family has some special devotion. In this shrine space there is a small pavilion used for family prayers and celebrations, and a place to keep religious vessels and accessories.

At the other end of the enclosure, farthest from the shrines, is a kitchen-garden and space to keep a pig or graze a pony or buffalo. The rice barn and kitchen are close together near this space, and then come the pavilions or living rooms, each a separate unit set apart (one for the parents, one for unmarried women, widows, and older girls, and perhaps another for relatives and children). In one of these lesser pavilions the looms are kept for weaving family sarongs. There is a pavilion for receiving and entertaining friends. The number of pavilions may be greater or less than these, depending on the status and affluence of the family.

The village of Ubud is the art center of Bali, where tourists come to buy paintings of village life done in traditional style—slim, bare-breasted girls planting rice, tooth-filing ceremonies, circumcisions, weddings, illustrations of the Legong, Barong, and Ramayana stories. It is pleasant but not great art although Bali has some clever artists. It is limited in subject matter, in treatment, symbolism, and color (red, blue, yellow, black, and white, with dull browns and greens mixed from these pigments). But with the flow of foreign visitors almost stopped the painters of Ubud have little incentive to work today.

There is a mass of tourist-class wood carving to be bought cheaply in almost every village, but at Mas, in back rooms, wrapped in rags, we saw some lovely pieces done with love, great skill, and a measure of genius, waiting to be bought by some stranger with an eye for excellence.

Of all the artists of Bali stone carvers are best occupied, being always busy building or renovating temples, carving statues and ornamental gateways, or decorating the walls of rich men's houses.

They use only one kind of stone, a conglomerate of volcanic ash the color of pumice, which they dig from river beds in blocks and slabs. The stone is soft when first cut and can be carved with a knife, giving the artist every chance to indulge a facile fancy in the matter of gods' heads, demons, monstrous animals, female figures, flowers, and arabesques. One Bali craftsman, a young Brahman whose father is a high priest, carves sculptures for the Christian missionaries; and poised above the entrance to the cathedral in Den Pasar are angels dressed as Legong dancers, while in a bas-relief of the Passion of Christ, Pilate studies the Jewish evidence by electric light, with a motorcycle standing by the door of his office.

We passed the morning in this manner, coming by way of Sanur (the famous beach of Bali) where Japanese contractors are building a luxury hotel in skyscraper style for tourists, although work has stopped and the site is surrounded by high wire fences and is guarded by soldiers. An international airport is planned, with a freeway running straight to the hotel, and the site of a harbor for overseas liners has been chosen, although no work has yet been started on these projects. So we came again to Den Pasar.

Toward evening, after the siesta, Wideh came to take me to his home. As we walked through the town two trucks overtook us, filled with young men and women waving Indonesian flags and singing. They were going, said Wideh, to a place in the hills where members of the Young Nationalist Movement were holding a seminar. He said that there was now much political activity among young intellectuals and students, and the purpose of the seminar was to organize a drive for membership all over Bali and to teach group leaders how to manage meetings, for in this they were falling far behind the Communists.

No sooner had the trucks passed and the black dust blown away than we heard drums and bugles, and a procession entered the main street led by two boys and a girl beating drums, flanked by two men carrying banners, one the national flag of Indonesia and the other the red flag of the Communists, with a golden hammer and sickle in the top corner. Behind them came two buglers, then a group of women and girls marching in files, perhaps forty of them, followed by a contingent of boys, some so small that they skipped alternate steps in order to keep up. Then came files of men, two hundred or so, marching quietly and in good order, unsmiling, and seeming embarrassed. People stood silently by the roadside, watching. There was no comment, no expressions of approval or resentment. No exchange of greetings or recognition.

We followed them and when they turned into a sports field (beside the jail) saw that there were a thousand or more men, women, and children already assembled, sitting in orderly rows on the ground, waiting for these people to arrive; and as they came into the field there was clapping and genteel murmurs of approval for the smartness of their marching. There was a rostrum set up in the field, flanked by the two flags and fitted with a microphone and public address system. After what I had already seen of Bali this seemed orderly, unreal, dull, and colorless.

What is a Communist? A political fanatic? Someone who is puzzled or hungry? A small boy aged eight or nine who wishes to overthrow the state? In Jakarta a priest had said to me, "The Communists are cunning and insidious—they never come out into the open." This all seemed open enough, a thousand people sitting on a playing field looking a little sad, especially the small boys.

There is a set of gamelan instruments behind the rostrum. Wideh says that it is the custom of the Communists to provide food and entertainment after their meetings. The money, he says, comes from China. One wonders where the Balinese gods fit into this grim, unjoyful, and unforgiving religion that was hatched in a London slum.

We met Wideh's father in a side street selling coconut wine from a bamboo tube; a middling, nondescript man with long gray face (needing a shave), irregular but big teeth, and fingers alive and articulated like spiders' legs. I was surprised to see him peddling, believing him to be a tailor by trade, but Wideh said that wine-selling was a casual occupation shared with friends who band together to earn a small fund of money with which to buy extra rice for feast days and temple celebrations.

The men—they call themselves a club—make the wine together, then each man on his appointed day must sell a pipe of wine and put the proceeds into a common fund. The customer buys it by the cup and drinks it standing in the street, which we did, while Wideh's father told us that he had been fishing that day, having risen before dawn to walk ten kilometers to his favorite place, where he caught three small fish and brought them home for the evening meal. Now, for two hours, he had been selling wine but soon would have sold his quota and would go then to his *bandjar* (an association of neighbors) to discuss the funeral feast of a member recently deceased.

Like most low-income Balinese, Wideh's father spends his surplus time and money in arranging and providing food for family feasts, anniversaries, and temple ceremonies, so that no matter how hard he works he is never able to accumulate possessions and is always poor, although not oppressed by the condition, knowing no other and seeing little likelihood of ever achieving even a relative affluence.

When we had finished our drink Wideh brought me to his father's house, squeezed among others in an alley way that earlier had been a residential area for minor Dutch officials and mixed-race families, so that the houses were built bungalow fashion and not in the manner of the Balinese, having contiguous rooms under one roof—although there were ancestral shrines in the small backyard.

In each of the three bedrooms the only furniture was an old pedal-operated sewing machine, a chair, and an unsprung bed without a mattress, but with a roll of sleeping mats lying upon it. Wideh's father lives with his wife in one of these rooms and makes women's blouses on the sewing machine. In the second room Wideh's young sister makes shirts and shares the living and sleeping space with a younger sister and brother. She is a pretty girl, fifteen years old, and she was at school long enough to learn to read and write. She has a colored postcard portrait of herself on the wall at the foot of the bed. A brother-in-law lives and works in the third room, making trousers. His wife, who is Wideh's older sister, also lives in this room with two of her six children. The other four children live with her husband's brother in a village near Den Pasar. This sister has been to hospital to have herself sterilized so that she will have no more children.

The brother-in-law who keeps the four children, as well as a wife and three children of his own, is a male nurse in the hospital at Den Pasar. In the afternoons and evenings he conducts a private medical practice in his own and neighboring villages and works far into the night. His patients are poor and pay mostly with food, so that he is well able to feed his brother's children as well as his own.

In this environment and against this background of little learning and historic poverty, Wideh has laid down his own disciplines, followed a road to goals of his own choosing, and become a Bachelor of Arts. The small front room of the house, used as the family reception room, is his study and bedroom. It contains a rough table, three visitor's chairs, some artificial flowers, a photograph of President Sukarno, and a locked wardrobe. The wardrobe is Wideh's. His status symbol, it contains his books, his spare shirt and set of underwear, the old cotton jacket, and a broken tennis racquet left behind many years ago by some Dutchman. When he daydreams he sees a new black jacket hanging in the wardrobe which will be kept for "social," that is, for functions Wideh will attend as a faculty member of the university and as a senior government servant when he gets his Master's degree.

We had a meal in the Chinese café near the bus stop, then went to Wideh's *bandjar* to listen to a broadcast from Jakarta of an international badminton game between Indonesia and Pakistan; but there was time to spare before the match began and we could sit and drink lemonade and chat with people who came to meet Wideh's foreign guest.

Every Balinese man belongs to a *bandjar*. It is a community extension of the home and family circle and membership is compulsory when a man marries. Each family pays a subscription and the *bandjar* runs its own bank, makes loans, supports a temple, owns a gamelan. It helps to arrange and finance weddings and other family celebrations, temple festivals, and cremations. It organizes community feasts and lends facilities and equipment for family parties. Each *bandjar* has its meeting house where members and their families gather in the evenings to eat and drink, talk and gamble, and take it in turn to act as cooks and waiters. The leader of the *bandjar* is elected by the members and approved by the gods, through a medium.

Wideh is one of the few unmarried men in this *bandjar* and is a member through his mother's family. She was sitting cross-legged among friends on a low platform that ran along one side of the club house, playing cards, an angular, fleshless woman with high, wide cheekbones. Several such groups were gambling, mostly elderly folk of the working class—the women wrinkled (one, even, without a blouse) and chewing betel nut; men sipping palm or coconut wine—the cards greasy and limp from long use. They played mechanically, for infinitesimal stakes, bursting suddenly into surprised, harsh laughter when a game turned unexpectedly upon a single card.

A few late workmen ate their evening meal of rice in the farthest corner, where a door led to an outside kitchen. Other men sat together talking on an open veranda facing the street, some with favorite fighting cocks in cages at their feet. Girls, busy between the kitchen and other parts of the *bandjar,* bringing food or drinks to their elders, were watching Wideh, hoping that he would look at them. At last he smiled at one, then winked at me and said that this was the girl whose wrist watch and ring he wore, adding smugly, "Now that girls may have the higher education their minds begin to spread and they look outside the rich men of the village for a man to marry and choose a good student." When he has his Master's degree he will want to take a wife, and the girl who gets him knows that she will enter into the new Indonesian hierarchy of academicians, army officers, and senior public officials.

We were sitting with a very old man who, said Wideh, was a member of Den Pasar's ruling family, a son or cousin of one of the minor wives of the late rajah, and one of the few members of that family to survive the big war between the people of southern Bali and the Dutch. This was in 1906 when the rajah, his wives, children, staff, and personal attendants all died together in one astounding encounter in the main street of Den Pasar.

The old man had the aristocratic face of those who live to great age austerely, although the illusion went when he opened his mouth to laugh and showed bare upper gums and spare, horselike, lower teeth stained black with betel juice. He sat in a wicker chair, leaning forward, thin-bearded chin on crossed hands (three curved fingernails each two inches long) resting upon a walking stick.

He would have been a youth when the Dutch, already long ruling in Java and the greater islands of the Indies, decided to arbitrate and bring order among the quarreling rajahs of Bali, some of whom had sought Dutch help in dealing with their neighbors. The battles which followed were brief, grotesque, monstrous encounters between two unequal civilizations: one brilliantly alive, imaginative and unrealistic; the other dull and deadly efficient. The Dutch expedition against the rajah of Den Pasar (Badung as it was then) lasted five days during which time there were two battles separated by a series of recitals given by the brass band of the Dutch command.

The first battle took place at Sanur, where the Dutch landed. A small army of Balinese spearmen attacked them and were quickly eliminated. The old man had been among those who went from Den Pasar to Sanur to meet the invaders and had fought all day, but in the evening went with friends in a canoe to a hiding place along the coast. "They had guns and bullets," said the old man, "and we had spears with golden tips, and the gods gave us no help."

Three days afterward, with his friends, he went back to Den Pasar; but before reaching the town they met people running away, who told them that cannon balls fired by Dutch ships, six kilometers (three and a half miles) out to sea, had fallen on the rajah's palace, setting it alight, and that the Dutch army from Sanur with its brass band blowing was now marching upon the town.

The rajah and his family prepared themselves for battle by dressing in their best, wearing ceremonial krisses with gold handles inlaid with jewels, and family ornaments of enormous value. When they were ready the rajah led them from the palace riding upon the shoulders of an attendant, another holding a gold umbrella over his head. His wives and other women followed together with sons, husbands, brothers, and even the smallest royal children, the women armed with spears and with their hair hanging loose as if going to a cremation.

Turning a corner of the main street, not far from where the Hotel Bali stands, they came suddenly upon the Dutch, whose commander, taken by surprise, called his soldiers to a halt and stood looking in amazement. The rajah's little army continued to advance and, coming close, ran to attack the Dutch with spears and krisses. The Dutch soldiers, to protect themselves, fired their rifles. The rajah fell dying in the middle of the street while his wives and daughters gathered around him and stabbed themselves to death across his body so that their spirits might ascend together to the holy mountain.

As fast as men or women were wounded by the Dutch guns, the Balinese themselves finished them off with kriss cuts and stabs so that they would not live to become prisoners of the horrible foreigners. Those who were not shot by the soldiers killed themselves, and in the end the rajah's little brother, a boy of twelve, led the remnants of the royal force in a last advance and was shot down, together with the rest. Broken spears, golden krisses with jeweled handles, purple, pink, and orange silk sarongs, patches of blood, beautiful bodies, all lay quiet in the morning sun in the main street of Den Pasar. Blood and hate and blind stupidity—even here in this little island of the gods, this paradise, this little world of marvelous make-believe. Blood and hate and blind stupidity. "But," said the old man, "if we had had a cannon that would shoot six kilometers the Dutch would never have taken Den Pasar."

A group of army officers came in, off duty and dressed casually, seated themselves at a table, and bought beer. Then, after consulting quietly together, they asked us to join them. When I had been introduced one of them remarked that the old man must have told me the story of the rajah's battle, adding, "Perhaps it will help you understand why we Indonesians are suspicious of foreign powers who want to help us solve our problems. What begins as assistance quickly becomes interference and ends in wicked tyranny. We have had enough of that in the course of our history and now would rather muddle in our own way than ask for help."

Inevitably, we spoke of the possibility of war over Malaysia. I said that it seemed ridiculous and beyond belief and credence that people as basically simple as the Balinese and the Australians should war against each other, having nothing, even theoretically, to gain and everything to lose; and that in general terms the same applied to all of Indonesia and to the people of America and Britain. I said that most Westerners found it difficult to approve the belligerence of Indonesia's leaders, to which one of the officers answered coldly, "In Australia you have no understanding of the meaning of leadership. You are ruled by performing walruses who sit up and clap their flippers together whenever they hear a band play 'God Save the Queen,' and bow to the ground like peasants when a voice is heard in Washington." I felt ashamed and angry and was ready to remonstrate when someone switched on the radio, and a rowdy announcer, talking from Jakarta, took charge of the *bandjar*.

Immediately there was tension. The officers bought more beer and settled down to listen. Young men and some children came in from the street, and the girls from the kitchen found places for themselves. Wideh said, "Everyone in Indonesia will turn to the radio tonight to hear this game, for we are the champions at badminton, and Pakistan is next." It was, he said, the final match of a series, with the decision depending upon this particular game.

The play went against Indonesia from the beginning—it seemed that the volatile favorite was off his game, making spectacular mistakes and errors of judgment. The people of the *bandjar* were quiet. The officers looked disappointed and moody. Wideh scowled, and the girls looked frightened. Even the card players sat like statues, listening. The announcer had lost his professional heartiness and now sounded confused and full of genuine despair, inventing unlikely, far-fetched excuses for the Indonesian players, snatching at imagined moments of hope, begging them to be careful, calling their shots for them, groaning when they missed. There was no mention of the other team, no suggestion that the Pakistani players were giving a good display. This was no longer a sporting contest, a badminton match, but a matter of national pride in which victory was an essential need, an urgency, a necessary reassurance that Indonesia and its people are of some account, able to hold their own, to be accounted superior in at least one twentieth-century activity.

When it seemed that the match might be lost the announcer began to shout hysterically, "Pray, pray, pray," and immediately a young man in the *bandjar* stood up and began to address the gods in a loud voice. Others joined him, mumbling, intoning, even some of the officers; and from that moment the game changed and the Indonesian players made no more mistakes but won every stroke, so that even I, who had no great interest in the game, became excited and thought it almost a miracle.

When victory came the announcer was weeping loudly into the microphone and shouting incoherent apostrophes, invoking the President, the people, God, and the glorious Republic. Then a band played the national anthem and everybody in the *bandjar* stood. The officers stopped cheering and beating each other on the back, and when I looked at Wideh he was smiling and crying.

In the morning, when he came to the hotel, Wideh brought a small, good-looking man of middle age saying that his name was Ida Bagus Alit and that he would spend the next two days with us. Alit smiled and I liked him immediately and was glad that he would be with us for these two days; then as we drove out of Den Pasar he said that we were going to the town of Klungkung to see a temple ceremomy and that he, being of the Brahman caste and consequently of a priestly family, would be able to explain anything that puzzled me.

"For many centuries," he said, "Bali was a colony of the great Javanese empire—when Java was the most civilized part of all the Eastern islands; and when the Mohammedan invasion brought about the downfall of that empire in the fifteenth century, its priests and the remnants of its royal family, together with scholars, artists, and the chief men of government, fled to Bali and settled here. The son of the last king of Java made himself king of Bali and established his court at the foot of Mount Agung, and Klungkung became one of the main centers of his government. Here," continued Alit, "the ancient religion, art, and literature of Java have been preserved in their pure state, uncontaminated by Moslem or other foreign influences that have overlain Java for the past five centuries."

It took an hour or more to drive to Klungkung; but long before we reached the town we began to pass truck and busloads of people from all parts of Bali, dressed in their best, coming to take part in the anniversary celebrations of the founding of their mother temple. "To replenish their identities," said Alit, "at the fountain of their first beginnings, the place where their ancestors established themselves with the gods which came with them from Java, and where their spirits now congregate on festival occasions."

Closer to the town traffic clogged the roads: cars, horse-drawn carts and gigs, people on foot and on bicycles; processions of women in single file carrying on their heads great silver dishes, filigreed, filled with intricate arrangements of flowers and fruit, rice cakes, sweets, some with whole chickens, ducklings or geese, decorated and hung with tassels of fresh young palm leaf or festoons of animal fat trimmed into floral shapes and geometrical figures. Many of these offerings, carried with stately grace and great care, elegant and ingenious, had taken days to design and make ready, and some were accompanied by large groups of people led by a musician.

In the open forecourt to the temple, opening from the main street of the town, local pony carts came and went like taxis, bringing townsfolk; trucks and buses and a few cars parked along the sides, and a food market did much business. People came and went continuously in groups, a flux of color against the dust-colored walls of the temple and the black volcanic ash underfoot.

Men entering the temple wore scarves or sarongs draped round their buttocks, and Alit sent a boy to borrow one each for me and

Wideh (he had his own with him) for it would have been improper and ill-mannered had we gone into the temple not dressed according to custom. While we waited for the boy Alit explained the pattern and plan of Bali-Hindu temples which vary, as do temples of other sects and religions, in some details though conforming in general to a tradition of design and architecture.

Every temple of the larger sort is an enclosed rectangle, open to the sky and divided by a wall into two parts, the first being a courtyard. In one corner of this there is a tall, wooden tower housing a drum or gong called a *kul kul,* used to rouse the town in time of crisis. Also in this court are sheds where pilgrims rest, prepare food for themselves or offerings for the gods, and store musical instruments and other such luggage as they may bring with them. Flowering trees grow in this court, giving shade and fragrance.

To pass into the temple proper one must go through a huge ornamental gateway of sculptured stone, with a flight of high steps leading up to it, and walk between two giant demons called *raksasas* (who eat people, dead and alive). Today being a feast day, these demons were decorated with colored aprons and wore flowers on their heads, looking hideous. The two halves of the towering gateway are identical, signifying the equal halves of all unities: soul and body, good and bad, male and female, day and night. So the people pass into the temple proper, the place of the shrines and community worship.

When the boy came back we wrapped our sarongs about us and went into the forecourt, following the crowd, and came to the gate through which people were passing to and fro, those unburdened making way when women came with heavy, decorated offerings on their heads, and the elders helping little children to climb the high steps.

A gamelan was playing in one of the pavilions, and the murmur of prayers mixed with music made a unity in which we moved slowly among the people, finding in a little while a place to sit. So we rested on stone steps and I spoke with an old man who claimed that he was a hundred years old, which may well have been true for his skin was like papyrus and he had no teeth and was bent like a tree on the seashore.

A little way to one side of us a group of sixty or seventy people were gathered before a shrine, the women kneeling and behind them men sitting cross-legged, with a priest among them, dressed in white, praying and ringing a silver handbell. In a while they went away and another group came to take their place.

This shrine before which they sat was a platform of brick and stone with steps leading up to it, and on the platform there was a small, square house with wooden double doors, over it a thatched roof supported with corner posts. A narrow pavement ran round the house and this was crowded with offerings, put there by women who moved up and down the stairway to place their decorated bowls and trays in this space before taking their places among the people praying.

When they were settled before the shrine the priest stood and sprinkled them all liberally with holy water from a dish in which flowers and flower petals floated; then he moved among them, splashing water on their hands to wash them, and as he passed, each person took a few flowers from the dish. The priest returned to his place facing the shrine, and sitting among the people rang his silver bell and began to pray. Each pilgrim took a flower or petal between the tips of the two middle fingers and with it touched his forehead, then flung the flower toward the shrine. Three times they did this, bowing before the shrine; then the priest went once more among them distributing the holy water, which they received in cupped hands and sipped three times, then three times wiped their heads with it.

The priest faced the shrine once more and prayed again, taking more flowers from his dish, and again he went among the people and put a flower behind the ear of each one of them, and afterward pressed a grain of soft rice between their eyebrows. "And this," said Alit, "is the sacrament of Holy Contact between the faithful and the god who is their beginning, their ancestor, the collective spirit into which they will be received when they die."

In the temple at Klungkung there are many shrines to many gods, each with its devotees, so that the courtyard was busy with groups coming in and out, praying at one shrine and another, bringing their offerings—among them a group with a buffalo head so decorated with flowers, sheaves of rice, and festoons of palm leaf that it seemed strangely appealing. Girls were going about taking some small part from each offering, collecting them together in a cleared space before each shrine so that later the climax of the ceremony of sacrifice might take place. When this time came the priest would take a fan and gently waft the essence of the offerings toward the invisible gods resting in the shrines. Next day the offerings would be taken away and eaten in a ceremonial feast.

There was much to see and later there would be dances, recitals by the gamelan, processions, seances, and feasts, continuing for several days; but Wideh, who had been away on his own for some little time, came with news of a cockfight to be held in a village not far away, so we left Klungkung and, after driving no more than two or three miles, saw a row of pony carts at the roadside, and a footpath leading into a coppice, which we followed, passing through a small clearing where four or five hundred bicycles were parked, leaning one against the other. A little farther along we entered another clearing, sheltered from the sun by a rough covering of cloth which formed a kind of marquee with open sides.

Hundreds of men were crowded under this shade, forming a ring round a circle of bare earth, most of them squatting or kneeling on the ground but some walking about carrying fighting cocks in tight-fitting satchels of woven coconut leaves, which enclosed them completely except that their heads and tail-feathers protruded. Other men had their birds beside them under the latticed bell-shaped cages, and some carried them about in their arms like babies, stroking them and softly massaging their chest muscles.

"This cockfight," said Alit, "is for the rice harvest, which cannot be started until a blood-offering has been made to the spirits, just as the rice cannot be planted until the fields have been purified in the same way."

Wideh made a face and said sourly, "Maybe this was true before but it should not be so in a modern country. Better to put fertilizer on the fields and do away with the gambling." But later he put a hundred rupiahs on a big white cock which was cut to pieces in a few seconds.

If cock-fighting is ever forbidden in Bali the pattern of life will be altered for peasant and nobleman alike, for a fighting cock is as much part of his possessions and takes as much of the time and mind of a Balinese man as a new wife might. He concerns himself with its diet, aiming not only to toughen its muscles but to reduce the weight of fat in its viscera and so lessen the bird's internal heat and susceptibility to fatigue. He trims its feathers so that none protrude to provide a beak-hold for some other bird, and crops its comb, ear-lobes, and wattles for the same reason. The bird is his constant companion; he carries it in his arms while walking about the courtyard of his home, he takes it with him to the clubhouse, and if he is not able to be with it all the time he sets it in its cage by the roadside so that it can see the people passing and not be lonely.

Alit said that men of his caste should not be present at cockfights but for my sake (he said smiling) he would accompany me, so we made our way into the crowd and room was made for me close by a little table where the timekeeper and the referee sat cross-legged with a gong between them, and a dish of water with a small saucer of coconut shell with a hole in it, which is a device for timing the count-out of a defeated bird. (When the bird keels over the timekeeper puts the saucer in the dish. The water coming in through the hole fills it so that it sinks, and this signifies that the stricken bird has been defeated.)

Men now were walking about on the outskirts of the crowd displaying their birds and making matches for them, or holding them high and calling out challenges and wagers which were quickly taken up. Some, already matched, were busy binding on gaffs, winding woolen thread around them so that each fighting cock carried a five-inch steel blade, razor sharp, bound to the spur of its right leg. In a small bamboo shrine, hung upon a pole beside the ring, there was an offering of flowers and rice to the cockfighting god, to ensure that no owner would be cut by one of these murderous, blood-letting, sacrificial knives.

These preliminaries were conducted decently and with proper decorum, without shouting or jostling or ill-mannered argument: but when the referee tapped his gong and called the first contestants into the ring there was a quick tightening of tension, and excitement flared and crackled as men reached forward, stretching and straining, to make wagers, holding out handfuls of paper rupiahs, shouting like stock brokers mad with money-making.

The first two birds were brought into the ring and faced with each other, their owners holding them by the body and provoking them one against the other while the onlookers yelled louder and made more bets and called to each other across the ring waving money. Then the owners lifted their birds and walked once round the ring holding them above their heads while the betting frenzy increased. Then again they faced the birds in the center of the ring, in a small square marked with chalk, plucking at their neck feathers and patting them between the legs to irritate and make them angry, opening their beaks and spitting into them until the cocks, exasperated, ruffed their neck feathers and glared at each other and struggled to escape their owners so that they could fight.

Men yelled now, trying to make last-minute wagers—a man jumped up and down beside me shouting, "The white, the white, who'll take two hundred against the white?" Other men screamed, "*Hidjo! Hidjo!*" (the cock with the green tail feathers) and tried to back the bird for sums rising from a few rupiahs—covered superciliously by big bettors—to amounts of several thousands.

The referee tapped the gong and the two owners withdrew, leaving the birds bobbing and nodding in the ring, their beaks almost touching the dust, eyeing each other evilly. The shouting stopped. There was silence around the ring. One bird leapt and there was a flurry and rustle of feathers, and an anxious "Ah," from the crowd, in unison.

The birds turned and faced each other again, bobbing and bowing. The colored cock leapt once more and the white bird rose to meet it in mid-air, legs extended. When they returned to earth the white bird faltered and the crowd sighed, and soon a red stain began to spread along the white bird's thigh and when it tried to move it staggered stiffly to one side.

The crowd shouted and the white bird's owner glanced toward the referee, who nodded almost imperceptibly and lightly touched the gong. The man ran swiftly into the ring, picked up his bird and blew into its beak, then set it down again. But the heart had gone out of the white cock, and the crowd shouted for a kill. The colored cock strutted for a second or two, uncertainly, then jumped and struck. The white bird buckled, shook its head, and slowly leaned over, fluttering one wing, then fell sideways like a sack. No one stirred until the gong rang and the owner of the colored cock walked slowly into the ring, caught up his bird, and walked round solemnly, holding it above his head. The owner of the dead bird took his up carefully so as not to cut himself on the steel spur, then went among his friends and was swallowed up. Straight away the crowd began to bet on the next main.

We stayed an hour and saw six or seven fights (or mains) each lasting less than thirty seconds, with breaks of several minutes between for ceremony and betting. In one main two cocks, reluctant to engage, were put together in a wicker cage and goaded, and when it seemed that they might fight the cage was lifted; but one bird ran away (the crowd laughing) and when the owner caught it up he cut its throat for shame.

I made a few small wagers and so found myself caught up momentarily in the excitement of each fight, but the winning and losing seemed so much a matter of chance, and the consummation so swiftly cruel and merciless that I soon tired of participation and found more pleasure in the general spectacle.

On the outskirts of the crowd some other men were gambling in small groups, playing a game in which one of them concealed a number of counters (five or less) underneath his hand, leaving his friends to guess and bet upon the number hidden. They played furtively, using Chinese coins for counters, but every so often were disturbed by policemen who, if they caught a player, took him into custody for gambling illegally. But the gamblers had boys watching and when warned they simply stepped into the cockfighting crowd and gambled with religious sanction until the police went away. It was only the old, slow-moving men who were caught and carried off.

One giant of a man, selling patent medicine, stood among the food vendors—wherever Indonesians collect there is food to be bought—and soon he had a small audience who saw him first stick a scimitar into the ground to mark his pitch, then take bottles of medicine from a basket and set them out in rows upon a square of canvas. When this was done he reached into a sack and lifted out a live python, seven or eight feet long, which he hung across his neck and shoulders, and when this was accomplished to their mutual comfort he unrolled a colored diagram illustrating the insides and circulatory system of a man. He now began, with wide dramatic gestures, to explain how blood runs through the body, entering every limb and organ, so that though a snake might bite only a man's toe or finger, its venom would inevitably be carried into his heart and head and so strike him dead or—here a dramatic pause and painful grimace—send him mad.

The audience, mostly little boys, stood fascinated, but when the big man took three strides forward and plucked his scimitar from the ground and stared at them the timid stepped back a pace or two. He stopped and took up a bottle of the medicine, drawing the cork with his teeth, then stood, scimitar in one hand and bottle in the other and the python peering eerily over his shoulder, staring at them.

"Observe," he commanded, and without further ado he scraped the skin of his forehead with the scimitar until blood ran. Then he held his arm up for all to see, and said, "I will now command the snake to bite me," which he did, and the python fastened onto his arm while he watched it, looking at once fierce and stern. The small boys were horrified.

Then roughly he brushed the snake away and splashed the magic medicine quickly and liberally over his wound, drank what remained in the bottle at one gulp and glared at his audience while he stuck the scimitar back into the ground. "See," he said, "I do not die. The snake cannot kill me," and with that he struck the attitude of a man doing the Pentjak (Fighting Dance) and began to go through the motions of engaging an imaginary enemy.

When they saw that he had finished his performance and was not going to die the crowd began to move away, but he turned swiftly and, picking up the scimitar again, faced them and began to expatiate upon the miraculous attributes of his medicine while a young man took up a number of bottles and moved among the people, offering them for sale.

I bought one and Wideh frowned and said, "You are foolish, for the snake has no teeth and that stuff is rubbish." But I answered that the man must sell his wares before he could buy rice for himself and that the price of one bottle was little enough to pay for such entertainment. But it was clear that Wideh thought me foolish, even for a foreigner.

We bought food[3] from the vendors and when we had eaten went back to Klungkung to see the famous courthouse—a great pavilion standing back from the main street on a platform of tiered brick, built to a height of fifteen feet or thereabouts above the level of the roadway. The building is simple and stately, with stairs leading from the main floor to a higher platform where the judges sit on gilt chairs flanked by stone serpents. But it is the ceiling of the pavilion which makes it famous, being covered in its entirety with harrowing and hideous cartoons predicting punishments that await miscreants and inadequate people when they get to hell.

[3] It may be worth noting that although I took whatever food and drink were available or offered during my journeys, I never at any time had stomach trouble.

A thief writhes forever in a vat of boiling oil. Prostitutes walk a plank stretched over a flaming inferno, to be decapitated afresh each time they reach the end of the ordeal. Liars are clawed continuously by tigers, and women who abort themselves have their breasts gnawed at by rats. Men and women who have no grandchildren hang forever in a burning bamboo thicket.

After dark we went again to the temple and saw the same scenes as before, but in the half light and shadow of shrines lit by oil lamps the mysteries seemed more mystical; and with vision limited, sounds and scents came more acutely to the senses so that passing through the first courtyard we sniffed the frangipani strongly and could hear gongs booming and the clear ringing of the gamelan above the murmur of people praying and singing hymns.

In the temple court itself the visual patterns seemed more compact and composed—solid blocks of shadow becoming lost in the night sky—and on the ground fractured by patches of bright light, with sharp outlines around the shrines where lamps hung and priests in white still prayed and made offerings of flowers and incense to invisible deities.

We moved closer, caught in slow-moving tides of people drifting between pavilions, and came eventually to rest beside a shrine hung with streamers and banners of woven palm, where an old woman with red flowers in her hair sat against a post moaning, in a trance. A priest prayed and held his hands in the incense smoke while men in the press of people sitting around him called out loudly, shouting sudden, meaningless ejaculations, swaying from side to side and looking upward with strained faces and unseeing eyes.

In a nearby pavilion, women and children watched anxiously, eyes upon the old lady (a *dewa* or priestess-medium said Alit, whispering), and suddenly she went rigid and began to speak in a high childish voice. The priest answered, making a dialogue, speaking through her to the unseen god and getting answers, while the people watched and listened, their faces eager. He sprinkled more incense into the brazier burning at his feet and began to rock to and fro. The people in the pavilion copied him, some of them lifting up their faces and making strange noises. A man jumped up and hung onto a post, shouting, but was quickly pulled down.

The old woman went on for a while, then stopped as suddenly as she had started. The priest rang his bell and sprinkled holy water all around. A file of girls in golden costumes came through the crowd and went past, intent upon their own business, dancing with slow, stately steps, followed by other girls with offerings and a man carrying a ceremonial umbrella.

Then on the other side of the temple a great shout, and the shrieking of women and children, and a scattering among the crowd. Alit said, "The Barong will come out soon and dance among the people, and perhaps there will be a Kris dance." But although we waited for an hour there was no Barong, and after speaking to some people Alit said that maybe they would do it tomorrow. So, being tired, we drove the car into a quiet street and slept in it.

CHAPTER 9

Extract from *Indonesia 1963,* published by the Department of Foreign Affairs, Jakarta

> The tragic poignancy of the eruption of Mount Agung on Bali lay in the fact that it occurred within days after the climax of the ceremonies connected with the Karya Agung Eka Dasa Rudra . . . clearly, in some respect, and in spite of all the efforts the Bali Hindus have made, men have not yet succeeded in restoring the balance of nature in purification and renewal which bring harmony and happiness to mankind.

"The Karya Agung Eka Dasa Rudra," said Alit, "means the Great Rite of the Eleven Directions, and these eleven directions are the eight major points of the compass together with Up and Down and Center, making eleven directions which encompass the whole of the universe, the center of which is this mountain, the Bali Gunung Agung, or great mountain of Bali."

We had been driving northward for two hours, having left Klungkung in the thin, rain-washed light of early morning, and were now skirting the foot of the holy volcano, Gunung Agung. We would soon be climbing to the rim of its sister mountain, Batur, to take a last look at the smoking cone which is the landmark for the whole south part of Bali; then we would cross the spine of the island and lose sight of it.

I had taken advantage of the early start to read the reports that

Miss Jo Abdoerachman had lent me in Jakarta of the recent eruption of Mount Agung and the disasters and relief work which followed. And from these reports and other government accounts, and extracts of letters which she had written to Red Cross headquarters in Geneva, I had reached the conclusion that the Balinese are, indeed, far removed in mind from what we believe to be the realities of this day and age.

There was, for instance, the officially sanctioned opinion that the Bali Agung eruption occurred because mankind has not yet succeeded in restoring the basic harmony in nature. And Miss Abdoerachman herself had said, in a report to Geneva, that "the Balinese are steeped in tradition and are closely bound to their deities, local shrines, and the souls of their ancestors living in these shrines."

Commenting on the difficulties of administering relief work immediately following the eruptions and the earthquakes which came after, she had written that "the biggest problem in connection with these disasters is not the physical work to be done but the problem of getting the victims psychologically adjusted to realize and accept the fact that the disaster will completely change their lives . . . they cannot accept this and consequently we get very little cooperation from them, even though they do not, themselves, know how to cope with their situation. They put up a resistance to everything we try to do for them which suggests a change from their past way of life."

I looked at Alit and asked, "Is this true?"

He replied, "First of all you must understand that when the gods first came to the island of Bali it was flat and had no place high enough for them to live on with the dignity proper to their status. So the gods themselves made Gunung Agung, the greatest of the great, and its sister, Gunung Batur, and the lake that lies between them, which is the home of the water gods; and these places are the most holy in the whole world—for Bali is the center of the universe and the home of all the gods—and must be venerated accordingly."

He said this without smiling, and I looked at Wideh to see if my leg was being pulled, but he looked disinterested and obviously found the conversation distasteful.

Alit continued, saying that every family in Bali has an ancestral shrine in the great mother temple of Besakih, on the slopes of the Gunung Agung, where its members come to worship at the times of the great feasts and anniversaries, in the presence of the high gods. It is there, he said, that the most elaborate offerings are made. There the richest gifts are given to the water gods when cattle and pigs are blessed by the priests, garlanded, then taken in decorated boats into the middle of lake and dropped over the side to drown. Ducks, geese, and hens are hung with stones, slaughtered, and thrown into the water wreathed with flowers, to please the spirits who live in the depths of the lake.

I asked if this were still true today and Wideh said impatiently, "I tell you, this place will always be a museum. Neither the people nor the government want it differently. The people will not change and the government is happy enough to keep the island as a tourist attraction for foreigners." Alit said that the ceremony still takes place every ten years—the time being measured by the Balinese calendar which has a year of thirty weeks, each of seven days—and that on these occasions the gods remain on earth for ten days so that everybody may have an opportunity to pray to them in the mother temple. In the old days, he said, a tiger and a black monkey were also sacrificed but now there were few of these animals left in Bali.

"We believe," said Alit, ignoring Wideh, "that just as sickness and health are two natural and contrasting states of man's condition, so good and veil are two extreme states of nature. And we believe, also, that men by their misdeeds can upset the fine balance of nature and thus create disharmonies which make for catastrophes such as volcanic eruptions and earthquakes and periods of pestilence or national calamity. Bad things happen in nature because of our misbehavior, and man brings upon himself all that befalls him."

Several times during the past century the Gunung Batur has erupted but nobody could remember when the Gunung Agung last became angry; and when in February, 1963, there were murmurings deep down inside the mountain, people said only that the gods were whispering to each other, and they ignored official warnings and remained in their villages. But in March there were three eruptions, with fire blasts and streams of lava, and a rain of stones and ash blackened the sky so that the people in Sourabaya, 350 kilometers (210 miles) to the west, could not see to work at noon, and the whole of eastern Java, beyond Sourabaya, was clouded with dust for a week, with everybody sneezing.

"After the first big blast," said Wideh, "many foreign journalists came to Bali, and when they saw the sufferings of the people they played strong, sad music on the heartstrings of the whole world. But when relief came and the government tried to help the villagers they were ungrateful. They wanted to be left alone with the gods, to suffer and make amends, and to be forgiven. It was like Miss Abdoerachman said, the world wanted to help but the people would not cooperate."

The Philippines sent a medical team which worked on the mountainside with an Indonesian medical regiment. The French sent drugs, the Canadians gave tents to house the homeless, the Australians flew in utility trucks and a plane-load of tires (at the time of the eruption only thirty percent of all vehicles in Bali were road-worthy). The Americans sent equipment to set up temporary schools, and the Thais sent rice.

Then Alit said, "To begin with, the governor made much of the foreign journalists and encouraged them to write sad stories of the problems and sorrows of Bali, hoping that America and other rich countries might provide ships and money and farming machinery to help move the homeless people to other islands and resettle them. But the President became angry and said that these stories made it seem that Indonesia was unable to manage its own affairs, and he told officials on Bali to stop the publicity and work harder to solve their problems themselves."

We climbed up past Bangli and came to the mountain town of Kintamani with its narrow main street, crowded with farmers and traders and pony carts, running along a ridge, with Agung and Batur beyond. On the rim of a high valley there is a café where we stopped, and as soon as we got out of the car we were pestered by young girls, some selling cheap cotton *batiks* and others offering melons and dark-green, thick-skinned oranges. They pulled and plucked at us, thrusting their goods into our hands, until Wideh shouted angrily and made them step back while we climbed a flight of stone steps to the café, which is set on a ledge above the road.

The girls followed and sat on the top steps saying that they were hungry and that we should buy from them so that they might eat, but although some of them looked wild, and wore shifts fashioned from flour sacks (relics of Red Cross relief), the others were dressed decently enough and none looked hungry.

We stood for a while trying to ignore them, looked across the basin in which Batur and Agung stand, traced the courses of great lava flows and areas of blast where nothing green remained, and guessed at the size of a huge scar on one face of the mountain. The land around us lay under a foot of black ash in which indentations had been scooped, and green corn was growing in them; but no fields were yet fit for rice planting.

While we waited for coffee the café manager came and stood beside us and spoke of things he had seen in the worst weeks of the cataclysm: black rivers of boiling mud and water rushing into the valleys to swell and flood other rivers already blocked with lava and great stones thrown out of the crater; bridges smashed and swept away; roads broken; houses collapsed; rice fields inundated and destroyed; and soon afterward a plague of rats looking for food.

"Refugees came up this road from the valleys," said the manager, "carrying whatever they had been able to save. Some families had their total possessions on their heads—women with tables, chairs, mattresses, and sleeping mats, children carrying kitchen things and water pots, men bringing the ceremonial dancing costumes and instruments of the gamelan. Some people wore several sets of clothing, one over the other, but many had left everything behind."

It was a pity, I said, that this had happened at the time of a great festival when so many people had congregated on the mountain, and the villages were full of visitors.

"It could not have happened otherwise," said Alit. "Time moves in cycles, as shown by the movement of the sun, moon, and stars, and the flow of tides and the great winds, and each cycle has its own need for a harmonious and natural completion. For this reason we in Bali have our periodical rites of purification and spiritual replenishment to restore any upset in the balance and harmony of nature during the period of each cycle of time. Some of these rites are held every Balinese year, others at ten-year intervals, and the Great Rite of the Eleven Directions is held once in every hundred years."

"They picked the wrong year," said the café manager, "and it was this that caused the eruption." We moved into the café and he sat down with us and continued to speak while we drank our coffee. "The gods were angry because we had forgotten the year of the Great Rite. In fact we had missed it altogether last time so that it had not been celebrated for two hundred years. Then when the priests and officials met to decide upon a date some said 1963 and others said 1964, so they took their dispute to the governor at Den Pasar, who decided for 1963. But even as he put down his pen after signing the decree the mountain rumbled, and many of us knew then that a mistake had been made, and we sent a delegation to the sultan of Karangasem [within whose sultanate the mountain stands] asking that a Barong be held, and the gods be asked to approve the date or give another."

He shrugged and pulled a face. "The sultan was away and our delegation spoke with government officials who said that the Tourist Department had printed many books and pamphlets announcing that the ceremonies would be held in 1963, and no change could be made." He looked up and faced across the valley. "You see what happened. No sooner had the ceremonies ended than the gods showed their displeasure. Agung threw out fire and hot stones and ashes which covered more than a quarter of Bali, and filled the temple of Besakih with ash and debris so that many shrines were broken down and the temple made desolate."

Alit looked at me and said, "What he says is correct, and that is why many of the people would not accept food and clothing or the medical care provided by relief organizations. They felt that they had sinned and must suffer all the punishments that the gods had sent them. Some went back to the mountain to ask forgiveness, to pay their last respects to family deities, and to collect relics which they could put into new shrines when they were resettled."

The café manager said that he had been on the mountain with a search party two weeks after the first great eruption, and had come upon corpses of people who had been caught unawares and dehydrated in a flash fire and others completely cooked or scorched through to the bone, looking hideous and hairless, some of them eaten by dogs. In exposed places houses and trees had been blown flat by the blast; in one such place his party had come upon a miracle.

"It was in a place," said the manager, "where the ground was covered with lava not yet cool, and no single tree left standing, and every house but one flattened to the ground. This house had been protected by a big stone, not only from the fire blast but also from the lava flow which had been diverted to either side; and the house was intact except for a hole in the roof and the door jammed so that it would not open.

"We had a man with us, from this village, and when he saw the house standing he was afraid and told us to come away, and when we asked why he was frightened he said that the village people had left a sacrifice in this house as an acknowledgment of the sins of the people, and it was clear that the gods had understood and had spared the house for this reason. We asked what kind of sacrifice had been left but he would not say, so we went and, finding the door jammed, broke it open and found a boy, blind and lame, who had been left there to appease the gods. His mother had left food with him, and rain water had come through the hole in the roof to make a puddle of muddy water at his head, so that he could drink, and because the door had been jammed and the boy could not wander out into the lava flow he was still alive, although thin and ill. So we brought him away with us and the governor took him to Den Pasar."

We bought oranges and melons from the girls, then went north through high country, past dead forests and fields smothered with ash, and in villages almost abandoned were called after by children holding out their hands for money. After a few miles we stopped to empty the carburetor and clear volcanic grit from the petrol pipe, then drove on through cleaner, more peaceful country and began to descend toward the northern shore of Bali through farmlands with fields of coffee, maize, and soya beans, and pigs grazing on pasture land.

I learned more about Alit. He had finished his schooling during the Japanese regime and had been put to work in a fish-canning factory. When the war ended and the Dutch came back he joined the revolutionary army and became a district leader of the home front, organizing intelligence and supplies for the guerrillas. He was caught and spent the last months of the revolutionary war in prison, and when peace came he joined the government service as an information officer, working among the peasants. He is married and has six children, and written in his memory are the words of John Kennedy of America: "Don't ask what your country can do for you but rather what you can do for your country."

We came then, in the afternoon, to Singaradja, the northern capital and the point of departure for those victims of the eruption who are to leave Bali and settle in other islands. Before they board the immigrant ships the government gives each of them gifts:

For each man, one hoe, one axe, one crowbar.
For each woman, one kettle, one cooking pot, one basket of rice.
For each person, one plate.
For each child, one writing book and one pencil.
For each community group, a school chest (from America) containing writing books, pencils, crayons, slates, chalk, drawing paper, erasers, and a blackboard.

The Plan (always the Plan) is to settle at least fifty thousand homeless Balinese in Southern Borneo and Sumatra, where there is plenty of good land, moving them in community and village groups complete with gods and gamelans. A few thousand have gone, but many have come back, lonely over there, cut off from the mother temple. Others stay in the camps and many have gone to live with relatives in other villages.

Perhaps the money spent on sending soldiers to Borneo could be used to make this transmigration more efficient and effective. Perhaps the people will not be happy anywhere but in their own land, in daily communion with their deities and the spirits of their ancestors. And they hate the sea, are frightened of it, its loneliness, the evil spirits which haunt it.

At the point of embarkation a coastal ship was waiting offshore while the people came to it in lighters. Three fishermen on the beach took no notice of the silent drama being played, but busied themselves dragging a turtle from their canoe. They were naked except for sarongs drawn between their legs, their wet skins shining and alive. A little girl came and walked into the water until the tide lapped at her thighs. She stood and prayed, then dropped flowers upon the sea, an offering to Vishnu, the water god. She washed her face and wiped her hands upon her hair, then went back to her family and boarded the lighter.

We turned away and drove south, to Den Pasar.

Extract from a letter
Written at the airport
Den Pasar

When next in the city will you please buy a gentleman's black jacket, lightweight but respectable and suitable for wearing on "occasions"? It should be of a size that would fit your younger brother, although loosely, and of a style more formal than he might like to wear. You could put a sober, dark tie in one of the pockets. The parcel should be sent by air freight to Mr. N. Wideh, in care The Manager, Qantas Airlines, Jakarta. Please do this as quickly as you can with convenience—it is a matter of keeping faith.

Now let me tell you about Alit and his uncle.

It was yesterday in Den Pasar. We had lunched, Alit, Wideh and I, on goat meat and rice and a fish of some kind, and because I had ordered too greedily there was much left over. Alit, a respectable public official, called for a banana leaf and wrapped up the remnants of the food saying, sensibly, that this would provide part of the evening meal for his six children.

Wideh asked how many children I could claim, and when I answered for two he said disparagingly, "You are not very strong in bed." To which I answered that I had little opportunity to beget children and in any case was a heavy sleeper. Alit, looking glum, shook his head and said, "I, too, sleep soundly, but when I shut my eyes God comes down and we have another baby." He has been a droll and sober-sided companion.

We went to his house; and his uncle, an old and holy man, a famous reader of ancient stories written in lontar-leaf books, told my fortune. A gentle fat man with a childlike smile, he set his paraphernalia about him on a small table top, peering all the time over a pair of half-lensed spectacles: first a lontar-leaf book of old Javanese Astrology, then a basket of eggs and a small brass tray of flower petals (bougainvillaea and hibiscus) together with two incense sticks and a box of peppercorns.

He took bougainvillaea and passed it through the incense smoke, then the hibiscus. He prayed for a clear view of the landscape of my life and asked me to make a money offering, which he placed upon the petals. Then he prayed again and afterward took a peppercorn from the box and pressed it into the ball of my thumb until I could have cried out. He asked if the pain were hot or cold and when I said neither, but very sharp, he shut his eyes and bowed his head to the table. Then looking up at me he said, "You suffer from pains across your shoulders," which is true, although my own doctor says that it is simply old age.

He then asked politely if there was anything I wished to know about my family, so I asked of my eldest son, at which he took up another lontar-leaf book and began to follow the ancient script with his long, curved thumbnail. After a while he looked up and said sadly, "Your son is troubled in his sleep because he does not show sufficient respect for his ancestors." After reading a few more lines he added, "He does not care about money, whether he has it or not, and his head is too weak for arithmetic." It seemed to me a fairly accurate summing up except the bit about his being troubled in his sleep. He went back to his book and after a long time said, with an air of some surprise, "He has a mark on his elbow." I asked if this had any serious significance, and after further study and the passing of flower petals through the smoke of the incense he replied that it was most likely the place where an evil spirit had entered the lad.

I must have looked discouraged for without further questioning he announced that my daughter would become famous at the age of thirty-two. I appreciated that he was delicately making amends for my unsatisfactory son, and respecting his sensitivity I assumed paternity of this gifted but fictitious daughter without any feeling of guilt.

He asked hopefully if I could give him the actual time and date of birth of every member of the family according to the ancient Hindu calendar, and was disappointed at my ignorance on this matter. Alit was clearly embarrassed and scandalized, for it seems that no legitimate Balinese would be without this information. But they gave me the peppercorn to keep in my pocket, saying gravely that it would give me inspiration in my sleep.

You ask in your last letter, "Do you begin to see the light and find the answers to questions that puzzled you when you set out on these travels?" To which I reply that I set out to discover Indonesia and myself and tend to become confused on both counts and feel at times an affinity with the Arab of whom Lawrence wrote in his *Seven Pillars* that "there was a constant depression with him, the unknown longing of a simple, restless people for abstract thought beyond their mind's supply."

I find myself in sympathy with any people who want to live their own lives as the Indonesians do; in intimacy with their wonderfully relevant and entertaining gods; with an innocent attitude toward efficiency; and with an occasional shortage of rice. I begin to believe that they should be permitted to continue to live as they wish; that we might modestly expect their gods to protect them from local and imported evils as well as we are able, and for less consideration (their gods being seemingly content with the music of the gamelan, a dance, and the blood of a fighting cock, whereas we look for both decent gratitude and the right to choose their companions).

But I see also that we must insist that they let other people do the same. It seems quite simple—but only to simple people. Perhaps the problem lies in leadership. The need for leadership, in many places, less arrogant and prideful of its own rightness and more responsive to the real needs and wishes of the people it professes to lead (perhaps we suffer from too much leadership). I am sorry, I did not mean to preach but simply to answer your question.

I have enjoyed being in Bali in spite of the absence of clear answers, and here, as in Makassar, have felt that Indonesian patriotism is largely local, with independence seen as freedom to be (in this case) Balinese rather than Indonesian. The larger loyalties are linked by two threads—confidence in Sukarno and the common history of discordance with the Dutch.

Even in this I was put out to discover my ignorance in the matter of Dutch rule in Bali (having become accustomed to the "three centuries of suppression and exploitation" engraved on the heart of every Javanese). Although it is true that Holland had Bali in its sphere of influence all that time, there was no large-scale occupation or sordid warfare until the sudden, ghastly drama of Den Pasar (repeated at Klungkung and elsewhere) early in this present century after which the Dutch seemed ashamed and left Bali much alone except for a few nominal officials, many of whom became devotees of Balinese arts, dancing, and drama, and helped encourage and preserve the uniqueness of the country.

President Sukarno's mother was a Balinese, and he himself provides the kind of mystic image that they approve with enthusiasm. There was never any doubt about their loyalty to the revolution. Local patriots answered his call and fought the Dutch with practically no assistance in 1945 (among them Wideh, who watched ducks and the Dutch with equal vigilance, while Alit organized central intelligence for the guerrilla army).

I went with them this morning, early, to the monument of their local hero, a colonel who defied the foreign enemy as tens of thousands of golden-hearted heroes have defied invading armies since the beginning of history, and have died in doing so. The action was romantic: a gesture made in the extravagant language of the Ramayana. The hero, I Gusti Ngurah Rai, son of a village nobleman, led a "long march" of the local guerrilla troops across Bali and congregated them upon the slopes of the holy mountain Gunung Agung, where they prayed and pledged themselves to death and glory, determined to be heroes, to sacrifice themselves and spill their blood on the foundations of the new Indonesia. And indeed they did, for many of them under Colonel Rai died in a gallant, theatrical stand on a hilltop, being shelled by Dutch troops from below and bombed by the single Dutch aircraft from above, until the last man expired crying *Merdeka* (Freedom) when they might all have been lying quietly in bed, hiding out in some village—except that the whole merit of heroism is in its dramatic impractibility. "Ninety-six dead men lay," says the official proclamation, "on a field strewn with the flowers of the nation, warriors, heroes, their bodies decorated with the bullets and bomb splinters of the enemy."

The colonel was cremated with full military honors and the assistance of fifteen priests, his body being enclosed for burning in a sarcophagus shaped like a water snake with wings; and a band played slow grave music as his soul was set free from the elements of the flesh. Now the Balinese have their own hero of the revolution; their own legendary deliverer from the Dutch.

Is it then that these gallant, individual idiocies are the only eventual protest against the monstrous stupidities of mankind *en bloc;* that only by choosing to die can one demonstrate the right to live? Is this why God Himself, in the body of Christ, had to die?

I must go now—we are being called to the airplane which takes me back to Jakarta for a few days. I have met a man here who lives in Palembang, in Sumatra, which I make the base for my next journey. He is from the West Coast of America, an engineer working on some construction project for the Indonesian government. He has invited me to stay with him for a few days. It will seem strange to live Western style again, even for a little while. I am not even sure that I will like it.

M.

PART V

Jakarta-Sumatra

CHAPTER
10

The journey of man through time,
from ape-likeness to god-likeness,
is a journey of the soul.

Each material gain made on the way,
however good in itself,
is incidental.

It is the evolution of man as a complete being
that is important;
the blossoming of the heart . . .
not a change of hats.

Oh Bian Hiang

In Jakarta the air was brittle with heat and the sky the color of metal. When I reached Kebajoran the sun was just down and Nah had gone to market, but her niece helped with my luggage and laughed with pleasure and surprise when I gave her the little silver brooch I had brought from Bali. But there was a shyness between us and she went from my room uncertainly.

There were letters and messages on the table, among them a card asking me to an exhibition of paintings by Javanese artists and to a party where I might meet some of them and other people whose names were mentioned. When I asked my host about them he said that I would find these people interesting, for they represented a variety of intellectual opinion in Jakarta.

I took a bus and because it was full, with people hanging to the door handles, I climbed up beside the driver with another man and a small boy who sat squeezed between us, staring straight ahead seriously and refusing to answer when I spoke to him. But the driver smiled and shouted some pleasantry which I could not hear above the engine rattle and the clatter of loose casings, and continuous gear-changing. It was hot and smelled of motor oil, but less sweaty than it would have been packed tight and standing inside among so many people. And for all their apparent decrepitude the buses of Jakarta are fast and efficient so that I came in ten minutes within walking distance of the place to which I had been invited.

The streets are dark in Jakarta, rough, and for the most part without sidewalks, and where these exist there is a custom (for which I never found explanation) of leaving the inspection holes in them uncovered, so that anyone walking at night may choose between the chance of a broken leg or being knocked down by an automobile, for it is unsafe to use the sidewalk and dangerous to walk on the road.

But I came unscathed to the gallery to be met graciously by a young Chinese who led me for a little while among painters and writers, local intellectuals, a miscellany of embassy people (compulsive collectors of art), and other foreigners with their womenfolk, and then introduced me to a woman of Medan (in the northern part of Sumatra) who, although beautiful, looked angry.

In a little while when food was passed around I went to her and found that she had been trying for more than a year to get away to Holland, to stay with relatives, and had hoped that after many tedious and vexatious interviews and much correspondence with the immigration authorities permission would be granted.

She had been refused nonetheless and was furious and cursed Sukarno (that unmentionable man, that beast, that murderer), and could not eat the dinner for the force of her anger. Although I found pleasure in the food, it being the best I had tasted in many weeks, I could appreciate her disappointment and was sorry, but thought her language excessively dramatic—and in any case doubted that the President had dealt personally with her application. But I had not heard the worst, for she then said viciously that she had found a picture of *that man* and had torn it into pieces and stamped upon it, and had scattered the fragments from her window crying, "Monster, monster," half hoping to be arrested. There had been no policeman in sight, however, only a man selling nuts, and he had gone trotting on his way, laughing.

I was rescued by the young Chinese, who gracefully led me to meet other people and to try some Yugoslavian wine, but as soon as I decently could I asked about the angry woman and learned she was of a family with some Dutch blood, and that her brother had been an officer of a rebel regiment which had gone against the government in North Sumatra. Some Sukarno men had come one day and, finding the young man asleep in his father's house, had taken him out and shot him dead in the garden, in the presence of his parents and this woman—his sister.

Historically, a trivial incident. The executioners probably had no feeling in the matter—no more than if they had been shooting a rabbit—and by now have forgotten it, or in vague retrospection perhaps feel faintly sorry for the young man they killed in his father's garden. They may even remember the horrified girl who watched them, then screamed and ran to embrace the body hysterically. They would be awed if they knew anything of the hate they had planted that day.

I was glad when someone asked me, "What do you think of this picture?" It was a big, bright canvas, much more than merely expert, alive and vital, done with certainty and assurance: "Boats on the Beach at Tegal" by Affandi, perhaps the most famous Javanese painter, well-known in South America and Europe, where his work shows at the main festivals. There were two smaller and more subtle works by Patti, and one by Rusli, both fine and highly civilized painters who see and feel the universal verities with Javanese senses and so produce great paintings that speak all languages.

Our host had much fine art to show and I was pleased to have come, for in these pictures and the people who painted them I saw yet another Indonesia, one that could be met on a familiar level and discussed without allowances on either side; and I wished that the people of the world could always meet on these levels of common longing and respect.

The food finished, we helped choose a picture for one of the embassy men who was leaving after five years in Jakarta, then moved out to take coffee in a small courtyard, where I sat with this young man and one of his superiors, a man wise, slow-speaking and careful of expression. In a while a priest sat with us, a Dutchman, and afterward an Englishman from the Borneo oil fields came with his coffee and joined our conversation.

Speaking to the young man who was going home I said that he must surely be pleased and in a sense relieved, for the work of a diplomat in Jakarta must be difficult and unrewarding. To which he replied, thinking as he spoke, "Well, yes and no. Yes, because it is always good to go home, and no, because most of us Americans who work here in Indonesia like the people and the place very much, and although the situation makes ordinary relationships and attitudes difficult to maintain, we feel that we are making some kind of contribution to the stability and development of the country."

The Englishman said, "As long as you think that you are doing good, any place is bearable, but I don't believe that you can do much about the economic chaos and the political confusion in this country simply by being here and paying a few of the bills; all you do is provide a platform and a target for the Communists."

The senior diplomat kept quiet and let the young man answer. "I don't know that I go along with you all the way. The political situation here is very fluid because they are trying to find a system that will work the way they have in mind, but it is not confused; and although this 'God will provide' economic system would drive a Western economist crazy it has yet to be proved that it won't work out. As for the Communists, we figure that so long as they hate us we must be frustrating them by being here, and from where I sit this is as good a reason as any for hanging around."

"The official view," said the older man, "is that while we are here, offering help wherever it seems proper, we are giving moral support to those sober elements in the community who will have to take on the Communists if and when a showdown comes, as we think it must."

I said then that I was of two minds on the question of the American position in Indonesia. As an example of know-how and efficiency, big thinking and generosity, the image is impressive: but a big United States embassy in Jakarta, seemingly at work to influence Indonesian relationships with other Asian countries, provides the Communists with their biggest propaganda asset against the West, and the most effective herring to distract attention from their own activities and inadequacies. So long as Americans continue to play the major Western role in Asia (the traditional villain's role) the Communists need do nothing about the real issues, and nothing positive to prove their own capacity to play a useful part in building up the country. All they need do is tie a tin can to the villain's coattails and bow when the crowd laughs.

"We used to be the villains," said the Englishman, "and up to a point we still are, but you Americans have taken the major role and the kicks along with it. We have no illusions left. We are here for business and there is no love or idealism on either side. If oil, for instance, cannot be got out of the country at a profit, political or financial, we British will pull out without any soul-searching and set up shop elsewhere. We don't want to civilize or save anybody any more."

The young American seemed disappointed, finding no answer to this attitude but saying that to accept it seemed like quitting, and an empty acknowledgment of defeat. But the older man said that it is the job and duty of diplomats to always believe that there is hope, and to hang on until ordered out, trying to hold back disasters until a dam can be built to contain them.

The Englishman had much to say and spoke without malice, simply, yet with the assurance of a man who has made up his mind and will not be budged. He said that everyone must admit the present regime to be administratively inefficient, but this was no cause for surprise since most governments are inefficient, especially new ones without experience. It would be reasonable, he thought, to expect the country to be running moderately well in a generation, provided that the President or some stable group could keep the state propped up while the necessary foundations were poured and allowed to set.

But he had doubts that the President, in spite of undoubted political genius, would be able to keep the country going, "For he runs the place," the Englishman said, "like a Wayang show with himself as the Darlan,[1] manipulating mythical characters in mythical situations and conducting the orchestra at the same time—it just can't work." We were all silent and discouraged, recognizing "truths" that were part true, having hope and faith shaken.

"Then there's this Great Father image which he cannot afford to tarnish by bringing in the stringent economic measures necessary to put the country on its feet. And this transmigration plan!" He had interpreted our silence as admission of defeat and now turned rhetorical. "Simply to resettle the minimal population increase of Java each year, one and one half million, will take half the national budget, while half the foreign earnings of the country is needed to meet payments on the foreign debt."

The priest spoke for the first time, diffidently, almost shrinking as we turned to listen. "The Father Image is not to be mocked for it is necessary in this country to give the people a sense of security and confidence; and as for talking like a Darlan, that is the language that the people understand, the voice they have listened to for three hundred years, their own voice, the voice that could not be raised elsewhere than in the puppet shows and the Wayang plays. It is the only voice they recognize as authentically Indonesian, the only voice they will trust until they have learned that foreigners can be friends as well as masters.

[1] The Darlan manipulates the puppets, conducts the orchestra, and tells the story in performances of the Wayang Kulit.

"The President is an idealist, and like other idealists who start movements of national liberation he has become a politician in order to direct the machinery and preserve the principle which makes the idealism materially effective for the people. The outside powers—" he looked at each of us— "can help create a climate and an international situation in which this idealistic force can develop and become creative, but they an also help to hasten the transformation of the original idealist into a ruthless individualist, by interfering without understanding—by forcing the idealist, by their opposition or resentment, into making undesirable allies."

The elder diplomat approved. "That is precisely the way we see it, Father, and what we are trying to work at. But it's tough going, and some of the Indonesians don't make it easy."

The priest said, "I think that it might be particularly difficult for the Australians. It means that your leaders must stand up and say that your point of view need not always be dictated by material or traditional interests, that you are not always right in your assessment of situations, and not always morally immaculate. It is possible that in some attitudes you could be wrong and Indonesia could be right. I say, it is possible. Sometimes it seems that you Australians see no probability of human progress, that your leaders are simply administrators of a hide-bound system of survival."

The young American looked toward me, then took my part. "Why, Father, that's fine although maybe a little one-sided. There is this little matter of Malaysia." He looked around, pretending to be furtive. "Whatever the moral aspects of that situation the fact is cold and clear that it is being handled badly. Some might say lawlessly, and as someone said a while back, 'It is one of the main characteristics of lawlessness that, like most diseases, it is infectious.' "[2]

I acknowledged the assistance, adding that I felt there was danger in the encouragement of the mythological element in Indonesian politics, the building up of a belief that the leader is a mouthpiece or prophet of the ancient ancestral gods; that it is not his function to produce the mundane, everyday, material requirements of life which are the business of minor gods and village oracles, and that he is above mere practicalities. I said that the

[2] The remark was made by Morley, writing of Edmund Burke: "It is one of the most significant characteristics of lawlessness that, like most deadly diseases, it is infectious."

Italians and Germans and Japanese had made this mistake earlier in the century, and the South Africans seemed to be doing the same with their God-given directive to maintain apartheid without regard to the consequences.

"Well," said the Englishman, "Sukarno seems to carry this myth business pretty well into his private life and acts the part of the eastern potentate on a pretty grand scale."

"The reference is fairly trivial," said the older American. "Maybe the President and some other Indonesian leaders have expansive and oriental ideas of domestic life but it must be kept in mind that this man Sukarno is not only a gifted statesman but a Moslem, and must be evaluated from the point of view of the Moslem world, not from the point of view of Saint Paul or Calvin."

The priest said, smiling, "He is not a Christian and there is no reason why he should be expected to live like one, any more than the ancient Hebrew kings lived like Christians. He is more broad-minded in religious tolerance than many Christian leaders, and has done more for my religion than the Dutch government ever did here in Indonesia. He even gave us a quarter of a million Bibles!"

It seemed an odd comment on the President of a great nation, but a true reflection of the man, that being a Moslem and head of a state that is more than ninety percent Moslem, he should hand out Christian Bibles with genuine enthusiasm; and it is also a reflection of the kaleidoscopic id of the Indonesian nation that the Catholic church proclaims a spiritual alliance with the government of a Moslem country for developing its independence in accordance with a constitution which acknowledges the validity of Communism.

"We sided with the Indonesian Republican movement against the Dutch," said the priest, "even though most of us were born Dutch. And when the Republic was established half of us took Indonesian citizenship. We believed then, as we do now, that the only way in which white men can stay in this country for the good of the country, is to identify with the country; and this is the difference between the Church and other foreign institutions.

"We believe that if Indonesia achieves its goals without our intimate collaboration we will have no right to share in the fruits of its accomplishment. We are, then, committed to Indonesia as part of Indonesia, because we are committed to a principle of one people under God and to the belief that if man has a common destiny, other than destruction, mankind must collaborate to achieve it. And the strong must lead, not drive and criticize."

With a journey through the south part of Sumatra in view I went next morning to buy maps but found every bookstore crowded and people waiting to be let in as others came out, a few at a time. I waited in the street outside one store until the manager, looking through the window, saw me and took me through to his office and gave me tea. He said that a new school term was soon beginning and that every bookstore in Jakarta was busy, trying to meet the needs of the students.

It was difficult, he said, because the lists assigning pupils to particular schools and classes had just been released, and there was a last-minute rush to buy books to suit these allocations. Before the revolution less than ten percent of Indonesian children had gone to school, even at the lowest village level; now they all go and there are not enough teachers, classrooms, teaching aids, or books to go around—especially books—because before a national educational system could begin in Indonesia a national language had to be decided upon, and a whole range of school books from kindergarten to university written, or translated from other languages, and printed. It has been done but there are still not enough books or enough money among the poorer people to buy them (I had met a nun earlier who told me that she had managed to build a village school in one of the outer islands but had run out of money and had no books). Yet I was surprised at their cheapness in Jakarta and bought an atlas, made locally and color printed, for much less than I would have spent in New York or Sydney.

The book seller said that every printer in Jakarta keeps his presses running almost night and day, until he runs out of paper, which is rationed because its cost is in foreign currency. The government decides what proportion of imported materials may be used for official publications, school books, and other educational works, newspapers, and general publishing.

The busiest printers are those who publish ministerial speeches and pronouncements and ideological material for official distribution; but from the publishing point of view textbooks of all kinds sell best, followed by translations of simple American Westerns, and Chinese novels which deal with regional heroes who war against corrupt government officials, feudal warlords, or brutal dictators. The Chinese books are written in Hong Kong and, although aimed at the Communist government in China, can be read as having relevance to the situation in Indonesia, the book seller said cautiously. The government begins to look closely at this kind of popular fiction and its popularity among the Chinese of Jakarta.

We moved quickly to less slippery ground when I asked what payments and royalty arrangements were made for these foreign books, to which he answered happily that there were no royalties and that the method, in the case of books by Western authors, was simply to select a paperback and pay a local academician or government official fluent in English to translate it for a flat fee of about $50. The Chinese authors will sell their stories for a lump sum, but reserve the title to resell the same manuscript as often as they can find new publishers for it, so that everybody makes a little money—which in these difficult days is as much as one might expect.

He said that he sold a good many "social" books and showed me a batch of current best sellers: one on *Mothercraft,* another entitled *A Clever Cook* and a third called *Setting the Table and How to Serve Your Guests.* There is, it seems, a regular demand for these books among women whose husbands have moved into the new social and domestic category with "international" contacts, and who find that they must entertain foreign visitors or local people who have been abroad on government missions or in diplomatic posts.

I find this interesting, this inevitability of compromise, the need, especially among women, to conform. In today's world almost any process of modernization involves an element of Westernization. The problem is, how much can new nations take from the old without becoming contaminated and dragged onto the wrong track?

The thought seemed moderately worth pursuing until the book seller went to his shelves and came back with a book on duck keeping, another on pigs, and one on fishing and fish breeding. "These do well," he said, "even in Jakarta, perhaps because town dwellers as well as village people need to raise food for themselves nowadays; and the fact that they are put out by a United Nations agency means that we don't have to pay anything for the right to translate and print them."

He smiled widely, content.

I came to the Foreign Office by *betjak,* without haste, but before I could sit down I was bustled away to keep appointments made suddenly possible after weeks of waiting.

The deputy minister for higher education and science is a physician, a psychologist, a professor of psychiatrics (with European degrees in these subjects), and a brigadier general of the revolutionary army. He said, "Knowledge divorced from intellect is a problem of the age everywhere, and a dangerous manifestation of nineteenth-century democracy and the systems that stem from it. One of the evolutionary errors that we are trying to avoid here is that of creating a class of professional men and technocrats that does not understand its proper function and responsibility to the state and to mankind in general. We understand the dangers of dictatorship, but a basic weakness of the current democratic concept is that it gives too many people powers and freedoms that they are not capable of using sensibly."

He is a dignified, slim man, overtaking middle age gracefully; he speaks neatly from behind a mask of calm that does not hide a mind ranging continuously and far past matters of the moment.

"Here in Indonesia we have plenty of problems, one of which is to direct our revolutionary dynamism into productive channels, particularly in matters of political development and national economics. It is mainly a psychological problem arising out of centuries of suppression, which has left us with a consciousness of inferiority in economic and technical fields—a consciousness that can produce its own distortions and break out into wasteful resentments.

"When scientists and academicians in the United States ask me what they can do to help Indonesia, I reply, 'Talk to us and try to understand us. One of our great needs is for a strong body of educated and informed Indonesians with close and intelligent foreign contacts, men and women who will have a stabilizing influence on our political development.' "

A member of his staff said, "We would like to be able to send thousands of people abroad each year—students, graduates, technicians, artists, and professional people—but we have problems of overseas currency and just cannot afford this sort of thing. At present there are two hundred Indonesians studying at universities in the United States at the expense of various American agencies, and this is wonderful; and we have a number of students in Australia and New Zealand under the Colombo Plan; but mostly we must contribute to the cost of sending and supporting students overseas, and this is inhibiting."

The minister for social affairs, acting also as minister for basic education and culture, is a woman, a lawyer, and a leader of the National Congress of Women. She received me graciously and with good humor, surrounded by advisors, both men and women, and attended by smiling young girls serving coffee and cakes in a family atmosphere. After an hour I felt that some specialist should be sent from the West to investigate and document what the minister called "the mobilization of women for the advancement of Indonesia and its revolution."

One of her colleagues, a woman member of the National Parliament—a true feminist if ever I saw one—said, "Indonesian society is generally stable because we have large families and lack easy communications, so that social units do not fragment because of members leaving home to work elsewhere. There is, too, the traditional feeling of family solidity and ancestor worship which holds our communities together. But we know there will be strains and breakdowns when education opens up new avenues of work for our young people and they begin to move about the country and make new relationships and become more individually self-contained and personally responsible. There will also be an inevitable weakening of religious ties and practices as the family and community structure weakens and as secular education destroys confidence in old beliefs and customs. All this has happened in the West and you have not yet found an answer to the problems that it raises."

The minister smiled and said, "The women of Indonesia are available and organized to play whatever part is asked of them in the building of our nation and the reconstruction of our way of life. We have forty-one women's groups representing all female sections of the community, and delegates from these groups together form the National Congress of Women, which in turn is a member of the National Front Organization, which is the executive arm of the President, Our Great Leader.

"These forty-one groups are organized mainly on the basis of natural affiliations or according to occupation: each political party has a women's group; each profession, the universities, students, government workers, and factory hands; the armed services and the police have their wives' groups and so do the farmers. Even the village mid-wives have their own group and send their representatives to the National Congress.

"You see, then, that the organization of the women of Indonesia is simply a part of the interlocking organization of all human resources in the Republic, from the President down to the simple village mid-wife."

On the active side of government there are twenty-six women members of parliament, including cabinet ministers. In the Law Department women judges share normal legal routines and deal with all juvenile crime, the aftercare of young criminals, and delinquents. Women's groups have the responsibility of establishing and supervising welfare centers, orphanages, kindergartens, homes for handicapped children, and similar institutions and are allowed to raise funds and run lotteries.

A shy man leaned forward diffidently to catch the minister's eye, and when she nodded graciously he said that one of the most important activities of the women's organizations was to establish village social committees and to control their activities. Then, seeming to feel that he had overreached himself, he drew back, leaving further explanation to the women.

"The purpose of the social committees," said the woman parliamentarian, "is to develop and motivate a strong sense of social consciousness within the village and to extend the traditional practice of *Gotong Royong* [or togetherness and cooperation] into new and progressive collective activities."

Committees are encouraged to raise their own finances (there is little enough to spare in the national treasury), and the Minister spoke of villages where each family gives a daily spoonful of rice to the common store, which is later sold in the market, and the money put toward a first-aid center; and of another place where each man plants a "social banana plant" and gives the fruit of it to the committee to dispose of for selected purposes.

At the Department of Justice a lawyer said that the Republic had inherited a legal system devised by a colonial power for the purpose of exploiting the country, and that the new need was to devise and write, in the Indonesian language, a set of definitions and a code of justice related to the new national constitution and philosophy.

He said that all departments concerned with the interpretation and administration of law, including the Police Department, were busy with revisions of the criminal code and gave as example changes that now make it illegal for the police department or prosecutor's department to hold people in jail indefinitely, without trial, as was possible, he said, during the days of the Dutch and still is in some neighboring countries. There were overtones of unction in his voice but later I sought opinion from less partisan sources and found that there was some justice in his comment.

I asked, tritely, about the incidence of crime and he said that Indonesians are, by and large, tractable and law-abiding people and that much minor wrong-doing or dispute is rectified by village officials and religious tribunals. In the matter of common crime the jails and courts are busy in these present days with an epidemic of minor thievery, a reflection of difficult times in which, he said, poor workmen who earn no more than fifty rupiahs a day—enough to buy one bare meal for a single person—may find it necessary to steal so that their children might be fed—for in the alley ways behind the Hotel Indonesia there are children and old people who die of hunger.

A man at the Health Department said that the eradication of malaria is well ahead of schedule and that eventually this achievement will add an annual two million people to the normal population increase and so create more problems than malaria does itself. He went on to say, quite unemotionally, that if the President persisted with the Malaysian confrontation, war might take care of this additional population but that it is cheaper, in fact, and more practical to let people die of malaria, since it is weak children and the least robust adults who succumb to the disease whereas the pick of the men are lost in war. He spoke seriously, seeing the problem purely as a paper one and was brightened only by the recollection that with Indonesia's withdrawal from United Nations the malaria eradication program, mainly financed and directed by the World Health Organization, would probably come to an end.

A doctor with a less academic approach said that he thought

death in war preferable to death by disease because the warrior was sure of a reward in heaven, and that to die for the President in Malaya was a more attractive possibility than drearily to die of malaria in a village. To which the first man answered, "Either way it is God's will, so why worry? The cause of death is simply a statistic."

Later, at dinner at the house of one of these men, I saw craftsmen and laborers busy with considerable reconstruction, making many modern alterations to the place, much of it on Western lines; but the alterations were carefully planned so as to leave an unimpeded pathway for ancestral spirits to make their way, without confusion, through the premises.

At dinner, a lady told me how, when the revolution against the Dutch began, she was with her husband and children in Sourabaya, at the eastern end of Java, and that he immediately joined the revolutionary army and instructed her to walk the eight hundred kilometers (480 miles) to Jakarta to seek refuge with her parents. This she did, begging as she went, but one child died on the way. I find it more and more difficult to have categorized opinions about these or any people. People are people, strange and marvelous, and spiritually beyond the reach of politics and journalism.

CHAPTER 11

You can take it from me, there will be no fighting. Indonesia will not go to war over a patch of jungle: we have enough jungle of our own right here in Sumatra.

Governor of the Province of South Sumatra

Leaving Jakarta by air next morning we flew across the harbor and saw two ships heading out to sea along a pathway of silver sunlight. The man beside me said that one was going to Jedda, in sand ballast, to pick up pilgrims returning from Mecca, and the other was carrying troops for Kalimantan. I do not know how he knew these things. In a little while he added, "The people do not want to fight, they wish only for peace. There are too many other things waiting to be done."

We crossed the water which separates Java and Sumatra, then flew above unbroken jungle. After an hour the man beside me pointed downward and said, without much interest, "The Musi River." I looked past him, and down. The river is a brown snake and the earth is a green curve—there seems nothing else down there. But while I watch, the airplane turns like a bird, and under the wing a long way down, is Palembang—a narrow fringe of red roofs stitched along the edges of the river. (The guide book says that in the middle of a little lake on the edge of the town there is a pavilion resting among pink water lilies. Here the Sultan used to sit with his favorite women and children, listening to music and the splashing of water from fountains.)

One of the governor's minor aides came to the airport, looking at his watch because the airplane was late. He had come to make sure that I would go straight to the meeting place outside the governor's office and listen to His Excellency speak to school children, "because," said the aide, "today we are celebrating the President's birthday."

The governor had almost finished when we got there, but the gist and pith of his remarks came clearly through the peroration. He spoke gently, a solid, fatherly soldier figure in general's uniform, turning his head to take in, affectionately, four thousand boys and girls in white who stood watching him solemnly, in a block.

"Your parents were slaves with no nationality. You, children of Palembang, are Indonesians. Our President has given you a nationality, an identity. For this you must always be grateful to him, and especially today, his birthday." The mayor, wearing a soiled white shirt and no tie, led the applause. He looked respectably shabby, although happy, standing on the platform with the neat commanders of the army, navy, air force, and police. The director of education came to the microphone—small, diffident, gray. (The best-dressed men in Indonesia are in uniform.) He nodded toward the leader of the army band, then led the children in birthday songs for President Sukarno:

"Great Indonesia"
"My Country"
"Forward Without Fear"
"One Country, One Nation"
"The Five Principles of Pantja Sila"
"Hurrah, Hurrah, We Are Very Happy"

When they had marched away proudly the governor took me to his office to talk about my visit. But first we spoke of Geneva, Paris, Rome, and other places where he had served diplomatically. As we talked he looked out of the window, across the rough-grassed paddock where the children had been, toward the background of unkempt streets and dull houses; and there was a faraway look in his eyes as he said, almost to himself, "I think that I prefer Venice to Vienna." Then he swung back and said wistfully,

"The Department of Information here calls Palembang the Venice of the East."

Palembang, on the Musi River, was a city of consequence and a center of Islamic culture and commerce long before Europeans came to the East. Today, downriver past the oil refineries, where tankers lie at anchor and thugs wait by the dock gates to waylay simple sailors, there is a settlement of Arab traders whose ancestors were established on the outskirts of the city six hundred years ago. In those times there was an Islamic university at Palembang with teachers from many other parts of the Mohammedan world, and academicians from Peking came to visit when the Mongols ruled in China. Even before that, in the seventh century, Palembang was a center of Buddhist learning and scholarship.

Today the town of 125,000 people wears none of the garments of glory and wisdom, but being still the main market and export center of southern Sumatra it remains economically important; many rivers of the inland flow into the Musi, draining the jungle not only of rain but of much of the commerce that comes out of it: rubber, tobacco and coffee, ebony, palm fibers and spices. Years ago the Dutch put a bridge over the river and ran a railway out from Palembang across swamps and low-hilled jungle to the opposite coast to help carry this commerce. The railway, workaday and now beginning to wear out, still runs, but the bridge has gone, destroyed by confused enthusiasts in the recent years of war and revolution, and rebellion, and is not yet replaced.

The governor said that he would give me a guide, Mr. Effendi, and that I might go where I pleased so long as he went with me, "Not that we wish to inhibit you in any way, but with the political situation being what it is we must take reponsibility for your safety." He was apologetic. "There are hot-heads in all countries and here, especially among the young people, there is a spirit of nationalism and revolution." I thought fleetingly of the six songs sung by the children and wondered at the possible relationship between their singing and my safety. But I was not then, or at any other time during my travels in Indonesia, conscious of any fear of personal danger from people so naturally gentle.

Mr. Effendi came, and as we walked out together he gave me his card, which said that he was a bachelor of science (Audiovisual-Educational Film and Television) at the University of Indiana, Bloomington, United States. He said that he was delighted to see me, that he had studied in the United States for a year, had given many talks to women's clubs and Methodist church groups, loved America, but was hungry the whole time he was there because the "American people do not have chilies to put into their food." His ambition was to return to the United States as information officer for his own government and to be stationed in Washington, D.C., which, he said, must be the most beautiful city in the world.

"Better than Palembang?"

He looked suddenly sad. "No, it is not better than Palembang because I am an Indonesian and I love my country. But there is not much for a bachelor of science [Audiovisual-Educational Film and Television] to do in Palembang. I have no camera and no film and have only the books I brought with me from America, and I wish very much to do more study so that I can help my country." He looked at me and asked hopefully, "Maybe you could send me some books on photography and film-making. I wish to be modern." Then he laughed uproariously as though the whole of life was a joke (I became accustomed to his use of this safety valve during the next few days), then said that we must first make a trip on the river because "Palembang is the Venice of the East, but much better than Venice because here many of the houses float in the river."

The city itself is not so skittish but stands flatly on dry land, its main street wide and packed tightly with single-storied, white stone buildings occupied by Chinese store-keepers. There are footpaths to give a sense of permanent respectability, but no trees, so that the city has a sparse look, not unpleasant after the many-patterned muddle of Jakarta, and on the surface more settled, middle class, and sedate, although these may be inappropriate claims to make for any equatorial Eastern seaport.

The three speeds of the city flow easily in the street—ox carts, *betjaks,* and elderly, domesticated buses—and the general tempo is that of people going unworried about businesses to which they have long been accustomed, not driven by inner tensions or any sense of desperate competition; but the sun above is a white-hot disc, and this makes for lethargy.

There are no political slogans in the streets of Palembang, only a billboard beside the offices of the Department of Information from which the usual ill-drawn "Crush Malaysia" cartoon hangs torn and tawdry. But there are several cinemas, all showing Afro-

Asia films, and the deficiencies of official propaganda are redeemed in part by their posters. One six-sheeter shows a Chinese woman, posed heroically in rags (one breast almost exposed). She carries a rifle in one hand and with the other points dramatically (and with unconscious cynicism) across the street to the Police Depot. The film is called "Song of Freedom." The Japanese offer "Love in Bali," and the Philippines counter with "Be My Love." From Africa there is an Algerian desert drama of war "Against the French Imperialists." The poster for this film also has a partly exposed woman carrying a gun and pointing to the other side of the street. Mr. Effendi seemed inclined to dismiss these films and said that American movies used to be shown in Palembang, but since the trouble with Malaya these have been banned, which he thought a pity because, "It is important that East and West should make cultural exchanges."

I asked if he would take me to the little lake on the edge of the town where a pavilion rests among pink water lillies, but he said that the lake had been drained and sprayed as part of the malaria eradication program.

We turned from the main street into a pattern of narrow alleys that run down to the river, the way at first being dry and dusty underfoot and drab and the alleys no more than five or six feet wide with the sun slicing down between the roofs in sharp knives of light. We came into a market full of life and color and smells and made a way among stands, stalls, and tiny boxlike shops showing baskets of garlic, artichokes, and spices. Mr. Effendi helped himself to a handful of chilies (seeming to have license because of governmental status) and, grinning, split one with his fingernail and chewed it vigorously, saying, "They don't have these in Bloomington."

We moved slowly, in a press of people. The women's multicolored clothing made patterns, continuously shuttling in and out of shadow and light like threads in a loom. As we went on the way narrowed until there was only elbow room. Slabs and slices of buffalo and goat meat lay exposed on wooden trays, alive and bright with shiny green flies. Yellow-eyed chickens tied by the feet in pairs hung head down from bamboo poles, blinking. There were small salt fish in panniers, big live fish swimming in shallow trays, baby sharks, and wrist-thick eels. A little old woman bought an eel, and the vendor, laying it on a block, hacked its head off while it wriggled, flicking blood onto people passing, making them edge away.

Closer to the river the footway narrowed still more and the earth was lost under a rotting morass of meat and vegetable refuse, black and slimy, with only the heavy scent of spices to make the stench bearable, so that I was glad when we spilled out of the market into harsh light on the river bank, itself many feet thick with decaying rubbish, in which goats scraped and scooped, searching for edible pieces. People were coming and going across the dark-brown river in canoes and little dinghies, in many the women rowing and the men sitting back reflectively in the stern seats shading themselves under umbrellas.

They came from the river city, on the opposite bank, where Palembang spreads itself domestically in a fringe of floating houses, shops, and offices which reach upriver for a mile or more; on this other bank where we stand, edging the solid city, are the factories, warehouses, freight yards, coal wharves, and a little silver-domed mosque.

We bargained for the use of a small sampan with an outboard motor and sat cramped in it, out of the sun under a calico canopy, while the boatman went to buy benzine with the money we had given him. When he came back we went upriver, fighting the swift flow, with a small boy sitting in the prow to fend off clumps of weed and water-hyacinth and debris brought down by the current.

As in the main streets of the city there is a pattern of three in the traffic flow on the river: first, small personal craft, like water bugs crossing and recrossing from suburban shore to the city proper, mixed with the slow domestic traffic of household commerce, food vendors, petty tradesmen, the postman, doctors and nurses on their rounds, and people visiting. Then bigger craft which keep to the middle of the stream, steadily heading up- or downriver, sometimes linked in line and being towed by a single power boat. These barges, or family houseboats, belong to people who live inland and whose business is transportation mixed with their own farming, so that they carry cargoes of coconuts or copra, baskets of coffee beans, parcels of tea and tobacco, rice in sheaves, livestock and poultry, logs, and blankets of untreated rubber for the factories or merchants' markets. Then there are deepwater praus sitting among little ships like broad-breasted swans, or tied to small wharves, unloading cargoes from the Moluccas or Sulawesi and the far-out islands—ships such as I had seen building in Pallengo out of Makassar.

An Ambonese sailor leaned over the stern of such a ship, speaking with a girl who stood on the wharf with a baby on her hip, fidgeting as though anxious but reluctant to leave. From the distance the sailor seemed self-consciously flippant, but we went past quickly and lost sight of them. I tried to remember a verse I had read somewhere, written by the Sumatran poet Chairil Anwar, telling of a sailor who had met and left a girl in some such port; but I could remember only a few lines:

> That time
> I was really a fool,
> Willing to make love to you,
> forgetting that sailors
> Can suddenly be lonely on the sad sea . . .
>
> My life is spent
> Between the stern and the helm;
> The limitation increases the unity of memory.

Anwar was of the "generation of '45, those who came to fruition during the revolution and found expression in the hard years which followed immediately afterward. He died in 1949, when he was twenty-seven years old.

We passed the coal wharves, where the railway to the mines has been rehabilitated with United States aid, and saw, too, that there was much business at the rubber mills, with river ships from the villages waiting to unload—the governor had said that the dispute with Malaysia was a blessing in disguise, because now the chinese merchants of Palembang could no longer send Sumatra's raw rubber to neighboring Singapore for treatment and final marketing by their friends and relatives, but must treat the rubber here in the local factories and then export it directly to the users, thus giving Indonesians the benefit of foreign currency earnings and a middleman's profit to boot.

The floating homes along the river are simple clapboard cottages built on bamboo rafts, with heavy cross-bearing logs a foot in diameter to raise the floors above water level. Some houses are shabby, some smart. Some have white picket fences and new-painted doors, curtains at the windows, and a small green parakeet in a wicker cage hanging on the narrow front verandah. Others, with owners less self-conscious, are drab and unpainted. But all have a single common feature: a long pole on a swivel, with a circular, fine-meshed fishing net hanging from it, and either an old woman or a girl-child dipping it continuously into the river, then swinging it into a projection of the house which does service as a yard. They empty the net of a few fingerlings and put them into a tin. It seems a job for those who are past, or not yet up to, other household tasks, for on this and other river trips made later, I seldom saw adult girls or agile women fishing in this way, although there were men fishing from canoes in deeper water, using draw nets, and others going around fish traps along the river bank.

A blown-bellied dead ox came floating by, drifting past a girl who stood waist deep in the river, cleaning her teeth. She dipped her brush into the dark-brown water as the ox went by. Behind her, on the little verandah of a house, a woman ladled water out of the river to bathe a baby, pouring the water over its head, ignoring its cries. Dark-red dragon-flies were everywhere hovering and darting an inch above the stream.

A river peddler stopped us and undid a shawl to show little wooden boxes from Jedda, Chinese vases inlaid with metal dragons, gold-painted fabrics from India, an ivory statuette, a small pot of the Soong dynasty, slightly chipped, a thousand years old. A pity not to buy it all, but I am no collector and Mr. Effendi is poor. So I took only the gold-painted cloth, paying cheaply for it.

There is natural rhythm about the simple life of this river city as there is about most self-contained, subsistence-level communities, a standard and pattern of living dictated by the environment and what it can provide. It has its own validity and dignity, which have little in common with the modern Western way of life. When such people are forced or encouraged to follow and adopt Western ways and standards too quickly, and without the full capacity to do so, they achieve only a limited parody of Western living which makes them dissatisfied and jealous of the West. Like Adam and Eve they gain new knowledge and find themselves naked and ashamed.

The achievements of the modern mind are beyond analysis by those who have no grasp of the language of mathematics and may be summed up in such symbols as the mushroom cloud—the ultimate pessimism, the nemesis of man. In Palembang I saw a symbol, equally significant although infinitely more modest, that seemed to me to signify the ultimate in optimism—a pellet smaller than a lentil, white and crystalline, with such potential power as may make it soon possible for the earth to feed all the millions with which man's fecundity can fill it. An unostentatious symbol—a pellet of synthetic urine.

The thought might seem objectionable and extravagant, but it is a fact and one of consequence; at least, that is how it was explained to me by the engineer with whom I came to stay, on the outskirts of Palembang, at the new fertilizer works.

At first I found it strange to be in a modern house with hot and cold water, a shower bath, air conditioning, drinks in the refrigerator, and, even more dramatic, hot meat and vegetables to eat; and in the evening people coming in for drinks, to talk tennis, bridge, American politics—straight talk spoken with strong, sure voices of certainty, with no doubts, at least not on the surface. I enjoyed the experience but felt almost a stranger. One does not always realize what happens to the mind in even a short time of negative and innocent conditioning, or see the measure of the length, depth, and breadth of separation between races, ways, and manners. I could literally see no connection between the gentle Indonesians among whom I had been living, and these kindly Americans with whom I was now visiting.

I escaped from having to weigh answers and hold opinions by listening to a man from Seattle who had played some major part in designing and building the fertilizer plant and was full of enthusiasm for its beauty, simplicity, and usefulness. He told me that Urea—even the name is economical—was rapidly changing the aspect of agriculture from America to Russia, that there were seventy plants operating around the world, between them producing something like four-million tons of this fertilizer.

Its advantage over most other standard fertilizers is that it is cheap to make and can be produced almost anywhere at low cost. It contains about fifty percent nitrogen, which is the basic fertilizer, can be used as a livestock food as well as a soil conditioner, and is easily transportable.

So keen was this American on the project and his part in it that he put down his drink and, although it was night time, went with me to see the plant, an enormous but neat arrangement of power units, pipelines, and huge tanks which constitute, in effect, a set of mechanical kidneys costing $30 million devoted to the apparently simple process of manufacturing the equivalent of solidified urine from air, water, and natural gas piped from the oilfields.

"Ten such plants as this," said the enthusiast, "and President Sukarno could treble the national rice crop in one year without any additional irrigation and so solve his immediate food problems. This would eliminate the need to import rice and other grains and would cut down speculation and inflation on the food market." I was prepared to look impressed and to make appropriate comment, but he went on. "That is not all. He could improve the cotton crop, could begin a major maize-production program using new seed strains that have been developed here in Indonesia, could raise the carrying capacity of pasture lands and so increase the livestock population and its quality. After that he could use any surplus output of Urea in the manufacture of plastics and synthetic fibers and in such industries as paper manufacture and the making of Polywood products."

I feel helpless and noncontributory in the presence of this kind of visionary. I stand mute, wondering why it is that the whole world is not provided with comfort, food, and clothing, almost for nothing. I feel that I should be playing some part in it, something within my unmechnical capacity. I could be happy sweeping the floor of a temple of this kind, knowing that I was playing some small part in the mystical processes of creation, adding something to the sum of mankind's happiness. To do such would seem to me as real and as significant as following some simple occupation in a missionary hospital in the jungle or in a great cathedral in which people could find inspiration or consolation, as required. What more could one ask than to be allowed to play a part in feeding the whole of mankind?

I carried these thoughts with me as we went around the great plant, so clean, orderly, and efficient. We came to the main storehouse, where hundreds of tons of these tiny, life-giving pellets lay in huge bins waiting to be bagged. My companion stopped talking and I, too, felt awed in the presence of this vast simplicity. Then he said quietly, breaking the silence, "There are more than three thousand tons of fertilizer here in this store."

My friend Andi Bahruddin of Makassar came to mind, with his schemes of making the south of Sulawesi a rice bowl for the whole of Indonesia—if only he could get fertilizer. I said, wondering if my question would be stupid, that the need for fertilizer all over Indonesia was so great and so urgent that I was surprised to see so much lying here, and was there some reason why this should be so?

He said, "String," and when I looked blankly at him, continued, "We have no string to tie the bags. No string, no fertilizer. Simple." He then added a four-letter word and turned and walked back the way we had come.

I did not feel that I could intrude upon pain so personal and so great, so I kept silent but when we came again to the house where I was staying, and had taken a drink and entered once more into the atmosphere of solid certainty, I took another man aside and asked him to unwind the riddle. He said that the matter was simple. The United States government had collaborated with the Indonesian government to build the plant, to get it running, and to hand it over to the Indonesians. This part of the bargain had been kept, and the Americans were due to leave very soon. In the ordinary course of operations the contractors had used up all the initial supply of bags and string and it was now up to the Indonesians to replace the stocks and keep the plant in operation. But the string must come from overseas and the government did not have the foreign currency to pay for it.

He said, "One does not criticize—that is too easy. But it is clear that these people have still a few things to learn. First that great works are an aggregation of exact details, that efficiency is interdependent. Wars have been lost for want of a horseshoe nail, and ships sunk for the lack of a cent's worth of tar."

He said also that the Indonesian technical staff was completely competent to run the plant and that the American construction and production bosses would have no reluctance on that score to hand it over and go home. But in the back of their minds will be a niggling fear that before very long something will go wrong in one part of the plant (whoever might be running it) and that of necessity the maintenance engineers will take a part from some other section of the plant, and this will go on until nothing works any more and the plant will stand idle. The answer, he said, does not lie with the engineers or chemists or plant supervisors, but with the politicians and departmental administrators who make the plans and the rules.

Before the night was over I was taken to the oil refineries, lit like a city on the edge of the river, toward the estuary. We crossed in a launch, past giant tankers anchored in the stream, and spent a little time with some of the Indonesian staff in the company club room.

The oil fields lie inland in jungle still lively with tigers, elephants, and rhinocerus. They were first tapped in 1890, since when Anglo-Dutch and American interests have developed them and built the refineries, and nominally still run them though a planned process of Indonesian takeover goes on, and the relationship between the government and the companies, although codified and theoretically fixed, is ambiguous.

New agreements have been reached by which the companies may extend their operations in partnership with the government on a limited profit-sharing basis, and these arrangements are no doubt satisfactory to the companies so long as the political and economic structure of the country remains stable. One of the men said, "The companies are putting up $50 million, and if they could not see profit they would cut their losses and get out."

But this alliance is uneasy. It lacks any real confidence or delicacy of affection. It is an unsentimental convenience on both sides. The Malayan matter has already affected the operations of the refineries by cutting off substantial markets, and the result is a partial shutdown and a reduction of employment and profit—for which, of course, the Communists will blame the companies and the British and American Imperialists.

People who work in the refineries live secret, isolated lives behind high wire fences, keeping to themselves, cut off from domestic or social commerce with Palembang. The feeling between Indonesian and foreign members of the staffs is friendly and respectful although national attitudes on both sides make candor difficult. The Indonesians are sensitive to their inability to take over the industry completely and resentful of their present dependence on foreign capital and equipment to develop the oil fields, and to market the increasing variety of products and by-products internationally.

The foreigners, for their part, feel that they are here on sufferance. Any personal feelings they may have for individual Indonesian colleagues are colored and pushed out of shape by the ideological pressure pumped out of Jakarta. The Indonesian schizophrenia undermines all interracial relationships. There is no way of completely admiring a person who represents the enemy.

The Indonesian engineers love their refineries, have a sense of possession, are proud of them and of their own capacity to make them work. They mutter and grumble about the Malaysian confrontation and its effect on the efficiency of their operations. The governor called them all to Palembang, together with the staff of the fertilizer plant, and asked two questions: "Do you approve of the President's policy of confrontation against Malaysia? Are you prepared to fight for it if necessary?"

The answer in both cases, inevitably, was yes. I asked one of them if he truly meant yes and he said, "So long as we have cause to doubt and fear the intentions of the British in Malaya and Kalimantan, and the ultimate extent and effect of American interference in Southeast Asian affairs, we must follow our President and be prepared to fight, whatever the cost. Better to be dead than to be slaves again."

Going back across the river, past the tankers, I asked my host to give me an opinion of the situation and his assessment of its significance.

He said, "The oil industry is Indonesia's biggest income-earner by far and provides whatever economic foundation there is for national development. Without the income from oil the President's plans for a greater Indonesia will remain forever on paper. But the oil industry is also an irresistible challenge to the Indonesian Communists and they will not rest until they have removed all foreign influences from the local operation, even if it means putting the industry out of action for a while or bringing in the Russians to help run it.

"In this situation the individual is helpless and ineffectual and has no part in the real battle which is going on behind the scenes between international oil and international Communism—a battle of giants that has no sentimental connotations of any kind and no loyalties except to the material ideologies represented. If you sum this up the position is: the President cannot build his Utopia without money from the oil industry; the oil industry cannot operate efficiently in Indonesia without political stability; political stability depends on what the Communists decide to do.

"But this, again, is not in itself the real issue. The big drama, of which this is only one act, is the struggle taking place between

Communism and Western capitalism for the body and soul of Asia and Africa.

"If President Sukarno understands this and is, in fact, acting with full awareness of the high stakes and the consequences, then he is not only a political genius, as some foreign diplomats maintain, but a man of prodigious courage and confidence. If he can make use of international oil to Indonesia's advantage, and at the same time keep the Communists from tearing the local industry to pieces for its own purposes, Indonesia may be able to solve its problems and go ahead—may even give a lead to the emerging nations. But if he fails, the future of Indonesia is very dark and dubious, and Sukarno's dream of a glorious middle way to human happiness may be the beginning of a very horrible nightmare."

It sounded logical enough, but frightening and perhaps farfetched, but I am, perhaps, naïve for I can never bring myself to actually believe in the unmitigated power of these mysterious, inhuman forces that are said to shape and bend the destiny of mankind and the course of history—the armament kings, the international financiers, the enormous industrial combines. Yet they exist, and they have power, more deadly perhaps than the evident power of unashamed dictators.

I said as much and another man said, "Maybe you remember that when the British embassy was burned by the Communists in Jakarta, a little Englishman walked up and down in front of the rioters blowing defiance on a set of bagpipes, inviting them to attack him. At the same time there was a meeting between oil company representatives and members of the Indonesian government going on across the road, in the Hotel Indonesia, to decide on contracts. The meeting adjourned for a little while so that the delegates could watch the embassy burning and the little man playing his bagpipes. In a while a British oil man said, "This is not our business. We are wasting time. Let us get back to our meetings. The future of Indonesia is what matters and that depends on us."

On the other side of the river I looked back at the refineries, lit like a city. The great installations, cylindrical, square, triangular, linked with lines of pipes. Everything tidy, in place, and potent. This plus that equals something predictable and probably useful, and the profit margin is *x*. I thought, this is good. It means something. It is achievement, and in part it may excuse the excesses which go to make it, just as any work of creative genius may perhaps excuse the excesses of the artist. And although those who direct these things make monstrous profits at the expense of everybody, they also dole out huge sums to make possible works of mercy, of scholarship, culture, and refinement, which is more than was done by feudal rulers who built the great palaces, temples, and monuments of Oriental civilizations.

Clearly something is happening to me on these journeys. I had not expected to be comforted or inspired by the sight of oil refineries, but suddenly it occurs to me that these and the fertilizer works are the first manmade things I have seen in Indonesia that make real sense. I am still not sure that I like this kind of sense but I now see more clearly and admire the enormous achievement of the technological civilization of the West. The pity of it is that it has outstripped its own religions, lost sight of its gods, and no longer has any spiritual significance.

CHAPTER 12

After two days the governor sent a message to say that arrangements had been made for me to go inland, to a place where immigrant colonies from Java and Bali were being resettled. The journey by rail and road would cover a thousand kilometers and take several days. Mr. Effendi would be my companion and I must meet him by the barrier at the railway ferry station no later than five o'clock the next morning.

It rained in the night and the sky, washed clean, was sparkling with stars as I came in a truck through Palembang an hour before dawn. The air was clean and cool, the streets were fresh and still wet, studded with black puddles through which we plunged and bumped. We drove alone in the long street although women were already beginning to gather on the narrow footpaths by the market, black shadows lit mysteriously by little flickering tongues of yellow light from tiny oil lamps. They moved like characters taking their places on a dark stage, squatting by baskets of oranges and bananas, setting out trays of flat bread and biscuits, nuts and rice cakes.

We stopped in a laneway filled with silent people, some standing in mounds of baggage, others pushing their way through toward wharf gates, bumping people with luggage, looking over their shoulders for bewildered, still sleepy children. Men were lighting cigarettes and coughing. My driver said that I should be careful of pick-pockets and sneak thieves. Through the wind screen we saw Mr. Effendi coming toward us. His smile seemed to say that we were on the threshhold of adventure. Mr. Effendi is a determined optimist.

A wire gate slid open. People picked up luggage, bed rolls, bundles—one woman with a basket of chickens—and began to shuffle down the ramp and onto a little launch with wooden benches. There were no gangplanks—the aged were lifted aboard like children. When we cast off a man, unshaven and not wearing any uniform, came round to collect the ferry fares. Nothing on the little launch seemed to have been cleaned since the Dutch left.

An upriver sampan slid by, silent, black, and bulky. We passed the unfinished bridge, stark like a gibbet against the dawn sky. At the station small boys were sleeping, curled on the bare ground like cats, each in a pool of pale golden light thrown from a stump of candle. When they heard us on the gravel they sat up blinking and offered sweets and cigarettes for sale, but sleepily. When we were settled they came again, more briskly, to do business.

This is the first train of the day, the express that goes to the southern tip of Sumatra and connects there with a ferry which takes passengers across the Sunda Strait into Java and so to Jakarta. The main daily train. The locomotive was made by Krupp in 1911. Of ten coaches nine were boxcars with bare plank seats and unglazed windows; these filled quickly with passengers spilling out onto the observation platforms, where they sat on luggage. The other coach was a restaurant car with an annex to seat sixteen first-class travelers on canvas-covered lounge seats. We found our places here among army officers going to Jakarta (their men were behind in the boxcars).

They greeted us with good humor, each man shaking my hand and saying his name while one, a rocklike, bull-necked lieutenant, clearly the company clown, called cheerfully, "Crush Malaysia—Ever Onward—No Retreat," a Sukarno slogan used daily on the radio. As other passengers came aboard he thumped them affectionately, laughing; and when a Chinese woman with two children stood in the doorway, hesitating, he took their bags and hoisted them into the rack and found places for them, while Mr. Effendi explained to the others who and what I was.

A businessman came, then a Christian minister with a young man who proved to be a student and a catechist. For half an hour or more the coach was noisy with the crude exuberance of soldiers; then the sun came in suddenly to flood the dull woodwork of the coaches with live light. There was a hoarse, high-pitched, ridiculous whistle and Herr Krupp slid forward smoothly. I shut my eyes to sleep, hearing the soldiers talk distantly of Kalimantan, helicopters, and paratroopers.

The train guard woke me to check tickets and travel permits. A young policeman stood beside him with a Tommy gun (for shooting tigers, said the lieutenant). Mr. Effendi was showing the soldiers a copy of the college magazine from Bloomington, pointing to a picture of himself standing beside a television camera in a studio. A brown hen ran squawking through the compartment and the Chinese children pounced on it, chattering instructions at each other until they caught it. The owner appeared silently in the doorway of the compartment, took it from them, and disappeared again.

Mr. Effendi, like a latter-day Marco Polo, took up his story again, explaining that in America rice must be planted and harvested within four months, from May to September, because for the rest of the year the weather is too cold and dull, with fog and snow and sleet. He says, "Because of this a meal in a Chinese restaurant in America costs $10, but in Palembang only thirty cents, which is why the Americans must work so hard."

This talk of food makes everybody hungry and bundles are brought down from the rack, opened up, and food discovered. The big lieutenant goes to the dining car and comes back followed by a boy with coffee in glasses. I have bread dipped in melted butter and sugar. We share everything. We have become a family. Outside, the landscape alternates between untidy savanna coated with tall coarse grass, and clumps of untidy rubber trees bled almost to the point of anemia.

The minister, an Englishman, said that he was going back to his mission station near Bengkulu on the west coast, where he had a church and school and a number of catechists like the student sitting with him. He said the government gave willing assistance to Christian missionaries and was generous within the limits of its means, giving subsidies to help pay teachers' wages and providing material needed to build schools.

However sceptical one might be, he said, about advances made in other directions since the revolution, no one could deny the almost miraculous achievement in education. In this southern part of Sumatra a thousand classrooms had been built, with the government providing money and material and the town and village people giving land, labor, and subscribing additional finance.

The soldiers listened to this praise from a foreigner, smiling and nodding approval, especially when the minister spoke of the number of young people who trained to be teachers, knowing that after graduation they would be poorly paid and sent to pioneer in far-off villages. The colonel in charge of the soldiers said, "There is no fear for the future of education here in Sumatra. The people will keep building schools, and many young men and women want to be teachers." Then he added, "My wife is a teacher of English at our university in Palembang."

We talked a little more of these things, the colonel saying that twenty-five of his officers were studying law at the university and others were attending courses in religion and morality at universitites in Java. He and his wife had begun an English-speaking club in Palembang and held meetings in their house so that people could practice English conversation. Then he became distracted with other talk between his officers and Mr. Effendi, who was saying that he had traveled from Chicago to Washington in a Pullman car, air conditioned and completely silent, and the train had stopped only twice in five hundred miles unless it had halted in the night without waking him, it came and went so silently. "But you can have no idea how cold it is in Chicago, beside the great sea. I could not take my clothes off for the three days I was there." Mr. Effendi was being circumspect, balancing his evident enthusiasm for America with patriotic reservations.

The missionary continued talking to me, saying that there were scarcely two thousand Christians in and around Palembang and there seemed little likelihood that the faith would make much headway among Asians for at least two generations yet, and possibly longer. It offers little else at present than a set of abstract truths alternative to those already held, and to Asians it seems a lonely religion, without the social and domestic merits which bind village Moslems and Hindu-Balinese so closely into spiritual communities. The Christian emphasis on education is in its favor at the present moment, but this is regarded rather as an aspect of general Western culture than as a singular attribute of Christianity.

He said, "We must understand that religion is a living thing with these people, a way of life, a link as strong or stronger than blood ties, just as Christianity was centuries ago before Christians became affluent and individual and obsolete. A village Indonesian who renounces the community faith ceases to exist for that community. This is why many missionaries especially discourage girls from becoming Christian, even if they come to our schools, because conversion is the social end of them unless they leave their homes entirely, go to live elsewhere, and marry a Christian man. If they don't do this their lives become a tragedy of loneliness with no future.

"We had one such girl who begged to be baptized but we refused her because she was promised to a Moslem boy in her village. She persisted, saying that she would go to Java and teach there in one of our schools, so we gave in. Her brothers went to Java and brought her home. She ran away again and they followed her to Jakarta and killed her. In their eyes they were saving her soul, just as the Inquisitors 'saved' thousands of Christians from hell by burning them alive."

The colonel came back and sat with us, saying that it was good for young officers to hear first-hand accounts of other countries, and that the bull-necked lieutenant would soon go to America for two years to do a quartermaster's course. He spoke of the problems of running an army that receives its weapons and equipment from several sources—the United States, Russia, Czechoslovakia, the United Kingdom, and Australia—then said that he was on his way to visit two units, one of them engaged in regular military training and the other occupied with civic missions.

When I asked about these he said that most of the men were working in the transmigration resettlement areas, making roads to link them with the coast, building bridges, leveling land for new settlements; but he had other units occupied with the beginnings of a rice-growing project and some men working a quarry to supply stone for a new tourist hotel. He sent for lemonade and settled himself.

"You see, we of the army have a twofold role. We are the defenders of the fatherland and protectors of our nation, but we are also the hands of Our President or, as he himself says, "A Tool of the Revolution. Using us, Our Leader can make roads, plough the land, build new villages, sow crops in the jungle. We are not merely professional fighters, we are servants of the people. We are not an unproductive burden on the taxpayers but producers, developers, helping to make the country rich, yet ever ready to defend it."

There is no self-consciousness in these speeches. These people are natural rhetoricians. Furthermore, they mean what they say although some (not many) have reservations about the capacity of their politicians and top administrators to provide the stability and the means to make their words productive. The colonel said, "Foreigners may think that we talk too strongly and perhaps we do, although we are not a militaristic people and have no real desire to fight. Our custom is to solve all problems by discussion and we have the will to do this, and to accept decisions that are reached honestly; but there are people we cannot trust and it is because of them that we talk loudly."

The train came to the top of a hill and stood a while, sighing, while Mr. Effendi told how he got lost in a department store in Chicago and was sick riding in the elevator. With a chirrup the train took off again and, gathering speed, went away whistling with ridiculous high-pitched hysteria, and this, together with the clatter and rattle of wheels and creaking coachwork made conversation no longer possible, until coming down once more to flat land we slowed and, bumping over points, came to a siding to wait, inexplicably.

In the yellow light of late afternoon we reached Kotabumi, a provincial market town and regional center of administration. A ragged boy chased a trio of outraged and disarranged geese from the railway track and let us through to the station. At the level crossing gates an ox-drawn benzine tanker, perhaps holding fifty gallons, waited patiently, the driver sitting on the shaft picking his teeth. On the other side of the track a girl in neat Western dress sat on a bicycle watching us pass.

The hotel is a frail wooden-framed structure built around a pressed-earth courtyard to which access is gained by way of a tunnel from the narrow street. There is a laundry across the way and when we had stripped off our clothes, filthy with engine soot, sweat, and dust, Mr. Effendi threw them down in a bundle to a boy who stood in the street, waiting. We sat, then, at a bare table on an upper veranda taking tea with the proprietor, a huge fat man with a close-shaven skull, several stomachs, and a harsh clanging voice. He showed us a shiny illustrated magazine called *China Pictorial,* turning the pages slowly so that we could see the pictures, and when there was one which featured Chou En Lai he held up his thumb and said, "Good man." He sent for more tea and sat scratching the black nipples of his fat breasts and clearing his throat of phlegm, telling us that he was also headman of a neighboring village, admitting that there was little progress there but that the hotel made him wealthy.

I went looking for somewhere to wash and found a dark, loathsome bathhouse with the floor thick with black slime through which I picked my way like a fastidious cat, looking for a lavatory, and found three middens (without bowls or fixtures of any kind) and a fine dun-colored pony mare tied to a ring in the wall beside them, so that they could not be used without moving her, which I did, feeling sorry for the beast being tied there, for the stench was almost unbearable. It seemed ignorant, too, of the owner to have her standing almost to the hocks in stagnant water, although her clean and polished coat showed that somebody took great care of her.

I drew water from a deep well, pulling up a bucket by a long rope, then found a corner where I could wash myself, and talked to a soldier across a low wall, who seeing me uncertain handed me a tin that I could use as a dipper; then stripping off his own clothes he borrowed my soap and lathered himself an inch thick from head to foot before handing it back.

The mayor of the town came to fetch us to dinner, a young man with many gold teeth, wearing the neat khaki of a provincial official, with a pistol at his hip. When Mr. Effendi had explained the purpose of our coming he took us hospitably to a café where, in a private upper room, a meal was set out splendidly: for each of us was a whole boiled chicken, a fish, goat's meat broiled on skewers and dipped in chili sauce, a great colander of cold rice, and a dish of marvelous bananas. Mr. Effendi ate in traditional fashion, with his fingers, allowing only the right hand to touch his lips, gathering up the rice in a wet wad and stuffing it into his mouth while holding his head bent over the plate. I thought it an untidy and inefficient way of eating, but he seemed to gain more savor from the food this way than in using fork or spoon, and I suffered nothing in the matter. We were watched by half a dozen minor town officials who, before we had done, were encouraged by the mayor to eat all that remained, so that in half an hour there was nothing left. Later I learned that the mayor owned the café and that we were to take all our meals there at the town expense.

Having eaten we went then to the house of the Bupati, Achmad Samad, chief government officer of the region, to meet other officials, all of them young except the police chief, a gentle and reflective man newly returned from his pilgrimage to Mecca and wearing the white cap to prove it. He hoped that we would find time, he said, to visit the kindergarten built and financed, for the common use, by policemen of the district. The Bupati listened, smiling, while he said this.

I had already been told of the Bupati Samad and knew something of his reputation as a man who thought much and planned precisely for the future of his region, much of it still little beyond the most elementary level of development. He had formerly been a policeman under the Dutch, and then the commander of a guerrilla battalion against them during the revolutionary war, a hero of the liberation, but also an efficient and intelligent leader in this period of reconstruction. He spread maps and charts on a table and told me, "The old men talk politics but the young people talk progress; that is why I am surrounded by these men who have yet to achieve their ambitions. They will work and not ask for ease or dignity or great rewards." Then catching the eye of his police chief he smiled and said, "He begins to go gray but he has a young heart, and in any case the job of a policeman is to be a father to the people."

He said that the major project for the region was an airfield which would bring Kotabumi within an hour of either Palembang or Jakarta. There were two major irrigation schemes under way and these would dove-tail into a collective rice-growing scheme, for which he had also put aside 150 tons of Urea, the new fertilizer. He planned to revitalize the old village silk-worm culture and extend it into a cooperative project with a modern spinning and weaving mill, and as part of this plan his agriculturalists had planted thirty hectares of mulberry trees. He was trying to improve the village rubber industry by centralizing rubber processing on the big plantations taken over from the Dutch. Meanwhile, the main market part of the town was being rebuilt as a community project financed by the shop-keepers themselves. The rebuilding, which involved pulling down the old wooden shops and dwellings and replacing them with concrete structures, was being done with local labor under the supervision of a twenty-three-year old engineer graduate from the university at Palembang. The new main square formed by these buildings would be known as Merdeka (Freedom) Square. He had it all pat, with plans and diagrams done with colored inks, and it sounded real. I could hear Mr. Effendi speaking on the other side of the room, and then I heard a voice say, "Forget Malaysia, we are too busy here."

In the morning, before dawn, I heard a man groaning and sighing as with pain or great sorrow, and sat up to listen more clearly, for the noise was almost alongside me and I feared that Mr. Effendi might be sick, but flashing my torch I saw him sleeping peacefully; then it came to me that the man in the next cubicle was saying his first prayers for the day. I got up and cleaned my teeth in a glass of tea, and went down to the well and washed. It was not yet daylight and the air was quick with little shivers.

Soon after sunrise we went to the mayor's café for a breakfast of raw eggs and rice, then inspected the reconstruction work in the marketplace, which was busy with little colored buses loading for trips to outlying villages, people buying and selling, and boys on the tops of the buses tying down bundles, baskets of live poultry, bags of cement, bicycles. Drivers pushed their last passengers inside and leaned against the doors, compressing people into every inch of space, leaving young lads to hang on outside as best they might.

Humped white oxen, steered with a cord strung through one nostril, trudged in the streets scuffing up dust, dragging carts with solid wooden wheels cut from whole tree trunks. In the center of the square, standing on the step of the little Independence Monument, a great, long-bearded, tolerant goat was being patient with a young buck feeling tentatively for a fight. Three nannies and two bleating kids foraged among the buses for dropped vegetable scraps, disinterested in the outcome.

We looked at the town hospital (thirty beds) and talked to the physician, a shy man one month fresh from medical school and as yet uncertain of his skills or his authority. He has a daily outpatient clinic, copes with infant and maternal walfare, town and village hygiene, and health education. Surgery, X-rays, pathology, and the like are dealt with in a bigger town, 150 kilometers (ninety-miles) further south. He says that there are three hundred thousand people in his region, and he the only civilian doctor. It could be true, and not unusual in an area of this kind, but I could find no authentication of the estimate, nor of the statement that he was the first civilian doctor to be stationed in the area for several years.

The doctor has a young Javanese wife who, while waiting for her own baby to be born—she is heavily pregnant—takes charge of the town kindergarten, to which I went with the benevolent police chief, nominal father of the whole project. We watched the little children come forward one by one, unaffectedly and without hesitation, to recite or sing or do a little dance; and he said that a policeman's work begins in the kindergarten and that the building was also used as a parent-guidance center, where people could come for instruction in domestic health, hygiene, diet, and the like.

He stood beaming on the children and I found it moving to see him so sentimental, and the little teacher, herself not much more than a schoolgirl, so clearly full of love for the little ones, so gentle with them, proud when they performed well, tender and encouraging with the shy or handicapped, herself carrying her baby inside her and seeming conscious of motherhood as already a reality.

When we sat in his office at the depot beside the jail (the prisoners all working in the fields or on town projects) he said that his main preoccupation was with the education and training of the 240 policemen under his command and that the objective was to fit them to assume practical and moral leadership in the region. They go to lectures each day for instruction in the state philosophy, religion, and the work of other government departments, and eighty percent of their time, and of the prisoners' time, is caught up with community projects. The wives of policemen have their own association and they, too, have instruction in social and community obligations.

I begin to become more understanding and tolerant of what, in the beginning of these travels, seemed overmuch like an intellectual and physical regimentation rigidly imposed by the state. I see more clearly that people stepping directly from servitude to democracy in a single generation may well need methods of social education that are more disciplined and single minded than those acceptable to the settled civilizations of the West, where an understanding of democratic principles and practices has been developed through centuries. The paradox and the danger seem to be that the more critically impatient and interfering the West becomes with this tendency to social regimentation in the East, the more solidly will the East be obstinate and resentful and ungrateful in its attitudes toward the West.

More and more it becomes clear that the people of Asia and Africa cannot be treated as dangerously irresponsible delinquents, but as adolescents who have been badly treated in childhood and need careful rehabilitation, not only for their sakes but for ours, for without their own self-imposed disciplines these people can bring us all down into confusion together.

A train pulled into the station as we passed through the town. It had come from the southern port of Pandjang, where the railway connects with a ferry boat from Java, and the whole boxcar section was crowded with immigrants making for one of the resettlement areas further west—they would leave the train a little way along the line and finish their journey by truck and on foot. They had piled their furniture and household belongings onto the roofs of the boxcars, so that beds, tables, and chairs made platforms and cages for smaller goods, and for dogs, pigs, and cages of poultry. Men clambered up to straighten this top hamper and take water to the animals, while others leaned out to buy oranges and other food from vendors on the station.

Only two passengers left the first-class coach: a portly man approaching middle age, dressed overwell for such traveling, with a fine lightweight suit, white silk shirt, and panama hat, carrying a swagger stick with an ivory handle; the other, a man of no account, ill-kempt, carried the baggage and was presumably his servant.

Later, resting on my bed, I heard martial music and marching commands given sharply, but in Japanese, and was puzzled by this, knowing that the sound could not be coming from the radio because there is no electric power in Kotabumi in daylight hours (the fuel for generation is conserved for night use only, and the power comes on in time for the evening radio news from Jakarta and is turned off after the news at night). I got up and looked over into the street, but it was siesta time and I saw nothing but a few lean chickens and a man asleep with his head on his chest, so I went back to lying on my bed but was irritated because I wanted to sleep and could not because of the marching music and the officer shouting. But in a while it stopped as suddenly as it had started.

In the cool of the evening when people were about again I went down to bathe and found the well-dressed newcomer, together with the hotel keeper, in the courtyard looking at the dun-colored mare, now being held on a halter by a small boy, while the serving man stood beside his master, carrying a small case. When I had done washing and was going back to my room they called me over. I found, then, that the pony belonged to the hotel keeper and that the man had come from Jakarta to buy horses, it being partly his hobby and partly business. When I had studied the animal and given an opinion as to its shape and conformation, apparent sagacity, and age, the stranger nodded, saying that he would think about it and decide before the train left for Palembang in the morning; in the meantime he would like to see other ponies of good quality, suitable either for racing or breeding, for which he would pay well. He spoke with authority, and the hotel keeper waved his hands and said that he could look anywhere within fifty kilometers (thirty miles) of Kotabumi and would find nothing to compare with the little mare standing there in the courtyard.

The stranger turned away and spoke to his servant, who fumbled with the little case, and suddenly a band began to play, with the voice shouting commands in Japanese. The mare flinched and backed away. "My tape recorder," said the stranger, "a transistor—the music is played by the band of my old regiment." He tapped the side of his leg with the ivory-handled swagger stick.

I said, "And the voice of the officer?"

He looked almost shy. "Yes, it is me. I have been an officer and I like to feel that I am marching again with my soldiers, giving orders and seeing them respond." He looked a little sad. "To be an army man is a fine life but limited, and I am a man of much imagination."

Later, when he came with a bottle of whisky and sat on the veranda outside my cubicle, I asked why he gave his commands in Japanese and he replied that they sounded more military and aggressive in that language than in English, Dutch, or Indonesian—and this seemed to me reason enough, if a man wished to play at soldiers. The tape recorder, he said, came from Singapore, where he had "contacts"; in fact, he knew a man who had lately imported a stallion from there, paying for it with smuggled rubber, a crime for which he could be hanged. He added that there was much interest in pony racing in the bigger cities of Indonesia, where it had replaced such traditional gambling sports and games as cock-fighting and bull racing. He owned a dozen ponies, kept a stud, and was writing a book to be called *Horses and the History of Man,* the theme of which would be that, wherever the footprints of man have been uncovered, there also have been found the foot-prints of his most faithful friend, the horse. I question the truth of this, but sentiment is frequently more satisfying than accuracy.

He turned the tape recorder on again and sat tapping out march time on his thigh, echoing the orders *sotto voce,* seeing himself back on the barrack square sharing the unaccustomed freedom to be proud of a new-born Indonesian identity. He switched it off suddenly and said, "Three years ago I was an officer of the National Army. I played my part in freeing our people from the oppressors and in stamping out the errors of rebellion here in Sumatra and in Java. I have done my duty; I have served the people and the President. I could do no more."

He looked proudly into the distance.

"The regiment advanced me money to build houses for the army, and now I am rich. I have a tourist playground with self-contained bungalows, a swimming pool, and am partner in a race track and a golf course. I have interests in the spice trade and in rubber and copra buying. I wish to serve my country, but to be successful in business it is necessary to cheat, to bribe, to buy the officials who can issue permits. There is no more glory—we have become Westernized. When I go to Jakarta to do business I no longer stay with my brother; I stay at the Hotel Indonesia."

I was about to protest that this was an unjust and illogical parenthesis, but as he continued it seemed to me that he was merely indulging in a penitential soul-scratching, common to men who, finding simple ways to riches, feel at first uneasy.

"Some of us are caught," he said, "between the sweet desires of the heart and the bitterness of truth." He poured me a drink and then helped himself. "We have Sukarno. He is Our President, Our Great Leader. He has made us. He has taken the three thousand stars that are the islands of Indonesia and has made them a single great constellation, with one name, one heart, one nationality. We are all patriots, every one of us—the army, the politicians, students and their teachers, farmers and fishermen and shop-keepers, the

Communists, the rubber smugglers and the black marketeers. Sukarno has done this. Without him we are nothing and there is no Indonesia."

His eyes began to water.

"Many people in the northern parts of Sumatra and Sulawesi have been trading for centuries with Malaya and the Philippines and feel closer to those places in culture and commerce than they do to Java. And because many northern people are also Christian they have resented, in the early stages of independence, both Moslem domination and the power of Communists in Jakarta, and they rebelled against the central government.

"In those days people left their villages, abandoned the fields, and gathered together in bands to fight the government army. My two brothers were rebel leaders. I was an officer in the central army. There were many on opposite sides like me and my brothers and many sons fighting against their fathers. It was the same in America at the time of the Civil War.

"We did not want to fight. We met and sat together, full of love and sorrow and understanding, trying to find agreement, pleading, reasoning. We asked them to put their arguments to the parliament, but they refused, saying that they had no confidence in self-seeking politicians in Jakarta who spent their time maneuvering for personal advantages. So we had to fight, and many were killed on both sides with no advantage to anybody. Trade stopped and the rice fields were neglected. Children went hungry, and people were eating even the stems of banana trees.

"I was a soldier and had my duty, but my commander permitted me to take a portion of our own supplies to the villages and give them to the wives and children of the rebels—half of a cassava root or sweet potato for each child. When they held out their hands for more I said, I have no more to give you, no tears left to cry over you, no sighs. And when the rebellion was over and the little children could be given rice again, many died because their stomachs had shrunk and they could not take proper food.

"Sukarno brought the fighting to an end. He made his declaration of a national policy that would give dignity and equality to everyone. He made the promise of an amnesty and the civil wars came to an end. One of my brothers is back in the central army; the other is dead. Now there is Malaysia.

"Many of us do good business in Singapore but if Sukarno says that we must fight Malaysia then we must do as he says, even if it means fighting against our friends in America and Australia, as we fought against our own brothers here in Indonesia during the rebellions. And if the President retreats from this position, many will be ashamed of him and he will lose face."

He looked at me and lifted his hands a little helplessly. "So, when you travel around Indonesia you must not look for the differences between my countrymen and yours, but for the sameness. Our skin is a different color, but if you cut my breast you will find that my heart is like yours, it beats, it bleeds."

CHAPTER 13

The truck came early in the morning to take us inland to a migrant settlement: me, and Mr. Effendi, local officers of the departments of transmigration, agriculture, and information (all young men in their twenties), two laborers in case we needed digging out of the mud, a driver, a man returning to a far village and me. When we were ready the driver put his hand upon the gear lever and said, "Great and good God protect and bless us on this journey and keep us safe from tigers." When we had gone a few yards I said tentatively, "Will we see tigers on this road?" He shook his head and said no, the tigers had moved back further into the jungle since the bulldozers came into the district, but he was accustomed to saying this prayer and nothing was lost by it.

We made the usual enquiries of each other regarding wives and children: how many? how old? The young man from the transmigration department answered that he was newly married to the daughter of a Javanese settler, and was able to feel that he had the approval of the President, who had asked all officials to help assimilate the immigrants. He said that her family were volunteer settlers who had come privately to Sumatra, and that people of this class succeeded in the enterprise more surely than those who came because of misfortune or extreme poverty by way of some government scheme. Many of these were reluctant refugees, illiterate, lacking confidence, and given to apathy, and without the desire or spirit to start a new life, and there was little likelihood that the plan to immigrate two million people from Java by 1970 could succeed if it depended upon moving people of this kind. But free settlers had both the will and determination to make good, and when roads and other communications were better advanced there would be, he thought, a great inrush of young and ambitious families anxious to take up the government offer of fifteen hectares of arable land when most village Javanese had been raised on holdings of half an hectare or even less.

"We have problems but in the end we must succeed. There are millions of people ready to work and there is plenty of empty land to be settled. It is a matter of time. Our people must become accustomed to the idea of immigration, and not only of settling into new racially exclusive communities but of becoming assimilated into existing villages, to build them up and make them more solid and prosperous. We need to raise money for more roads and irrigation. We want to build local agricultural colleges and training centers. It will take time but it can be done: if we have peace."

A little way out of town we came to a plantation and drove through stands of dappled, delicately slender young rubber trees, planted precisely and kept neatly clean from undergrowth. The property had once belonged to a Dutch company but had been neglected through years of war and revolution and finally abandoned by them. Now it was owned by a Javanese businessman who had brought it from the government. The young man from the Agricultural Department said that the Dutch had employed three hundred men but now there were thirteen hundred workers with their families housed and fed on the estate.

It is difficult to pick out threads of relevant fact from a tangled pattern of half-truths and persuasive propaganda, and figures have little meaning without more precise information. The estate produces fifty tons of rubber a month and the manager buys fifteen hundred tons from local villagers. "Production is much better than before," said the young man, "and the profit is going back into the country instead of being sent to Americans to make them richer than they are already."

In Palembang the governor had told me that he had persuaded local rubber growers and exporters to donate the cost of building dormitories at the university. "It is not the policy of the government to substitute local capitalists for foreign exploiters," he had said, "and our businessmen must learn that they must not only earn the privilege of becoming rich but must pay for it continuously, remembering that the natural resources of the country belong to the people, to be exploited on their behalf."

We headed, in burning heat, toward the mountains, and although the road was rough and the ride bumpy and uncomfortable I felt exhilarated, being among fundamental things: simple people, the earth, great shapes of trees and hills, and big white clouds against the sky; the landscape a collaboration between men and nature. Slopes lined with orderly patterns of pepper vines; ranks of stiff-armed kapok trees posed like a corps de ballet on the sky line; coffee beans yellow, green, and red spread in carpets by the roadside; patches of gawdy, orange-colored corn. Coconut palms pointlessly tall but always graceful, goats on the roadway, chickens, slow oxen, children going to school with their few books.

In a small town that seemed at first deserted we found the men of the place gathered under a rough shelter of palm branches by the roadside, sitting on benches and with a blackboard set up among them with an agenda written on it; so we stopped and, having exchanged courtesies, discovered that they were holding a village meeting to deal with the matters listed so neatly (by the schoolteacher), and were invited, if we so wished, to stop a while and listen.

The building of a new school topped the list (inevitably) followed by questions of food production, the repair of the road, and the cleaning out of fire hazards in the jungle. These seemed straightforward, as did the domestic matter of distributing the government's free issue of kerosene—one bottle each week to every family. The secretary, stepping aside for a while, said that there had been some discussion about the standard of dress, the progressive faction feeling that there should be an attempt at improvement in keeping with the new identity and dignity of Indonesia and its people.

The major issue of the meeting, making for much discussion, revolved around a stock of rice held in common, collected by the townsfolk, and amounting to five hundred kilograms (eleven hundred pounds, roughly). Many of the older men, led by a gray-beard wearing the headgear of a Hadji, were anxious that the rice be sold and the money used to rebuild the mosque, which had become shabby and unworthy of its purpose; but others, driven by the spirit of the new Indonesia and anxious to make gestures, thought that part of the money might be lent to the people of a nearby village who badly needed a new roof for their school. We left before the matter was resolved but called again some days later, on our way back, and found the issue put aside until another hundred kilograms of rice had been added to the common store.

"You see here," said Mr. Effendi, "the real Indonesia of *Gotong Royong,* mutual help, togetherness. In the cities we fill the wind with words that become meaningless like prayers repeated without thinking; but here in the villages words take root and produce deeds." The trip was having its effect on Mr. Effendi. He had stopped talking about Bloomington and had coined a new catch phrase, pointing to pepper and coffee plantations as we passed and saying, "Dollars everywhere you look, riches growing all over Indonesia, how beautiful is my country."

When we had gone further and were on the edge of a bigger town, a tire burst, and leaving the driver and laborers to mend it we went to a café and found there three men in uniform drinking coffee by the glass. They proved to be the big men of the district—the army and police commanders, both sergeants, and the principal civilian official. They were ready to leave and go about their business but stopped to greet us decently, and afterward, while we were still waiting for the truck tire to be fixed, they took us around and about the town.

They showed us how the river had been dammed to form a chain of family fish ponds, with one community pond bigger than the rest, which is fished once a year and the catch sold in the market. The money from this is used to provide vocational training for village girls. We saw, also, a new satellite village built to house the police and their families, a community coffee-tree nursery, and a first-aid center with a permanent medical attendant, trained in Palembang.

The market seemed too large for the town but they said that merchants from Palembang and Kotabumi came on Sundays to buy pepper, coffee, rubber, and rice and to offer cloth and clothes and manufactured goods, and on those days about ten thousand people from nearby villages filled the town. They had in mind to build stalls and pens to make the livestock market tidier and more orderly, and had notions of a community hotel. The policeman said, "We are beginning to live like other people, it is a strange experience."

This was all evidence of the village activity that had been explained to me in Jakarta. There it had seemed theoretical and suspect; but here it seemed real, and the answer seemed to be that where the initiative lay in the village things were being done: that the country people, working inside the limits of their own economy and knowledge, were achieving all that the central government could suggest to them and were capable of more if the state could provide the major public works, communications, and credits.

The little people of Indonesia are doing their bit. The young men who represent the government in the country areas are inspired, have visions, faith, and a clear, creative understanding of what they are doing. Other young men sitting in offices in Jakarta, writing their war propaganda, sowing hate, betray them.

Soon after leaving this town we turned off the main road (which had been gravel-faced and pitted here and there with potholes) and followed a less-used track leading into the resettlement areas; and now I understood why the Bupati of Kotabumi had provided so rugged a truck to make this journey. The ruts were so water worn and deep that, in spite of a two-foot clearance, the underside of the truck scraped continuously along the middle ridge of the roadway, and the undulations in the ruts were so eccentric that within half an hour the muscles of my stomach were tight and twisted and my entrails tied in knots.

There were no more villages, only a solid block of high jungle hung with creepers and great stands of bamboo and the thin twisting ribbon of unmade road like a brown string dropped on the green. Here and there a few fretful birds protested our intrusion. Then a family of monkeys moved away from us, looking down over their shoulders, swaggering with impudent, disdainful gait through latticed space, reaching out feet and hands, without looking, to clasp branches which swayed gracefully with their weight: movements as smooth and complete as perfect phrases, self-contained statements as clear as if made on a printed page. They freeze, stop, and stare in a fixed moment of being. One is aware that there has been an exchange, an occurrence.

It was dusk when we came to the settlement and climbed painfully down from the cabin of the truck, tired, to meet the men in charge and be shown a bunk in the police barracks. To lie for a while stretched out, then to bathe, to feel the air cool with the soft coming of night. To take tea, to eat, to sleep.

There was a tiger. It came in the night and took the dog tied up outside, and nobody heard a sound. In the morning when they found the dog gone but the chain and collar intact, the grass flattened a little, and drops of blood making a trail into the bush, the policemen were surprised and went about talking in whispers to hide their excitement. They said that dry weather was bringing jungle animals to the river; that thirty-two tigers had been shot in the Pendopo area, round about the oilfields, in recent months. It would be necessary, they thought, to take precautions to protect the settlers' livestock.

It is five years since the first immigrant settlers came to this area from the poorest part of South-Central Java, the periodic dust bowl just below Jogjakarta, from which "starvation stories" had come each year to cheer foreign correspondents bored with handouts from the Foreign Office in Jakarta. The hungry Javanese make good headlines year by year, being politically more interesting than hungry Indians and Arabs, and this makes the President extremely angry with the foreign press, which, he says, gives hypocritical headlines to this "congenital" disease, left untreated for centuries by the Dutch, and studiedly overlooks any praiseworthy progress being made in solving Indonesia's multitudinous difficulties.

Many of the early immigrants went back to Java, disillusioned, unable to accommodate themselves to the demands and disciplines of pioneering: the living in sheds together, the lack of permanent water, the new rice fields plagued with insects never seen before, more voracious than those known in Java. They said, "Better starve at home among our own people than alone out here in the jungle." The newsmen wrote, "Indonesia's transmigration plan merely transfers poverty from one place to another."

They were mainly middle-aged folk who went back, too old to change their ways—and who could blame them? It was a time of trial and error and the mistakes were frequently fundamental. But most of the young stayed and later were joined by veterans from the colonial and civil wars, men who were offered land and a new start in the settlements when they were demobilized from the army. These were more of the mind for such an operation, for they had been living hard since their school days, battling and living light or off the land since leaving their own homes to join the students' army or some guerrilla band. Many of them had nothing to go back to, after the fighting, but work in the family rice field, so that pioneering with the prospect of owning more land than all of their relations put together was more their meat. These men married and came, having nothing whatever to lose and everything to gain. Being young and soldier-trained and in vigorous condition they could work, and did, and began to make life in the wilderness look better.

The next immigrants came also from Central Java when the great God Mountain of Merapi blew its cone and smothered the land for miles around with ash and rubble. Many families, made landless, listened to tales of land for the asking in Sumatra and were encouraged by the knowledge that other people from Java were already there, growing rice and maize and making money out of pepper, speaking their own language, following the ancient customs. They would not be alone in the new land.

We took the truck and went among them in the cool of the morning, in a lowering landscape of unlit jungle green, and mauve clouds heavy with wetness pressing down around the hill-tops. The locals looked at the sky, smiling hopefully, sniffing distant rain.

We sat in a lean-to shelter alongside a man's house, small but solidly beamed. Heavy bunches of bananas were hanging in the kitchen, papaya, beans, and rice sheaves. He was a man of about thirty, of peasant stock, who had been a soldier, had hidden out in the hills, had killed a few Darul Islam rebels; not a really bright man but not dull, and he was doing pretty well. He said that he had been three years in the place and in that time had built this house, moved his family out of the community buildings, and had made the garden and put a fence round it. Now his family ate all it wanted, and had not been better fed before. As for himself, he was busy: had grown half a ton of rice over and above the family requirement and sold this to a trader, had fifteen hundred coffee bushes coming into bearing next year and these would make him richer than anybody but the headman of his father's village back in Java. Already he was in a more substantial way than any government official hereabouts, although without any but the merest education. (Mr. Effendi looked thoughtful, and I could see opposing pictures forming in his mind, mixing and making confusion for him. First the sophisticated, and, for him, unreal life of Washington, then the ease and natural dignity and plenty of rice of a rich man in Sumatra.)

The man gave us big, fresh bananas to eat, tea, and biscuits made with sweetened cassava flour. When we left my guides said that he was typical of the veteran settlers, most of whom were doing well but were purely peasant in their outlook. They would not, for instance, put money in a bank but, having sold a crop or livestock, would buy golden ornaments for their women and use these for storing their wealth. If, later, they wished to buy an old truck, a bicycle, or farm tools they took their gold to town to trade with.

Apart from this little impatience with the old ways these young officials were well pleased with their work and with the immigrants. They said, "The President should send us the homeless and the hungry from Jakarta and we will look after them, give them land, teach them to use it to grow food, get fat and raise strong children who will praise them in their old age. We have the space, they have the people—let them all come." It is not so easy, for peasants or for city people, to tear themselves up by the roots and transplant successfully in a place that has nothing but untamed land; no decent roads, no permanent water, no doctor, no power supply, no telephones, no local traditions to cling to or find comfort in. Those who stay are brave, especially the women.

They stand at the gates of the little houses, with expressionless faces and sad eyes, watching us as we drive by, at each gate a woman with a baby on her hip or in her belly, and three, four, or five naked children jumping up and down and screaming shrilly with excitement as we pass. The houses are small but strong; the gardens are fenced and full of growing things. The men are in the fields, and the older youngsters are at school.

Schoolteachers came with the settlers from Java and helped build the school. When we came to it there were a hundred children inside and a hundred waiting outside under big trees. These were seven and eight years old, waiting to begin their lessons at ten o'clock, by which time the younger group, inside, would be done for the day. We were taken inside, protesting that we ought not interrupt to see new desks, carpentered with care from rough bush wood. Six little children sat squeezed in each, their feet not reaching the bare earth, watching with wide eyes as the teacher put each one's name on the blackboard, pointing to the child, saying its name, then writing it. Some were shy and hid their eyes and giggled; others looked surprised to find, suddenly, that they had an existence outside themselves, that these letters on the blackboard belonged exclusively to them; others looked around at their playmates, pointing to themselves and then to the blackboard, as if to say, "That's me." A miracle of discovery.

When we had seen enough of this settlement we drove further inland along the broken road and came to a wide river with no motor bridge, where we left the truck and crossed on logs. Then we followed a cart track for an hour and came to a place where men were clearing jungle and leveling land with machinery—provided by the Japanese as war reparations.

Here we turned along a foot track and came suddenly upon a line of huts built of rough-cut slabs and roofed with thatch; no fences, no gardens. In front of each hut stood a tall bamboo with a palm-leaf streamer hung from it, and beside the pole was a little shrine with a few rice grains laid inside. There were pigs sniffling in the rough grass. I knew, then, that we had come among the Balinese refugees from Agung.

They numbered two thousand, had come through the Red Cross camp at Singaradja in Bali, each man with his hoe, crowbar, and basket of rice, to these little wooden huts put up by the government. No temples yet, no red-brick gateways and shrines to ancestors; but they had written through the school teacher to the Department of Religious Affairs in Jakarta, asking that a Bali-Hindu priest be sent to them.

It was the schoolteacher, Nyoman Gania, recently of Bangli, who told us this as we sat in the single unlit room that is his home, with his wife, sister, father, mother, and two children; other Balinese, some in ceremonial costume, looked down on us from fuzzy, grubby photographs nailed to the wooden walls.

He said that they were not unhappy but would be more content when they could get a gamelan together and teach their children to perform the ritual dances. It was the spiritual and mystical elements of the old life they missed most (a few families had already gone back to Bali) and the lack of any real connection with their past. It was not loneliness, not the remoteness of this strange place that worried them—they had each other for company—but the absence of any familiar spirits.

They had no news of the outside world except when letters came from Bali and such gossip as might be gained when they went to the Javanese settlement on market day; but the government had promised them a transistor radio so that they might listen to the news.

The village policeman came with other men, and Nyoman's wife put a platter of fresh-boiled ground nuts on the table between us. The men spoke of building a temple and a school and said that their first rice crop was almost ready for reaping. They talked of starting a community rubber plantation and of planting coconuts, but this was future work, to be done when food supplies were more certain. To see them sitting there in the rough room with its bare earthen floor, planning a new future, was to be sitting in on the story of man-the-indestructible, always building—a culture, a civilization—losing it, pulling it to pieces, moving on, starting again, creating his own glory, his own pain.

But it had begun to rain, fat globular spots, and it would take an hour to walk back to the river and the truck, so we left with thanks and good wishes, and shaking hands all around went into the wet. Nyoman came a little way, looking around the skyline smiling, and pointing to a mountain wreathed in cloud said, "This is our Gunung Agung, the navel of our new birth, our holy mountain. Our children will look up at it and say to each other, 'The souls of our ancestors dwell there with the Gods.' They will build a temple on it and make offerings to the gods and to the souls of their ancestors—we who were the first."

Next morning, after breakfast, I stood on the roadway saying goodbye to my host, the young man in charge of the transmigration settlements. He said he was glad that I had come to visit this part of Sumatra to see what the people and the government were doing to build a new nation. He asked me to tell my countrymen that Indonesians wished to be friends with us because "we are all the children of one father, God." He took my hands between his own and bowed his head, saying, "You have been in my house, sat with me and eaten my rice, and I feel comfortable in my stomach."

Extract from a letter
The Lily Pond
Palembang

Mr. Effendi was precipitate or deliberately misleading in his statement that the old sultan's lily pond had been drained as part of the antimalarial campaign—perhaps he regarded my interest in pink lilies as frivolous in this age of Indonesia's emancipation and advancement;

but I have said goodbye to him and sit here in the sultan's pavilion writing to you while swifts flitter in and out in pursuit of evening insects. The water in the pool is still and the lilies are folding for the night. It is so quiet I can hear the flicker of the swifts' wings, and drips from the lily leaves falling back into the pond.

I reached Palembang again last night, tired after twelve hours in the train (we were delayed by elephants on the track and some damage they had done to the signaling system) but pleased with the week spent among country people. Being with them brings a feeling of reality. One sees the possibility of achievement within the immediate means of the country, and the grand, extravagant dreams that will take a generation to come true fall into perspective.

With each of these journeys I see more distinctly the outlines of Indonesia's complex national personality and understand more precisely the predicament of the Western world in coming to satisfactory terms with this nation on a foundation of mutual respect and equal dignity. We of the Western world must face the unpalatable fact that in building our own civilization we shamefully misused these and most other Asian, African, and South American people for many centuries. We are responsible not only for much of their present national insufficiency but for their irascible nationalistic attitudes: we are in debt to them.

Given time, the ordinary, hard-working, and intelligent people of Indonesia will put the national house in order and create a system of government and administration which will give practical as well as inspirational leadership; but this will not happen in ten years, perhaps not in twenty, and the problem of the West is not only to be certain what it expects of Indonesia, but to be patient and helpful while this is being achieved.

These Indonesian people won their freedom fighting with bamboo spears against Western rifles, guns, and bombs given to the Dutch; we owe them more than sympathy.

I'm sorry, my dear, to be preaching again (even among the lilies). The train of thought was triggered by a conversation I had an hour ago with a Peace Corps boy from California and an Australian Voluntary Graduate (which is much the same thing except that the Australians are privately organized, few in number, and have no official status). They are both working here in Sumatra.

The Australian in this case is a countryman, product of farm and agricultural college. He is thoroughly happy here in the back blocks of Sumatra, working on a district research and experiment station as assistant to an Indonesian agricultural officer. He takes exactly the same pay and conditions as the other employees and lives at the same economic and social level—at the Jakarta black-market exchange rate he earns about $2 a month, but on the local market this is adequate to live by, Asian style. His subject is pasture improvement and he runs an experimental and demonstration project. He says that the farmers among whom he works are strictly conservative and traditional in their farming beliefs and methods but are prepared to change their ways if new methods are shown to be better than the old. He feels that this will take him another two years to demonstrate; in the meantime his own folks back in Australia need his help on the family farm. This poses him a problem, but he thinks that he will ask the Indonesian government to renew his contract for another two years so that he can keep faith with the peasant farmers of this part of Sumatra.

The American, Paul, has been less lucky. He came as a sports instructor when the President was anxious that Indonesia should show up well in international games, but the young of Palembang showed no great enthusiasm for weight-lifting, athletics, and volleyball, at which Paul is expert. They are commercially minded by tradition, an Oriental trading people, given to contemplation and the weighing of profit. Prowess in sport (except, perhaps, at badminton) carries no social rating. Paul says that the people of Palembang wouldn't play ball of any kind, and this bothered him. He really felt useless and unwanted and was ready to go home. But he had also majored in English at Pasadena, and when invited to fill a sudden vacancy in the English department of Palembang University he took it, and found a place for himself in the Indonesian scene.

He is doing fine now, and likes it, confessing shyly that the students are right along with him and tell him that he is their best and favorite teacher. This has made him reevaluate his own attitude and motivation, and he sees that he came to Indonesia looking for some kind of personal experience, although wiling and anxious to contribute to the Indonesians within the framework of his own satisfaction. Now he feels that he must give, and want to give, not what he thinks they need or should be given, but what the people want for themselves. He does not want to go home now—too many young people have become dependent upon his decency.

I was reminded, when talking to these boys, of an incident occurring on an earlier journey, when a member of the Peace Corps, offended and confused by "Go Home Peace Corps" scrawled on walls in the town where he was working, went to the rector of the university at which he taught and asked for an explanation. The rector said, "My dear boy, we like you very much. You must take no notice of the slogans. They are purely political and have no personal implications of any kind. We would be distressed and disappointed if you decided to go home."

The young man—his name, I think, was Smith—pointed out that, being the only Peace Corpsman in the district, he had no alternative but to regard the matter personally and felt that the rector could ask the police to take some action; but the rector repeated, with a suspicion of impatience, that it was purely a political matter, having nothing to do with either the police, Mr. Smith, or the rector, and that to pursue the matter would be an embarrassment. Yet, when a few days later another scrawl said blatantly, "Go Home Smith," the police went into action immediately, arrested a score of young Communist students, and put them into jail without hesitation, saying they had committed a personal and ill-mannered attack upon a citizen of a friendly nation. It is, clearly, not easy for us to deal with such people.

Tonight I am invited to dinner with a middle-class family from the north of Sumatra. I am told that both dog and rat meat are on the menu. Mr. Effendi says that field rats, which feed almost entirely on rice, are more palatable, tender, and delicate of flesh than are town rats, which feed mainly on market garbage. He thinks that my hosts, being well-to-do and decent people, will give me field rats. He has written down a recipe for what he humorously calls "Hot Dog Palembang," asking that I pass it on to you with his respectful good wishes, which I do herewith:

> The dog should be short in the legs so that it has not run about too quickly, which gives a dog tough sinews and adds a rank flavor to its various glands. The dog should be bled and disemboweled, then spitted on a bamboo stick and part roasted with its skin still on. After about half an hour or perhaps a little longer (depending upon the species of dog and its age) you must withdraw the spit and take away any superfluous organs. Cut the meat in pieces and take away the skin. Now fry the meat in coconut oil with garlic and split chilies. Give it to the guests with rice and chili sauce.

Tomorrow I go back to Jakarta to begin a tour of Java.

P.S. All USIS libraries in Indonesia have now been closed by order of the American government, and the Peace Corps project is to be terminated in protest against continuous anti-American demonstrations staged by the Young Communists. One can understand the action and sympathize with it while wondering if it is a sign that the United States has finally and officially lost patience. If this is so the local

Communists have won a victory at the expense of tens of thousands of students, like my sad little friend in Makassar.

It is said that the United States ambassador presented the USIS books and office equipment to the Indonesian government and that the government gave the equipment to the Young Communists, who have taken over the USIS premises in Jakarta as an anti-American propaganda center under the title, "Friends of the People's Democratic Republic of North Viet Nam."

PART VI

Jakarta-Java

CHAPTER 14

. . . it is clear that there will be only two forces left in the field, namely, the PKI and Nasution . . . and Indonesia will be a Socialist State in 1970.

D. N. Aidit
Chairman of the PKI

. . . if we should be attacked from outside within the next ten to fifteen years we will not be able to put into the field a modern armed force . . . we pray for the best . . . we should keep our umbrella ready before it rains.

General A. H. Nasution
Chief of staff of the Armed Forces

Turn your heads as you pass,
Avert your eyes
All you nice Western ladies and gentlemen
Who love Indonesians—
We shall die soon enough
From a surfeit of words:
We do not need
The slow poison of your pity.

Soejono
Clerk

There was a message from Soejono to say that he had tickets for the soccer football semifinal at the main stadium, that the game was between Bandung and Jakarta, and that the President might be there because he is a graduate of the Bandung Technical College. As it happened he was unable to come, and ninety thousand people were disappointed, but an official with a loud, vulgar voice read a presidential message which said:

> Physical as well as mental strength is imperative for the molding of the new Indonesia. Sport must be a tool used to achieve this national purpose; consequently, the attitude of all Indonesian people toward sport must be based on the Political Manifesto of August 17, 1959 . . . etc.

It was good, exciting football, which Jakarta won by a narrow margin, for although Bandung played the prettier game its team seemed to lack the hard finishing edge of toughness that the city players showed. Soejono said that neither the comparative standard of play nor the result had anything to do with the President's Political Manifesto, but that the outcome of the game merely demonstrated the difference between playing for love and playing for three thousand rupiahs a month, which is what a good player can command in Jakarta. He seemed in tetchy humor and out of patience with all ideologies, saying, "It is no good the President preaching at us about such matters, we are just as civilized and up to date as the Americans in these things. A footballer anywhere makes a greater social contribution, makes less mischief, gives more pleasure to the public, and makes more profit for his employers than a university lecturer does and should therefore get higher pay."

A Foreign Office car came soon after seven o'clock the next morning to collect me (these courtesies continued to pursue and amaze me through the months of my stay in Indonesia), and we went, first by devious streets, to a strange part of the city that I had not visited before; but the expedition was no part of my itinerary. The driver, who seemed secretive, said he had been told that benzine could be bought for the officially fixed price at a certain service station in this part of town, and this alone was reason for our early start and the detour from the usual route into the city.

We found a line of like-minded motorists long before coming within sight of the service station and, taking our turn, were an hour and ten minutes getting our fill, although twice, while waiting, we were offered immediate service at black-market rates. It seemed ridiculous to engage in such capricious inefficiency in the capital of one of the biggest oil-producing countries in the world, where a gallon of benzine is normally cheaper than a cup of tea. And it seemed sillier still to see, a few minutes later, "Go Home British" scrawled along the wall of the Shell Oil headquarters in that city.

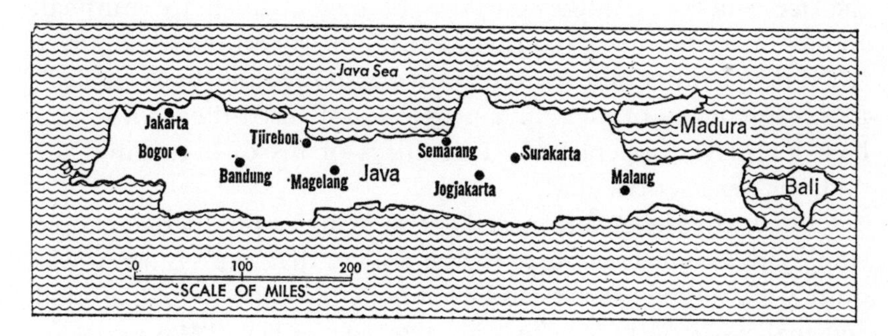

To be in the Indonesian capital, even for a single day, is to lose patience with the Revolution. The national administration cannot expect to be taken seriously if it brings itself almost to a standstill, unable to maintain essential services, because it is busy building national monuments and staging the extravagant charade of "confrontation." The simple caption to it all is "Muddle," although the word seems hardly adequate to describe administrative anarchy of such formidable proportions.

To a foreigner, loving Indonesia and the Indonesians, Jakarta is a horror city, a travesty of earnestness and honest aspiration, a place to leave gratefully, glad to be away from the inefficiency, the confusion, the crude schoolboy scrawlings on walls (a perversion of the true courtesy of the Javanese). Within hours of landing in Jakarta the traveler is anxious to get out, to give up the attempt to get anything done, to see officials who are seldom in their offices, being half their time busy with other jobs. Foreign correspondents live and try to work in this environment; it is no wonder that they are instinctively biased and hypercritical.

I tracked down a man I had been hoping to see since first I came here (we have mutual acquaintances in the United States), a government man with five hundred people under him, and found him collecting his issue of rice, checking its weight on scales set up behind his offices. He looked up and smiled. "This is the day we all appear on duty, this and pay day, so the government is sure of our attendance, if not of our services, at least two or three times a month." He carried the sack of rice to his car and put it in the back beside his briefcase. "On any other day it is unlikely that half the staff will show up."

Driving out to Kebajoran to deliver the rice to his home he said that for many people a government job was a kind of dole, with the rice issue more important than the wages, which are minimal. In most cases the work required of a junior government employee left time for other and more lucrative activities and business dealings, while many of the senior people simply used their offices as a base for private operations. Two-thirds of his own earnings, he said, were extracurricular.

I asked why the government kept so many unproductive people employed, and he said that it was policy, that the system works quite well, nobody starves and everybody has time to look around and make a little money to add savor to the rice. "We are poor but we don't go hungry. God looks after us." Nor can anybody in a government job be easily dismissed. There must be three distinct warnings. Then, if the head of the section persists, the case must go to a tribunal, and if the decision is against the employee he must be found another job before he is paid off. The system is humane but inefficient. The ultimate question is, Which is most important, justice, mercy, or efficiency? It is difficult.

He put me down at the office of an assistant to the minister for people's industries, where I began again the processes with which I had become more and more familiar with each visit to the capital: first to listen to the story of the vision, then to search for its modified reality. "We must not disguise the problems," said the gentleman who received me. "It would be foolish to do this. In our department we have a multiplicity of difficulties, each of which will take a generation to overcome. Our task is to make a hundred million peasant people industrially self-supporting. Let no one tell you that this is easy."

He listed the main problems neatly, ticking them off on his fingers (the man had been educated in Japan, was precisely analytical, and spoke a meticulous brand of clickety English). "There is the ethnological problem which revolves around the fact that we are a conservative yet highly individualistic people. We do not change our ways easily nor do we care to standardize; after all, in a society in which most of one's possessions are homemade the expression of individuality tends to become a challenge if not a fetish. And in the matter of conservatism I offer as illustration the fact that our people prefer to use teak wood for building and furnishing although a teak tree takes eighty years to mature, is heavy and expensive to transport, and is hard to work.

"Then there is the infrastructural problem—" he must have seen uncertainty come into my eyes for he hesitated and explained— "the problem of providing roads, harbors, harbor approaches and installations, up-to-date railways and such major utilities by which raw materials, power plants, and finished products get from one place to another. In one port we have electric generators lying on wharves where they were put by ships' winches, but we have no lifting equipment nor transport heavy enough to take them to the place where we wish to start an industry."

Like almost every other Indonesian official he spoke freely and frankly, making no effort to disguise the mistakes and the weaknesses, but pressing onward with a fantastic belief in the power of faith to move generators, build dams, establish factories, and keep the nation fed and free. "We are naturally an industrious people and once we are able to coordinate the components of supply, production, and distribution we will be able to meet most of our own needs in regard to textiles, leather, ceramics, and timber, which means that we will be able to clothe and house ourselves without having to depend in any way on imports of foreign materials. At the same time, with the aid of new irrigation systems and increased fertilizer production we will become entirely self-supporting in foodstuffs."

When I asked about immediate problems he said that his department had eighty thousand factories requiring supervision and assistance in matters of finance, supplies of raw materials, research, labor training, and mechanization. Some of these were state undertakings and others were private or community enterprises begun by village cooperatives, veterans' groups, or private operators. His department was also responsible for the allocation of foreign funds and the issue of permits to regulate the supply of imported raw materials. "This," he said, frowning, "involves us in police activities, for there are unscrupulous people and traitors who will betray the Revolution for the sake of personal gain. These people get our assistance in many ways and we give them permits to import raw materials, but instead of using these materials to operate their factories and produce goods for people to buy at reasonable prices, they sell them on the black market and make big profits without producing anything."

He seemed so disappointed in his fellow countrymen that I felt sorry for him and said that in my country many people had become rich during the war by cheating in this and similar ways while their own sons were fighting on bitter battlefields, but that this was the way of man and always would be while the devil roamed the world, tempting the weak to evil. To this opinion he agreed, nodding his head, and sent out for cups of tea. While we waited he explained that the policy of his department was based on the five principles of Pantja Sila, which, he said, might concisely be defined as "Belief in one supreme God, just and civilized humanity, democracy which is guided by the inner wisdom in a unanimity arising out of deliberation, while creating a condition of social justice for the whole people of Indonesia—or to put it more concisely still, God plus private enterprise."

There was more he might have told me, and indeed he seemed willing to continue as long as I would listen, but I begged to be excused, saying that General Nasution had agreed to receive me and that I must go or else be late. At this he got up quickly, looking respectful, with a peremptory gesture sent a boy to fetch a *betjak*, and came with me to instruct the driver in detail by which route I should be taken to see the general, prophesying trouble if I were late on the driver's account.

A mad woman in make-shift uniform, long hair hanging wildly down her back, stood by the roadside directing the traffic outside Merdeka Barracks, saluting cars that seemed by appearance important, shouting threats and insults at any who ignored or laughed at her. Regular police stood by smiling. A white priest on a motor scooter hummed past swiftly, sun-ripened face red beneath solar topee, his soutane pulled up over his knees to let the breeze play about his body. Over in the parkland, by the partially built Freedom Monument, anxious boys marched up and down with their eyes on Malaysia.

There were no guards on the barrack gates, no challenges. I went in and walked about looking for someone who might show me where to find the general and was directed to the office of a major who greeted me affably and said the general had a busy day and could only spare an hour for my interview. I was alarmed at this for I had little to ask and nothing to say to the general. There is no point in asking questions of such people. They are committed to replies already given in their speeches, their books, and repeated day by day in the newspapers and on the radio. I already knew by heart the standard answers to the questions of Malaysia, inflation, American aid, the Communist problem, neo-colonialism, imperialism, and the people's sufferings. I wanted no more than to meet him for a few moments, to make a private assessment of this man who stands in the shadows waiting for the day all Indonesia dreads yet knows must come—the day when the President is no longer invulnerable, when there is room at the top for some other power and authority to govern and shape the way of Indonesia. The general, waiting in the shadows on one side of the stage, watches the aging, spot-lit hero miraculously act out his virtuoso fantasy. In the shadows on the other side of the stage stands another man, Aidit, Chairman of the Communist Party of Indonesia. The whole audience is aware that the two men wait there. They know that when the man on the stage hesitates or falters both will step forward to keep the show going, each claiming to act in his name for the people of the nation.

General Abdul Harris Nasution, minister-coordinator for national defense and security, chief of staff of the armed forces, has a score or more of other offices and titles, a random handful including deputy chief of the Board of the National Front (under the President), member of the Supervisory Council of the Antara News Agency, supreme advisor of the Indonesian Students' Council, and deputy chairman of the Committee for the Improvement of the Pilgrimage to Mecca. His influence and authority, through these offices and others, are spread widely, if thinly, over the whole landscape of the Indonesian scene. Yet in such a country as this, where a generous measure of flamboyance and dramatic emphasis is an essential element in the make-up of heroes and leaders, this man's discretion seems to border on the edge of coyness and self-effacement.

His answer is that he is a soldier, a servant of the Republic and the President, yet talking with him I could not feel certain whether his seeming simplicity is, in fact, natural and unaffected or is a careful political discipline. Of all the Indonesian leaders he carries most comfortably the label "enigma." Ask whether he is strong or weak and no one will answer. The most precise assessment likely to be given is that he is careful, and he is honest.

He came, smiling frankly, from behind the big table to shake hands, indicated a deep armchair, and then sat facing me in a similar chair. A bronze bust of the President stood between us on a pedestal. An army photographer came in and took a picture of us in this pose. When the photographer had gone the general made a restrained, almost apologetic reference to Australia's obsolete foreign policy, saying that there could be no profit in living in a past that had made walls of what were once horizons. The great revolutions of this age—French, American, Russian—have expended their energy and impetus, and only a new revolution can lead the people out again beyond these walls so that the progress of man toward his ultimate destiny may continue. That, he said, was his opinion.

He went on to say, not waiting for any lead or question, that President Sukarno is trying to do this and that "it is the first duty of every Indonesian to support him, whatever other loyalties may seem to have claims on us." He leaned forward. "When we were forced to go to war over West Irian, the rebels in Sumatra and Sulawesi, although in dispute with the government here in Jakarta, came back into the fold and were united, lovingly, with all other Indonesians under the President. The same is true of our troubles with Malaysia. Our people, aware of the dangers of neocolonialism, are united in the face of this threat from the British Imperialists, simply because the President had explained this to them in their own language and has made it clear.

"We of the armed forces are an inseparable part of the Indonesian state and society, involved in its difficulties and deficiencies—we must be ready to use the hoe as well as the rifle, blackboards more often than bombs. For this reason you will find as you go around the country that great numbers of our armed forces are engaged in civic missions, busy with major construction works, operating production and marketing cooperatives and loan societies. You will find officers acting as provincial governors, as executive heads of departments, as coordinators of the national effort at all levels."

General Nasution is the organizational head of the National Front, an interlocking political and administrative machinery headed by the President. Its function is to organize all human forces required to carry out the developmental policies of the ministries. It keeps a central registry of all volunteer "citizen forces" set up to provide for district and village defense, law, and order, including the "Crush Malaysia" volunteers. Among other functions is that of keeping the national conscience and watching public morality, and its members are encouraged to investigate and report on suspected evidences of disloyalty, corruption, black-marketing, anti-Sukarnoism, and the like.

This puts General Nasution, at least technically, in charge of all the regular and volunteer fighting forces in the country, plus the police, all organized work forces, and a comprehensive amateur spying system; and it is in this context and against this background that he has become a symbol of strength and stability, and an apparent barrier against whatever power ambitions the Communists might have. It is envy of Nasution's theoretical control of all the national armament, extending from elite paratroop battalions down to the village Home Guard, that makes Aidit ingenuously ask the President "to arm the peasants for the defense of the fatherland against Imperialist encirclement." If there is ever to be a civil war, Aidit is anxious that all may have an equal opportunity to be in it.

But this is Indonesia, with a paradox in every situation (in any case the President is clever and cunning), so it is commonly said that Nasution's National Front is "a nest of Communist intrigue and activity," used by the party as a holy robe beneath which it hides its hands while manipulating provocations and inquisitions, all aimed at undermining the general and those who would support him if trouble came.

General Nasution is a nice man, a religious man, generous and fair in all his dealings. He might even be called a simple man (within the decent meaning of that word), but he is certainly not stupid. He has written books and made many speeches, all of which quote and support the President. He says nothing against the Communists, utters no word that might set the delicate power-balance trembling in Sukarno's hand. Little is known of what goes on in this man's mind. No conservative observer is prepared to prophesy whether or not he will prove to be the strong man of the Right when and if the moment comes for one to appear. The answer might lie in his certain knowledge that if the Communists come to power General Nasution will disappear from public life.

I was surprised, seeing him glance at his watch, to find that we had indeed been talking together for almost an hour, and I got up quickly, apologizing for taking his time. But he said he found it helpful and relaxing to discuss the problems of the country without feeling forced into apologetics. Then he gave me a parcel of his publications, saying that he had arranged for me to spend a few days, if I wished, at the Staff and Command College at Bandung, and that I might feel myself free to see him whenever I wished.

In the evening, at an official speech-making, I met Aidit and his deputy, Lukman—who was brought up an exile in West Irian and seemed a simple, decent man, a Communist of the sentimental kind, more heart than mind, although others in the group wore the worried look of uncertain but determined rank-and-file believers.

Someone was speaking to Aidit. He listened with the blank, ungiving stillness of those who are either stupid or ruthless—an outwardly soft, round, almost flabby man with guileless face and the clear, innocent, merciless eyes of a child. I felt cold. Yet when we were introduced he smiled pleasantly enough and was briefly gracious, inviting me to call on him when I could. But he soon excused himself and walked away with his retinue, self-assured, conscious of authority.

CHAPTER
15

We drove up past Bogor in blinding rain, the black landscape lit erratically with lightning flashes (for a second we saw dappled deer in the palace gardens, huddled under trees). The great humped back of Gunung Salak leaned over us, seeming to sway from side to side as we twisted our way up from the hot coast onto the Java plateau, threading through a hundred hills covered with tea plants and summer bungalows. Our lights slid over them, back and forth with the swing and sweep of the car, driven smoothly and at high speed by an army driver. A woman lieutenant, chubby and smooth-skinned, with wishful brown eyes, cuddled down in the front seat singing softly:

> Clear moon, bathing naked in the stream,
> See the crocodile lying quiet, close by.
> Don't believe the words he whispers,
> With his lips or with his heart.

She sings mischievously to the tune of the Malayan national anthem. Indonesia is the moon and the crocodile is Tunku Abdul Rahman. But underneath is the ancient erotic symbolism—the moon always a woman bathing in a stream, and the crocodile (or tiger) a man waiting to take pleasure of her, tempting her with soft words and sighs to love. The lieutenant is said to be an efficient and strict officer. When she speaks the tip of her tongue slips in and out between her lips.

A colonel, returning to the Staff and Command school at Bandung, had offered to take me that far (a matter of something over a hundred miles) and so set me on my journey through Java, which he described with a lavish cascade of mixed metaphors as "the body and soul of our nation, the getting-bed of most of its millions—450 people to the square kilometer against an average twenty elsewhere in the country—the hammer and anvil of its history of war and civil war, revolution and rebellion, and the cradle of the great Republic of Indonesia."

The lieutenant wriggled in her seat and sang:

> My eyes store your image
> As my father stores rice in his barn.
> When the harvest is finished
> You may ask if I will marry you.

The colonel said, "The general speaks very well of her and has recommended her promotion to the rank of captain. She is in command of all the service women at the school and is very firm with them, but motherly. We say that she is a good soldier."

I asked if the ordinary problems of accommodating army families was not complicated by the Moslem custom of permitting a man four wives, to which he answered that the army had its own rules in the matter, recognizing only one wife with her children. It was not, he said, that the army set itself above customs sanctioned by Mohammed but simply that it could not transport, keep, and accommodate a multiplicity of families for each soldier in a garrison. But it is true, he added, that most of the high command are men of austere and tightly moral attitudes, monogamous themselves and given to asceticism.

The lieutenant turned in her seat to ask if I were married, then said she hoped that I would have time to visit the female officers in their mess and take a meal with them, for they would like to learn more about my country. The colonel nodded approvingly, then came back to the matter of Java (he had been told to brief me and give background to the bits of knowledge and impressions gathered on my earlier journeys).

"However much you may travel in the outer islands, however far from Jakarta you go seeking the real Indonesia, you will be drawn back inevitably to the center, the vortex of the Revolution, in which is concentrated most of the history and the hope of the

Indonesian people. Here, in Java, we have kept alive, through centuries, the anxieties, the longings, and the desires of a nation in chains. Here we have kept faith in ourselves and in our leaders. Here the traveler can lay his hand on our heart, can see and feel the physical, living fact of Indonesia's being."

The lieutenant had stopped singing and was silent until she said good night at the gateway to her quarters at the college.

Bandung, capital of the province of West Java, a big city with no center. In Dutch days it was sometimes called the "Paris of Java" (according to guidebooks) but there is nothing visible today which would give validity to the simile. Yet in the soft light of a rain-washed morning it has the clean and decent look of a respectable West European city of the early twentieth century, which to all physical appearances it is, with wide streets given to business and solid, square buildings with a middle-class dignity and architectural seriousness matching the period. It was also a tourist and summer place, with a zoo and a girdle of parks and gardens where a brass band played on Sundays, and clusters of little satellite towns full of boarding houses and holiday hotels furnished with teak and bamboo, pianos and aspidistras. There is not much of this elegance now, although an enormous and beautiful public swimming pool has been built since, and the band plays there now, instead of in the parks. The boarding houses and little hotels have lost luster and become a little dull, and the pianos are all out of tune.

Bandung is the center of Java's domestic industries, a city of textile mills, tanneries, dye works, kilns, machine shops, and engineering works. The nation's biggest technical schools and colleges are here and training centers for designers, mechanics, and artisans. It has research laboratories, the small-arms factory, and the national telecommunications center.

In Bandung, in 1925, a young man named Sukarno (nicknamed the Fighting Cock by his schoolfellows), having studied architecture, graduated in civil engineering. He was also a private student of political science, made speeches against the Dutch, was put into prison for eight months and then brought to trial for taking part in the planning of a rebellion and inciting the population to take part in it.

At the trial he made a speech in his own defense which laid the foundation of his future as a Nationalist and revolutionary leader.

He spoke in the name of the little people of Indonesia, "who for three centuries have gone hungry, living miserable and tragic lives because of the concentrated exploitation of their country by foreign rulers."[1] The speech, under the heading "Indonesia Accuses," later became one of his published utterances. The Dutch judges, hearing it for the first time, sent him to prison for two years.

Twenty-five years later, in 1955, he made another speech at Bandung, foreshadowing yet an ultimate step in his own progression and full-flowering as a leader of men. This time he spoke not as a young, uncertain rebel defending himself for crimes committed against the government, but as President-Supreme, Commander-Prime-Minister of the Republic of Indonesia, Great Leader of the Indonesian Revolution, Main Bearer of the Message of the People's Sufferings, and Judge of the High Court of Mankind's Conscience.

He spoke, too, not only for his friends, the little people of Indonesia but, as a world leader taking shape, for the suffering one and one half thousand millions of Africa and Asia. The occasion was the opening session of the first Afro-Asian conference and the speech was entitled, "Where Do We Stand?" In making delegates welcome, he prayed that they might "strike sparks of light from the hard flints of circumstance . . . give guidance . . . point out to mankind the way it must take to attain safety and peace." The "Fighting Cock" was moving to the top of the highest haystack to crow his challenge to the old order from the new.

He coined a new phrase, "The Spirit of Bandung," made clear new objectives, produced from the conference a new Decalogue which he called the Dasa Sila, or Ten Principles for the Promotion of World Peace and Cooperation. He says in 1965 that "the spirit and principles of Bandung have acted as a spur and an inspiration to the peoples of Asia and Africa as they struggled and fought for their national independence . . . have been a torch in the hands of the Asian-African peoples, lighting the path of their struggle to build a new world, guiding them in their dealings with one another and with the world around."

So Bandung may become famous as the cradle of a new civilization. Maybe with that ultimately in mind the main street was renamed Africa-Asia Street. But it looks as Dutch as ever it did, for

[1] A Foreign Office official paraphrase of the original speech.

in Java in general and Bandung in particular the foreign masters made their best attempt to settle into the landscape and make homes for themselves. In the other islands they had shallow roots, their influence was superficial, their imprint less than skin deep. Bandung has wide streets and walks; the shops on the main blocks have plate-glass windows. Its essential Dutch neatness gains it the President's prize each year for the nation's cleanest city. It is good to have pride in a city where one first went to jail.

The colonel from the Staff and Command school sent me by army truck to my first appointment; and when we came close to the place the driver set me down so that I could walk in the streets a little way. The stores were beginning to open, and young men were spreading sheets of paper on the pavements to set up piles of colored cloth on them for selling. A blind girl, dressed in brown rags, sat among them, holding out her hand; quite still, like a statuette or a painting, her face fixed, smooth, flawless, entirely without expression. A few yards from her an old man picked unmusically at a rough, home-made zither, making quick pinpricks in the covering background of traffic sounds, for the streets were busy with cars and covered carts drawn by ponies, each pony walking in the shade of a high canopy hung out over the shafts.

Extract from *Indonesia 1963*
(published by the Department of Foreign Affairs)

> As regards the textile industry, the main emphasis at the moment is upon building up spinning capacity in order to catch up with weaving capacity which, if operated at the full, could come close to meeting a bare minimum of domestic requirements.

The office I came into was a huge, rectangular room containing fifty-seven desks or tables. Two men sat at one of these tables playing chess while another stood over them, watching. I joined him and nobody moved. At another table a girl pecked at a typewriter with one finger. In the middle of the room a man sprawled in his chair, smoking and reading a newspaper. In a corner, in the shadows, an official interviewed a man who sat upright on a straight-backed chair holding a briefcase on his knees. There were no other people; only forty-three empty desks and tables standing quiet in the gray, unlit room.

One of the chess players moved a pawn, then looked up at me and asked, "Whom do you want to see?" I held out a letter of introduction written by a deputy-minister in Jakarta, addressed to the Regional Inspector of People's Industries in Bandung. The chess player looked but refused to take it, saying that the inspector was in Jarkata and no one had authority to open the letter. I opened it myself and held it out, but he ignored it. I said that my visit was approved by the minister, backed by this letter of introduction, and that I only wanted to see something of the industries centered on Bandung, especially one or two textile factories.

He was timid and uncertain. He had no authority to arrange for me to visit factories. I must get what information I needed from Jakarta. I held out the letter again but he backed away, then stood up excitedly saying that my visit had been arranged by a political enemy intent upon getting him into trouble. He said that I was a foreigner, that having seen the factories I would write that they were inefficient, and he would be blamed for taking me to them. I replied that he was more likely to get into trouble for disregarding the minister's instructions and *not* taking me to them; but I felt that I should go away and not be a nuisance. The other man moved a bishop, then stood up and said, "Please come back a little later, we will arrange something."

There are 360 textile mills in and around Bandung plus training centers for staff at all levels. There is much up-to-date testing and research equipment, some of it a present from the United States. Most key personnel have had some overseas experience.

With over a hundred million people to clothe, however simply, Indonesia has a textile problem, complicated by the fact that it grows no cotton of consequence and must import almost all the yarn it needs to keep the mills busy. The import permits and foreign currency allocations are issued on a priority basis. In Bandung it seemed that orders for cloth from the mills were filled first for the army, then the police, the Railway Workers Union, members of the telecommunications department, other government agencies, and finally for private buyers. One factory produced only gray unbleached shirting and a tough, black trouser material, both exclusively for farmers and laborers. I do not guarantee statistics, but I was told by officials that the lowest wage for a junior textile worker is three hundred rupiahs, and the best about one thousand rupiahs, a week plus an adequate rice issue and six meters (seven yards) of free cloth each month. It is possible to make do on the lowest wage and to live with an essay at dignity on the highest.

When I went back to the Regional Office I was smiled at and given a cane chair to sit on. The chess players sat on either side of me and the man who had been reading the newspaper joined us, but without sitting down. They had prepared an itinerary and read through a list of fourteen factories. They were happy. The way was clear. I was a friendly foreigner and should see everything: I would not write bad things about Indonesia (nor did I wish to, and neither did I wish to see fourteen factories).

We went to a textile mill built originally by the Dutch but confiscated and sold by the government to a Chinese financier. It was clean, efficient, and capable of the complete operation of spinning, weaving, and dyeing but was working at sixty percent of its capacity because of the shortage of yarn. It would be back in full operation, said the manager, as soon as the currency problem was straightened out in Jakarta.

Afterward, we went to one of the biggest state-owned mills, also taken over from the Dutch. The manager was "busy for a little while," but a deputy was found who could show me the plant and recite the necessary figures: nearly 4,000 workers, 1,096 looms, 37,000 spindles. Very big. It would be possible, said the deputy, to install automation and so dispense with most of the workers, but Java has an enormous work force and it is better to keep people employed than to spend money on new equipment. "In Dutch times the workers wore their own clothes in the mill but now they have three sets of overalls each year."

The weaving room is impressive in a way that anything big and symmetrical is impressive: the 1,096 looms laid out in series, the biggest weaving room in Indonesia, he said. It is filled with the sharp clack, rattle, and a slap of shuttles against a waterfall roar of machinery. Ten more factories like this would take care of Indonesia's textile needs. We walked the length of the enormous room. Like the other factory, it was neat and orderly. Whole banks of machinery were idle. In normal times the mills work three shifts a day, seven days a week. Now it was working one shift a day for only two days each week. A temporary slackening due to a shortage of materials, said the deputy.

He asked if I had seen the model of the planned extensions to the mills, displayed in the Blueprint Hall in Jakarta. I smiled wistfully to myself, thinking of the four friendly girls who had guided me that day, and said that I had indeed seen the model and thought it excellent and impressive. "The mills will be four times bigger than they are now, and equipped with the latest overseas machinery." He was seeing visions. "At the moment we cannot begin to build the extensions because the farmers need the land for growing rice."

We finished the tour and were standing at the main gate when the manager came, at the head of twenty other young executives, trotting at the double. They turned into the gateway, in line, and halted by the flagstaff, standing to attention until dismissed in brisk military fashion. He was a pleasant young man, a graduate of the textile training center. He had been to India for experience in mill management. "It is better here," he said. "Nobody is hungry in Indonesia. In India they die while working."

He was disappointed that I had already been around the mill and was about to leave. As we shook hands I wanted to say that I was sorry to see the place running down and coming slowly to a standstill. But while I was still thinking he said, "We are making great progress in Indonesia. No doubt you have seen many of the new buildings going up in Jakarta. Before long it will be a beautiful city. At present we have a little trouble but it is just 'politics.' We will soon get over it."

> In Bandung the Institute of Ceramics has the main task to carry out experiments with various kinds of clay, with several methods of baking, coloring, and glazing them. It has a large staff of young engineers trying out latest methods and mixtures of glazure. Several of them have attended special courses in England in this field.
>
> *Arts & Crafts in Indonesia*

A quiet woman in a white coat, senior instructor in design at the institute, showed me what was to be seen. We picked a way among bins of clay, men grinding and mixing them, students working at potter's wheels and then through sheds stacked with work waiting to be fired. It seemed workmanlike and professional. The kilns were cold. The woman said softly, "We are waiting for spare parts and for chemicals from abroad."

We sat and drank tea, and she said that the institute had done much to encourage villagers to improve and extend the range of their local pottery. The government had set up central kilns and workshops in many parts of Java where there were good clays of several kinds, and a number of young village artists had taken courses in design so that the range and pattern of objects being made was improving all the time. What had been for generations an almost primitive village craft was becoming a village art. Not only that, but the decentralizing of these simple industries helped create secondary employment opportunities in rural areas, raised family living standards, and simplified distribution problems. She said that I should go to the village of Plered, forty miles from Bandung, where I would see a whole community of four hundred families occupied and thriving in the pottery business.

The colonel was good enough to lend me a truck. He said I should start early in the morning and, having seen Plered and its potters, should go on to view the huge dam being built at Jatiluhur. He sent a young captain to keep me company, a slender, shy youth from round about Bogor.

We went north through postcard country framed on all its edges by banana plants. Long green valleys terraced in steps to the hilltops. Water in rice fields reflected the sky and white clouds. Men walking along the edge of the road, each with a hoe on his shoulder, and diminutive women were going to the family fields in groups under wide umbrella hats. Boys flew kites with long, wriggling tails. A fish merchant was coming back to Bandung in his rickety truck from coastal villages in the north, where he had been to buy the catch for next to nothing, since the fishermen have no other means of livelihood and must take what he offers.

We turned off the main road to cross a plain, heading toward an eroded, grotesque range of hills worn down to rough columns and cores and jagged craters, and so came by a stony wadi into Plered, clinging to a hillside.

The houses of Plered are stacked untidily together like a batch of unpainted wooden crates, the spaces between them making a maze of laneways just wide enough to walk through. The most substantial building is a small pilot factory with two kilns, set up by the government to show the people round about how best to develop and expand the traditional pot-making industry of the villages in this district.

The manager of the factory sells a range of clays gathered from the area. He explains changing methods and new glazes, gives guidance on design and advice about extending the range of products. In an open booth across the laneway is a display of these village potters' virtuosity, a variety of household ornaments such as were popular a century ago: glazed oxen, dogs, goats, unimaginable birds, modest madonnas (for the tourist trade) and decorous village women with water pots. Then comes a section of domestic ware, water jars, vases, jugs, dishes, and drinking vessels, crudely utilitarian, roughly-made without grace.

There are forty or more "home factories," each shared by several families; bare sheds with earthen floors, wheels sunk into the ground so that the potters sit on the earth to work, spinning the wheels by hand.

We walked through the village, in and out of houses and sheds, past groups of girls and women pounding clay in stone or wooden troughs as though husking rice. We watched an old man shape huge water jars (echoes of Ali Baba) who said that he was a specialist and worked alone, making five of these each week, and was paid 450 rupiahs for each of them, which put him in a higher wage bracket than a professor at the university (although he must grow his own rice). He got up and began to stamp a mass of wet clay with his feet, grinning and dribbling crimson betel juice from the corner of his toothless mouth. A happy man.

Next door, in a family factory, the ground was spread with unfired work, mostly domestic ware, with five silent people around the edges of the room occupied with the making and shaping of things: an elderly man making teapot spouts (the pots lined up beside him waiting to be made masculine); a boy busy with kitchen dishes, shaping them in a mould; a pregnant girl, detached, dreamily making indentations in ashtrays with one lingering finger; a young man painting pots with lead oxide and being patient with a baby, crawling in the dust, wanting to touch and taste the bright, deadly coloring; and the mother sitting nearby making up wet clay. In a room not much bigger than a cupboard small boys sleep at night to guard against thieves and the depredations of rats.

The home-factory kilns are simple brick ovens fired with wood, the temperature guessed at or known by instinct, for this is an ancient trade. The good work of the government men will perhaps help raise standards and widen the variety of articles made, but until there is money available for new equipment, controlled-temperature kilns, and materials for modern glazes, the industry will stay geared to the primitive means and materials which have always been close at hand.

It is the same with other community industries: in villages

where people make roof tiles, building bricks, earthenware drain pipes; where they shape and stamp out simple cutlery from scrap metal, furniture from rattan, lamps from strips of tin. The pattern of domestic industry is traditional and the people are receptive and ready for improvement, but the country is still geared to a peasant economy; there is a gap at this level between ambition and capacity.

But climb the weather-worn heights behind Plered, and on the other side look down into the Tjitarum Valley to see the twentieth century at work: the huge, raw wedge of the Jatiluhur Dam rising out of the river to span twelve hundred meters (3,937 feet); and the concrete towers of the power station rising higher than any mosque. Great gray-brown scars on the ground, mountains eaten away by machinery, rock faces shattered and collapsing in thick slices, followed by the roar and wind blast of explosions. Power shovels, caterpillar tractors and traxcavators, motor graders, fifty-ton rollers, all the paraphernalia of modern technology mercilessly tearing at the earth's surface. And over it all, like banners, fly long intertwining plumes of dust thrown up by mammoth dump trucks (each one lugs thirty tons in a single loading) as they take the earth away on figure-eight traffic tracks to dump it elsewhere: men reshaping the landscape to meet man's needs.

French firms are doing the job on contract; and for each French engineer and technician there is an Indonesian counterpart (they are sensitive people, unhappy at having to call in foreigners to do these jobs, anxious to seem already capable). There are tensions in spite of politeness on both sides, and the work falls behind. But it is big, and when done will change the way of life of millions of West Javanese.

Wet-season flood waters will be directed into an irrigation system which will water half a million acres of farmland. Two crops will grow where one grew before, adding three hundred thousand tons of rice each year to the West Java crop. Seven hundred million kilowatt hours of electric power will fan out through Bandung and Jakarta; already the pylons begin to stride over the hills toward the capital. The potters of Plered will have their power kilns; fish will swim in three thousand million cubic meters of stored water; Jakarta will have sanitation; there will be a peoples' holiday center here at Jatiluhur, with water skiing; and the President, on his monument in the middle of Freedom Field, will be flood lit all night long without dimming the people's household lights.

Ten thousand villagers (*Gotong Royong*) helped dig the main ditch which takes the water to their fields and on to Jakarta. An army civic mission unit played its part. The Indonesian engineer in charge of the whole operation, a graduate of Bandung, says that eleven thousand laborers are employed on the project and that work goes on twenty-four hours a day, the only kind of "rock-around-the-clock" permitted by the President—he laughs as he says this, in case I misunderstand that he is joking. There is a little lag in the work at the moment because the Bung has ordered that some equipment from Jatiluhur (and elsewhere) be transferred for a while to help fix up roads in Jakarta and Bandung before distinguished foreign visitors arrive for the tenth anniversary of the Afro-Asian conference.

Standing there, looking down on this, I found it strange to reflect that not so far away, a little eastward, the remains of Pithecanthropus erectus were first found, the Java man—the missing link—who walked upright half a million years ago when Europe was under ice and these hills were high mountains covered with jungle. He hid from the saber-toothed tiger here in these hills, and hunted primitive pachyderms where bulldozers and dump trucks change the face of nature. One becomes dumb, awe-struck by the achievements of this twentiety-century civilization in which we live; the capacity and magnitude of the mind of modern man, descended from the same stock as Pithecanthropus, who was half ape. But one is horrified and struck dumber still by modern man's capacity for a stupidity so fantastic that, having come this far, his survival is allowed to swing on the whim of any idiot who can press a button.

We went to the dam and were permitted to lunch at the Frenchmen's canteen and suffer the agony of having to choose between three French dishes after months of cold, unsalted, clammy rice laced with taste-destroying chilies, and a glass of red wine instead of cold tea. Afterward I went to the washroom and looking out of the little window could see a fine stretch of water in the bed of the valley, the beginnings of three thousand million cubic meters. When I flushed the toilet no water came; but the practical French had left a bottle of eau de Cologne on the window ledge.

CHAPTER 16

On the third morning of my visit I left Bandung a little before daylight.

The other eight passengers in the little bus seemed surprised to find a foreigner traveling with them, although they responded promptly enough to my "good morning," and squeezed up willingly to let me in. But once I was settled on the back seat between a youth and a stack of baggage they made no attempt to talk. In any case it was too early for conversation, so we sat mute, each inside himself, knowing that with the long day to fill with each other's company it was best to begin sparingly.

We went westward out of the city, heading across country to Tjirebon, a secondary seaport and naval base; after that we would follow the coastal road to Semarang, capital of Java's central province, where I would stay a few days, the total of this leg of the journey being some 250 miles from Bandung. We traveled by *Suburban,* a small bus which carries a fixed number of people on intercity routes, not stopping to pick up passengers indiscriminately at villages or along the road as other buses do.

The colonel, like all Indonesians, had thought it strange that I should choose to travel unaccompanied, but he understood when I said that only by making myself dependent for help upon the people I met along the way could I hope to begin to know them; only by making myself less than they could I expect to establish any truly human relationship with them—for it seems to me, after many years of living among people of another race, that any talk of real affection or understanding spoken from a position of superiority, real or imagined, is so much wind and rubbish. So he had let me go alone, with the understanding that I would call on local army commanders along the way if I needed help, and that I would return to him at Bandung in two weeks' time and spend a few days with his officers on a field exercise of some kind "to see how we work with the village people."

When we had been two hours on the road we stopped at an eating place to have breakfast, after which we walked up and down, stretching our legs and getting acquainted, then went back into the bus ready to be civil and communicative. Two women and a child sat in the front seat with the driver; three men sat in the seat behind them: a sugar merchant, a young judge, and a buyer of hides and skins for a leather exporting company. In the back seat beside me, was a student with his young brother and the pile of baggage.

The stopping place had been at the top of a dividing range, and we nosed down now toward the coast, through tea plantations and stands of young rubber trees (thin and spindly, yet with the incipient grace of adolescent girls), then came through teak forests and fields bristling with stiff cassava plants to the outskirts of Tjirebon, where we were stopped at a road block.

A policeman peered in at us and asked for the driver's license, which he took and went away with behind the bus. The sugar merchant said that it was a routine matter, an attempt to prevent overloading and the use of unsafe or unregistered vehicles. He said that the whole motor-transport system of the country was in bad shape since currency restrictions had stopped the importation of spare parts. The number of road-worthy vehicles diminished each week, which meant that the remainder were worked even harder and they, too, soon broke down; in any case, overloaded trucks and buses damaged roads and broke bridges, and for these reasons the traffic check was necessary.

The policeman came back and passed the driver's papers to him through the window and waved us on. The sugar merchant leaned forward and said, "How much?" Without looking around the driver replied, "Fifty, it is nothing," then moved into second gear.

The merchant turned back to me. "He had the money hidden in the license. It is better to pay a little. If the driver refuses to contribute to the police funds he will be made to take his bus for a technical overhaul, which will take several days and cost a lot of money. His license will be sent to Bandung for checking, and this might take three months. As it is, everybody pays a little, and no time is wasted." It seemed reasonable until a few miles further on we came to a bridge with broken bearers, sagging so badly that it must soon collapse; and a little further on was a truck so overloaded that the back wheels were beginning to buckle. When we had passed the overloaded truck the skinbuyer spoke.

"You see what bribery does—it just encourages the breakdown of all efficiency and order. It was not like this in the Dutch times. The country is falling to pieces. Foreign ships are coming here to Tjirebon or to Sourabaya because the warehouses in Jakarta are full to overflowing and there are not enough trucks running to clear cargo from the wharves."

The sugar merchant said disgustedly, "Jakarta, Jakarta, there the trouble lies. Everywhere else in Indonesia people get on with their business, trying to build up the country, but in Jakarta they bring us down with their plotting and political games."

The student was wriggling, and while the others went on talking he turned to me. "These old, middle-class men who used to work for the Dutch are all the same, always complaining because they can't make more money at the expense of the people and live like imitation Europeans. They would rather go back to the old times and be comfortable themselves than help us to get justice for everybody. They are worse than foreigners."

As the student stopped speaking the skin buyer was saying, "In the old days we had bread for breakfast and maybe a little meat and jam, but now this is too expensive and we can only have rice. At night we could read a decent newspaper and magazines from Holland and America or England and listen to nice music on the radio or visit friends and talk freely about anything; but not now. The newspapers print only government speeches and the radio makes government talk all day long; it is illegal to complain, so why go visiting—there is nothing to talk about."

The judge spoke, choosing his words slowly. "It is the nature of men to complain as they get older and to say that things were better when they were young, for this is how we all excuse the failure to achieve our dreams and ambitions. Our fathers were able to criticize the Dutch, but now we have nobody but ourselves to blame for the way things go in our own country, and this makes us bitter and ashamed."

I asked if he found difficulties in applying the security and emergency regulations aimed at suppressing antigovernment talk and demonstrations, to which he answered that justice is an abstract concept subject to practical pressures. "In such times as these," he said, "a judge must come to terms with his conscience or give up the job. A thief can be sent to prison for a day or for five years or anything in between, depending upon the amount stolen and whether under trivial circumstances or as the result of planned burglary. But a man with no rice field, no money, and many children may steal simply to be sent to prison, where he will be fed and clothed while the government supports his family. It then becomes not a simple matter of crime and punishment but of dealing with a complex social and political problem in which the judge must do what he thinks best for everybody.

"A judge must also be sensitive to political aspects of justice in these days of political emergency. It is a criminal offense to join in subversive talk, to hold illegal meetings, to belong to proscribed political parties, to read various foreign magazines, or to listen to Radio Malaya. But many otherwise law-abiding people do these things, and if somebody reports them they must be arrested and tried. A man who is not involved politically might be sentenced to a single day in prison simply to teach him a lesson, but a man with powerful political enemies who press the case against him may be put in prison for a year for listening to Radio Malaya. If a judge is to remain in his job and do the best he can for the people, he must know when to bend before political winds, remembering that his job is to uphold the laws, whether he agrees with them or not."

The skin buyer said, "The government makes laws to cut us off from the rest of the world and from Western culture. In my town we had an English-speaking club which met every week to read English and American magazines and technical publications, to discuss them and learn something, but now we are afraid to meet. We had a Rotary Club, but it was banned because the Communists said it was an instrument of Capitalist propaganda. There is nothing left in the small towns for an educated person, only the shadow plays, which are for peasants."

The student spoke up so that the men in front could hear him. "These white Indonesians have the American idea of culture, the culture of *Time Magazine* and Rotary clubs. They forget that this culture [he spoke the word viciously] despises all colored people, including themselves. They are so much in love with this culture that they complain because they cannot get magazines which tell lies about our country and our President. What right do these American barbarians have to tell lies about us, to demand that we stop demonstrating against them when they never cease to slander our leaders? By what right do they claim to be able to tell us what to do, how to run our country, what standards we should set for ourselves? What makes them think that they are so much better than we are? No American will get hurt in a demonstration in Indonesia because we are decent people, but plenty of Americans get beaten up in their own country, especially if they are colored. Let them mind their own business and keep their culture to themselves."

Flat, shadeless fields stretched far on either side, patterned green, yellow, and black with blocks of high tasseled sugarcane, squares of stubble, and patches of fallow land; and across this toylike landscape went a tiny locomotive pulling a string of rickety trolleys of stacked cane to a long white-washed mill built on the edge of a stream. Men in the fields with broad-bladed hoes were digging deep trenches, and behind them women came with arms full of sugar stick for planting. For a few moments there was quiet, broken only by the distant whistling of the locomotive.

The judge sighed and said, "It is not so easy to draw sharp lines between good and bad. Politicians, teachers, journalists, even religious leaders must oversimplify things because they have not the time or capacity to teach people each detail of truth. So they telescope complex ideas into slogans and catch-phrases that can be learned quickly and to which people respond like Pavlov's dogs, without even understanding the whole and complete meaning of the ideas that the catch-words represent. The slogans soon become more real than the ideas, and more deadly, because they are more simple and direct; they do not ask people to think or to examine more than one dimension of a situation. Slogans simplify life and make it easy for us to feel that we are doing a reasonable thing even when we know we are doing wrong.

"Students write on a wall 'Yankee Go Home.' You ask them what this saying means and they tell you, 'The Americans are Fascists and Imerialists.' You ask again what do these words mean and the answer is, 'The United States seeks to rule the whole world with a dollar dictatorship.' So it goes on. Each question can be answered with a slogan and the final slogan is always, 'I am right, you are wrong.' It is the same on all sides. The Americans claim that they seek only to make the world safe for democracy. What kind of democracy do they mean? They are fighting to contain Communism! Is there only one democracy, only one kind of Communism?"

The student leaned forward. "You are right. We have our own kind of democracy here in Indonesia, 'Guided Democracy,' and we have our own kind of Communism, 'National Communism.' We could probably make them work together if other people would stop interfering and making trouble. The Americans try to justify their aggression in Vietnam by claiming to defend Asia against Communism, but we are trying to defend Asia against Imperialism. And there is more justification for our confrontation of Malaysia than there is for the United States interference in Vietnam. We fight against foreign white armies, not against Malayan villagers."

The skin buyer turned in his seat and spoke directly at the student. "The Communists have some good ideas and they work hard, but they should not shame the rest of the Indonesian people with their childish demonstrations. If we want the Americans to stay out of our business we should stay out of theirs and not try to tell them how to deal with their Negro troubles and things like that."

The student, smiling slyly, answered, "It is the Young Moslems who demonstrated against the United States about racial discrimination, not the Communists. Maybe you get this wrong information from Radio Malaya." He turned to the judge, joking. "How much jail will you give him if I report him for listening to Radio Malaya?"

The judge was uncomfortable. "Our President does not want us to argue and fight among ourselves but wishes us to be united in the struggle to build our country. It is *Gotong Royong* that will solve our problems, not political arguments."

But the skin buyer said sharply, "Everything is politics, even the President's kidneys."

The women in the front seat moved for the first time, nudging each other and whispering; then one of them made a remark to the driver and he laughed and said, "A man can get along with imitation kidneys but there are other parts that he has to look after more carefully."

"The Americans even tried to interfere in that matter." The student turned to me. "The President was going to Vienna to see the doctors and he appointed Saleh to be Prime Minister while he was away, because Saleh is a Nationalist and a Socialist and a smart businessman and wouldn't do anything too crazy. But this didn't please Subandrio, who was passed over, and it didn't please his wife, and it didn't please Aidit because Saleh is supposed to be a Murba man, even though he denied it, and the Murba Party is Trotskyist and opposed to Aidit's ties with the Russians and Chinese.

"But because the American press has to criticize everything that the President says or does it took up this story about Saleh being behind the Murba, and being anti-PKI, and that he is secretly storing away money in foreign banks, and this made the President angry and played right into the hands of Aidit. And suddenly three Peking doctors turn up in Jakarta to treat the President so that he doesn't have to go to Vienna, and Saleh doesn't get to be acting Prime Minister, and the Murba Party is driven underground, leaving Aidit and the PKI on top. If the Americans had minded their own business the President would have gone to Vienna, leaving Saleh in charge."

The skin buyer said sarcastically, "You seem to know a lot about the President's kidneys, maybe you read *Time Magazine*." But nobody laughed, and he went on, "The President never wanted to have an operation in Vienna because it has been prophesied that he will die by the knife, so he arranged, himself, for the Chinese doctors to come."

There was an uncomfortable silence; then the judge said, "Who knows the truth about these things? Most of it is rumor and gossip. It is not the people's business, it is politics. We should keep silent."

We came to a small town and stopped while the driver bought benzine at the bus depot. The women got out and went to the rest room, and the sugar merchant bought oranges and handed them around. A wagonette passed, pulled by a pony, with a man driving and a boy beating a drum. Hand-painted signs hung on the side of the wagonette saying that a film show would be given in the evening by the Department of Information, and the films would be about the Thomas Cup badminton matches and transmigration.

On a hill, behind the town, a tall tree reached up into the pale blue sky, higher than the others, its topmost branches stripped of leaves by flying foxes, who hung in clusters like black fruit along the bare boughs, chattering at each other, then dropping off to circle the tree, seeking another place to hang, complaining with thin, plaintive screeches as they planed around and around on red, angular bat wings.

The women came back and we left the little town, sucking oranges and settling ourselves in our seats and talking more easily to each other. The student said that he had an arts degree from the Islamic University in Jogjakarta but was reading for a doctorate at the Catholic University (although he was a Moslem). Meanwhile he was also helping his mother, a widow, to run the family business and had been to Bandung to get a permit to buy cement. He hoped to be able to go to Mecca soon to do some business and make the pilgrimage—he smiled as he said this—and then to Rome to see what it was like. When I asked how he could do this he said that his family had business connections in Singapore and that "the money could be arranged."

The road was in fair condition, it being the dry season, and we made good time, passing for a while through dusty country with the sea on one side and white-scarred hills on the other. Smoky fires were burning all along the landscape and the skin buyer said that lime burners were at work, that it was an occupation which occupied whole villages in these parts, while people of other villages were fisher-folk. A small boy, emptying himself into a canal, watched us go by. The traffic seemed thicker here (we had passed half a dozen private automobiles within a distance of fifteen kilometers (nine miles)), and the sugar merchant said that people were traveling more since the roads were free of rebels and bandits for the first time in twenty years. We left him at the next town, where he had business with some of the mills, and he said that should I pass through there on my way back I might stay overnight with him and look around.

The farm and village people use oxcarts built like caravans, with plaited walls and thatched roofs and pulled by two oxen which wear wooden shoes to protect their hooves; these make click-clacking noises as they walk. We passed many such carts parked by the roadside, their owners loading timber or stones or working the fields and the oxen being treated kindly, tethered in the shady overhang of the cart roof, with bales of fresh-cut grass to chew on while waiting.

Towards evening, having passed through a forest noisy with monkeys, we came to a car inextricably in a ditch, with two nuns in white habits standing helplessly by while a group of men and boys struggled unsystematically to back it out, the wheels spinning and smoking and the engine screaming, while the men shouted impractical instructions at each other. The driver would have passed by but the skin buyer said that he should stop and see if we could help the nuns. We found a broken shackle bolt and the steering gone. Also, one of the nuns was ill and on the way to hospital, so we took them to the next town, where they said they could get help.

I left the bus at Semarang, which is a city with a skin disease, or so it seemed, for the paint on every building in the main street hung in strips and flakes as though nothing had been done to renovate or clean the city for decades—and this is probably true. But I found a restaurant and had a good Chinese meal, while a boy cleaned my shoes and another came with books to sell. He knelt beside me, handing up book after book silently, holding the title page open and watching my face for signs of interest. He tried me with a space-man comic, then Lenin's *Thesis,* published in the Indonesian language in Moscow, *The Clever Mother* (a textbook on baby care), and a guide to English conversation written and published in Semarang, and beginning: "A Travel by Train—Where you are going for a stroll." And this I bought.

A tiny, wrinkled woman with two stumps of legs terminating in wooden blocks waited at the door of the restaurant, begging. Then a blind man passed by, selling lottery tickets, his free hand resting on the shoulder of a young girl who walked ahead of him. A funeral procession went past, about a hundred men in a compact cluster, many of them wheeling bicycles. The coffin, its curved top covered with a white pall, was carried on the shoulders of six men. As it came abreast of the restaurant the procession stopped and other men relieved the bearers. Two of those who had been carrying the coffin came into the restaurant for lemon drinks and, having swallowed them, went hurriedly after the cortege.

I asked the waiter if I could call a taxi, and he said there were few to be had but I might find one at the railway station. As I was thinking what to do, a jeep pulled up and a man got out and came straight to me, speaking my name and saying that I was expected (the colonel had sent a radio to the local commandant) and would I please come to the hotel, where a room was reserved. Also, the governor of the province would be happy if I would go to his house for dinner.

He lives on top of a hill overlooking the town, with the sea as his horizon, in a big house that could have been decorous in colonial days when it was the residency but now has a domestic air and feeling of family. When I came up through the garden, in the dark, and mounted the wide stone steps, children raced past me calling that I was coming, and a member of the governor's staff came out, and after him a pleasant, dignified woman, the governor's wife, who took me in. Other men, guests, officials, and visitors of one kind and another, sat about the wide veranda, a servant going among them with coffee and fruit juices. Women were setting a table for a meal in an inner room where a young girl was sewing.

I could see the governor in an annex, at a long conference table with a dozen other men, and I watched someone tell him that I had come. He sat with me a little while, then excused himself, saying that the meeting was important but would finish soon, leaving him free to have dinner, and that afterward he would take me to the provincial fair. It was a homely, unaffected welcome to a stranger from the governor of a province of twenty million people. While I waited, one of his staff, speaking affectionately of him, said that he had been a schoolteacher in his youth, a member of the President's Nationalist Party in the days of the struggle against the Dutch, then a town mayor, now governor. It was no easy job, either to fill or to keep, for the province is strongly Communist and most of the mayors and high officials of the district are members of the Communist Party.

It was here and now, on the edges of Central Java, moving closer each day into the heart and drama of Indonesia's being, that I began to understand how finely balanced is the spiritual and emotional machinery of this enigmatic, paradoxical republic; and how cleverly and delicately has this strangely great man Sukarno maintained the equilibrium of a national nervous system that is subject to the most diverse and violent influences. More and more he takes shape as a composite of medieval Oriental potentate and modern Marxist, an identity in many ways unique and, for Western pragmatical minds, difficult to assess or comprehend.

And here is a problem, for in spite of the speeches, proclamations, manifestoes, and syntheses of ideological aims, Sukarno stands before the world as a symbol of a nation that has not yet found itself or its true image, but remains in a state of nature, shapeless as a vagrant wind, as yet no more developed in substance than the models in the Blueprint Hall in Jakarta. And it is in Java that Indonesia needs to create an intelligible and acceptable character for itself, here that a fusion must first take place between the revolutionary ardor of the Communists, the traditional patriotism and loyalties of the Nationalists, the religious disciplines and social order of the Moslems, and the modern sense of efficiency and practicality of the armed forces. It is here that the key struggle for Indonesia goes on, behind the smokescreen of Malaysian confrontation and the stage-managed divertissements of the capital.

The people of Central Java have elected Communists to public office all over the province, as mayors, councilors, members of the national parliament; Sukarno has appointed a Nationalist governor above them; the army keeps a crack paratroop battalion in Semarang; the principal religious universities are at Jogjakarta, which was the revolutionary capital in the early days of the struggle for independence and is still the center of Javanese cultural and historical tradition, governed, nominally at least, by the last hereditary sultan. The governor of Central Java lives with a cage full of life tigers.

We went to the fair and walked proudly in the crowd without escort ("I need no police with guns to protect me from the people"), going slowly from one pavilion to another: more models, plans, diagrams, and graphs showing farm and plantation production targets for ten or twenty years hence; exhibits of machinery, new kinds of seed, samples of fertilizer, home-made smoke pumps for rat extermination (the governor gave a demonstration and the crowd pressed around, laughing and cheering him on). He pointed out on plans and dioramas where new dams would be built, new reservoirs, canals, power lines. A new harbor is on the list, factories, a tourist center, railway electrification, a sport ground.

"Everybody can be employed in the Revolution," said the governor as we pressed with hundreds of other people into the Social Welfare pavilion to see disabled war veterans, fitted with artificial limbs, swinging hoes and hammers and lighting cigarettes; blind girls typing; blind men pressing pants; retarded children playing dexterity games; deaf and dumb children lip reading. A group of women sewing army uniforms seemed normal enough but the governor said, "Prostitutes—the trade increases because many young men cannot afford to marry at the moment, but these women must still learn to work for the revolution."

There was a little lake, with paddle boats for the children, and the Semerang Police Band in a rotunda played music left behind by a British Regiment at the time of the troubles in 1945 ("Nothing is wasted," said the governor). The band played, "There's an old mill by the stream, Nelly dear." I was undecided whether to laugh or cry; but the governor hurried into an enclosure, pulling me with him, toward a stage set up against a lath and canvas replica of the great Hindu-Javanese temple at Prambanan. Here we sat, between the police chief and the general commanding the Central Java army, to see an excerpt of the Ramayana played by a troupe of visiting actors. The gamelan gongs, drums, and metallophones overlaid the music of the police band, and poor anemic Nelly was forgotten in the splendid excesses of Ramayana's stylized sex play, bloodshed, magic, and monumental violence. But when the show was over for the night and we made our way out, shuffling through the dust, leaving the debris behind, the band was playing "Auld Lang Syne." It seemed odd.

> "I feel like Dante in his *Divina Commedia*. I feel that our revolution has also suffered all kinds of tortures from all kinds of devils, all the kinds of sufferings of the inferno . . . so that later we can enter Heaven. At present we are still in Purgatory, we are still being purified . . .
>
> Extract from the *Political Manifesto*—Sukarno

As we walked through the corridors of the big district hospital the surgeon was saying, "We realize that we seem foolish in the eyes of the West; that our grave economic problems, the shortages of water, electric power, transport, and the other essentials of modern life, the comparative poverty and even hunger at times and in some places, might all be readily overcome if we would abandon our principles and our philosophy. We know that if we were prepared to admit that we are wrong in our political and economic attitudes, wealthy friends in the West would rush to help us. But this we cannot and will not do because we believe that we are right, that we must follow our destiny, and that our President truly represents the mind and heart of Indonesia."

We looked in for a moment at the operating theater, equipped much as the Dutch had left it. The air conditioning broke down five years ago and is not yet fixed.

"In the Western world science is for the scientists. They work in laboratories, proving that man is cleverer than God, that they can unravel His mysteries, work better miracles, and make bigger bangs than the Bali Agung or the eruption of our own Mount Merapi. In Indonesia science is the servant of the people, and scientists are concerned only with the welfare of the masses." He realized that he was sounding sanctimonious and went on quickly, "We believe that we are on a track that leads to universal human happiness, but we are aware that the West does not agree with us nor understand what it is we are trying to achieve. We are truly sorry for this misunderstanding but there is nothing we can do but go on and suffer if necessary."

This surgeon is not a stupid man. He does not give the impression of being a fanatic, and he is certainly not an optimist. He is a doctor with a European education and degrees. He hates working with inadequate equipment and is critical of much administrative and political mismanagement. But he goes along with the President and with the continuing revolution, body and soul.

"We made the revolution, we doctors and lawyers." We were drinking coffee in his office. "We formed the bulk of the intellectual revolutionaries even before World War II. We were the ones who had received a European education and lived on approximately the same level as the Dutch. When the revolution broke out in Java it was largely directed from the hospitals at Jakarta, Semarang, and Sourabaya. Doctors were the link between the revolutionary leaders and the village masses. Doctors commanded army units and became generals. Today, in the national cabinet, there are five physicians, including Doctor Subandrio."

There is another side to this picture. Before the war there were three thousand doctors in Indonesia, half of them Dutch, and a quarter Chinese or other foreigners. Most of them went, leaving less than a thousand doctors for a hundred million people. The years in between have been full of fighting. Hospitals and equipment have deteriorated, become worn out, and there has been neither time nor opportunity to train replacements for the doctors who went away.

A slim, antiseptic senior nurse walked me through the maternity wards. "We have seventy beds and, at the moment, 102 patients, mostly emergency cases from the villages, whose complications are too far advanced for us to do much about them." She spoke as though there was nothing unusual in the circumstance.

I saw some of them, two in a bed, wearing ordinary village clothes and sharing a single blanket. There is no linen for sheets and gowns. Two doctors average ten deliveries a day besides dealing with their private patients. The nurses are immaculate and their dormitories irreproachably neat and clean. There is some dissatisfaction among them because their food ration has been reduced again.

"I will show you the mid-wifery training school," said the senior nurse. She looked perfectly serious but I knew that she was laughing inside. We went into a room where fifteen trainee nurses were gathered around a life-size female effigy, lying with its knees drawn up in position for an immediate delivery. A nurse-instructor with her hand inserted through the back of the effigy worked a rubber doll slowly down through the uterus, explaining the physiological processes of parturition. The students moved over to make room for me.

When the doll had been delivered and the placenta examined and disposed of (it had been brought fresh from the hospital delivery room to complete the demonstration), the senior nurse sat me down to cakes and fruit drinks and said that these girls would train in general nursing and infant welfare for three years and would then be sent to rural areas to take charge of maternity wards and infant welfare clinics. Part of their work would be to teach village mid-wives the elements of hygiene and asepsis. They were attractive girls, one of them an ex-Legong dancer from Bali.

"At present," said the senior nurse, "there is more reliance on magic than on medical attention when a village baby is born. The mid-wife is called and goes straight from her housework, or from the garden or rice field, to the house where the child is to be born. Her equipment is the traditional bamboo knife and some hair or twine with which to bind the cord. The placenta is kept under the mother's bed in an earthen pot for forty days, with a coconut oil lamp burning beside it. Then it is buried under the floor. In most places our nurses must start teaching the mid-wives to scrub their hands before going to work and to boil the bamboo knives." She said that in the past few years the infant mortality rate in Central Java had been reduced from two hundred per thousand to eighty per thousand. More and more lovely babies. More and more problems for the politicians, the agricultural experts, the transmigration people.

I spoke to another doctor in Semarang, a Chinese, who has been busy in the field of eye diseases, working on theories which correlate the incidence of blindness with aspects of malnutrition, especially in children of preschool age. He has forty-five clinics in Central Java, and a program of research worked out in collaboration with the World Health Organization and UNICEF. He was sick when I saw him, not expected to live much longer, and was disappointed that his work would be restricted by the President's decision to withdraw from the United Nations, but he did not complain or criticize.

I met a woman doctor who had created a milk service for children, teaching the villagers to milk their working cattle and the goats (a thing they had not done before). She arranged a collection, refrigeration, and distribution service with the help of local village authorities (including Communists) and set up clinics where mothers could get free milk for their children as part of a general child welfare and medical service. UNICEF was in this, too, and United Nations agencies kept the transport system going and provided the equipment.

> Continuing his *Manifesto* speech the President said: "After we have been cleansed, we can enter the happiness of the Paradise of a just and prosperous society."

CHAPTER 17

> Surakata and Jogjakarta [have] always been the heart of the island. There lived and still live the true Javanese, the people of heaven's mercy, cherishing their old traditions . . . they lived and live, in their world of custom and formality, a life unintelligible in its inner workings to the Western brain, impenetrable to the Western eye.
>
> J. F. Scheltema in *Monumental Java,* 1912

The Bupati of Magelang (south of Semarang), a fat young man not yet thirty, took me to the top of the great Buddhist monument of Borobudour, where we sat looking out over rice fields and coconut groves toward Merapi, sharp against the blue sky with a thin wisp of white smoke floating like a silk scarf from her shoulder.

The number of her eruptions is unknown but their violence might be measured by the fact that debris almost buried this huge Buddhist monument centuries ago and so devastated the surrounding land that it was left desolate for generations.

The history of Java is so misty that no one can say with certainty what happened at any time, but it is known that Borobudour was built during the eighth and ninth centuries, and that it was uncovered from the jungle and volcanic ash by Englishmen in the early nineteenth century when Stamford Raffles was lieutenant governor of Indonesia. How long it had been buried and unknown—a monument roughly two hundred meters (219 yards) square and almost half as high—is anybody's guess, although three hundred years is the figure most used.

We sat on the highest terrace, on the rim of one of the seventy-two stone stupas, each of which has the shape of a calyx (or chalice) inverted to cover a calm statue of the Buddha. Each stupa is fifteen feet high and latticed so that pilgrims may put their arms through and, by dint of stretching, may drop an offering, a flower petal, into the extended hand of the man-savior who sits inside on a lotus cushion.

The base of this temple-monument is a rectangle of four galleries lined with a sculptured biography of the Buddha from birth to death: his pilgrimages, miracles, alms-givings, exhortations, fasts, and acts of charity. They depict also the successive metamorphoses into animals, birds and fish, so illustrating the oneness of all created things. Three circular tiers rise above this rectangular base just as man, created and animal, rises in stages from lower to higher planes of comprehension, freeing himself from the insistence of the senses and the rashness of passion, to achieve a beatitude of self-purification and truth. Above these tiers, at the very top of the monument, is a huge but perfectly proportioned stupa which might have been a reliquary for a holy fragment of the Buddha: perhaps one of the 84,000 stupas built throughout Asia to contain fractional remains of the Indian savior centuries before Christ. The whole is an astonishing monument to contemplation.

Each year, on the night of Buddha's birthday, which is also the day of his enlightenment and his death, thousands of his followers climb barefoot, in procession, to the top of the monument, carrying candles, chanting and praying, admitting their involvement in a truth too big for man's comprehension. Among the devotees walk monks in saffron robes and women in white saris, making a thin twining chain of candlelight from the earth up to where the topmost stupa seems to pierce the floor of the firmament. They stay all night, uniting themselves through prayer and contemplation with the Infinite, of which man is part and in which lies the answer to the riddle of his being.

The fat young Bupati was saying that when the Communists rose against the government in 1948 (to be put down swiftly by the army) they took all of the town officials, who were Nationalists and Islamites, and shot them in the square. The Bupati's father was among those killed in this way. Then he pointed out to me the plain where, between 1825 and 1830, the Javanese Prince Diponegoro fought many battles with the Dutch garrison from nearby Magelang during five years of determined and spectacular revolution. When we went down into the plain he showed me a few stones close to a village which, he said, was the remnant of a little mosque which stood there in those days and where the prince said his prayers before going into battle. It was his intention, he said, to build a memorial mosque here in his honor, in sight of both the Temple of Borobodour and Mount Merapi.

Diponegoro was the son of the Sultan of Jogjakarta by one of the lesser wives, a woman, it is said, of low descent. The prince was religious and he hated the Dutch, who were infidels and interlopers; also, on the death of his father they appointed his young half-brother to the sultanate, and for this his hatred became harder.

In 1825, after much soul-searching prayer and deep study of the Koran in sacred caves, he raised the banner of revolt in Central Java, and for five years thousands followed him in warfare against the Dutch to such extent and effect that the garrison at Malang was reinforced repeatedly with fresh soldiers from Holland and thousands of native troops from the other islands. Eventually his chief lieutenant was captured, and Diponegoro offered to negotiate a truce in return for the freedom of his friend.

There is a big stone house on the outskirts of Magelang, a low rambling place with a huge portico, supported on slender columns, which covers a marble-tiled patio. At that time it was the headquarters of the Dutch governor. A wide lawn slopes down from the house to the edge of a deep gully in which a little river runs. On the other side the land rises to a level plain edged with clumps of bushes and trees. Merapi dominates the background, and scattered about the lawn in front of the house are stone statues (including a Buddha) and animal sculptures taken from Borobudour and other monuments and temples in the district. At one corner of the lawn there is a large ficus tree. The scene might well be the setting for an operetta.

Historical pedantry does not greatly interest Indonesians. National tradition has been shaped by legends and fables and perpetuated through shadow plays and colorful ceremonies so that any account of local events is likely to reflect mood or point of view rather than a particular devotion to accuracy. What I know of Diponegoro is not out of a book but was told to me by an old man, one-time Bupati of Malang, who lives in the residency and looks after the relics of this Prince who became the inspiration and patron saint of Indonesia's latter-day revolutionaries.

We were on the lawn, looking across the river toward Merapi. "He came across the plain," said the old man, "on a big gray stallion. He was wearing a white *djubah* [robe] and headcloth, and had a gold kris in his girdle. Four of his bodyguard rode with him and one of them carried his standard, black and red, with a motto embroidered in silver thread. 'There is one God and his prophet is Mohammed.' There was a troop of his special cavalry up there behind the trees, waiting for him to come back. They always wore black and were called the night raiders. The Dutch were afraid of them and would not go out after dark.

"The Prince and his bodyguard crossed the river and came up under the ficus tree, where some Dutch officers were waiting to take him to the General. They would not let the bodyguard come any further so the prince dismounted and came with two of the Dutchmen across the lawn to the house."

I went with the old Bupati across to the portico, and when he had found a key we entered a small room in which there was a table and four rush-covered chairs. On the wall behind one of the chairs was a portrait of the Prince on his stallion.

"This is the room where the Dutch general and two of his staff waited for Diponegoro. They sat on those chairs, at that table, and signed a treaty. Then the General went to the door and gave orders for soldiers to arrest the Prince and his bodyguard. It was a trick that the Javanese never forgave. On that day the Dutch planted the seed of their own defeat, even though more than a hundred years had to pass before President Sukarno declared that their rule over Indonesia had come to an end."

The relics of the Prince are kept in the next room—the white robe, the kris, the banner, a great wooden war drum hollowed out of a tree trunk three feet in diameter and covered with ox skin; a simple teapot and four earthen cups such as peasants use; a reading stand with a book resting on it, a commentary on the Koran and the Islamic faith. There is a low bed on which the prince knelt to pray and lay down to sleep.

"They sent him to Makassar into exile, among people who have no love for the Javanese, for this was the way of the Dutch—to set the people of the islands against each other, using Javanese soldiers to put down rebellions in Sulawesi, Sumatra, and the other islands, and bringing soldiers from these places to put down revolts in Java, so that all Indonesia was divided and could be ruled with a few Dutch troops."

In offices and public buildings throughout Central Java, and in other parts of Indonesia, portraits of Prince Diponegoro and President Sukarno hang side by side, the two great leaders of Indonesian Nationalism and revolution. Sukarno, then, is no political upstart but an authentic Indonesian hero, the extension of a legend, who has followed in the tradition of three centuries of other heroes who rose against the Dutch, first on one island, then on another: heroes exiled, put into prison, executed. Sukarno finished what they began, achieved what generations of rebel chieftains and princes had fought for.

Looking at Indonesia and its history from the Borobudour and the Diponegoro room in the residency at Magelang, one is able to understand Sukarno when he says that he did not make the revolution but explained it to his generation, made it clear, brought it up to date, and related its fragmented legendry to a modern political concept, codified its philosophy and aspirations, and created a national unity from its frequently antagonistic components. A man of these achievements is not to be treated disdainfully however much he may remain a paradox to Western minds. It is, moreover, possible that our own vision of history and the ideal future is too fixed, too inflexible, and too limited.

The present sultan of Jogjakarta, a descendant of Prince Diponegoro, lives in the old family palace and is the only hereditary ruler in Indonesia to retain royal status and to head a provincial government. The local council over which he presides is dominated by Communists, and the official handbook put out by the council states pointedly that he continues in his position because his "rule up to now is still desired by the people." He is also a minister in the Jakarta parliament, and a Nationalist (it is said, also, that he has thirty-one brothers although his father died a young man).

The fact that one man can be, at the same time, an hereditary royal ruler, head of a Communist-controlled province, and a member of the national parliament is not so much a reflection of the accommodating tractability of the local Communists or the flexibility of Indonesian politics as it is a sign of the tensile strength of tradition and national sentiment in Indonesia; for in 1946, soon after Sukarno had declared the independence of the republic and set up a revolutionary government, the sultan offered Jogjakarta as its capital and gave the new government his help and protection for five years, until the country was freed from the Dutch and the government of the Republic could set itself up in Jakarta.

His palace is a kilometer (three fifths of a mile) square, the walls two and a half meters (eight feet) thick and six meters (nearly twenty feet) high. There are five gateways, one of which is ornamented with two great snakes facing in opposite directions with their tails interwined. According to the handbook this intertwining of the tails makes the two snakes "feel as one," and this signifies the year in which the palace gate was built. To clarify what might otherwise seem an ambiguity the book explains that "the value which the Javanese give to the snake is the figure eight, and the value given to 'feeling' is six, so that two snakes feeling as one makes the figure 2861 which, read backward, becomes 1682 which in Javanese corresponds to the Western figure 1775, which is the year that the gate was made and the palace completed." The book is written and published by Javanese Communists. One doubts if Marx would have been amused.

The Sultan, Hamengkubuono IX, is pleasant and easy to meet, sleek, Western in dress and manner, such a man as might be successful in public relations. We had a drink, our photograph was taken, and I was led on tour by a servant, through high-walled courtyards and wide pavilions where, for two centuries, the sultans of Jogjakarta have received official visitors and foreign monarchs with all the dignity and ritual of near divinity (glass-fronted showcases are full of regal teapots and other dusty, cobwebbed junk, gifts from visiting kings of Asia and Europe). A royal coach built in England by Victoria's coachmaker is kept, together with the palanquins in which sultans and their wives were carried to marriage. In another pavilion are two great gamelans, each of fifty or more pieces, sacred, played on feast days. Huge brass-bound chests, each left by a dead sultan, contain their sets of personal puppets, used in court performances of the shadow plays. Holy krises rest in shrines with lamps burning eternally before them, tended by virgins who remain from childhood until death in the royal service, offering incense each day at these tabernacles.

Much might be made of such wonders and curiosities, but after many weeks of living in Indonesia my mind had no more room for gold-covered holy krises or for any other of the laborious and affected ornamentation of make believe. Nor was I much impressed with the breathless story of that ancestor whose kris had such prescience and accurate capacity for self-propulsion that it could seek out its master's enemies and cut them down. There is a limit to one's capacity to make do with whimsy.

The immediate reality of a thousand university students using one pavilion of the palace as a lecture room seemed more exciting and significant. I listened to their lecturer, a lawyer, and watched them scribbling their notes on the legal system where formerly sultans had doled out justice or punishment with a movement of the head or hand, too dignified to speak. Flocks of sparrows flew in and out among them, arguing. The voice of the lecturer echoed off the marble floor. I admired, in passing, the red and gold decoration of the carved teak-wood ceilings. My guide crouched down each time he came close to me, a reflex action habituated by the traditional practice of walking on one's knees in the presence of rank or authority. But the students looked directly at me, some smiling, others with simple curiosity and even resentment.

The national university of Jogjakarta (there are several others in the city) has twelve thousand students and is named Gadja Mada after a famous Javanese prime minister who, five hundred years before President Sukarno, saw a vision of greatness and power in a political and economic union of the islands of the Indies and, before he died, went near to achieving this and so set a mark for later patriots and statesmen to aim at.

The empire which he made included most of what is now Indonesia, and the kings of central Java who ruled over it had alliances with China, Siam, Cambodia, and Vietnam (mark these things well). But the empire became soft inside with an excess of luxury and spectacular extravagance, and when Gadja Mada died the writing was already on the wall. Islam was making inroads through Sumatra, and then the Europeans came like predatory ants from all directions with their superior armaments, determined avarice, and flexible morality to erode the empire piece by piece. Within a hundred years this first Indonesian empire had come, flourished, and died; but dying it left seed in the ground, in the hot eruptive soil of Central Java, in the minds of a race of people who thrive on fable and legend, who drink mysticism with their mothers' milk.

It is a mistake, then, to think of current Indonesian behavior in terms of twentieth-century Western political conventions built on pillars of modern military and economic power. Nor is it sensible to look exclusively for answers in Jakarta. Unless one follows the thread which binds Bung Sukarno back to Gadja Mada and the Prince Diponegoro one cannot find any comprehensible answer to the present-day riddle of Indonesia, because the riddle is not propounded in Western terms. It is not simply a matter of, "When is a Communist not a Communist?" Or, "Could the Indonesian army control a Communist uprising?" Nor even, "What is the strength of Islam in this situation?" The Communist, the colonel, and the pious Moslem are likely to be one and the same man.

For Indonesia, aspiring to an adequate place in the modern world, the danger lies in this longing to return to earlier glories, to seek and achieve greatness before all else and at any price, and to win splendid victories over demons or to meet defeat with the accustomed flourish: it is the gestures that matter; cost is of secondary consequence. There is a common saying in Indonesia that a Javanese would rather have a new suit than a full stomach. It will take time for these attitudes to change.

There are three little museums in Jogjakarta, each housed inadequately in a shed. The Historical Museum is a haphazard collection of stone fragments collected from ancient monuments. There is no attendant and no catalogue. The Army Museum and the Museum of the Revolution are housed in outbuildings belonging to the sultan. They contain, between them, a touching collection of obsolete weapons and firearms, make-shift cannon fashioned from metal piping, torn uniforms and worn boots, dog-eared snapshots of guerrilla groups, and a metal box full of grotesque scraps of radio equipment which may have been either the central command's communication system or the Freedom Radio transmitter (neither the attendants nor my guides could do more than scratch their heads in answer to my enquiry). There is a sedan chair in which the ailing commander in chief of the Revolutionary Army,

General Sudirman, was carried about the battlefields. There are his slippers and his sword.

The principal exhibits in the Museum of the Revolution are a small, plain, wooden kitchen table and a low, square, plank bed with a bare framework of metal rods for hangings. The table was used by the revolutionaries for meetings of the cabinet under Doctor Hatta. Doctor Sukarno sat on the low bed and wrote the declaration of independence. One day these relics will be displayed with proper dignity in the National Museum, which is to be part of the Freedom Monument now building in Jakarta.

Meanwhile, this trivial, pathetic collection of debris truly represents the material capacity of the Indonesian people to wage war at that time. There could be no more stark an illustration of the paucity and simplicity of means by which the revolutionary government achieved its victory over a well-armed European enemy.

Objective commentators will say that world opinion beat the Dutch, and that the drama was played at a time in history when victory for the revolutionaries was inevitable; and this is doubtless true. Even Sukarno was unsure at the beginning and it was members of the underground movement, including Aidit the Communist leader, who persuaded him to make the declaration of independence when he did. The timing was right and the victory was won: the barefoot army beat the armed oppressor; the buffalo conquered the tiger as had been prophesied centuries ago; good triumphed over evil, the Prince Diponegoro and all the other heroes of Indonesia were avenged. This is epic stuff, material for extravagant fantasy with overtones of the miraculous; but in the heady ecstasy of triumph there is a tendency to forget that miracles can only be worked when the necessary elements for success are in conjunction.

I went back to the palace at night, and approaching one of the pavilions through a long perspective of columns saw a girl sitting cross-legged on the marble floor in a pool of light, like a lotus flower on a pond, body upright, head bent forward, hands resting relaxed in her lap. I joined a small, indistinct group standing in the shadows, mostly young men and girls wearing the workaday practice clothes of professional Western dancers. They smiled and showed me where they had put a chair for me. They were some of the ninety students of the National Academy of Dancing, their classroom being this pavilion in the palace. The sultan, their patron, had suggested that I might care to watch them practice for the annual examinations.

Shadows at the back of the pavilion showed where gamelan players were getting ready, and soon a single bellsound, seeming to come from far inside the darkness, rippled across the pavilion. Without seeming to move the girl suddenly became conscious and totally aware, like a wild creature surprised, and a few seconds later I sensed that she was moving, although time went by before I saw that her fingers were unfolding one by one with the slow, mysterious inevitability of living things in process of becoming (leaf buds silently breaking open). Then with one hand still resting in her lap, the other opened joint by joint and her forearm began to flow upward archly, while long, thin shafts of sound pierced the dark silence like knives. Slowly she came to life, limb by limb, as we watched, no one moving.

Seen in this environment, separated from the gaudy decor and dress of public performance and the distraction of an audience full of its own life and vitality, the dance took on a pure lucidity of line, a sharpened definition of that which was being communicated. The dancer seemed involved in a personal act of faith, of total contemplation, approaching ultimate unity with the Infinite. There is nothing equivalent to this in the Western artist's striving for self-expression, for personal interpretation, and for statement of opinion or emotion.

Afterward, when several dancers had practiced their examination pieces, some of them, whose teacher had been a Martha Graham student in New York, danced other pieces using traditional outlines but a fresher choreographic grammar to speak of contemporary matters. They danced excerpts from new dances based on stories of guerrilla warfare, a football game, the suffering of villagers during the Japanese occupation.

But the night took fire and left its mark on my mind when a young girl, not yet thirteen years old and hardly formed in womanhood, came forward from among the columns onto the marble floor and with plastic fragility made the simple, simulated movements of a woman planting rice flow like clear, clean, running water.

At the end of the dance she stood, scarcely moving, with a scarf held before her face to signify a woman weeping, and it seemed that the eternal sorrows of the human race hung about this child, standing solitary in the great, dimly-lit, empty pavilion. And I, too, felt myself near weeping for the sorrows that could come to these sweet people of Indonesia.

When they had finished I went with some of them through the palace grounds to a forecourt bounded by high walls, where the sultan's gamelans were being played to celebrate the festival of Sekartan, Mohammed's birthday. The great space was crowded like a marketplace with thousands of people gathered round a brightly lit pavilion ablaze with hanging oil lamps and candelabra holding flares and torches and the lights from scores of food stalls.

The two royal gamelans, one on either side of the pavilion, played alternately, each group of players dressed in the sultan's uniform, tight turban, jacket, and patterned sarong. They had started at sundown and would play until close to midnight without interruption, watched by thousands of townspeople sitting on the ground, while others walked about the forecourt among the food sellers or gathered in groups by the high walls, talking.

The night was warm and soft to the touch, the sky was alive with stars and a slim new moon. Bats flittered about the palm trees in the courtyard. But the slow, desolate, five-note melodies of the gamelan and the funereal thump of a great slack drum gave the calm an enervating melancholy.

A little before midnight a hundred young men wearing pantaloons, maroon tunics, and red tabooshes, came with litters and long poles to carry the gamelans to the mosque, where for a week they would play all night in honor of the prophet. More men came with flaming torches and others with spears, all dressed in the sultan's uniform, and for a while there was the confusion of forming all into a procession, which eventually set off along a winding lane made by the people and led along the edge of the palace wall, past an open bazaar, to an old and honored mosque.

Strangely, at the head of this cavalcade of holy instruments went a quartet of fifes and drums, playing a merry jig that surely must have first been heard in Raffles' time, when the British had a garrison in Jogjakarta and the main street was named Marlborough in honor of that monumental duke (and, strangely, still is). The tune seemed certainly too frolicsome to have come from Holland, although when the British went a squadron of Dutch dragoons were stationed in the palace to be a ceremonial bodyguard for successive sultans.

After the fife band, stepping lively, came spearmen and torch-bearers, then twelve men with baskets of food, then one of the sultan's brothers dressed richly (deputizing for His Highness, who had been called to Jakarta by the President), and the chief Iman of the mosque, wearing white and with a heavy gold chain hung about him, then other dignitaries, followed by the holy gongs under umbrellas and the other instruments of the gamelan carried upon the shoulders of the young men in their maroon tunics. When the procession had passed the people followed after it, but being tired I went to the hotel.

CHAPTER 18

I went for a walk at dawn, when the city was gray and those who slept in the streets were stirring and saw a young woman in rags, with two children, washing themselves with water that trickled in slimy drips from a waste pipe under a house. The children were teasing each other and laughing, but the mother had no smile on her face. I was ashamed to give her money but called the oldest child, put a few rupiahs into her hand, and went on quickly, remembering a conversation I had had with an Australian journalist in Jakarta soon after arriving in Indonesia.

It had gone along these lines:

Author:	How long have you been in Indonesia?
Journalist:	Nearly two years.
Author:	Have you been able to get around and see much of the country?
Journalist:	No, not very much. Most of us are pretty well tied to Jakarta, although I did manage to get to Central Java for a couple of days last year. Just a quick trip there and back.
Author:	Well, that would be interesting. It's the center of Javanese history and culture. Did you see anything of the Ramayana or the Wayang plays, or meet any of the painters and dancers or musicians?

Journalist: No, I went down especially to do a piece and get some pictures about the famine and the beggars. There were thousands of them from the dry areas, blocking the streets of the big towns. I think that Ganis [a Foreign Office spokesman] was annoyed about me going.

Author: Have you been anywhere else in Indonesia?

Journalist: No, everything of importance happens in Jakarta. I daren't go away for more than a day or two, at most, in case anything breaks. But I'd like to. It's an interesting country.

Author: But you went four hundred miles to see the beggars and the hungry people.

Journalist: Yes, it was a pretty good story.

Much is written by Western writers about the poverty and hunger in Java (Asian writers find nothing of novelty and little of drama in this subject, for hundreds of millions of Asians being hungry is as much a part of life as being cold is part of death); and many of these Western writers suggest indignantly that Sukarno is more concerned with building monuments than he is with feeding his people. It would be idle to deny that people starve in Indonesia, although the proportion of hungry to satisfied people in the Republic is much less than it is in India or China and possibly not higher than it is in parts of South America and elsewhere nearer home.

The hunger belt in Java is an area south and east of Jogjakarta where the soil is impoverished, the rainfall scanty, and the population excessive for the capacity of the land. There are no industries. In a good year the people grow enough rice to see them through. In a drought year they go very hungry, the old people and little children die, and tens of thousands of others go begging in the streets of Jogjakarta, Surakata, Semarang, and Sourabaya, the big cities of Central and Eastern Java. It is what the colonel in charge of the malaria eradication campaign (and others) calls the working of the natural law of survival and population control.

The Dutch scholar Scheltema, who lived in Java for thirty years at the end of the last century, referred to the attitude of the colonial government in this matter when he wrote, ". . . endeavoring, after periodical visitations of worse than customary want, misery and famine, to secure progress and prosperity in the island by appointing long commissions with long names, toiling long years over long reports that leave matters exactly where they are." This is no excuse for present hunger but it suggests that the President is not solely to blame, and that Java's periodic famines are not, essentially, an element in the current political differences between Indonesia and the West.

Everybody in the Republic, from the leanest peasant to the President himself, realizes that the answer lies in transmigration on a fabulous scale, plus huge land reclamation schemes. Either would absorb the entire budget of the country for several years; meanwhile, the only people who have anything to gain from "pretty good stories" of starvation are the local Communists, who have a vested interest in seeing that calamities of this kind are published far and wide, especially if the blame can be aimed at President Sukarno and non-Communist members of his cabinet, for by this means the day of Indonesia's collapse into the arms of Marxism is brought closer.

It was a priest, an Indonesian from Flores, who asked me, "Is it a crime to be poor, a wicked thing to be hungry when crops fail and there is nothing to eat? It is sinful to starve to death when there has been no rain for a year and the rice is thin and rats swarm all over the land?" We were riding in a hired jeep, going down to a town in the center of the dry part.

I said, "We of the West believe that the function of modern government is to see that people have enough to eat and can be looked after when they are sick and protected by the law from any kind of exploitation and oppression." It sounded trite and smug, and I blushed as I spoke, while still believing that what I said was basically true.

But he answered, "We had Western rulers here for three hundred years and in that time we starved very often but they did nothing for us. But now there is a Communist council in this part of Java and they gather up the hungry people and take them in trucks to the cities where they can beg or find scraps of food in the markets or can pick up bits of junk and sell it for a handful of rice. Or they can live with friends until things get better."

The driver said, "I came down here last full moon and thousands of rats were streaming across the road. If one was killed by a truck the others stopped to eat it. They would stare with their red eyes into the headlights of any truck that came after and refused to move until they had eaten the dead one." He went on, "The mayor and the police and army chiefs and men from the offices came and helped the people to put poison in the rat holes, but some of the people ate the poison because they wanted to die."

The change in the landscape came suddenly. At one moment we were driving through the green Java of wide rice fields, guardian mountains, running water, a man driving ducks to graze, women in line reaping, a man digging with a hoe, another ploughing; the cycle of peasant life, always in motion. Then over a hill, into a dry river bed, and the land was suddenly desolate. The earth was gray, cracked, fractured. Not even a lizard was alive. There were sparse, brittle stalks of stubble, no leaf on any tree, no green weed, dry rice terraces which had the look of antique amphitheatres in Asia Minor.

In a hollow by the side of the road a group of women with buckets and earthen pots clustered around a puddle, the remains of a lake, muddy, thick with scum. These were the stubborn ones who had stayed through the year-long drought. There was a second, smaller pond, five or six yards long and two yards wide. Children were washing in it and drinking the water with their cupped hands. A buffalo with washboard ribs plodded toward it, dragging a small boy by a halter. The animal walked right into the pond and stood in it. It nuzzled a clearing in the scum and began to drink. Then it pissed. The children shouted and thumped it ineffectually with their fists but it took no heed, only switched its tail as if flies were worrying it. The small boy was crying with shame and rage as he kicked at the buffalo with his bare, clay-covered feet.

Coming to a town we passed a procession of thin, dessicated people scuffling along the edges of the broken road, carrying with them such household goods and pieces of furniture as might help them to set up house elsewhere or which might be sold and the money used to keep them alive until rain could bring the rice fields back to life. Some of them carried their things roped to their backs, others had them swung on poles. A man wheeled a table and two chairs on a bicycle, a second man with a bicycle had window frames and a door. A family with a pony cart piled high were heading toward Jogjakarta.

The priest said, "If they can get to one of the big towns they can pawn their things with the Chinese for rice, and at least there is water in the towns. It is better to suffer together in the streets of the city than alone in an empty village. But if they want to stay here they can sell the furniture and these other things or raise a loan on them at the mayor's office."

The driver said, "The mayor buys up their land and whatever else they have to sell and sends them to the towns, where the government has stores of rice for the refugees. If there were enough trucks they could bring the rice here and distribute it around the villages, but the way things are it is easier to take the people to the rice."

"In Semarang," said the priest, "the Communists have organized refugees into bands of beggars and help them to set up road blocks along the main roads so that they can stop the traffic and make travelers pay to get past. If the drivers won't pay they turn over their trucks or cars and strip the wheels off them. But they only do this in places where the local authorities are anti-Communist, so as to create trouble and make the President angry with them for bringing the country to shame."

There was a transmigration office in the town that we came to, a wooden shed, but few people using it, and these seemed skinny and sad: people making a last gesture of despair rather than of hope—giving up rather than making a fresh start. The man in charge had little enthusiasm for his job and no inclination to talk about it, and to every attempt at conversation said, "You must ask the mayor, it is his business, I am a clerk." I could understand the refusal of this man to become involved beyond the mere business of filling in forms, could appreciate his reluctance, a stranger to the district, to let himself begin to have opinions, to feel deeply, to take sides, to try to work out where the answers lie, to allow himself to become, personally, part of the desolation and aridity.

"He is afraid," said the priest as we drove away. "He is afraid that the Communists will make trouble for him if he speaks to strangers, so he says nothing, does nothing but what he is paid to do. It is not his business. The big landowners use the famine to take a tighter grip on the peasants, and maybe some of them work in with government officials to encourage the people to sell their land and houses and leave the district. The Communists try to break the grip of the landowners by buying the houses and taking over the peasants' land themselves. They say they are helping the people to get land reform; that is why they organize the begging and the hunger demonstrations. Maybe they are doing good, maybe not. Who knows? Communists cannot be trusted."

The driver said, not unkindly, "You are a priest and you must be against the Communists, whatever they do."

The priest looked at him and asked, "Are you a Communist?"

The driver eased himself in his seat and spoke, looking straight ahead. "No, there are enough people who think they have all the answers. I am like the clerk. I do my job and mind my own business. It is best. More people should do the same."

The priest sighed.

I opened a pack of cigarettes, and they both took one. We drove on silently.

We threw a loop around the dry area and, having come east from Jogjakarta during the morning, curved northward in the afternoon with our sights set on Lawu, a ten thousand foot volcanic cone on the boundary of East Java. Near the foot of this mountain there is a village where I could stay, arrangements having been made vaguely by uncertain mail some weeks earlier. The driver would take the priest on to Sourabaya and come back for me in two or three days.

The history of this village begins in the days of Prince Diponegoro, when a certain man of Surakarta (also called Solo after the big river which flows nearby), a trader and landowner of some substance, became impatient of the continuous confusion and unrest caused by Diponegoro's warfare with the Dutch and decided to move to quieter parts.

This man, whose name was Mita, gathered twenty families together, having himself a wife and one daughter, and, gaining permission of the sultan to settle new lands, led them eastward, carrying their goods and chattels in ox carts. They left behind their old landmark, Mount Merapi, and traveled until they came comfortably in sight of Lawu. Their journey, measured in a straight line, was no more than thirty miles, but there were no roads and much of the way was through uncultivated country and dangerous jungle.

Breaking out of the jungle they came to the edge of the plain on which Lawu stands and followed a stream which ran along the edge of a teak forest. Toward evening of that day they camped and on the following day examined the land, its area, substance, and contour. The place seemed suitable for a settlement, having clean, volcanic plain for rice fields, streams to give constant water, teak for building, and a mountain to look up to for encouragement and inspiration. Here they built their village and called it Sekaralas (Flower of the Forest).

Mita's brother-in-law was of the party, a strongman by the name of Wirjoatmadga. He is said to have fought a white tiger with his bare hands and killed it, for which feat he is still regarded as a holy man, his tomb venerated and visited by people with petitions. He helped Mita build a big house of ax-trimmed teak, the planks being each a foot wide and two inches thick. Alongside the house they built a rice barn and behind that a kitchen, stalls for the oxen, and a place for the servants to sleep. In front of the house he made a paved courtyard and set up two brick pillars as a gateway, after the Hindu fashion.

The twenty families intermarried, and other relatives and friends came from Surakarta to join them. Today, after 140 years, the community has split into four hamlets with a total population of four thousand people. The only direct descendant of Mita, through his daughter, is the wife of the present headman, and they live in the house that Mita built.

We came to it by a cart track which we had followed for some miles, and having left me there with the headman's son Jon, a man of thirty or thereabouts, the driver and the priest turned back, leaving me once more among strangers. But I felt in no way apprehensive, for I am at ease with country people, who share the same spirit anywhere in the world.

He took me first to meet his father, who was in one of the other hamlets, a mile away, supervising some business of the rice bank, and as we went he explained this. Because it is the nature of the Javanese to be generous and extravagant, he said, it is necessary for a community to safeguard itself against squandering an entire rice crop in feasts and hospitality between harvests, finding, when the time comes around again for sowing, that there is no seed. It is the custom, then, in well-run villages for the headman to organize a rice bank in which every family deposits sufficient grain, at each harvest, to ensure that it will have seed to plant for the next. When sowing time comes around a man takes what he needs from the bank and after the harvest pays back this amount with interest, so that in normal seasons there is a surplus of rice in the bank. This is lent out at interest to families in which there is to be a wedding or some other occasion for special feasting. Or if there is a rice shortage elsewhere the village committee may sell part of the surplus and replace it later at a lower price.

He said that each of the four hamlets had a rice bank and that his father supervised the affairs of all of them, although the handling of the rice and the bookkeeping was done by a village committee in each case. There were, he thought, about two hundred tons of rice in each of the four rice banks, and this was sufficient to see them through a year of misfortune. When I asked if his father had some special gift or experience in commerce of this kind he said that until his retirement thirty years ago the old man had been head evaluator for all government pawn shops in the district, a position of responsibility and status, adding that the pawn shops were set up by the government to protect peasants from extortionate money-lenders and unscrupulous merchants who before they were established, would advance money on rice crops at usurious rates of interest or mortgage and so turn the villagers into debt-ridden serfs.

The old man, Prijosusilo, had been headman (Lurah) of Sekaralas for the past thirty years, and although the office is elective there had never been any suggestion of replacing him, and it seemed that he might die in the job, for he was now over eighty and frail. Of himself, Jon said he had been to Agricultural High School at Jogjakarta and to the Gadja Mada University; then he worked as a government agricultural extension officer, afterward taking a job as staff supervisor on an American rubber estate in Sumatra, where he married an Australian wife and had two young children, Krishna and Chandra. He had come back to the village to look after the family lands, for although there were other sons they lived in Surakarta and were married to town-bred women.

"My father is an old man, and things are changing quickly. The government's land reform program has become political business, and if we are to stay ahead of the agitators we must use the land more efficiently than we used to." We were walking through the fields, between rice paddies and patches of young corn. Further out on the plain dark green blocks of sugar cane underlined the mountain. "My mother inherited the original family lands and my father had a good grant because of his government job, but land reform laws have now limited each man's holding to seven hectares [about fourteen acres] so that big landowners have had to split up their holdings among those who previously had little or no land. Even so, our family still has enough. My father and each of his four children have seven hectares, and he has an additional ten because he is the Lurah and receives no other payment for the office; but to make this amount of land return the same as the original family holding we must farm it by more modern methods. Where we used to be able to plant part of the land and leave part fallow, we now must plant it all and this weakens the soil, so we have to use fertilizers and better seed and follow a different calendar of planting."

He looked at me. "This might not seem difficult, but you must remember that our whole way of life has been built around the cycle of rice growing. Our social life and our religious customs are all interwoven with it. You can say that the cloth of our culture is woven of three threads: belief in God, the way of the people, and rice. Our religious feasts are fixed to fit in with the planting and the harvest, our marriages take place when there is little work to do in the fields, our health and our prosperity depend on the rice crop. You have to understand this when you speak of changing the ways of planting and harvesting and the timetable of the rice cycle."

He said that Javanese women are more conservative than men in these matters because by custom they plant the rice and reap it, and the act is bound up with ancient fertility rites and beliefs that are part of the thinking of women. In a neighboring village there had recently been trouble because a young man who had been to college wanted to change the rice planting method. This man said that instead of planting the rice in rows spaced evenly apart, the women should plant two rows close together, leaving a wide space between each set of two rows. This, he said, would allow for easier weeding, irrigation, and fertilizing. But every woman continued to plant the old way until three young husbands uprooted their wives' plantings and did it themselves in the new way. Their wives left them, and the village was split in its sympathies and indignations. There were disputes, and many people became sullen. But at the time of the harvest each of the three men produced twenty percent more crop than any of the women.

Jon said he was the only man in the four hamlets to own a steel plough and that he had given demonstrations to show that it did the work in less time than a wooden plough and was easier for the oxen. After this the two men had asked him to buy steel ploughshares for them when he next went to town. He had used fertilizer on his maize and the stalks stood twice as high as any other on the plain and the cobs were bigger; but some women passing by, looking at it, said it was too tall and that the wind would blow it down on the ground. They laughed without malice and said that he was a city farmer.

Rats had been at a patch of young maize and many shoots were gnawed through and wilted. He said it was little use one man doing anything about it and that the whole village would have to make war on the rats and destroy all females nursing litters in the burrows. A boy went past carrying a catapult in one hand and five dead rats, by their tails, in the other. He said that he was taking them home for the cat.

We talked of these things walking through the fields, and Jon said that sugar, grown as a cash crop, brought three times as much money as rice, so that if the rice yield could be increased by using new seed, fertilizers and better planting methods, less land would be needed for rice and more could be used for sugar. He said, too, that he was raising turkeys from eggs sent from Australia and was breeding milch goats so that the children could have milk.

These things may seem trivial to people for whom agriculture is big business, but for three fourths of the earth's people a hoe and a patch of land no bigger than a back yard are inseparable from existence, the only source of food, clothing, self-respect, and position in society. It is all that stands between them and beggary, and the Communists make land reform their main political platform in rural areas. In the cities they demonstrate against the United States and Britain, but the issues mean nothing to a farmer whose enemies are the landlord, the Chinese merchant who holds a mortgage on his rice crop, and the local officials who collect taxes and bribes. So in rural Java the Communists organize demonstrations against landlords and student riots against the Chinese and make accusations of corruption against officials who oppose them.

In the abortive Communist uprising of 1948, when town and village officials were methodically rounded up and shot, those of Sekaralas (Flower of the Forest) were on the list; but because the village is remote and far off the main highway it was near the bottom of the list, and government troops caught up with the execution platoons on the outskirts of the village and shot them dead with as little discussion as the Communists would have shot Jon's father and his friends.

We came to the rice bank and waited for Jon's father to finish, and when the last sheaves were weighed and entered in the ledger and the barn door was locked with a key that hung at his waist, we walked back with him through the fields, a mile or more, to his house.

I stayed there for three days and was refreshed with good simple food, a clean and decent bed, talk about crops and livestock, and the bringing up of children. Jon's wife said that village women had been horrified and whispered among themselves that she was a poor mother because she gave her infant children no rice or tea for breakfast but only fruit and eggs and allowed them to sleep alone in separate beds away from their parents. Nor did she flatten the little girl's skull at its base nor have her ears splayed outwards, and this meant that her hair could never sit neatly in a coil at the base of her neck, and when she married her earrings would not hang properly. After two years of watching her grow the village women are still solicitous and surprised that the children are still alive and seemingly healthy.

There is one automobile in the four hamlets, belonging to a rich man who took it in settlement of a debt, but it is used only in emergency or when the owner has impressive business in the market town of Madiun, thirty miles to the east. There are eight radios scattered among four thousand people and nobody buys a newspaper except the schoolteacher, who is a foreigner from East Java and the only known Communist in this community.

In the evening of the third day I sat in the yard of a farmer's house watching the family squeeze sugar from cane. Two lumbering oxen lurched around and around a circle, harnessed to a shaft with plaited palm and wooden yokes, their interminable walk turning two steel cylinders in upon each other. A boy, black with sugar juice, sat feeding lengths of cane between them, watching the sticky sap run into a bucket underneath. Others of the family, and their helpers, were tending four vats set into a mud and brick oven, a skeletal old man feeding the fires with shredded cane while women cooked the juice, clarifying it with lime before setting it aside finally in rings of bamboo to solidify into soft brown discs of sugar.

A row of children sat along the steps of the house, each little girl with a baby brother or sister on her hip, and the small boys darting to the mill every minute or two to pick up bits of sugar and bring them back to share with the infants. Women were coming, in the dusk, to the well by the roadside with pitchers and round pots, and a boy walked by bringing oxen from the fields. A mist crept around the foot of Lawu making the mountain seem an insubstantial image in the sky; everything seemed sharply outlined against the pink horizon—even the red and orange flames flickering from the oven fires, throwing up spirals of black smoke and soft flakes of soot.

I sat among men, beside a little quiet one with a sad face and faraway eyes, and because they used the old Surakarta dialect I could have no part in their conversation, although this did not worry me. I was at peace, glad to be free of obligation, pleased that I did not have to speak or listen or give an opinion but simply to sit and be part of this uncomplicated scene, not searching or explaining, not looking for answers to the things that trouble us all in this age overshadowed by the devil's hand.

Jon said they were speaking of the Wayang Kulit (shadow play) to be performed at his father's house that night, and that the man beside me was the Darlan, one of the most popular in the district, who would be giving the show. The man understood that we were speaking of him and looked at me and smiled. His name, said Jon, was Pak Darso.

When we came to the house for the evening meal there was a screen set up between pillars of the portico, and a lad was hanging a pressure lamp above and behind the spot where Pak Darso would sit to manipulate his puppets. Afterward, when we had eaten, Pak Darso came and took his place, sitting cross-legged on the floor in an attitude of prayer, and the lad hung sheaves of rice at each end of the screen, according to tradition.

The cult of the shadow play is older than anyone knows, rooted far back in domestic ritual to a time when each family kept flat puppet images of its ancestors to consult on occasions of household crises when calamity threatened or strange sickness came upon a member of the family and the elders were uncertain what to do. At these times the head of the family would fetch an ancestor puppet and throw its shadow upon the wall to create a visual presence which could be questioned. Then, in a state of mystical receptivity, he would "hear" the answer and speak it and so give the family guidance. The custom extended into community use; and the handling of the puppets became an occupation set apart, a minor priesthood, and it remains so, although the Darlan (whose title means "unfolder of wisdom") is now as much an entertainer and topical commentator as he is the mouthpiece of ancestors and gods. In this he has affinities with the story tellers, troubadours and morality play-makers of Europe's Middle Ages.

It was dark now and the paved courtyard of the house was spangled with little globes of orange light where women sat beside tiny stalls selling food and drinks and cigarettes, and people coming from the village appeared as black shadows out of a violet night, taking shape as they moved toward the arc of half-light thrown by the Darlan's lantern. As they came they found places for themselves, the senior people and the proud making their way up into the portico close to the screen, others finding room in the dark semicircle of audience forming in the courtyard itself, facing toward the front of the house. Small boys went round to the back of the screen where they fell upon each other like pups in a heap and went to sleep, while the girls stayed with their mothers in front of the screen.

A place had been kept for me immediately behind the screen with old Prijosusilo and his matriarchal wife and a few other people closely connected to the family by ties of blood or long friendship, and we had a table with sweetmeats, nuts, and lemonade within reach. But as there is no audience formality attached to the Wayang, no starting time or obligation to stillness or silence, I was free to move about and did so.

A small gamelan of seven instruments grouped behind Pak Darso made desultory sounds while he, having done with his prayers, was setting out the puppets, dipping swiftly into a deep chest to take them up, reciting at the same time their names and their part in the story that he would soon tell. Each puppet he set to the left or right of the screen according to its being "good" or "bad" in character, sticking each one firmly by its pointed stick-handle into a length of banana stalk set at the bottom edge of the screen.

He worked quickly, shuffling the flat leather images from hand to hand, selecting those needed for the story he had in mind to tell, and setting them in line according to the order of their appearance on the screen. Some he seemed to treat with more respect than others, bowing over them for a moment as he held them in his hand, and whispering a prayer or invocation before setting them in line among the others.

His wife sat behind him, a slim, sharp-featured woman with an intelligent face, suckling a child while she played one of the gamelan instruments with her free hand. She paused in her playing to shift the baby to the other breast, then lit a cigarette which she passed to her husband across his shoulder, placing it between his lips while he continued with his ritual. The Communist schoolteacher sat near the screen, at a table set to one side for the use of such village dignitaries, and I joined him for a while.

Seeing in me one of his own kind, a city man among peasants, he confided that the people of Sekaralas were backward, using the word "reactionary," and said that they were narrow, superstitious, and had no sense of solidarity with the peasants and working classes of the rest of the world. "They have lived so long in isolation," he said, "that they cannot understand that they are being exploited by the old landowners working hand in hand with corrupt officials." He helped himself to rice cakes and accepted a glass of coffee from one of the girls from the kitchen, then spoke about the necessity for a complete redistribution of land, and told me of an official in the district who had been found out in the matter of accepting bribes from big landholders and falsifying the register so that those who paid him could retain more land than that to which they were entitled.

"This man," he said, "was greedy, mean, and vain. He took money from all who would offer it for any shady business and with the money bought gold pieces and hid them in his house. But being a vain man he also bought many splendid rings for his fingers and displayed them foolishly like a stupid woman. He was found out in his doubledealing and put in prison, but when they came to take him to the courthouse he had hanged himself with strips torn from his shirt. In his house the police found forty-five million rupiahs in money and gold pieces, and they confiscated this and distributed it among the village committees.

"Soon afterward his wife called together some of this man's friends to discuss matters of business, and while they were talking the hand of her dead husband appeared before them on the table, and his voice came out of the air, saying, 'Look at my beautiful rings and remember what happened to me,' whereupon the widow died immediately of fright." I waited for him to laugh or to show some sign that this was a jest or a parable, but he shook his head reflectively and said, "It is difficult to change the ways of this generation, but the children will know better who their enemies are."

The Darlan embarked upon a prologue and introduced from among the "good" characters on the right side of the screen a king in conversation with his prime minister. He sketched out quickly the gist of their discussion and the direction of the plot, holding the puppets in such a manner as to make their shadows fall upon the screen, and by articulating their arms made them strike attitudes and postures simulating pride, arrogance, servility, and boastfulness. The king made his exit upward, toward heaven, while the prime minister went more conventionally into the wings. Other characters appeared: evil spirits coming and going at the bottom of the screen; villains making their entrances and exits at the left; a cavalcade of heroes and scoundrels, kings, their families and retinues, great fighters, funny servants, mystical birds and animals. The Darlan brought each to life, giving it character and personality, putting words into its mouth and passion into its actions, while at the same time improvising dialogues interspersed with topical allusions and directing the players in the gamelan behind him.

There are, I was told, some five thousand Darlans in Java, all artists of varying degree, all virtuosos, able to create and act a part for each shadow character in the play, to make a voice for it, a style of action, to relate it to experience and nature. Each Darlan weaves on his flimsy screen a tapestry of his own attitudes toward the eternal tragicomedy of life.

Like priests and schoolteachers they belong to the people, till their own fields, and take part in all things that effect the village. Yet their capacity sets them apart—the authority of their knowledge of all the legends and ancient texts (the lontar-leaf stories); their understanding of the mystique and morality of situations and attitudes; their sense of poetry, rhetoric, and rhythm, wit, and repartee; the calculated crudity of their earthly village humor set in mocking counterpoint to the pomposity of kings and other creatures of comic, insubstantial superiority. Through the long years of the Dutch occupation the Darlans played the part of prophets, kept the people in touch with the past, spoke against oppression with the authentic voice of their ancestors, kept up a mockery of foreign authority and a certain hope of ultimate freedom.

I went back behind the screen and watched Pak Darso tell his story with shadow characters to which he himself gave life and set them strutting, making speeches, hatching plots, disclosing motives—inventing an imaginary world and filling it with people of his own devising—and I remembered what had been told to me months ago in Jakarta, "Sukarno is the great Darlan, and we are all characters in his Wayang, his shadow play. We have no existence beyond that which he imagines for us. He directs our actions, speaks for us, conjures up demons for us to fight, shows us visions of glory hardly understood."

This man, close to the palace group, described how sometimes the President sits all night with his guests, watching the Wayang: How mentally he matches the situations of the shadow play with those of the contemporary political scene, finding parallels in plot and action and reaction, matching the characters on the screen to his own friends and enemies, projecting each shadow protagonist into some living hero or villain involved in the complex modern melodrama of which he is himself a principal author, as well as the central character.

Sitting among his followers, watching the shadow show, he weaves the speeches that have cast a spell about his people, using the poetical, magic, imaginative language of the Darlan, twisting together words of godlike wisdom and the common humor of the clown, a pastiche of philosophy, pathos, and slapstick, the old stuff of story and legend that the villagers understand. His story is the epic of the Revolution. He, himself, becomes the mystical king, the ancestral shadow speaking with the voice of authority, the ancestor-god, central figure of Indonesia's mythology and history, hereditary leader of the people against the foreign forces of evil.

Pak Darso made a number of quick passes across the screen with a puppet representing a soldier and so signified an army marching to war. At the same time, the king, riding on the back of the mystical Garuda bird (Indonesia's emblem), went to heaven to consult with the gods. A miter-shaped emblem appeared in the middle of the screen to indicate a change of scene. Jon's mother came to us with little cakes of rice mixed with nutmeg and the brown sugar of the village. The clashing of the gamelan as the army went off to war woke the boys sleeping around our feet.

They sat up and chattered, then lay down again and went back to sleep.

The old Lurah, like a dignified wraith, came from the shadows to sit with us. Earlier, I had seen him speaking with the schoolteacher, and now I asked him, diffidently, if he found it easy to entertain a Communist in his house, knowing that once they would have killed him in cold blood without a qualm and, if events moved in that direction, might try again and would do violence to him and his whole family.

His wife came and stood beside him and motioned a girl to bring coffee. He smiled up at her and then looked at me and said, "Day is day and night is night, and life and death go together as do good and evil, and we must learn to live with them both. This is what many Western people do not understand. They think that evil can be destroyed, forgetting that the act of destruction can be evil in itself and sow more evil. We are all characters in a shadow show, and we play the parts that are given to us. Only the Darlan knows how the story will end."

I watched for another hour but became tired and could not follow so I went to bed but could still hear the gamelan in my sleep. And when I woke before dawn the Wayang was still going. Soon after daylight I got up and outside found Jon and two neighbors going to the fields to plant sugar. I went with them, shaking a scorpion out of my shoe before setting out. The sun shone on the top of Merapi, and everything was beautiful.

CHAPTER 19

Extract from a letter
The Hotel Dana
Surakarta

Searching as usual for sympathy, I draw your attention to an extract from the notice that is taped to the shaving mirror in my room in this hotel.

> *Regulation* 4: It is the tabu here to fetch a prostitute at the hotel in accordance with the State Law 10/52.

The delicacy of the prohibition is perhaps better understood when one discovers that the hotel was previously the palace of the sultan of Solo's eldest son, Prince Dana, and that my room is in the wing occupied in less inhibited times by the prince's concubines—or so I am told by the professor of literature from the university here, who is also a member of the Town Council and has been appointed to guide me as required.

Across the street is the People's Cultural Center which, before the revolution, was the sultan's pleasure garden, open to the public on feast days upon payment of small entrance fees from which the wages of the concubines were paid. On these occasions the sultan and his women sat in a pavilion on the lake, richly dressed and ornamented, while the royal gamelans played; and when the people were satisfied with gazing at His Highness and the ladies they were permitted to view the birds and animals in the royal zoo and afterward to watch Wayang stories played by actors in the royal theater.

According to my guide, who is a good but lugubrious Communist, the sultans of Solo were always "collaborators and lackeys of the Imperialists" and even sent troops to help the Dutch against neighboring Prince Diponegoro and later patriots. It is not surprising, then, that at the first general election after the revolution, when there was a sixty percent Communist vote, the people immediately petitioned the government to abolish the sultanate.

The Town Council took over the royal pleasure garden, adding a cinema and cafeteria to the zoo and theater, and now, instead of the royal gamelan playing on feast days, loudspeakers howl and shout from morning until midnight everyday, interspersing recorded music with propaganda, public announcements, and relays from the state radio station. The sultan has become a colonel in the army and, having lost the revenues from the pleasure garden, cannot presumably afford to keep as many women as before; but in any case army regulations permit only one wife per soldier so the problem is solved for him.

When I booked in at the hotel yesterday, at noon, the loudspeakers in the Cultural Center were going full blast, and the voice of Doctor Subandrio, speaking in Jakarta, boomed from across the street. While I stood at the desk registering, I learned two new words from him, *Nefos* and *Oldefos* (cross my heart), meaning "New Emerging Forces" and "Old Established Forces."

The main railway line runs along the edge of the street, across from the hotel, and a locomotive whistle cut off the rest of the doctor's speech. It was a troop train, taking local volunteers to join the "Crush Malaysia" forces in Borneo. The boys in the train were leaning out of the window singing and shouting jokes to their friends standing around the gates of the Cultural Center. When the train had gone Doctor Subandrio had finished speaking and another voice was saying that President Sukarno has been proclaimed Champion of Islam and Freedom.

I was sorry to hear, a little later, from a businessman who had the next room, that Sukarno has ordered the nationalization of the oil companies. I know that this is quite logical in terms of the Wayang way of life, but if foreign experts at the oil fields and refineries find it impossible to work under the new management and leave Indonesia, the economic state of the country will become worsened, and the people will be asked to suffer still more heroically for the Revolution —although the President has lately said that "economics are for the people, not the people for economics."

My informant in the next room also says that the President has instructed that all owners of automobiles must pay a special tax to help finance the Malaysian operation. This will be a blow to many government officers in Jakarta who have been stationed abroad and who brought back automobiles which they can scarcely afford to run on their local salaries. I expect the Chinese merchants will buy them cheaply as a means of investing their surplus cash, for no one hoards currency or puts money in the banks any more.

I came to Surakarta yesterday, from the village of Sekaralas, and am making my way back to Bandung to stay for a few days with the army before returning to Jakarta to begin the last of these journeys.

I am glad that I decided to go to Sulawesi, Bali, and Sumatra before traveling through Java, for had I started here I would have traveled pessimistically the rest of the way and in the other places would have been suspicious of the people's faith in the future and sceptical of their present enthusiasms. Even though I have seen much that is beautiful and exciting in Java I feel that the island as a whole carries the brand of tragedy and gives off an air of hopelessness. It is like being in a house where somebody is dying of a horrible illness in a room upstairs. Members of the family wear brave, blank faces and go about their business as though nothing is wrong. No one mentions that there is sickness in the house; but the secret keeps showing through in supersensitive reactions to chance remarks, in unguarded references, and in a vague smell of decay that no deodorants can completely obliterate.

From now on I am impatient to get home; there is too much pity creeping into the affection which I feel for these people and soon it will become apparent. When that happens we will stop being honest with each other. Whatever they tell me and whatever I write will have little of genuine simplicity and less of true wonder in it. Pity is a poison.

Last night, in the ruins of the great temple complex of Prambanan, between here and Jogjakarta, I watched a spectacular performance of one of the Ramayana episodes presented as a formal ballet on an enormous stone platform in front of a flood-lit temple; a marriage of Indonesian culture and Western theatrical techniques, the brain child of Surakarta's leading surgeon, Doctor Suharso, who is a much-traveled man and a devotee of the Radio City Music Hall Rockettes in New York.

Four thousand people filled stone tiers overlooking the stage. The flood-lit temple, a thousand years old, towered in the background. Two complete gamelans and sixty singers made music in raised enclosures on either side of the backstage center entrance (a high flight of steps leading into a gateway). Two hundred dancers, dressed gorgeously, went through the grotesque, strutting representation of two armies opposing each other, and between the armies a girl and a young man (more exquisite, even, than she) made love balletically, with movements of eye, hip, and finger, each with one foot upraised and arms held geometrically.

I sat with the surgeon and his wife. They were entranced, leaning forward all the time, their eyes alight with love, watching the beautiful young man with the golden earrings, the winged helmet, and a quiverful of arrows. "He is lovely," said the surgeon, and his wife smiled—the boy is their son. He is going to be a plastic surgeon.

The Ramayana ballet performs for six nights during the week of the full moon in the four dry months of the year (July through October), and according to the souvenir program, "Each performance revives an epic of the glorious and mighty national culture . . . performed beneath a silvery tropical moon against a background of the mighty Civa shrine and Mount Merapi." It makes a remarkable and moving spectacle but I thought the presentation too sophisticated for the material, and felt that it lacked the drama and integrated reality of a village performance.

When it was done, and I had met the boy and praised the producer and his assistants, they brought me back to Surakarta, a matter of thirty miles, with Mount Merapi seeming bigger and even more omnipotent by moonlight than by day. On our way the surgeon said that if I want to write the truth about Indonesians I must first try to understand the factors that have combined to make the national character.

I agreed but, suspecting that this is his hobbyhorse, said that if he were willing and had time tomorrow we might speak of these things; so we have made an appointment for the morning. He brought me to the hotel and has not long gone, leaving me sitting on the edge of my bed on this soft white moonlight night, in an aura of superannuated concubines and a notice underlining State Law 10/52.

It is good to be heading in the direction of home.

M.

> Under the traditional feudal and colonial rule something was missing from every Indonesia—*dignity*—we all felt it, whatever one's personal achievements were, just as Negroes in America feel it.
>
> *President Sukarno*
> Quoted in Conversation

"You must understand, first of all, that there have been three basic historical influences on the Indonesian character." We were sitting comfortably in cane chairs on a stone-paved terrace, at the back of Dr. Suharso's home: the doctor, his wife, a constitutional lawyer (a gray-headed man of seventy or more), and myself. An old house-maid served us in traditional manner, on her knees, with coffee and fruit. As Dr. Suharso spoke, his wife and the lawyer exchanged nods and smiles as though they had watched the thesis take shape over the years, had heard it whittled and chipped by repeated argument to its present state of refinement.

"First there is the Hindu influence with its mysticism and the deliberate rejection of material ambition and possessions. The aspiring to nirvana, and a happiness that is achieved by ridding oneself of desires of any kind. This influence is responsible for the element of impracticality in the Indonesian character.

"Then there is the influence of Islam—the Will of Allah—an acceptance of the inevitability of things, and a belief that happiness is to be found in being satisfied with 'what is.' The creed of 'austerity in this life and houris in heaven.'

"On top of these two there is the third and contradictory influence, the legacy of the Dutch and the insistent example of the Americans and Russians, which inspire a 'will to achieve'—to conquer nature and to overcome all physical difficulties."

I said, paraphrasing the professor of literature who had been with me during the day, "There you have a portrait of the President, whose mother was Hindu-Balinese, his father an Islamite of Java, and his messiah, Karl Marx. But on top of the influences you have mentioned you must add a general belief in demons, wizards, witchcraft, astrologers, ancestral spirits, necromancy, hobgoblins of all kinds, and a multitude of gods, good and bad."

"In spite of your sophistication," said the lawyer, "you people of European stock also retain many ancient delusions left behind by successive waves of influence." His manner was urbane and there was a smile in his eyes. "For instance, you persist in believing that God was originally a Jew who became converted to Christianity and, even more strangely, that He has a white skin. And from this deduce that white-skinned people are more refined than those with yellow or brown skins, and that these in turn are more refined than people with black skins. Then, stemming from this folk fable, come hundreds of curious beliefs such as that which says that if a man is baptized with water he will go to heaven, but a man who is circumsized will go to hell. There are many such fantasies in which millions of white people believe implicitly and which we

Asian peasants know to be ridiculous. You believe, for instance, that money is a measure of merit, and poverty is either sin or a crime; that education is the equivalent of wisdom; you not only believe that might is right but that right is essentially white, that history has become rigid and that you will always be on top."

He brushed the cigarette ash from his vest and grinned amiably. "As a matter of fact I suspect that it is some deep-down instinct for self-preservation that is driving you white people to find a way to the moon, where your remnants may survive to plant your seed when we brown and black people have overrun your world."

I protested that he was leading us away from the point of the discussion, which was to help find some formula with which to decipher the pattern of paradox that Indonesia displays to the Western world. "Do we have to believe," I asked, "that Indonesia cannot help itself, that hereditary influences have the nation in chains, that it is like a deliquent adolescent who blames its parents for failure to cope with adult life or face responsibilities? Is there no other explanation for these seeming contradictions—the gentle courtesy and the organized violence, the personal affection and the public hate, the high-sounding resolution and the sad muddles of reality? Are the windy, belligerent speeches some form of political masturbation?"

The lawyer pursed his lips, looked over his spectacles and scratched his left temple thoughtfully. I was aware that I had been rude and waited to be reproved. When he spoke he said, "You suggest that I am leading us off the track. You believe that the answer to your confusion lies entirely in the enigma of our Indonesian ego. No, my friend, I do not lead you astray. I merely ask you to analyse the position from which you view us, to check your own myopia or, as your own prophet said, take the speck out of your own eye before you look for the beam in ours." Then he grinned again and said, "I also have been a Christian."

The surgeon, my host, to save me from embarrassment, began to speak of his work in the field of rehabilitation, saying that the desire to fit maimed and crippled bodies into the active pattern of society was a minor aspect of the revolution that has taken place in mankind's thinking during this twentieth century—a kind of penitential reaction to the sadistic and cynical violence of World War II, the mass executions, the gas chambers, and the atomic bombs.

His theory was that the grotesque excesses of two world wars so shocked the West that, for its own preservation, it devised the Atlantic Charter and agreed to the dissolution of its colonial empires and the unchaining of Asia and Africa. These actions and reactions have let loose a wave of creativity that, until it is harnessed, will continue to bring its own kind of confused violence and moral chaos.

"We live in an age," he said, "when the latest marvels of the West become obsolete before the people of Asia and Africa achieve them. We live in an age when the West rushes ahead materially at the speed of light but remains politically and philosophically in the age of the horse and cart.

"You people of Europe and America do not understand what is happening in Asia and Africa except in terms of your own self-interest. You are obsessed with preserving your system of living off the rest of the world. You do not really believe in equality except in the way that an English vicar believes in the equality of his gardener because they both love roses. You do not truly believe in the brotherhood of man. If your leaders did honestly believe in One-World, as John Kennedy did, then they would try to stop thinking exclusively in Western terms and would aim to match, spiritually and philosophically, the vision of your scientists and technologists. To use another Christian saying, you need to be born again."

The lawyer took up where the surgeon left off (they were enjoying themselves hugely, making the most of a captive audience, and I let them go on without interruption, for they were both men of intelligence and much traveled, with opinions that could be listened to without irritation). "The United States is haunted by Stalin and refuses to believe that Communism can evolve and change as every society must if it is to survive; and the British still cling to their old concept of a trading empire safeguarded by a string of naval bases—hence the Malaysian dispute. Both concepts are obsolete and make One-World impossible. If these two countries would just admit the partial validity of any other point of view but their own, in Malaysia and Vietnam, it would be possible to bring these disputes into the arena of calm discussion."

I disagree and said so, insisting that their arguments were too simple and one sided, seeming to suggest that Britain and the United States were alone responsible for the muddled state of the world. I said that Asians should also bring their thinking up to date, and that any twentieth-century concept coming out of Indonesia or elsewhere in Asia should be an advance on the Wayang way of thinking. "Keep the dignity of your old traditions by all means," I said, "but don't forget that dignity overdone becomes ridiculous."

They laughed, and we all felt that we had gone far enough, and to crown our discussion the surgeon's wife, a physician herself, said, "The answer for all of us is not in searching for ways by which to overcome each other, but by freeing the heart from the fears of the mind. The world's millions must demand human solutions from their leaders."

Dr. Suharso then played on the rebus for me and after that scratched out a tune on a violin. His wife went to her room and came back with a photograph, taken in Berlin, which showed her and her husband with Einstein and Tagore. Looking at it, Suharso said, "That was the greatest day of my life."

Among the many books, pamphlets, reports, and other research material collected during my five journeys from Jakarta, is a nine-page foolscap typescript that I came by, that evening, in Surakarta. It is headed: "Kegiatan PKI Dewasa ini (suatu résumé)," which roughly translated means, "Present Activity of the Communist Party of Indonesia—a résumé."

It is transcribed from notes said to have been taken during a meeting of Communist Party executives called to discuss party policy and ways and means of implementing it. The notes were taken on behalf of an anti-Communist group which has its own members inside the party, at least two of whom were at the meeting. A copy of the transcript was sent to President Sukarno and to a number of anti-Communist cabinet ministers. I came by the document under circumstances which incline me to believe that it is genuine, but as I had no wish to play at politics or be become involved in the domestic affairs of Indonesia, where I was a guest, I made no attempt to search out the authors. The following extracts are interesting in that they indicate the thorough efficiency of Communist Party planning.

Discussing the Indonesian Revolution in general terms, the meeting concluded that "since it was only concerned with a transfer of political power it failed . . . because a revolution must destroy feudalism . . . will destroy capitalism [and] will only be completed when we, the PKI, have succeeded in building a People's Democracy, and this is what we are working for." In order to achieve these objectives "the following actions should be taken:

1. Snatch the leadership away from the bourgeoisie.
2. Imbue the proletariat with the real meaning of revolution.

The power for taking over leadership of the Revolution . . . does not come from heaven, but *must be prepared.*"

Referring to this matter of preparedness, which is underlined in the report, delegates comment on the failure of the Communist uprising in 1948, saying that "Comrade Muso [leader of the uprising] could not integrate the power of the proletariat [and] did not unite the workers, the farmers, and the army."

The party although paying lip-service to the President's *Political Manifesto,* "only acknowledges a Marxist-Leninist revolution which aims at the foundation of a dictatorship of the proletariat." The chairman of the PKI, Comrade D.N. Aidit, said that in 1970 Indonesia will be a socialist country.

Scattered throughout the transcript are references to national leaders and assessments of their value or danger to the party. There is a satisfied note that Dr. Roeslan Abdulgani, minister in charge of all information services, has not been made a deputy prime minister; but the party is even more relieved that General Nasution was also passed over and admits that his appointment "would have been rather hard for the PKI [because] Nasution could have proposed to the President that he go abroad and then he [as acting prime minister] could have forced a *coup d'état.*"

A party member who traveled with General Nasution on a foreign mission at this time reports to the meeting that the general "kept silent in the airplane because he was furious about not being appointed deputy prime minister."

The document makes it clear that General Nasution is the party's pet hate and comments on the coming Revolution in these terms. "It is clear that finally there will be only two forces left in the arena to fight, namely, the PKI and Nasution. The middle groups will ask for protection from whichever of the two they consider the stronger side." In the same context it is suggested that Nasution will try to manuever the PKI into attacking first so that he can then step in as the defender of the constitution, but "the

PKI learned its lesson at Madiun and will not again be provoked into striking the first blow."

Having stated the policy of the party, commented on earlier mistakes, and discussed internal political alignments, the document comments on the extent to which the army is, or can be, infiltrated and notes that "the Central Committee is already working on the problem of the armed forces . . . already thirty percent of the armed forces is Communist [and] Dr. Aidit says that his talks and lectures to the armed forces have definitely increased the Communist influence in the army? . . . the army will not shoot the people."

The situation for the Communists does not seem so rosy among the peasants. "Many of our cadres cannot yet use arms," notes one delegate, while another comments that "the cultural and political level of our members in the villages is not yet of a high standard . . . this must be overcome quickly . . . the training of workers and farmers must be intensified."

On the domestic front it is suggested that Madam Hartini, the President's wife, should be sent to Russia or China so that she might be made more sympathetic to the Communist cause.

There are references to a four-year plan of organization and strengthening of membership, which began on August 17 (Independence Day) 1963, and the document lists agencies through which it will achieve these ends. At the top of the list is the Communist Youth Organization, described as "the right hand of the party; tough, militant, dynamic, and reliable." One of its specialties is the organization of demonstrations. Other in-party groups take care of university students, graduates, workers, farmers, and Chinese organizations which are "the source of the needed funds of the party, and represent the interests of the Chinese Communist Party."

There are interesting references to activity in the cultural field. Certain "nonrevolutionary" writers are listed, and efforts are to be made to "purify" the fields in which they work. There are to be slander campaigns against certain religious writers and campaigns to promote "revolutionary realism and revolutionary romanticism."

A delegate concerned with party organization in the educational field reports that "influence among university students did not have enough results . . . so the party starts now among boys at high school level . . . through sending active members and cadres among the teachers." It is this attention to detail which fascinates. There is a suggestion, for instance, that each section committee must organize "one choir for revolutionary songs with at least twenty-five members."

There is not, and never has been, much real secrecy about the organizational methods and the workers of Communist parties anywhere in the world: the pattern is similar to that taught in Moscow (or Peking or Belgrade, depending upon which brand of Communism you use), just as most religious or international business organizations have an international promotional center and a formula approach, with local variations. Even so I was seized with the sudden knowledge that I had seen, or known about, the kind of things that were mentioned in the document without actually relating them to a clearly conceived and efficiently directed plan. And the conclusion I came to, sitting in the People's Cultural Center reading this document, was that the most efficient organization I had so far encountered in Indonesia was its Communist Party.

I read the paragraph on Land Reform and remembered immediately the people around Sekaralas, whom I had left only two days ago; the Communist schoolmaster there; and the stories of organized begging told to me by the driver who took me down to the dry area. The paragraph read, "Always insist on forming local land reform committees, etc., in order to protect the small farmers [then] if you disagree with the way it is carried out, sabotage should be organized, and the word spread around that the committees are inefficient and oppress the people." It was as amoral and uncomplicated as the lay-out for a sales campaign.

Later, I went to a cheap little eating house, no more than a pleasantly decorated shed, near the railway station, run by some of Dr. Suharso's rehabilitated limbless veterans, and was well fed there as a guest of the establishment. Sitting opposite me, at the same table, were travelers just off the train from East Java, speaking of a demonstration in Malang (south from Sourabaya), where a group of Islamic students had wrecked the offices of the Communist Youth Organization.

The news surprised me, for the impression gained elsewhere was that religious groups had so far seemed unwilling to issue any challenge to the Communists, although there were whispers to suggest that the Imams and other religious leaders could not much longer tolerate the open love affair between President Sukarno and the party and still retain their own self-respect.

Such opinion as I had gathered seemed to be that Moslems had neither a rallying point nor the machinery to achieve a concensus of opinion or policy, while the Christian body was too frail and naked to risk exposure in the arena of revolutionary politics; but if Moslem leadership could consolidate and contrive even an elementary policy, stiffened with religious principles, then Islam could become a decisive and stabilizing factor in the Indonesian uncertainty.

True, one youth group demonstrating against another did not amount to an Islamic declaration of war on Communism, but the train travelers seemed to think that the wrecking of the Communist offices in Malang was a planned move in a game played for bigger stakes than local satisfaction.

I must have looked doubtful, for one of them, a dockyard worker from Sourabaya, leaned across the table and said, "Aidit will complain about this to the President, who will tell Dr. Subandrio to disband the Young Islam group in the interests of public security, but if he does, then all Islamic groups in East Java will stage a protest demonstration." I asked if he spoke from knowledge or if he was telling me a story, but he said that he held office in an active Islamic group, of which there were twenty-six in Java, and that the time had come for them to show openly and with collective strength that they were not prepared to hand over the Republic to the Communists.

"We are with the President," he said, "because he is a popular and constitutional leader, but he needs some guidance." He smiled as he said this, and the café manager murmured, "Sure, he invented guided democracy, so he shouldn't complain."

The man from Sourabaya went on, "He is aiming at the Yugoslavian brand of unaligned Communism for Indonesia and believes that Aidit will help him to achieve this, but Aidit won't because he is a model Communist and will settle only for straight Leninism. Like all Communists he will support anyone so long as they can help him reach his goal. Aidit can see himself top man in Indonesia, secretary general of the party and prime minister, with an old and impotent President Sukarno kept safely in the summerplace or at Tampaksiring in Bali, watching with his women the Wayang or the Legong dancers every night, talking with other old men about the great days of the Revolution."

The café manager got up and went into the kitchen, and I supposed that he wanted to be clear of this conversation, but the man from Sourabaya took no notice and went on speaking. "In this part of Indonesia we are realistic about heroes. We have been fighting the revolution for centuries, and millions of Javanese have been killed since it began, by the Dutch and the Japanese, by the English when they fought us at Sourabaya, and when we fought among ourselves. Moslems and Communists have staged rebellions and have failed for want of a purpose which we could all share."

When we had finished our meal I asked if I might walk with him to the bus station (he was going to his village to be present at the wedding of a niece) and, having said my thanks to the people at the café, left with him to continue the conversation. He told me that he was busy on behalf of the Islamic groups, organizing among the labor unions, and that they had beaten the Communists for control of the union in Sourabaya's biggest iron foundry.

When I asked if this activity went on all over Java he shook his head and said, "We would like to be stronger but there are difficulties. The Communists have a popular policy, good political education and organization, and plenty of foreign money to play with. They keep the rank and file busy stirring up trouble to make conditions in the country seem worse than they really are. This leads other nations to distrust us and abandon us, so that even the anti-Communists in the government are forced to turn more toward Communist countries for friendship.

"We Moslems have no policy except that God must be kept in the national constitution; and we get no money from outside. The Catholics are the only religious group with any political education, and they have to be careful because they are strangers in our midst and if they play at politics the Communists will say that they are working for a foreign power, and they will be banned and their foreign priests put in jail."

I told him, then, that I had spoken to many Christians, and without exception they had praised the President fervently and looked confidently to him for protection, to which the man smiled and answered, "With the help of the Communists the President is

Our Great Leader, Bearer of the Message of the People's Sufferings, Champion of Islam, Prophet of the New Emerging Forces. If, one day, he must decide between these titles and that of Defender of Christians, which will he choose? I tell you, we must be realistic." '

I asked him, "You think, then, that the Communists will win?"

"I did not say so. It's a question of what alternatives we can offer and how soon we can get organized. The communists have been in Java since 1920. They have good office buildings and social and political centers in most towns in Central and East Java. They know what their goal is and they train cadre leaders to herd the people toward it. We are not so sure what our goal is except that it should prevent the Communists from taking over the government of the country. But we are a long way behind."

We sat talking until his bus went. Walking back to the hotel I tried to sort it out: why do we want to prevent Communism from taking over in Indonesia or elsewhere in Asia? Why are we concerned with the fate of these people under Communism when for centuries past, while they suffered under our system of colonialism, we have not cared a tinker's dam for them? Is it that behind all this concern for a "free world" we are really only troubled about our own ultimate fate in a world that is becoming predominantly Communist? Do we need to be afraid? Do we need to interfere? I was finding it difficult to take stock of my own attitudes, and felt that I was, perhaps, tiring more than I knew after floundering for months out of my depth in matters for which my understanding lacks both width and wisdom.

Walking through the dark streets I wondered what I was doing here in Indonesia: why had I come? I told myself tiredly that I had come to find, if I could, some understanding of the Indonesian people so that I, and those of my own countrymen who could be disposed to read or listen, might find them much like ourselves in all essentials; not enemies, not people we must feel compelled to oppose because their leaders and ours are pride-bound to opposing philosophies. Instead of this, I find myself taking sides, dividing Indonesians into good and bad according to divisions and prejudices that have been ingrained in me by circumstances of birth, background and education, and that have nothing to do with the needs, desires, or requirements of any Indonesian yet born. How do we escape this tyranny, break out of this inherited accretion which keeps our hearts confined as if in plaster, which prevents the free giving of ourselves to each other except selfishly, as lovers give for their own fulfillment?

I stayed two more days and went to the Wayang in the People's Cultural Center, then was taken to a village and was received ceremoniously by the social committee. We made decent, honest speeches to each other, full of the longing to be loved and trusted, then inspected a new welfare center with an emergency medical clinic, a three-classroom primary school with an annex for retarded children, and a meeting place for village discussions. The area was a burying ground, and they showed me photographs of the ceremony of digging up the dead and removing them to make room for progress. It was done with much dignity, the village volunteer security force forming a bodyguard for the bones and all of the civic dignitaries in attendance. "We wished to show respect for our ancestors and to let them share in the new Indonesia that is growing out of the Revolution." I inspected the security force and took photographs of its commander, an ex-army sergeant who in stance and manner might have passed for a sergeant in any army in the world. His men are clerks and laborers, seven squads of seven, who guard the village by night and provide the core of a volunteer labor force at other times (they built the school and medical clinic). When working for the village, or on guard duty, they are fed by the community. The army provides a uniform and a rifle, with rationed ammunition. In Jakarta, Comrade Aidit and General Nasution take these rifles into reckoning when they total the logistics of possible future conflict. Aidit says, "The illegal forces in the country are more dangerous than the legal armed forces"; but presumably he is thinking of similar security groups which operate in anti-Communist areas.

Here, in this village the rifles are on his side. "We no longer observe the old religious holidays but keep May Day as our principal feast, and on that day we visit each other and exchange food; we also have ceremonies on Independence Day and on other national anniversaries." The chairman of the village committee is a quiet-spoken, dignified, scholarly man. He sat beside me while we had tea and rice cakes, at a long table, with other members of the committee; then he made a final speech thanking me for my visit and wishing for "understanding and cordial relations" between my country and his. I said that we were simple people, like them, and wanted only to be friends (there is nothing left for ordinary people to say); then he led me back to the jeep that had brought me, passing through a corridor of saluting village guards, with everybody standing back and clapping kindly, until I drove away knowing that any politician in the Western world would think, pityingly, that I was foolish and sentimental and blind to the simple, dreadful truth that all Communists are evil people. But one must learn to live with these ready-made convictions.

CHAPTER 20

Officers of the armed forces have a noble nature based on Budhi-Bakti-Wira-Utama [nature of devotion of the eminent hero] and should constantly maintain cordial and the closest relations with the people, and love them [so as] to constantly gain their trust and support.

from *The Identity of the Indonesian National Army*
(Official Army publication)

The bureaucratic capitalist circle [of the army] are preparing to rob the people of democracy.

D. N. Aidit

One would not immediately pick Paratroop Colonel Achdiat out of a crowd as a man preparing to rob the people of democracy nor, for that matter, as one who compulsively loves the people on any major scale. Standing with studiedly negligent elegance on the edge of the parade ground at the Staff and Command School of the Army, slim, left shoulder slightly lifted, cap to one side, an eight-inch ivory cigarette holder clamped at an acute angle between neat even teeth, he would pass tolerably well for a sun-tanned English film actor of the Beau Geste period, complete with wry, enigmatic smile and ebony-handled riding switch.

I had driven from Surakarta through the night in an army car to get to Bandung in time to join a convoy of officers going on a five-day field exercise to villages in West Java and had reported to Colonel Archdiat, in charge of movement and program, for allotment to a group which would take and look after me. With the usual Indonesian courtesy I had been allotted a place in the colonel's jeep, leading the convoy, and now we waited only for the officers of the course to take their places in other vehicles parked in line along the edge of the parade ground, each with its driver standing by the bonnet.

But the officers, ranking from majors to generals, were schoolboy busy, having photographs taken in groups, calling to each other to "come over here for a minue and be taken with us and smile please Subono, you won't be away long and she'll wait until you come back." Then, "squeeze in a bit, Achmed, and please take your hat off, major; that's it, but wait a minute and I'll take another." The colonel stood smiling tolerantly but looked at his watch while staff-clerk corporals and privates bustled about with lists, begging the gentlemen to take their places in the vehicles. He was called to come and stand in the middle of a group and "now here please Colonel have one taken with us." The smile, each time, merged into a proper similitude of paternal sternness, although he was younger than most of the others.

Another picture, another look at the watch, then a whistle. No more now, we must move on. A little, fat, full colonel with a wheezing giggle scampered about looking for his haversack while the others jeered and cheered, and the man who had hidden it doubled over with laughter. Then we were ready and everybody saluted everybody else, those left behind stood to attention, and we drove slowly out through the college gates. The colonel switched on a tape recorder, sitting on the seat between himself and the driver, and we edged our way into the stream of traffic to the tune of "Bye-Bye Blackbird" played by Benny Goodman.

Weaving through the city we raced a railway train to the crossing in the main street and got through with a drove of *betjaks* and pony carts (like a cow lumbering into a farmyard among hurrying ducks and geese) before the gates closed and cut off the rest of the convoy. While waiting for them to catch up, the colonel filled me in.

The role of the army in Indonesia is complex. It is a security force, an executive arm of the civilian government with its members in the cabinet, and a vital factor in political and social stability. Consequently, its officers must be educated not only in military matters but also in the political ideology of the Republic and its administrative and sociological structure. And because the basic military emphasis (in spite of the Malaysian confrontation) is on local defense, army training is almost entirely oriented toward the tactics of guerrilla warfare and the creation of a system of collaboration between the army and the civilian population.

"This exercise," said Colonel Achdiat, reluctantly reducing the volume of "Bye-Bye Blackbird," involves "everybody at the school. We are divided into three groups, and each group goes to a different part of West Java so that we can get a consensus of experience. Our group is headed northwest for about sixty kilometers (36 miles) and when we get there we will be split again into three smaller groups for billeting among the villagers.

"The purpose of this particular exercise is to give the officers experience in the practical aspects of collaboration with local authorities on the village and regional levels—human, economic, logistic, and social. They need to be able to estimate local resources in these categories and to work out systems of communication and liaison that will make it possible to use the resources effectively in time of trouble."

I had already done some study on the subject in Jakarta, where the army staff has been free and frank with information, allowing me access to documents that made no bones about the army's opinion of its own attitudes and capacities and its present role. One such document, surveying the capability of the armed forces to defend the Republic against invasion, says that in the event of a major war a powerful enemy would soon control the sea and air space of Indonesia and that the Republic would be forced back into a defense of its own territory, which would, of necessity, be confined only to Java, Sumatra, and Borneo, where the "most important lines of communication and strategic materials are located." The paragraph clearly writes off the air and fleet arms of the armed forces as incapable even of defensive action, and it is only necessary to glance at a map of Indonesia to catch the reality of this attitude.

In a paper headed "The Concept of Defense," the thesis is developed in paragraphs which read, "If a country attacks us our best policy is to prevent its forces from entering our nation. It would be better yet if we could attack them in their own territory and strike them there, destroying them at home, but at present we do not have that capability." And again, "If the enemy is moving toward our nation it would be best to destroy him *en route,* thus preventing him from landing in our country. It is possible that this too cannot be done at the present time." And going back much further, to 1960, and an address by General Jani, now commander in chief of the army, to a senior officers' course, there is his statement that "Indonesia could not possibly take part in a war between the two [power] blocs, a war which could break out any time."

This is not so much a serious or reliable assessment of the capacity of the armed forces to wage war as it is the reflection of an attitude toward involvement in war, and I thought it curious that in the mass of material put out by the army there is no suggestion whatever that the service commanders had at any time thought seriously of full-fledged operations outside the boundaries of Indonesia.

The relevant paragraph in "The Concept of Defense" document says, "We have a policy of active defense, meaning that it is not aggressive. Our view of war reflects the principles of Pantja Sila, that is, the Indonesian nation is peace-loving and wants friendship with all nations; it does not want war. Indonesia will go to war only when everything possible has been done to prevent war and when there is no other way to settle a dispute with another nation, therefore [sic], when Indonesia is compelled to resist in the national interest."

This, of course, is standard international double talk, the language of mass-media diplomacy, suspect from any source—the language which has made necessary the creation of a race of political commentators whose enormously important function it has become to interpret official and political new-speak to ordinary people. But in spite of an instinctive suspicion, the impression has remained with me that most of the top men in the services have an equivocal attitude toward the Malaysian campaign, recognizing it as a purely political maneuver of doubtful outcome, yet being forced to support it with some appearance of enthusiasm simply to match the ostentatious nationalism of the Communists.

And so the impression grew upon me during these journeys

that, whereas the top echelon of the Communist Party seeks total political power and plans only to that end (probably with the best of intentions), most of the army leaders, under Nasution, are genuine sentimentalists who want only to protect the Republic which they created for the people in the days of the Revolution.

For the army was, indeed, the People's Army, the first-born of the Indonesian Revolution, the first tangible national symbol of determined independence. It won the Revolution, not so much, perhaps, by what it achieved in a material military sense but by existing simply as evidence of an inchoate native Indonesia, recognizable by the rest of the world, evoking admiration at home and sympathy abroad. When independence came it kept control of the country and put down Moslem and Communist rebellions while the President experimented with various systems of government. It has stuck to him and to the country, seeing them as indivisible, and still considers itself the family watchdog, an essential part of a revolution which is by no means completed but which will continue until there is a reliable civilian machinery to take over its functions.

From the point of view of the army the Malaysian campaign is a nuisance, and the Communists are doing the country no service by pushing it. If pursued to the point where it flares into a proper war it would mean the destruction of the army in a war against the West; but to oppose the Communists openly at this moment would bring about a fragmentation of the army in a civil war. From everything they say, write, and do, it would seem that Nasution and the army commanders understand this very well.

So Colonel Achdiat was saying, "Our aim is to integrate with the people of the villages and to establish a relationship between them and the army on an organized basis so that they have a specific function in time of war and understand their role and responsibility. They will have to undertake sabotage against enemy installations, gather intelligence, work out a system of communications between the village authorities and the guerrilla army units. They will have to organize emergency food and medical supplies, some kind of first-aid service, transportaton, fire-fighting.

"If we are invaded we shall have to fight that kind of war, and one of the first laws of guerrilla warfare is that the army cannot win without the support of the people—they learned this years ago in Yugoslavia—and to get this support the people have to want their army to win because they trust it."

But it is twenty years since the declaration of independence and a new generation of soldiers and officers has grown up in a different political and emotional climate. They take the same grave oath of loyalty to the Republic and the President, obedience to authority, respect for all fellow-citizens, and are abjured to abstain from fornication, theft, idleness, alcohol, and opium; but a peacetime army of 250,000 needs work if it is to be kept out of mischief and, seeing this clearly, the army staff is concerned with defining and putting into action a purpose and a program which will hold this huge group together in a commonality of particular loyalty and honor. It is the possibility of this achievement that the Communists seek to prevent and undermine.

A motorcycle escort picked us up at the approaches to a small town and went wailing in front of us, until we turned into a barracks square and cut with our convoy clear through a mad, mock battle in which militiamen and civilian Crush Malaysia volunteers fought wildly, hand to hand, cheered on by children who ran in and out among the combatants screaming and throwing stones and giving swift, barefoot kicks at them, then running away fearfully.

The soldiers played on, unembarrassed by our cutting through their battle, a secondary wave of attackers now using us as cover from which to aim their mock shots at the imitation enemy defending one of the barracks buildings. Some hung to our vehicles, turning us into trojan horses; others, bedecked with twigs and sprigs of greenery, lay on their stomachs, wriggling from one imaginary piece of cover to another, then at a whistle leapt to their feet and charged extravagantly upon their adversaries, shouting and brandishing toy rifles, taking no notice of our reception by their own commanders and town officials going on within fifty feet of them.

It seemed a splendid fight and a pity to stop it, but the yells of the men, overlaid with an excited obligato of screaming children, whistles, and bugle blasts, drowned out our welcome so that an officer was sent to end the battle and exile the children beyond earshot.

We were now received with dignity, seated as in school, and made welcome with speeches while girls brought tea and small things to eat; then, with the general briefing done, they led us to the community meeting place to feed enormously on chicken and other meats, rice, and fruit, while the civilian leaders of the district made generous speeches of good will and welcome. Afterward we were dispersed and billeted among villagers.

I partnered the lesser general of the two in our party, a short, thick-set man of good humor who, when shown the room which we would occupy, chose for himself a narrow-planked divan on which to sleep, assigning to me the curtained family bed, hung with lace tied back with bows and spread with embroidered sheets and pillows. Hassan, our host, stood in the doorway anxious that we should be pleased with his wife's preparations for us, hiding two of his children behind the skirts of his sarong.

Before trying the beds we took coffee with him in the small front room of the cottage, attended by neighbors including a brother-in-law from next door, a cousin, and the village teacher and made ourselves known to each other. Hassan sat cross-legged in a chair beneath a colored lithograph of the great mosque at Mecca and the motto "Love and Peace"; a slim, sad-eyed man with a swift, shy, feminine smile, who listened while the others talked and kept our cups filled until the general yawned and said that he should sleep. He went then to his planked divan and I to the curtained bed, with a tiny oil lamp between us.

Hassan woke me before dawn, praying, then came with coffee. I got up, the stars still in the sky, and went to the village bath house, a well-like room with water pouring in through a pipe at one end, chest high, and out again by a tunnel on the other side, and so down a bank and into the river. The water was earth brown and warm from yesterday's sun, and came into the bath house after passing by gutters and bamboo pipes through other houses higher up, filling fish ponds and water tanks on the way and bringing down effluent; but by now my susceptiblities were disciplined and I stood under the flow without flinching.

We were in a village of some two hundred people, decent, frugal, peasant folk whose way of life, although spare, is pegged at a respectable level: a neat place held on a slope between road and river, its northern end bounded by wet rice fields and the southern end dropping away into a valley. The houses are all of an equal smallness, built of wood and stone and with tiled roofs, each house having a small forecourt with a fish pond and square, stone, water tank filled by the unfiltered overflow from the rice fields. They seemed decently although cheaply painted (a noticeable detail after the raw austerity of the villages farther east), with their insides furnished adequately, although in most cases sparsely, each house having a sitting room and principal bedroom in the front and a single large living and sleeping room at the back.

For the first two days I joined the officers and went with them about their business, seeing how they met together with the village committees, gave lecturettes, split into groups to analyse resources and requirements, made maps and plans of the area, discussed theoretical military actions, lines of communication, hiding places, and made an inventory of arms and weapons. Religious and political factors were noted, a census made and broken into statistics—so many men of fighting age, men trained in police or army ways, veterans with military experience, men skilled in certain trades and abilities, able women (especially those practiced in first aid). They discussed means by which the army might help to increase local food supplies and livestock and to improve communications.

Then, when I had watched enough, I walked from village to village with small boys leading me and found kindness and ready welcome in each place, tea or coffee or cold drinks, and people pleased to let me see whatever I would. In one place was a man making the little lanterns which hang outside each house, simple things of tin and four pieces of thin glass, with a piece of palm leaf twisted boat-shape to hold the oil. Next door, was a family making hats, the black, brimless *kopiah* worn by Moslem men and boys (made fashionable by the President). Then came two toothless old men sewing with hand-cranked machines, one making a woman's blouse and the other patching a coat.

In the weaver's house (he was away meeting with the officers) I watched his eldest sons make cloth for sarongs and drank thick, sweet coffee, the beans being crushed in a dish with a wooden pestle by the weaver's wife, a beautiful and calm young woman, mother of nine children, the last carried in a sling hung from her shoulder. Watching her I remembered that I had asked the doctors in Semarang to explain the serenity, the smooth soft skin, the calm, and the plasticity of Javanese women. Their medical concensus had been that their women seem young and desirable, even after bearing ten children and working from girlhood in the fields, because to keep their skins soft and clear, they keep themselves covered from the sun, wash only in cold water, and drink *Djamu,* which is an infusion of herbs and grasses; that they remain serene and uncomplicated because they understand and accept their position in society and give it dignity; and that they are so proud and busy attending to their children and their husbands that there is little room in their minds for inner conflict. They had said that the modern Western way of life gives many women wider opportunities for expression than before, but there was no gain in this for any woman if she denied herself the one great opportunity that nature gave her for herself alone.

In most of the villages there were slogans painted on the walls of courtyards, but these showed no belligerence. One read, "If I offend you, tell me, and we will pray together." Another addressed passers-by on behalf of the householder; "If we have done wrong to you, known or unknown, forgive us." A third declared: "We must help each other to stand strongly."

In one village there were no women to be seen, only a few old men; but as I stood talking to them a girl hurried by and the old men said that she was going to the mosque where all village women gathered with the older children, twice each week, to receive religious instruction from the Iman, and that this was the custom of the district, and no woman stayed away.

I came back from one of these visits to neighboring villages and sat in the forecourt of Hassan's house to make notes of things I had seen, and while I was there a woman came to the back of the house and went inside. Soon after this Hassan came out, sharpening a small, curved knife blade on a stone and said that the woman had a bad headache and had come to be cured. He set the knife and the sharpening stone down on the doorstep and took a small copper pot from his pocket, of the kind used in Eastern cafés for serving coffee, then took a leaf from a bush growing beside the house and put it into the pot, blowing upon it gently.

He called to the woman and she came and lay down inside the house with her head hanging outside over the step. Hassan prayed for a moment, then took the blade and made a small incision in the woman's forehead. Blood began to drop slowly and he moved the pot into position to catch it, watching closely. He waited a while, then rapped her forehead with his knuckles, listened, then prayed again, after which he looked into the pot. Then he took a piece of rag from inside his shirt, spat on it and dabbed it quickly on the cut in the woman's forehead and held it there to stop the bleeding.

I watched him, then, take the leaf out of the pot and examine the spots of blood that had dropped upon it; then he held it to his breast and prayed over it and quickly went to the edge of the rice fields alongside the house, scooped a hole, buried the leaf, and washed out the pot into the fishpond, where carp came eagerly to his hand, thinking to be fed. He returned to the woman and tapped her on the shoulder, at which she got up stiffly, paid him, and went her way through the rice fields toward a village on the side of a hill about a mile away.

Later, a man came complaining of pain in his thigh, and I watched Hassan's fingers feel along the man's muscles for several minutes while his lips moved as if in prayer. When he found what he was seeking he poured spirit onto a twist of paper, lit it, dropped it into his little copper pot and clapped this mouth downward onto the spot where his finger had come to rest on the man's thigh. It stuck there, held by suction, the man remaining unmoved. Then Hassan pulled the pot away and taking an open-bladed razor made a nick in the man's skin, causing blood to flow, which he caught in his pot, explaining to me that pain is caused by evil elements which enter, unknown, deep into the body and must be drawn to the surface by prayer and let out through the skin by bleeding.

I saw then that Hassan was the village Dukun (or healer) and learned later that he also was thought especially holy and called upon by most of these villagers to choose the days for rice planting and harvesting and for special family ceremonies. At such times he keeps vigil and prays at intervals through the night while those who have come for advice keep him company.

We talked again that evening when neighbors came to visit for a while, and Hassan, bidden by his brother-in-law, went into the back room and fetched a photograph of his father which he passed among us, so that each of us held for a moment this old portrait of a round-faced, stubble-whiskered, elderly peasant, wearing a tarboosh, his shirt buttoned tightly at the neck, looking steadfastly and without expression at the camera.

The schoolteacher said, "He was also a holy man and he was killed by a Gurkha when the British were here." We looked at Hassan, waiting for the story and, when he had whispered to his brother-in-law, he told it, speaking softly and in the local dialect so that I could not follow clearly until the general, seeing me in doubt, translated.

"It was during the time after the big war when the Japanese had given in, and the British were here to keep order. They had a troop of about fifty Gurkhas stationed in this area, but the villagers thought they were Dutch colonial troops or mercenaries and so treated them as enemies and did them damage at every opportunity.

"One evening some of these foreign soldiers came to Hassan's father, who was head of the village home guard, complaining that one of their men had been ambushed and killed on the outskirts of the village and that they must have three hostages to hold until the killer was discovered. The old man denied that any one of this village had been responsible, and much argument ensued.

"The leader of the Gurkhas then said that to gain satisfaction and make example he would shoot Hassan's father and, pulling out a pistol, pointed it at him and pulled the trigger, but the pistol misfired. Then the old man boasted that he was protected from bullets by the power of the holy kris which he wore at his waist, so the Gurkha pulled the kris from his girdle and struck him in the stomach with it and killed the old man there and then in his own garden."

He is buried in a corner, with his wife and some children of the family, at the edge of the rice fields overlooking the river. Next day, in the evening, I saw Hassan kneeling there saying his prayers.

It is deceptive, the gentleness that seems to lie over Java like a soft silken spread; behind the quiet, calm eyes and the serene faces of the people are sharp-edged memories of violence and disaster, death, war, hunger, and privation, back through generations. I was impressed by the neatness of this village until I found that almost every house had been built in the past five years on the ashes of a previous home burned to the ground by fanatical Moslem bands.

"The Darul Islam rebels came seeking help from these villages, wanting the people to join in the uprising against the government, but the people were loyal to the President and would not help them, so their houses were burned down, their crops pulled out of the ground, their oxen killed and eaten by the rebels." The General was lying on his back on the narrow divan, smoking a cigarette and looking at the ceiling, while I sat on the edge of my curtained bed listening to him. "Foreigners smile at the extravagance of our language and often do not understand what seems to them a strangeness in our actions and behavior. When Our Leader talks about the message of the people's sufferings they shrug their shoulders, but we know what he is saying because all of us have shared in these sufferings from before we were born.

"This is why we understand each other, why officers of the army can live and work as brothers with these village people, because we are the same as they, share the same history of oppression, feel the same pain and the same pride, face the same future whether it brings progress or yet more tragedy. The slogan you have seen out there in the other room, 'Love and Peace,' is no pious text, it is a prayer from the heart of the people."

On the fifth day we walked to a far village, all of the officers and a number of civilian officials from Jakarta who had joined us; men from the Foreign Office, the Treasury, and the Law Department, who took part in the exercise to gain experience of army methods and procedures, to study the administrative problems and implications. This is all part of the Nasution plan to integrate the army not only with the civilian population but with civilian officials throughout the whole complex structure of government. This is what the Communists seek to prevent. What the President thinks about it nobody knows.

I walked with dapper Colonel Achdiat, who told me that as a member of the student army during the Revolution he had taken part in a month-long march from Jogjakarta, through this country, almost to Jakarta, harassing the Dutch at river crossings and crossroads, laying ambushes for them, setting traps. The student army had no transport, no aerial support, no radio communication with headquarters, and no boots; it walked barefoot.

"We won our country from the Dutch, and we will keep it from any nation that tries to invade us, even if we have to go barefoot again and fight for another fifty years." I had long since given up trying to explain to anybody in Indonesia that no Western nation would want to invade the Republic so I said nothing, but merely walked on beside him in silence in the bright sunshine along the ridge of a long hill; but he seemed to read my thoughts and said, "We know that the West will not invade us for reasons of gain, but we are afraid that the West may want to save us in the light of its own diagnosis of our troubles and according to its own prescriptions, without asking us if and how we wish to be saved, and from what."

At the end of the ridge we looked down onto the village and saw the reception committee waiting in line to meet us, some thirty or forty men, women, and young people, representing each political and social group in the community: the Lurah, the schoolteacher, the policeman, the leader of the women's committee, youth group leaders. When we came down to them we passed along the line, each of us greeting each of them with a gentle Islamic salutation, touching finger tips together, then breast, lip, and forehead, a bow, a murmured "God be with you": acknowledgment of common kinship under Allah.

We gathered under a coppice of orange trees at the edge of a big fish pond, the guests sitting at tables that later would be filled with food. The Lurah spoke of the recent history of the village, the loss of life and property at the hands of the rebels, their coreligionists, and the progress they had made in rebuilding.

He spoke of their plans: of their vision of a new Indonesia without feudal or foreign overlords, with no divisions between the people, only peace, and time to build their own kind of society; not following Capitalist or Communist methods or ideologies, but finding something distinctively Indonesian, based on their own historical concepts of equality, brotherhood, *Gotong Royong* (building on mutual help from below), each village and villager contributing to an equal progress rather than trying to outstrip his neighbor.

"We do not ask for much from above, only peace. This is why we welcome you men of the People's Army to our village, because you are a sign of peace and a promise of protection. If you can give us this we will do the rest, for our needs are simple and our ambitions moderate."

When he had done speaking one of the officers (the fat one who played the part of the company comic) went back over the hill and in a while reappeared with a boy who led a male goat and two nannies down to us, the fat officer providing much extravagant pantomine until the procession came to a halt in the middle of the company. The general who was my roommate stood up and, when the laughing had stopped, made an amiable address of presentation, saying that the officers wished to integrate and make this contribution to the resources of the village, hoping that the animals would practice Gotong Royong (much laughter from the men and giggling by the women) and so prosper and increase to the profit of the people and the honor of the army.

Then, when we had fed, almost to excess, he spoke again saying, "After so many years of war the villages are poor but their hospitality is rich, and in all things that are good and in the tradition of the Javanese people they are an inspiration and a challenge to the leaders of the country who, with the help of the people and the People's Army [polite and approving nods all around] will resist the persistent pressures to follow the 'hot dog or vodka' philosophies which people inside and outside are trying to foist onto our country."

We went to other villages to make speeches and give goats, and in the evening we met in the market town to be entertained with music, singing, and dancing, first being led to the meeting house by an anklong band of lads beating bamboo tubes with sticks to a syncopated rhythm.

A chubby young woman dressed in black sat on a stool clutching a pink plastic shopping bag on her lap and looking for all the world like an oriental Britannia or Queen Victoria; she sang patriotic songs impassively in a high-pitched, nasal, wavering, Asiatic mode, using traditional tunes to words set by a local poet. She sang in a stolid contralto, "Let us all unite under the five principles of Patja Sila to Crush Malaysia and the Imperialist." The officers cheered and demanded more, pointing at me and calling out, "Sing for the Imperialist," then slapped me on the back, laughing like children. But she sang, instead, about land reform and the avarice of the big landowners, calling on us to arise and destroy them, at which the officers cheered more loudly and pointed to their fat friend, calling out in rhythm, "Crush him, crush him, his father owns a rubber plantation." And the villain doubled over, holding his huge stomach and shaking with laughter.

Other young women danced, then men, then children. A small girl danced the *pentjak* (a male fighting dance) and a man squeezed in beside me and whispered that this was not good because the child would turn into a witch when she got older. The Lurah made a presentation of bows and arrows to the officers' school, gave the general a fishing rod from the people, and gave a Wayang puppet to Colonel Achdiat. Then the officers sang in groups, comic and topical songs, the Lurah sang; I sang, the people cheered. Every little while I reminded myself that this was a serious military exercise.

CHAPTER

21

In the morning, taking leave of Hassan and his family, I set out for Jakarta with two officers who, having official business in the capital, were able to take me. We drove westward through the hills, past tea plantations, savoring again in recollection the simplicities of the past few days; and I said it seemed to me, a stranger, that the people of Indonesia needed, more than anything else, a time in which to breathe easily, to rebuild what had been broken, to put once more into motion the smooth rhythms of orderly existence and so provide a starting point from which to work toward the new accomplishments planned by the President.

They were silent for a while, but when we had gone some kilometers further and were coming to a town, one of them said, "We would like to have peace but like all other people in this world, whether in Asia or America or Europe, we have little say in these things. The ordinary people of the world, whether they be Indonesians, Americans, Chinese, or Russians, are pieces moved on a chess board by their leaders; it is all the same. Sometimes the leaders make a wrong move, and if they are too proud or stubborn or stupid to admit it they lose the game and their people pay the price. Then the board is set up for the next game and another generation gets moved around."

Again there was silence until the driver pointed to a black speck in the sky, coming closer, which turned into a helicopter swinging southward in long, looping curves like a hawk hunting. It passed above us, its sound diminishing as we separated; then coming into the town we drew up at a café in the market place, close to the bus station.

Hills hold Sukabumi as in cupped hands, rising all round in wet terraces of rice and the darker green of tea. High above the town, on a mountainside laid bare by an earthquake or slide, a rock face running with water shines like a sheet of glass in the mid-morning light; but the market place and the streets that run from it are dusty dry, and the light is harsh.

People were standing in clusters by the buses or sat in the cafés, waiting. *Betjak* boys hung about hoping to pick up passengers who might come with too much luggage to carry comfortably by hand. A few farmers were doing long-winded ritualistic business with the town merchants, although it was not a main market day; otherwise, the square was empty except for occasional ox and pony carts passing through and scavenging goats and some children playing in the corner under a clump of white-trunked warringen trees hung with yellowing, dry-season leaves.

A thick-waisted farm woman walked past with live fowls hung by their feet from her belt, encircling her like a feather skirt. Then a man came selling eggs and another with beans and melons. A beggar with no legs propelled himself swiftly toward us with wooden blocks tied to his hands to play the part of feet. When we had given our orders to the waiter he came closer so that we could put offerings into the tin tied around his neck. Then we were silent, having talked ourselves out on the way, the officers no doubt weary with the strain of making safe conversation.

Five minutes passed, and a bus came, and there was chatter and a little shouting as people claimed baggage from off the roof and *betjak* boys jostled to take it and to claim the passengers. A man looked up and pointed to the sky and others followed his gaze. The goats stopped meandering and shuffling in the dust and looked up too; and there was the helicopter again, but this time swinging low inside the ring of the hills, making a tight turn above the town before stopping to hover over the market place.

An ox cart crossed the square, the driver sitting half asleep on the shafts until people began to shout at him and point upward at the helicopter, and when he understood he jumped down and ran to beat the ox with his hand but the beast shook its head and plodded on without changing its gait. The children had come from under the trees and were standing with their faces turned to the sky. A waiter, coming from the kitchen, walked out into the square with a bowl of rice in one hand and cutlery clutched in the other. People in the cafés, left their food to the flies and came outside into the sunlight, looking upward.

A driver shouted to a boy on the roof of his bus, asking him to hand down baggage; but the boy, gazing into the sky with his mouth open, bag in hand, did not hear but suddenly looked down and shouted, "It's the President, the President."

The helicopter was dropping down. The goats, alarmed by the loud noise of its engine, lifted their heads high and ran with uncertain steps, bleating. A boy threw stones to chase them to safety. People were coming from everywhere, out of side streets into the square, lining its sides, eager, excited. The helicopter steadied and hesitated a few feet from the ground, its rotor beating up dust; then it settled gently in the center of the square and tick-tocked to a stop. Hundreds of men, women, and children stood around the sides of the square, watching as if hypnotized.

The door in the side of the machine opened and a young soldier jumped out, wearing the red beret of the Palace Guard. He let down a set of folding steps and stood back, saluting. There was absolute silence, then a sigh like a wind stirring trees, and the President stood framed in the open doorway like a statue. It was theatrical and eerie. The whole town seemed to catch its breath, to gasp and become perfectly still for several seconds; then there was a scampering and whispering that reached into side streets and alley ways as more and more people began to stream into the market place. The whispering grew to a sea sound with shouting and the high-pitched cries of children excited and partly frightened.

The President stepped down and came toward the trees where the children had been playing: tall, straight-backed, impressive; aware of himself and of his powers; playing a part, creating an image of greatness. The young soldier hesitated, turned to follow, then turned back again to the helicopter and reached up a hand to help a woman down the steps. The crowd spoke her name, "Hartini." She walked after her husband smiling, bright-eyed and very beautiful. A few other people came after her: a young man who may have been a secretary or aide; two white men who had the surprised, uncertain, bemused look of visitors caught up in something unexpected; then two young palace guards without arms.

He came into the shade of the trees and stood waiting for Madam Hartini and her companions while men, pushing through the crowd, brought chairs for them. Within minutes, it seemed, there were perhaps ten thousand people packed in the square staring at their President and his lady, whispering, nudging each other, standing on tip-toe, straining to see better. (At the café we stood on chairs and saw clearly above the heads of the crowd; other people were on tops of buses or looked out from upstairs windows.)

He wore a dark khaki uniform, the ribbons of the revolution, the familiar black cap, and he carried a baton. He sat looking around calmly, spoke briefly to his visitors, smiled at his wife. The townspeople in the front row, closest to him, looked awed and uncertain and were worried by the pressure of the crowd pushing them in toward the President.

Leaning forward a little he began to sing a Javanese song, beating time with his hand and encouraging those closest to join in. The crowd took it up but was interrupted by shouting and confusion in one corner of the square where town police and other men were forcing a way through. When they came into the little clearing in front of the President and had formed up in front of him, he held out a hand to greet them: the Bupati, the mayor, the chief of police, the army commander, and the judge, still straightening clothes changed hastily, making it plain that the visit was unexpected.

These greetings made, they stood to one side. Women in the crowd began to sing again, with the men joining in where they could, and the President, the Bung, their brother, their uncle, beating time. He called two little girls from out of the crowd, who hesitated shyly but were pushed forward and in a while, with encouragement and cajolery, sang sweetly although petrified with fright and excitement; when they were done he called them closer and put his arms around him and spoke kindly before letting them go.

I looked at the people close by and saw in their faces such devotion and joy that I was amazed: men and women, faces alive with delight, some crying with happiness, some praying. Whatever doubt I might have had about the power of this man, the gift he has of taking hold of the hearts of his people, the bonds of loyalty that bind them to each other, left me then. I could not believe it to be the evil fascination of a ranting, fanatical demagogue, but the genuine and rare power of a man who has the elements of both greatness and simplicity.

I, a Westerner, might feel afraid that this man can, and in my opinion does, make grave mistakes in the exercising of his greatness; but to his own people he is almost supernatural, a character out of the Wayang, who comes from heaven in a helicopter, sits before them like a sultan, and tells them what to do.

So now, in the market place, he called the five officials to ask if they had settled the troubles that had recently caused anti-Chinese riots in the town; had they repaired the damage and paid compensation to merchants whose stores had been broken into and looted? While they talked the crowd began calling for a speech and men attempted to assemble a public address system; the air was filled with the crackle and screech of amplified feedback and oscillation, which irritated him, for he waved the men and their apparatus away and called upon someone in the crowd to lead more singing.

Then he stood and began to walk back to the helicopter, the crowd parting to let him through, and as he went some drew back in awe and others leaned forward to touch, while a small boy walked behind staring up at him; Hartini followed, smiling.

The door of the helicopter closed on them. The engine spluttered and the motor began to turn, stirring thick billows of dust and grit. People moved back a little but continued to stare in silence until the machine, howling like a hurricane, rose off the ground. Then, even over the sound of the engine, I heard the crowd sigh as though released from an emotional imprisonment, and ten thousand faces stayed lifted up until the black dot disappeared, leaving an empty sky and silence.

We spoke little during the rest of the two-hour journey back to Jakarta, and in the quiet my mind went back over the month spent in these islands; in Sulawesi, Bali, Sumatra, and Java, months packed with impressions of people and events which, spread out for inspection, spelled out simple, clear things. They said that here were people with a highly civilized culture and many social instincts and characteristics that are in advance of our own; a people not educated to be egocentric, selfish, greedy, not ambitious to outdo friends and neighbors; a sensitive, creative people courteous to each other and kindly toward strangers.

They have been kept in a state of poverty, servitude, and technological ignorance for centuries but have retained their character and intelligence, and at rice-roots level have developed efficient systems of organization that can be adapted to raise their living standards to twentieth-century ones. The whole huge archipelago is rich in resources and economic potential. The people are industrious. Every necessary element for success is present. That much is clear.

It is also clear that in the context of their history their President is a genuine folk hero. His title, Our Great Leader, is valid all over Indonesia. Where is he leading them? That is not so clear; but I cannot yet go along with those who say that he is mad, like Hitler, or stupid, like Mussolini.

I talked to all kinds of people in Sulawesi, in Bali, and in Sumatra, and to people from the outer islands. At some time during the past centuries they have all warred against Java, and the resentments (kept alive deliberately by the Dutch) flared into rebellion, uprising, and revolt as soon as the Java-based republic was born. To deny the paternal patience, the clear-sighted perseverance and leadership, the achievement of Sukarno in uniting these proud and diverse people on the basis of a personal loyalty to himself is simply to be perverse. To write him off as anything less than he is would be unrealistic.

He won independence for his people and afterward gained West Irian (with the help of the President of America). Although both gains were political rather than military victories, with the world on Indonesia's side, the barefoot student army in Java and the dedicated guerrilla volunteers in West Irian gave these events the authentic Wayang flavor, a magical fairy-tale dimension, proof of the infallibility of a pure heart, faith in the gods, and a high-minded dedication—things not to be despised in any national leader.

In his next vision, which he called Maphilindo, the President saw a Southeast Asian Federation embracing the Philippines, Singapore, Malaya, and the ex-British possessions in North Borneo, with Indonesia as the cornerstone and senior partner. Theoretically at least this would have removed the last unsightly marks of Western colonialism from Borneo without bloodshed and paved the way for an integration of the ex-British possessions into greater Indonesia. But the British created Malaysia and destroyed this dream.

It was several months before the President saw (or was convinced by Comrade Aidit) that Malaysia was an Imperialist plot to keep not only North Borneo but the whole of Southeast Asia out of his sphere of influence and within that of Britain. The vision of Maphilindo grew dim and he realized that he had been swindled. He was understandably and dramatically angry. "We will," he cried, "crunch up Malaysia and spit out the pieces." It must have been maddening, without doubt, to be cheated with such swift, unprincipled, manipulative skill by so decrepit and decadent an adversary as Britain. He coined a new slogan and with the help of Dr. Roeslan Abdulgani made it a patriotic catch-cry, "Crush Malaysia."

In doing this he may have gambled more extravagantly than he realized at the time. The Malaysia issue gave the Communists the break they had been waiting for, a chance to redeem the mistake they had made in 1948 when they sparked off a premature revolution against the Jakarta government. At the same time the obligation to back this anti-Malaysia campaign with inadequate arms and insufficient equipment hung the army up in a stick so cleft that, in trying to extricate itself, it may yet split in two.

This does not mean that President Sukarno cannot win his gamble. Malaysia, the late baby of Britain's old age, is congenitally feeble and with Singapore's strength withdrawn is hardly likely to survive; and insofar as the Crush Malaysia campaign has the limited aim of "liberating" the North Borneo territories from neocolonialism and bringing them into the arms of the Indonesian Republic, there is still a rough chance that Sukarno could win this third trick of the series simply by persevering with the same methods that won him independence and West Irian. The rights and wrongs are fairly evenly distributed, and it is likely that only Australia (sadly irrelevant in such matters) would want to interfere with any enthusiasm in a jungle conflict between Britain and Indonesia.

But by moving the dispute out of the northern corner of Borneo and into Malaya proper, the President has stepped out of parlor politics into the major league where his ideological desire to "free" Malaysia from Imperialism is no more or less valid than Russia's "protection" of Eastern Europe from Capitalism, or the United States "safe-guarding of the freedom" of Southeast Asia against Communism. In this spot-lit arena guns and money on a major scale are the only effective currency; fine speeches, bleeding hearts, and barefoot armies are merely stage paper for cynical, ritualistic exchange. To win in this league President Sukarno must go into partnership with someone a little more materially substantial than himself.

His enemies in this situation are the sycophants big and little; those who want him to go in and lose and those who are paid to say that he can do no wrong. Together they egg him on to grasp at glories for which neither he nor his people are historically ready. The Indonesian people and their leader have not yet finished building the monuments to their own revolution, to their own freedom; much less are they ready to play the part of architect and builder to any other race and nation.

We were coming close to Jakarta when the officers, who had been dozing, woke; and one of them, sitting up and stretching, said, "Well, you have seen our President with his people. Do you believe that he will betray them to the Communists?" He was smiling, except for his eyes, which were anxious, and I felt that he was asking me to comfort him with assurances. But I shrugged and said that I was no expert in these matters and no prophet, and that it was mostly easier to start trouble than to stop it.

To myself I thought: the plot and the characters in a Wayang play may be manipulated all night long by the Darlan and made to weave marvelous tales of mighty heroes armed with magic powers, men in direct communication with the gods, themselves being demi-gods who defy giants, trick wizards, destroy by might or guile all who oppose them, and annihilate their armies. But when dawn dims the shadow images on his sheet the Darlan lays his puppets aside and locks them in their box, where they no longer have life or meaning. Men pick up their hoes and go back to the fields. Women return to their weaving. The night is for dreaming, daylight is real, even in Indonesia: even for the great Darlan, Sukarno.

PART VII

Jakarta-Sukarnapura

CHAPTER 22

Five days in Jakarta, uncertain, with nerves on edge. Deciding that the time had come to leave Indonesia, I had dispensed myself from the obligation to be tolerant and now found the daily trivial inefficiencies irritating. I had also complicated my departure by asking if I might quit the country by its most extremely easterly exit, by way of Sukarnapura, capital of West Irian, where a local service could put me across the border into the contiguous territory of Australian New Guinea, which seemed to me a logical maneuver in several senses.

In West Irian I could see the most primitive and undeveloped part of the Republic; I could watch Indonesia play the role of a colonial power (for, whatever polite words are used, the fact is irrefutable that the people of West Irian are Papuans and not Indonesian by race or nature or even by choice, whatever they may be by politics); and if I could leave Jakarta within the week I would reach Sukarnapura in time to attend the ceremonies celebrating Indonesia's Independence Day in its most remote province, in the capital newly named for the President. There may have been an element of sentiment in my reasoning, but this I excused by underlining to myself the good sense of being able to see how matters stood, comparatively, between these two territories, divided only by politics and an arbitrary line on the map, one side now governed by Indonesians and the other by my own people.

But the matter of travel to West Irian is complex and hedged about with administrative dubiety and uncertainties. There is a single flight each week and the service is reserved for passengers on government business. The Foreign Office had said, "Yes, go ahead, we will arrange it." The West Irian Office said, "It is difficult, unusual. Why can't you go the regular way, straight from Jakarta to Darwin?" The airlines office said, "We can promise nothing. The seats are allotted by government priority the day before each flight. It may take months to get you on and even then your place could be canceled ten minutes before take-off. Better you go the other way." They were all patient and polite, making allowances for a stubborn, irrational white man.

I said, "My ticket is endorsed for the next flight, and I have a Foreign Office priority to go with it. The Secretary-Coordinator of West Irian Affairs has invited me to be at the Independence Day ceremonies at Sukarnapura. I am prepared to sit at the airport all day, to sleep in the waiting room all night, if necessary." One after another they shrugged, went into inner rooms for consultation, came back, gave me other forms to fill in, asked for more photographs, told me to come back tomorrow.

I was not impatient. I had done all I wanted to do in Jakarta, had heard all the explanations, listened to all the dreams, had exhausted my capacity to absorb and to sympathize. So I waited for hours in offices only to be sent to others on the far side of the city for different signatures, another piece of paper. But no matter. I kept telling myself that there is no reason why people who have just been given access to the administrative machinery of this technological civilization should be adept with it. In any case I was a foreigner, little more than a tourist, less important than most other travelers—and I was being crudely persistent and difficult.

The time was not all lost. Waiting in the anterooms and offices I could sit and think or talk to other people also waiting. There was a Papuan student from West Irian, studying at the Teachers Training College in Jakarta on a government scholarship (in this office dozens of such young men and women went in and out). He said that many West Irian students, used to village food and plenty of it, were hungry in the capital and went to work to earn money but, although eating more frequently, missed much of their studies. He himself spent much time driving a taxi for a Chinese owner.

A pastor of the Papuan Evangelical Church, waiting for a permit to return to West Irian, had come to see his son, newly graduated in medicine. But the young man had joined the Confrontation volunteers and gone to Borneo to be an army doctor. The pastor was disappointed. "We thought he would come home and work among his own people. His mother had been counting the days until he came and she could be proud among the other women. But young men are restless these days and dissatisfied with village life."

Several families came with an official and stood together uncertainly in the foyer while he went away along a corridor. The pastor said, "They are from Central Java, going to start a new settlement in the mountains of West Irian, among wild people. It will be hard for them."

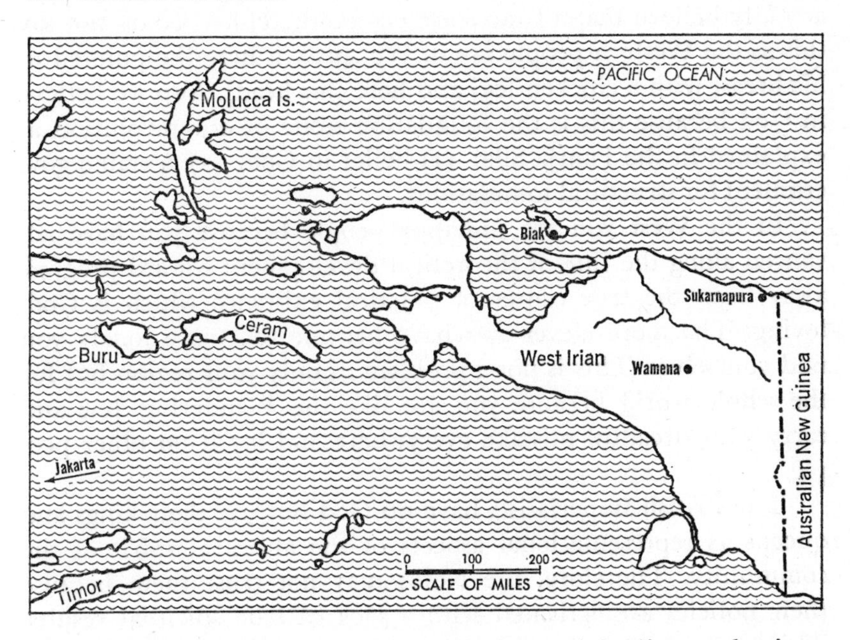

One morning I had breakfast with General Sutjipto, who is an elf disguised as a departmental administrator: a compact civil-military figure of middle age (gray tinge at the temple) tending to firm rotundity, short-sighted, bespectacled, benevolent. He smiles like a child, without guile, and speaks like the Congressional Record set to wild music.

"My friend, the people's confirmation of the will is accompanied by the realization which is dependent upon the executors of the task. This is important because we have to suit it with the outcomes that we have gained in order to turn up the geniality of the Indonesian Revolution, the Indonesian people, and the Great Leader of the Revolution."

I could think of no answer to this, so I said simply, "Yes."

The general's nonmilitary title is Secretary-General to the Conference of Supporters to the Revolutionary Leadership, Head of the Fifth Column of Supreme Operation Command, Secretary of the Coordination of West Irian Affairs. He is responsible to Dr. Subandrio for all that takes place in West Irian. His mission is to show the whole world that a non-white emerging nation can develop a backward, alien people with more efficiency and humanity than any white colonial power has ever done.

"We begin at the heavenly advantage that Indonesians do not despise any people because of his race, color or economics. We actually believe that all races are equal; therefore, we do not say this as the Western people say it. We speak it here [he pointed to his breast with a chicken leg] and here [his head]. Also we believe in God because this is the foundation stone of our revolution as explained in the Pantja Sila: (1) belief in God, (2) a stable government for structural foundations.

"In the West you are unhappy people because you have advanced along the line of theoretical development toward progress away from the true center of practical existence which is God-loving. The more clever you have become the more lonely you find yourselves. This is not a problem of only your region but for the whole world because you are like the Wandering Jew and carry your dreadful mistake everywhere and lay it on other people.

"The British Imperialists have no God but use their kings and queens as representational aspects of the ancestral spirit of the community. Therefore, the Nefos may not trust them because their policies are activated with a lack of true spiritual results. This explains the neocolonial project 'Malaysia' which was created to undermine our revolution."

There was nothing to be gained by interrupting, and for that matter the message, uninhibited by syntax, had a magic, flashed through with shafts of lucidity, which not only fascinated but shot home.

He scraped more rice onto his plate while vigorously chewing chicken and continued. "Americans have much respect for God the same as they love their old grandfathers. But he must not talk too much when they are doing business with the devil. He must hide behind the door. But still they believe in God and in consequence they are not so expert at politics as the British and make many big mistakes."

He led me then into a conference room rapidly filling with officials who wandered around finding their places by name cards set out on desks. As each found his place an attendant came with plates of food; rice, meats, and spices. Then a clerk brought each person a heavy package of books tied neatly with wide white tape, the main book being more than an inch thick and foolscap size—an outline of the general's plans for the development of West Irian.

There were, in the end, sixty or seventy men, representing other ministries and government agencies, sitting in the room facing Sutjipto, who stood at a lectern, beside a blackboard and easel. Models, photographs, graphs, and diagrams filled in blank spaces. Once more the dream, the vision splendid; this time in West Irian.

They picked at their food while Sutjipto spoke of "the duties that are burdened on our shoulders, the duties of the revolution, the self-propelling, self-acting, self-supporting confirmation of the people's will to reconstruct West Irian, to build up the power of cooperation, the democratic power guided by wisdom which guarantees the concentration of the whole national powers—people's powers—in gaining its goals, a spiritually just and prosperous society! The Imperialist-colonialist powers, concentrative powers, of people who are not willing to understand about the direction of our move must be swept away with a motto, 'All that spray will be torn, all that cross will be broken,' and for our journey let the dogs bark while the travelers pass."

This is lyricism, much of it borrowed from Sukarno, the master. There is nothing one can do but listen: even if it means nothing it is better than the stuff to which we are accustomed. But there is no point in repeating the program (and Sutjipto's lyricism is difficult to sustain in translation). The blueprint for developing underprivileged nations has become commonplace, familiar to every schoolchild.

In another generation the whole world will be one great working model of material efficiency; there will be nothing, anywhere on this earth, to amaze or take the breath away, nothing to love, nothing to pity; nothing to surprise or admire. It will then be time to move to some other planet.

Later in the day I took photographs of Nah and her niece in the garden behind the house, under the frangipani tree. The dove in its wicker cage, with its head to one side, cooed tentative enquiries. The green and purple lizard looked down from the top of the wall where it lay in the sun. Nah and the girl were excited, taken by surprise, insistent that they be given time to tidy themselves.

Nah scampered into the house giggling, and the girl ran into the cupboardlike room behind the bathhouse, her legs bared almost to the thighs under the mud-brown rag of an old sarong which she wore while working around the house. She came back in a few minutes wearing an ankle-length blue-brown *batik kain,* tight-fitting, a mauve breast cloth, and a black lace-work jacket. She broke a cream-yellow blossom from the frangipani tree and put it in her hair, then stood in the dappled shadow, hand on hip, looking at me with serious dignity as though we had never met before; as though this were a beginning and not an ending. For a moment I wondered if I wanted to go home.

In the evening Soejono and his wife came to say goodbye, and we went with my host for a farewell dinner downtown. I had not planned it this way; I would not have brought together for the occasion two men so dissimilar and in so many ways ill-matched: the faithful old revolutionary hack and a disillusioned post-revolutionary youth.

I fished around for a conversational gambit, trying to keep away from politics, with Soejono's wife helping, but we made no progress. Then the waiter came with beer, and the old man asked him for an evening newspaper. Soejono pulled a face. "Why do you bother with them? You can feel the freedoms dying around you one by one—no need to read the official obituaries."

The older man was unmoved, feeling no need to enter into any discussion or dialogue of justification. In any case he had never been one for words; the young man's cynicism bothered him no more than rain showers bother an old rock; and suddenly, after these many months, he seemed real to me for the first time. I had used his house each time I had been in Jakarta, had talked trivialities with him for hours, and only now, with my mind full of the journey through Java and what it had taught me, I saw the solid reality of him and of a life spent since boyhood in the service of the revolution, much of it in prison and in exile in the fever-ridden swamps of West Irian.

For Soejono the word "revolution" was singular and definitive, referring to something which had happened recently in Indonesia, a splendid victory that had somehow become dissipated, had blossomed magnificently, but had borne rotten fruit. He felt cheated. But the older man had asked nothing of the revolution except that it succeed. He looked forward to no Utopia, no sudden upsurge of prosperity, expected no personal reward. A quiet man, he saw himself simply as part of all the revolutions that have happened, one after the other, since the beginning of mankind's history—each one a shaking-off of shackles (no more than that), a manifestation of the human will to be something better than an ox, to seek some system of survival which would give protection and at the same time permit human dignity.

For him there could be no end to revolution. It was a continuing thing, a process, an expression of the energy and motive force that keeps propeling mankind forward, rocketlike, to the ultimate goal of total knowledge and a final revelation of its role in creation.

He had been part of this Indonesian revolution, had helped to make the Republic. He had felt, from the beginning, the ache, the longing, and the desire of his people for freedom and identity, and he had worked all his life for its alleviation. He could hold out his hands and say, "These fingers guided a pen to write pamphlets, they sketched posters, scrawled slogans on walls, dug trenches, drove trucks, cut rice for men in hiding, fired rifles when necessary; these hands, this body have always been busy with the simple chores of revolution." Alongside the questioning, self-driving Soejono he seemed a little dull and vague; but without his kind, Soejono and the rest of the hundred million Indonesians would still be in servitude.

When the waiter brought the newspaper he held it up to the light to read the headlines and the lead paragraph of the story he was looking for. Then he took off his spectacles and put them away, folded the newspaper, laid it on the table, and said, "Well, the Bung has disbanded the committee of the generation of 1945." It was as if a parish priest had said that the Pope had proscribed the Calendar of Saints.

A hundred guesses will dart around Jakarta. Dozens of reasons will be given, and although they will be mostly no more than journalistic opinions, many of these reasons will be headlined worldwide as authentic answers to the questions, "Why has President Sukarno done this thing?" Perhaps the 1945 group is secretly playing politics, lining up with other anti-PKI factions, getting ready to move with them into the power vacuum when the time comes. Only one thing is quite clear; Sukarno is still certain of the loyalty of the people; not afraid to keep even the most privileged and powerful cliques disciplined.

And he is a master at this political game, knowing all the moves and making them swiftly. For the second time within weeks he has disbanded a powerful group with deep roots in the soil of the revolution. First the Murba, a nationalistic nonaligned Communist party opposing the PKI. Now the veteran 1945's (both groups loyal to himself). There is a clue, a connecting link: Chairul Saleh, third Deputy Prime Minister, a big man in both groups. A lifelong revolutionary, a "Nationalist-Marxist," he imitates the President in minor mannerisms of speech and gesture and is chief rival to Dr. Subandrio for the presidential succession.

Furthermore, in 1945, when the Dutch were still in possession, a small group of young revolutionaries kidnapped Sukarno and induced him to declare the independence of the Republic of Indonesia. Saleh was of this group, another was Aidit the Communist. Saleh, a Nationalist, became third Deputy Prime Minister. Aidit became head of the PKI. Now, twice within a matter of weeks, powerful anti-PKI nationalist organizations with which Saleh is involved have been disbanded and driven underground by the President. At the same time Dr. Subandrio, who has no popular group support, moves closer and closer to Aidit and to China.

While Soejono and the old man were fitting these fragments of fact into a picture of possibility I was thinking of the two officers with whom I had driven back to Jakarta and how one of them had said, while they looked at me hopefully, "You see, the President will never betray his people to the Communists."

I walked home with my host, Soejono and his wife having gone their way by *betjak,* and we sat on the small brick patio in the starlight and talked far into the night, quietly, the house in darkness and the street lights dimmed to a glimmer (flood lights at the Freedom Monument draw excessively on the suburban supply of electricity). Now that I was leaving Jakarta for the last time he seemed to feel free to speak more openly and completely of his own beliefs; and as I listened, the image of a vaguely outlined minor government official faded and gave place to a real person who spoke to me now, out of the shadows, with the clear, true voice of the Indonesian people: even here, in Jakarta.

"We must trust the President, we have no alternative. The others do not matter, they are politicians and will fight among themselves for power and personal status. Except, perhaps, Nasution, who will try to keep clear of entanglements until he is needed to bring order.

"There will be mistakes and more suffering before we find which way to go, but if people leave us alone we will solve our own problems in our own way. The Western powers must accept this. They cannot force us to fit into a shape that they want the world to take; a shape that suits them best.

"The majority of people on this earth are Asians and Africans, and now that we have broken free from Colonialism nothing will stop us from taking an equal place with the white races; nothing, not atom bombs nor any other form of white warfare. We are too many for you, and you cannot win."

He stopped to light a cigarette and in the silence I realized that he was right; that the white West can achieve nothing in Asia and Africa unless it locks up its weapons and approaches the colored world with love and justice.

There is, for instance, no way for America to win the war in Vietnam: there is just simply no way for a Western power to win an Asian war except by becoming an occupying power—by continuing Colonialism and admitting that even the most advanced section of the human race is not big enough or intelligent enough to solve its problems except with ham-fisted threats of destruction.

Equally, the British must eventually lose the Malaysian game, regardless of Sukarno's by-play and its side effects. The Malayan people are Asians and sooner or later will take their country out of Britain's hands without particular reference to Sukarno or his opinions; in this context he is little more than a red herring. No interference by Western powers can achieve anything but a complication of the ultimate solution, delay, more death, and suffering for the Asians.

Soejono had said at dinner, "Let us Asians kill each other if we have no other way of solving our problems or finding our answers. Better to be killed methodically by a local terrorist who knows who and why he is killing, than to be wiped out accidentally by a foreign advisor who scatters death indiscriminately and without knowledge of our problems."

And Dr. Suharso at the Rehabilitation Center in Surakarta said, "Modern medicine and surgery have wonderfully reduced the number of completely crippled children all over the world, but power politics has replaced them ten times over with horribly crippled adults." And we had gone on to talk of the hypocrisy of power politics, the sickening fiction that one nation could "free" another by bombing it, that for one side to shoot its opponents in cold blood was tyranny while the other side could be "morally justified" in burning whole villages. We had come to the conclusion that God, in His misery, would find it easier to forgive the Communists who did not believe in Him, than the Christians who claimed to be doing His work.

The answers are not easy to find but if the West is proud of its superior level of education and understanding, then the West should take the lead and not stand pat on its achievements, leaving the colored world to catch up if it can. And taking the lead means that Western people must themselves find leaders who can see ahead, who have visions, and above all faith in the ability of humanity to find its way bravely through the dangers. White leaders have unsolved problems of their own, real problems that cry out for answers; it is presumptuous of them to claim the right to deal with the evolutionary problems of the colored races and down right criminal to attempt to deal with these problems by methods they would not dare use at home.

"The West can help us," said my host, out of the shadows, "but it should help us all, not try to separate us into pro-Western and anti-Western, into Communist-dominated and democratically-oriented. The West must let us find our own way; and the best it can do is to set examples and help us to reach up to them. It should not be concerned whether our director of agriculture or education or health is a Communist or a Nationalist, or even whether he loves you or not: that is our affair. If you honestly want to help us you must not ask questions. You must not demand that we love you. You must first earn our respect and then learn to return it."

Soejono had borrowed a car to take me to the airport. We went early because I still had doubts about my reservation, even though

General Sutjipto himself had assured me that it carried his signature; and there were whispers around the town that air services to Australia and its New Guinea territories might soon be closed down in protest against its support of Malaysia. I had no wish to be left stranded in Sukarnapura.

We made a call at the United States Embassy to return a borrowed book and passing through the lobby took a last look at the portrait of John Kennedy, bearing the inscription:

> This painting is a gift to the American people from the artist, Mohamad Thamdjid of Jakarta:
>
> "I am an ordinary man, a self-taught artist. I have painted this portrait of President Kennedy out of my strong and sincere feelings for the loss of a great man who worked for world peace."

An embassy messenger, passing through, stopped to speak. "Kinda nice, isn't it?" I agreed, and he went on. "Seems crazy to me that guys like these would think of burning down the embassy." I looked surprised. "Yeah, some of our boys been getting letters—'Remember what we did to the British.' " He shrugged and went on along a corridor, shaking his head.

When we came to the airport, the clerk, running his finger down the passenger list, said, "We don't have a seat for you." I was not surprised: I showed him my tickets, permits, recommendations. He went down the list again and shook his head. Without speaking Soejono gathered up my papers and, telling me to sit and wait, went away. A boy sidled up and under cover of the Communist daily paper offered a boot-leg copy of *Time Magazine.* In half an hour Soejono came back to say that a passenger had given up his seat for me. I said I would like to thank him but Soejono said, "He doesn't know about it yet. He's a student going back to West Irian and will be glad to have the extra week in Jakarta." I asked no questions.

We shook hands and he gave me an envelope. "This is for you, a souvenir that you may remember me. You have a good heart. One day you might wish to remind yourself that Indonesians are people like any other people. That we are not mad, irresponsible brown savages. That we can even learn to forgive white people, if they will help us to do this." Then he went.

CHAPTER 23

In 1969 the people of West Irian may freely decide: to remain within the Republic, to leave the Republic, or how is it to be?

President Sukarno
August, 1962

Leave 1969 to me.

Dr. Subandrio
May, 1965

"There is no question about it. We are already part of the unitary state of the Republic of Indonesia." Governor Bonay[1] seemed surprised that I had thought it necessary to raise the subject. A slight frown creased his forehead, his fingers tapped the arm of his chair, and he gave me a birdlike look.

He is a sharp, neat Papuan in a dark suit, with slender hands and feet and a thin moustache. He had received me pleasantly and we sat, now, in deep basket chairs on the tiled patio of the governor's guest house, overlooking a blue harbor ringed with deep-green hills and, below, the roofs of the little tropical town that had long been Hollandia and was now Sukarnapura, capital of West Irian, two thousand three hundred miles from Jakarta.

[1] Now advisor to the Coordinator of West Irian Affairs, resident in Jakarta.

Eliezar Bonay: born 1924 on the island of Serui near Biak on the north coast of New Guinea, son of a village headman, sitting on the patio, framed by canes of scarlet and orange bougainvillae against a background of yellow hibiscus bushes, where the Dutch resident used to sit with his favored guests and drink Bols, where the Japanese Commander held court, where American General Douglas MacArthur strode, godlike, back and forth issuing edicts that would send tens of thousands of men into one battle after another.

Through glass doors I could see into the reception room; there were deep chairs and lounges, a grand piano from Paris (the cook has scratched the names of the notes onto the keys so that his children may learn to play with more facility). President Sukarno looks down from the wall, his picture not quite covering an unfaded patch left by a larger picture of Queen Wilhemina that was once there. Prince Diponegoro rides his white charger along the opposite wall.

This morning I sat alone at the long table in an adjoining dining room and was served seven fried eggs for breakfast, and bread as well as rice. In three days' time a special flight from Jakarta will bring General Sutjipto and other officials to take part in the Independence Day celebrations. Then the house will be filled with important people.

Governor Bonay was telling me about himself—his rise from schoolboy to government clerk, to councilor, and so on until, with the change from Dutch supervision to Indonesian in 1963, the Great Leader made him the first governor of West Irian.

"When the Japanese first drove the Dutch out of our country we Papuans began to think of independence, and we looked forward to the end of the war so that we could begin to govern ourselves. But when the Americans came to drive the Japanese away they brought the Dutch back with them, white men helping white men, and we knew then that we could never expect help from the West but would have to fight for our independence and for every other step forward."

Then, in 1945, when news came of Sukarno's declaration of Indonesian Independence, Mr. Bonay knew where his road lay; knew that the Dutch would never give up their bit of New Guinea except under international pressure; knew that there was no help to be had except from Sukarno, and no possible future for the people of Western New Guinea (West Irian) except as part of the Republic of Indonesia. Had the Australians in the other half of New Guinea made any gesture of encouragement it was possible that the whole island of three million people could have been integrated and developed under the protection of the West, but Australia lives politically in the nineteenth century, has not the habit of initiative, is more conservative, even, than Mother England—is negative.

Eliezar Bonay, clerk in the Dutch administration, joined the Indonesian Nationalist party and, with others, began to create a network of liaison with other native independence groups in Dutch New Guinea. He made contact with Sukarno, using the crewmen of interisland trading ships to carry messages to and from Jakarta. He studied the President's writings; became his disciple; and when, eventually, Sukarno proclaimed his determination to take West Irian from the Dutch "before the cock crows on January the first, 1963," he was among those who, in the dead of night, all over the country, raised the red and white flag of the Indonesian Republic above Dutch government offices and patrol posts and on the highest mountain in each district. The Dutch had continued to promote him. In 1962 he was native assistant to the director of home affairs and in the same year went to Jakarta as part of a political delegation.

He met the President.

"He was my hero, my inspiration. When I saw him my heart jumped. I walked toward him in a dream. I whispered, 'Father.' Told him of my loyalty, to him and to the cause of Indonesian unity and the inclusion of West Irian within the Republic. One nation from Sabang to Merauke.[2] I said, 'We are your lost children, come for us, join us again with our brothers and sisters.' We embraced and wept together."

The President kept him in Jakarta to study the Indonesian system of government and administration; found him a Javanese wife; and when the Dutch at last capitulated, sent him back to West Irian to be its first governor. He renamed the little capital Sukarnapura in honor of his hero, the Great Leader, the Dispenser of Independence.

[2] Sabang, in the northern part of Sumatra, and Merauke, on the southeastern border of West Irian, are 3,300 miles apart, the most widely separated towns in Indonesia.

There are eight hundred thousand West Irians (the country is not yet fully explored, and there may be others not counted). A few hundred have been as well educated as the governor. Some few thousands may be more or less literate—the Dutch were concerned only with creating a class of minor public officials among the native people. The picture is much the same in most ex-colonial territories. Since the Indonesians took over they have established a university. Nine West Irians have become members of the Republic's House of People's Representatives; two others belong to the President's Advisory Council.

Hukum Jiri, paramount chief of sixty thousand West Irian savages, sat beside me in the Cessna wearing a khaki shirt, a tie, and cloth trousers. He had been to Jakarta to meet the President and was going back now to his people in the high valleys, having promised the Great Chief of all the tribes that his people would stop fighting and quickly strive to become civilized citizens of the Republic. Some of them might even volunteer to join the anti-Malaysian volunteers.

There are other tribes and other highland chiefs in the middle of West Irian, perhaps 150,000 people all told, maybe more, discovered within the last ten years; naked stone-age savages. Men wear only a penis gourd held erect with strings, and women (like little wrinkled apes) cover themselves briefly with sparse wisps of withered grass.

Hukum Jiri has asked the President to send clothing for his sixty thousand people to make them civilized (Adam and Eve, seeing they were naked, were ashamed). But in spite of such backwardness a young man of the tribe has gone to the new university at Sukarnapura.

We smiled at each other, nodded, touched each other affectionately, and pointed to features of the landscape we flew through so that we could share, however insubstantially. We had no language to link us, but the pilot, a missionary, had a smattering of the valley talk with which to pass our simple patter back and forth.

He lifted the nose of the aircraft slightly and leaving the lowland swamps behind, aimed upward into a great gray pass, between walls of limestone. Once through this gateway we leapt wide and wooded valleys, each higher than the last; came in another hour into a jumble of peaks rising naked from dark green jungle;

and, climbing to gain height, out of cloud cover, saw on the far horizon the main range with its highest peaks snow-capped.

Hukum Jiri touched my hand, laughed, and pointed. The pilot over his shoulder said, "Mount Sukarno, the highest point in West Irian." We turned into a wide, bleak and shallow valley and for the first time since take-off saw signs of human life: clusters of grass huts and little mission stations spaced out precisely—an iron-roofed homestead, a church, a school, and a shed or two; then at the end of the valley the flash of sunlight on aluminum which in a minute took shape squarely and became a squat row of government huts. Hukum Jiri beat happily upon his breast, chanting "Wamena, Wamena, Wamena."

We touched down and taxied along the grass runway, bumping, and stopped by the aluminium huts. A young man met us, Soedarno Kartodichardjo (age twenty-six), graduate in social and political science at the Gadja Mada University, Jogjakarta; he was now research assistant to the Resident of Wamena, capital of the Central Highlands (uncontrolled) area of West Irian.

As always, there was unfailing, simple courtesy: a room in the aluminum barracks, an iron cot, two army blankets, a candle, a nail upon which to hang my clothes. As I unpacked my haversack, Soedarno told me that he was busy planning "the first essential project of the coordinating committee to implement the President's four-pronged objective and directive for the social, economic, political, and cultural development and integration of the people of West Irian into the constitutional and practical framework of the unitary Republic of Indonesia."

We walked, then, a little way to where men were building a machinery shed or hangar and here met the Resident of Wamena, mending a wheelbarrow. He was a cheerful, practical man from Makassar who said, laughing, "Rome was not built in a day," and, having shaken hands, bent over the wheelbarrow again. When it was made work-worthy he gave it to a laborer to shift bricks.

But later in the day a giant Air Force Hercules screamed into the valley to drop machinery for road-making and earth-moving: three parts of a seven-ton roller, each lashed onto a platform, hanging in the air under huge parachutes; a tractor and a jeep. "Tomorrow they bring us a truck and a grader," said the Resident.

Two Dakotas landed on the little grass runway to unload

smaller gear, benzine, prefabricated aluminum houses, and huts; then a dozen soldiers, to join the Civic Mission Company already camped out beyond the tiny township, their task to start an agricultural and livestock experiment farm.

Parachutes and landing platforms were retrieved and stowed inside the Dakotas, which took off, back to the coast. A few dozen tribesmen with stone axes clenched in their hands, stood gaping at the take-off, disbelief printed on their faces.

Soedarno checked what had come against lists in his office and said that with three such aerial visits each week for three months Wamena would soon be a fully equipped developmental center and his "plan" could be put into operation. "We shall achieve in the next ten years what the Dutch never did. We will materialize material and spiritual well-being, awareness and mental upbuilding [social overhead capital] to carry out economic developments for the materialization of abovementioned, especially the need for food and clothing."

And as a coda:

"Our West Irian people must first clothe themselves, then plant potatoes and tomatoes and other vegetables. This is the beginning of my plan. Afterward we will have many model villages for the people, community farms, roads, resettlement schemes, etc., to show the old established colonial forces what is possible to do for backward and dependent people." Except for syntax the speech was familiar; it might have been spoken by a colonial politician or administrative official of any color or race.

I went along the valley to a Christian Mission Station, through tribal gardens of sweet potatoes growing in long, oblong mounds, divided by deep drains. The valley soil seemed rich enough, but the mountainsides were bare and bleak, eroded into bunkers, humps, and sinkholes.

The missionaries came to these valleys first, before the government, in the time of the Dutch. They came mostly from the United States and Canada, and some of the early ones were killed quickly by these savages they had come to save for Christ. Those who came to take their places report little progress: some children in the bush schools, some young men and women training to be teachers, nurses, Christian group leaders.

Tribal elders, as a politeness, gave seven children outright to begin a new school, but refused to let any others attend, saying they could spare no more to spend their time sitting inside, watching a white man make marks on a piece of board. If there were some magic to this that could be demonstrated, well and good, but it seemed unproductive. It seemed foolish that children should be so engaged when they might be minding pigs, gathering food, or learning to fight against other clans and tribes.

While I sat in the missionary's kitchen a naked old man came to ask if he might borrow a gun because three big cassowaries were destroying his garden. When, after much discussion, he went (without the gun) the missionary said that seventy-two men had been killed in tribal fighting in the past few days, and this man's brother one of them. The "cassowaries" to be shot were most likely men of the clan who had killed his brother.

The missionary's wife, feeding chocolate and cookies to her blonde baby, said that tribal fighting was a nuisance and inconvenient: "Our cook-boy was killed a few days ago, and now I will have to find and train another." The thought obviously displeased her.

Bedbugs living in the blankets fed well on my legs in the night, raising red lumps that irritated. I left, not envying the Javanese peasant families who were coming as pioneer settlers to help build a new Jakarta in this raw, remote, and primitive land.

Waiting for the missionary aviator to come for me I walked out into the valley and, looking up into the mountains, sheer and forbidding, thought back the way I had come, through the twisted ranges, the high barren valleys, the jungle and swamps between here and the coast, and wondered what desperation first drove people into this ultimate of isolation, separate from the rest of mankind; into this dreary desolation of wet and cold and primeval discomfort: How many hundreds or thousands of years ago was it that the ancestors of these tribesmen found their way here, and why?

When the plane came there was a white woman waiting alone on the edge of the runway; middle aged, slim, fair hair unkempt, blue eyes in a thin, sad face that might once have been fresh and pleasant and still held impressions of long-ago happiness. She wore a neat cotton dress, but faded, and carried a small traveling bag with a broken lock, a strap round it.

When she saw that I was waiting for the plane she laughed,

seemed excessively excited, almost gay, and asked a question in Dutch which I answered in German, in which language we began to converse quaintly (neither being sufficiently fluent to speak easily). Airborne, going back to Sukarnapura, she told me her story.

She was Dutch, from a small town in Friesland where her father was a parson. She had gone to stay in Rotterdam with an aunt who let rooms to students, one of whom was a Javanese. In time he asked her to marry him. She came to Java and was married according to the Moslem rite, to the distress of her parents—a few tears hung along the edges of her eyelashes—nor was she entirely sure in her heart if she were properly and decently married in the eyes of her own Lord Jesus.

They went to live in Sourabaya, where the young man, a marine engineer, was employed in the shipyards, and here made many friends among others who had similar ties with Holland. But when the Dutch left Indonesia most of these went too, and although she said nothing she secretly hoped that her husband would make the same decision. But he believed in the revolution and was proud to stay and work for it. Then, because he traveled a great deal, inspecting and working on harbor installations all over Indonesia, she was lonely much of the time, although two babies kept her busy.

They moved to a smaller town on the coast where there were few Western-educated people and were here during the Communist uprisings. Part of this time her husband was away, and at the height of the fighting, when the Communists were scorching the earth behind their retreat from government troops, she was alone in the house with her children and an old serving woman, the doors and windows locked and a loaded rifle ready, although she had never used one before. For three days they stayed inside, listening to the fighting, the mortars and rifles, and the sound and smoke of sugar cane burning in the fields.

As she told her story she seemed to be talking to herself, pouring out the misery and disappointment of her life, the longing for security among people of her own kind; not looking at me except to make some emphasis, but speaking as if to a priest or lawyer who would listen and, in due course, forget.

She spoke of her husband (*meinen Mann*) as though he were a child and she protecting him, even from her own unspoken reproaches. "A good man, so kind, so gentle. He does not fight." I could see him, quiet, almost obsequious, conditioned like a peasant by centuries of suppression to accept, not to fight, not to struggle. "We are so poor, we have not enough money to buy clothes, must always eat rice instead of bread."

She had a high, crying voice. A tight line of tension ran down the side of her face and along the thin column of her neck into the hollows. She seemed as sad and lonely as a statue.

Her husband had been brought here to West Irian to inspect harbors and shipping facilities around the coast, an assignment that might take months, perhaps a year. They have a house in the town but he is away most of the time and there are no other European women in the area. But a missionary family, passing through and hearing of her, had asked her to visit them in the valley. After several months she had come, to find that the missionary's wife had gone north, to Biak, to have a baby.

She felt let down and guilty for having gone: as though by needing someone of her own kind to talk to she was being disloyal to her husband. She tried to explain it all, but our German could not cope. As we came over the coast and headed toward Sukarnapura she closed her eyes and cried out sharply, so that the pilot looked around, "I am all alone . . . *Ich bin ganz allein.*"

When we landed there was a car to meet me so that I was able to take her the twenty miles into town, but there were others in the car and she was silent and politely smiling. When we let her out she ran quickly to embrace her brown, dark-eyed children. Later I came back and quietly left a few things on the veranda: some tubes of processed milk, some soap, a tin of cheese, a piece of printed cotton that would make a simple dress—things I had brought with me for gifts. Then I walked away, feeling as though I had left a few flowers on a grave.

CHAPTER 24

Independence Day At Sukarnapura

Let us make West Irian a sparkling emerald in the belt of Indonesia.

Sukarno

Yesterday we were all at the airport, drawn up on the tarmac to receive the President's flag—that is, the Indonesian officials, armed forces and police units, the youth groups and schoolchildren, and students from the university. We stood in ranks forming three sides of a square. Fortunately, there were storm clouds all around to block out the afternoon sun, so that although the plane was late coming from Jakarta (a special flight and we had long to wait), it was not unpleasant standing out on the tarmac. Inside our square were four lads and a girl, Irianese, dressed in white, waiting to accept the flag.

When the plane came it brought fifty students from Jakarta who, when they had disembarked, made a corridor through which one of them, a girl, escorted by four boys, solemnly and with great dignity carried the flag in a casket, carved and draped with a yellow satin stole, so that it was secret, hidden, almost sacramental. As it passed between the two lines of students a girl fainted and two soldiers ran to carry her away.

The group from Jakarta came forward and stopped, facing the

local party. The casket was passed to the Irianese girl and together the two groups slow-marched across the tarmac, those from Jakarta smartly, but the local ones with some self-consciousness, being less involved in the mystique of the occasion. A convoy of army trucks took them to Sukarnapura, where Governor Bonay met them in the residency with further ceremony, flanked by officials and service commanders. He took the casket carefully and laid it on a table in the guest pavilion, stood silently for a while, then bowed over it and stood back. Officers saluted; the Iman said a prayer. Young girls in the gay costumes of Java, Bali, Sumatra, and Menado were for a moment solemn, as if aware of being within the aura of a mystery, a presence. A man beside me said, "The President's flag is holy, like the sultan's kris." Sentries stood guard all through the night at each side of the table.

At dawn a thin mist of fine rain covered the town and hung in veils about the green hills. The road down to the parade ground was muddy and little rivulets ran in the cracks. A canvas shelter had been put up for officials, but troops and schoolchildren stood in the rain. On the edge of the parade grounds, unsheltered, is a temporary dais, a table and, a little to one side, a new flag staff. A few hundred Irianese cluster to one side of the ground, sheltering under trees.

There may be a thousand people altogether. (In Jakarta the President will soon be making his Independence Day speech to a hundred thousand at the stadium and to millions over the radio.) Here the rain gets a little heavier. The service contingents, facing us in long double lines, take out their capes and put them on. Irianese children shake their woolly heads and send shining drops of rain flying from them like silver sparks. A group of students in white tunics stands by the dais to receive the flag. The Irianese girls (unlike the slim, catlike Indonesians) are blocky, broad, and big-chested. The rain makes their thin tunics stick to their heavy breasts and thighs. Department of Information men are fussing with the cameras and microphones, trying to keep them dry.

In the center of the front row in our shelter is General Sutjipto from Jakarta, still smiling, although in a moment he must go down to the dais to receive the flag and make a speech for the President, in the rain. Governor Bonay sits next to him, chain-smoking and looking at his wrist watch. There is a fat admiral from Jakarta in white uniform, wearing a sword with gold tassels. He has a resentful look, seeming to hate this small-town stuff, wishing he were back in Jakarta among the big-wigs.

At ten o'clock exactly General Sutjipto leaves the shelter and goes down briskly to the dais. Thunder rumbles around the hills, and a thin wind sweeps over the ground. The general smiles and waves away an umbrella brought by a soldier. The soldier retires a few steps to the rear and stands under the umbrella himself. A photographer comes and crouches beside him, then a thin, shivering dog.

The wind comes again, bringing with it a scudding rain that makes the schoolchildren break and run to the shelter of the trees. Water begins to trickle through the official enclosure, making shoes wet and muddy. Women pull thin wraps more tightly around bare shoulders. Out in the rain the general sneezes. The admiral looks irritable and fiddles with the tassel of his sword.

Then far away the beat of motorcycle engines and the thin wail of a siren. The rain comes down faster and the general's broad shoulders are soaked. He takes off his spectacles and wipes them, still smiling. The powerful drumming sound of motorcycles comes closer and suddenly the cavalcade is creeping down the hill toward us, the outriders leading a line of white jeeps. Adults standing under the trees send the children back into their places but themselves stay sheltered.

The Irianese students who are to meet the flag smooth themselves and stand straight again. As the cavalcade drives onto the field we can see a girl sitting in a closed car with the casket on her knees. She wears long white gloves. When the cavalcade stops by the dais there is an uncertain pause and a soldier who has run around to open the car door looks up first at the rain and then at the general. He nods. The door is opened and the girl steps out. The rain stops. We all look at each other and smile.

The girl, escorted, walks toward the general, who now has a priestlike look. He takes the casket, reverently lays it on the table, opens it, and takes out a message from the President. The loudspeaker system has failed and nobody can hear what he is saying. He folds the paper and lays it to one side. A trumpet sounds across the grounds. His hands disappear into the casket and at the same time a drum roll begins, at first quietly, then, as he slowly brings the flag into view, louder, until it thunders in the ears. Four naval cadets step forward (the admiral has his head to one side and watches critically); they take the flag, neatly unfold it, then carry it opened, one at each corner, to the flag staff, bend it to the halyards, and slowly, slowly send it up, flickering in a fitful wind. A band begins to play "Indonesia Raja Merdeka Merdeka," the national anthem: "Great Indonesia, Land of the Free." Halfway up the staff the flag wraps itself round the wet staff and stops.

We are all standing tense, staring; schoolchildren with wide, white eyes. Even the soldiers, saluting, watch fearfully. The admiral is angry. The band hesitates. Then the flag frees itself and goes on up to the top, red and white waving bravely. The band follows it, proud and loud; and I suddenly feel that the President is, in part, forgotten; that it is the country, Indonesia itself, that holds them; that they are bigger than one man. Beside me a major wipes his eyes.

When the flag is made fast we all sit down and look at each other, laugh, make inarticulate sounds of joy and undefined emotion. The rest of the ceremony is relaxed and uninhibited. We offer each other cigarettes, and I am glad that I am not in Jakarta.

General Sutjipto, again beaming, hangs a medal around the neck of a tall, bearded student from the university—one who was in the party which climbed Mount Sukarno to plant the flag of the Republic upon its peak. The general stands tip-toe to the task, then clasps the young man to him, although his stomach makes this difficult. We clap and laugh. Photographers ask him to do it again so that they can get pictures. The clouds have blown away, and the sun smiles down on us. Steam begins to rise from the wet ground.

Now we go gaily into the town to the Council House, take tea, chat, make ourselves comfortable, then assemble again: this time in the street where the admiral is to take the salute of the Grand Parade. He is happier now; he gives me his visiting card and asks me to call on him in Jakarta. The dais has been brought from the parade grounds, and he takes his place on it.

I have a good position among officials who stretch in two lines on either side of him, facing the Council House. The atmosphere is informal. Small boys, playing at soldiers, strut up and down in the roadway. People take snapshots of the admiral. Three puzzled goats huddle in the doorway of a store across the street. A lieutenant in green battle dress and high-necked yellow sweater reports that all is ready. The admiral puts one foot forward, placing his hand on the hilt of his sword. General Sutjipto beams widely beside him. The governor throws down an unfinished cigarette and straightens his tie. The lieutenant salutes, blows a whistle, makes a sign. A band begins to play, and we all crane forward to look along the street. The sun beats down brightly on the squat white buildings. They sky is blue above the harbor.

The band comes first: drums, silver trumpets, saxophones, trombones, tubas, and two great sousaphones booming out the bass beat. They stop at the corner of the square to play for the marchers passing the dais: first a company of local volunteers, Irianese, each with an Indonesian flag fixed to a bush stick carried on his shoulder. Darker than Indonesians, heavier, woolly haired, they march stolidly but in good order, and the crowd claps. Then a company of women, fat and thin, led by a woman doctor. They wear men's trousers and shirts and look ridiculous. Indonesian women are too soft and sexually feminine, and Irianese bodies too untamed, for this unnatural and unimaginative disguise.

Nine tenths of the parade is amateur. Volunteer soldiers, naval and air corps cadets, troops mainly engaged in civic mission occupations. Then government workers led by their bosses, middle-aged, thick-waisted men wearing glasses, followed by clerks and office boys. They march untidily, wearing their own shoes, many without socks, some unshaven and needing haircuts. One young man, modeling himself upon Castro the Cuban, has hair hanging in ringlets and a beard, he carries a revolver at his hip and marches out of step. The crowd laughs and applauds loudly.

The director of education and cultural affairs leads his office staff, teachers, and senior students—a soft, short, shaggy man, his heroes being Aristotle and the President, especially the President. Yesterday, when we were talking together, he said, "Before we came to West Irian the natives were not counted as people. Now, after one year, they can look anybody in the face." A lawyer came next, head of the Justice Department; a 1945 veteran who fought against Dutch and Scottish soldiers in Sourabaya. He, too, looks odd in battle dress, marches imprecisely, but salutes smartly enough as he leads his staff past the admiral.

In Jakarta there will be thousands of troops parading past the President—young men like millions of others all over the world, black, brown, white, marching with the chill, deliberate, cruel look of professionally dedicated relentlessness; the negative, stamped-out destructive face of unquestioning, uncomprehending malevolence. Puppets whose function it is to kill on command. The confession of man's inability to understand himself or see his function in the plan and pattern of creation.

I am glad, standing in the dusty street of this little white-walled square, that I am not in Jakarta, where the parade will be arranged, calculated to intimidate, threaten, brag, boast, build up, and perpetuate hate. Here in Sukarnapura, a tatty little tropic town, the Independence Day celebration is a pleasant, positive thing, a simple display of loyalty and patriotism, sentimental, moving (the band plays slightly out of tune).

I have dust on my shoes, scuffed up by the marchers. People keep running in and out to take pictures of the admiral, who now looks proud, glad (like me) that he is here and not in Jakarta, where he would be one among hundreds of dignitaries, whereas here he *is* Indonesia.

But it seems that I am making another mistake.

As we break up and move toward the Council House to have food and refreshment General Sutjipto takes me by the elbow to show me a letter. It is signed by the leaders of the volunteer contingents, young men and women, and it requests the general to send them all to Borneo so that they may help crush Malaysia and rid Asia of Imperialism. These are ordinary, simple people, not Communists or fanatics or cranks. They are like us. We are all like us. We all want to be left alone to live in peace and do things that will make ourselves and those around us happy.

I brought my troubles to the director of education and cultural affairs, who had his boots off and was resting his feet after marching. "It is simple," he said. "You desire peace because there is nothing you can gain from war. You have everything, you are rich"—he was speaking of the West in general—"and for you war is a matter of defending what you have got, what the white world has taken from others over centuries. But for us war is revolution, a necessary prelude to reaching an equal place among the nations of the world. As long as the West tries to hold us back, to hedge us in, to keep a grip on our riches, we will have to fight, we have no alternative. The President has said, 'Do not sell thy soul for a plate of nuts.' If we are dreaming, it is our own dream, you cannot take it from us, not until you have killed every Indonesian and every other Asian and African."

When we had eaten we went, each one, to his siesta, but I could not sleep for thinking of what he and many other decent, generous men had said simply and in all sincerity to me in many parts of Indonesia; men I had found it pleasant to be with, for whom I had developed much affection. I got off the bed and found my note-book and wrote . . . they say that whatever success the West has achieved is flavorless because, to gain it, we have renounced the spiritual principles upon which our civilization was founded, and our way of life no longer has real meaning.

They do not want to imitate us. They see the danger; under-stand the sacrifice of personality and faith that must be made if they accept our measure and estimate of success. Instinctively they resist and resent our efforts to drive or cajole them along the way that leads to our kind of pointless prosperity.

They look at the record of our progress and believe that it offers little hope for the future. They say that we are spiritually sick, politically confused, and engaged in a mad race to chaos; that their own insubstantial dreams are more satisfying than our realities. They feel that any disaster they may bring upon themselves by ignorance, mismanagement, corruption, and inefficiency will not be as degrading as the indignities that the West has already in-flicted upon them nor as painful and devastating as involvement in our crusade against Communism.

They say that we have the power, and the right, to interfere overwhelmingly if and when our own domestic security is threat-ened by their weakness and mistakes, but until then we should re-sist the temptation to interfere in Asia.

This attitude does not seem to me unreasonable. Nor does it seem impossible to believe that there is still time, still a common hope, a shared faith in the ultimate capacity of man to achieve a universal dignity, permitting differences of personality, attitudes, and manners. Love is still potent, still possible of accomplish-ment.

Heroes' Field is a small clearing in the bush, at the foot of a high hill, about a mile from Sukarnapura. A broad gravel path leads down from the road to the far end of the field where there is a simple obelisk set on a platform. There are thirteen low mounds on the stony ground beside the monument and under each low mound, an Indonesian hero.

We drove out from town a little before midnight, with no moon and, coming over the brow of a hill saw, down below, blobs of orange flame: flares, marking the square outline of the field. Arriving, we parked our car at the roadside and joined the draggle of bulky shadows stumbling over the road to gather in untidy ranks on the rough, uneven edges of the field, seeing each other only dimly by the yellow-red fretting of the flares.

We whispered and peered at each other seeking recognition, asking if we were properly placed and what was to happen, for no one could see more than a few feet. Someone flicked a cigarette lighter, peering at a watch by its infinitesimal flame. There was a rustle among us, a susurration, and movements of expectancy.

Then, midnight and the drums.

Quiet at first, rising in a long crescendo. Behind us, up on the road, three sets of car headlights came on, throwing into silhouette a foreground of familiar figures: General Sutjipto, the admiral, and Governor Bonay, their elongated, caricature shadows stretched out along the ground.

Now, with the monument spotlit, we could see soldiers—two with arms reversed standing with bent heads on the plinth; others lined to one side holding wreaths of palm leaf plaited with flowers. But we, watching, remained in shadow, and near us was a smaller group, set apart.

The drumming diminished to a whisper and a trumpet clamored a call above it; and when the far-faint echo was spent the general stepped forward and spoke, apostrophizing the thirteen lonely men lying beside the monument in their gravel graves, without benefit of having lived long beyond boyhood.

He said that they were heroes, although in fact they were little more than a minor miscellaneous expenditure of the Propaganda Section, thrown away like farthings, spent as a gesture. There had been no hope of ever achieving that for which they were ostensibly sent. Young boys dressed as soldiers, dropped out of airplanes into West Irian as part of a propaganda game played by politicians. They fell into swamps, got hung up in trees, lost in jungle, were dead before they ever saw the Dutchman they had come to fight. Heroes? Why yes. And they should have the accolade, being brave boys, patriotic, ready to die for any idiocy clearly labeled "My Country."

Two thousand Indonesians were dropped or put ashore in various parts of West Irian. Hundreds of these were killed, others were captured or surrendered with empty bellies—lads never before out of sight of rice fields being dropped into untamed jungle to play-act as "bandit gangs," "Indonesian terrorists," "foreign infiltrators." The plan had been for them to organize and lead Irian villagers in rebellion against the Dutch, to make raids and commit acts of sabotage. Anti-Dutch underground leaders like Eliezar Bonay would help hide and supply them.

They could not have known that their adventure was as far-fetched as a Wayang play; as a military action, pointless, doomed to failure. But every country honors similar heroes, men who have died dramatically to substantiate some piece of political rhetoric; expendable men who provide corpses for statesmen to praise and priests to pray over.

General Sutjipto had finished speaking. A trumpet sang a slow, sad, simple phrase, four notes rising and falling. As it died another trumpet, far away on a hillside, picked it up. Then another, across the valley.

Governor Bonay went down the wide path, his shadow slithering along the ground ahead of him. At the foot of the monument a soldier stepped forward and handed him a wreath. He climbed five steps and stood before the obelisk with head bent, then went forward to rest the wreath on a ledge. The trumpets called to each other mournfully. A breath of wind stirred the tongues of torch flame.

Other men, detaching themselves from the little group near us, repeated what the governor had done, stepped forward, bowed to the general, then walked the long pathway to the monument, laid a wreath, and walked back again—a soldier, an airman, a naval cadet, the Iman, a Catholic priest, a Protestant pastor (we believe in the equal validity of all religions once you are dead).

Then a Javanese woman went; the man beside me whispered that her son was one of the thirteen. When she had placed her wreath she bowed low, almost to the ground, and remained so without moving for a minute or more. Then she straightened herself and stood looking up into the sky, to the stars hanging above the black bulk of the mountain; a tiny figure, almost like a child in the half-light, and the trumpets were crying. When, at last, she turned to come back to us, we sighed.

The drums unrolled their thunder again. An officer shouted. There was a slap and rattle of rifles as the guard presented arms. A bugle brashly called us back from the luxury of sadness. A car started and we all stumbled in the dark, up onto the roadway to reality, to report back for duty, all of us; to be told what to believe, what to think, what to do, how and why to die, leaving the thirteen lads alone in Heroes' Field. But they had achieved; had attained their greatness.

Before leaving Sukarnapura I took part in the opening of the new West Irian Council House. They buried the whole head of an ox under the memorial stone to give strength to the building. General Sutjipto shoveled the first earth over it, and the three versatile clergymen prayed over the ox head as they had prayed over the graves in Heroes' Field.

There were the usual speeches: Pantja Sila and its Five Principles, the Manifesto, Gotong Royong, the Unitary State, Our Great Leader, and the tyranny of the neo-Imperialists (with the general grinning at me). Afterward we shuffled through the building to look at models, plans, diagrams, and photographs of projects that may soon make West Irian a model province of the Republic. There was the usual feast, followed by dancing in the courtyard, with Governor Bonay and a Javanese lady leading a cha-cha around the fountain.

When I had crossed the border and was in Australian territory I opened Soejono's letter, a single sheet headed, "To a Foreign Friend," and after that:

When they put a rifle in my hand
And tell me to fire at you
I must do it,
Because it is too confusing
To have to choose
My own right and wrong.
But believe me,
If I kill you
I will not do it willingly;
And when they give me my medal
I will weep.

Sydney, 1965

INDEX

BOSTON PUBLIC LIBRARY
3 9999 00016 224 6

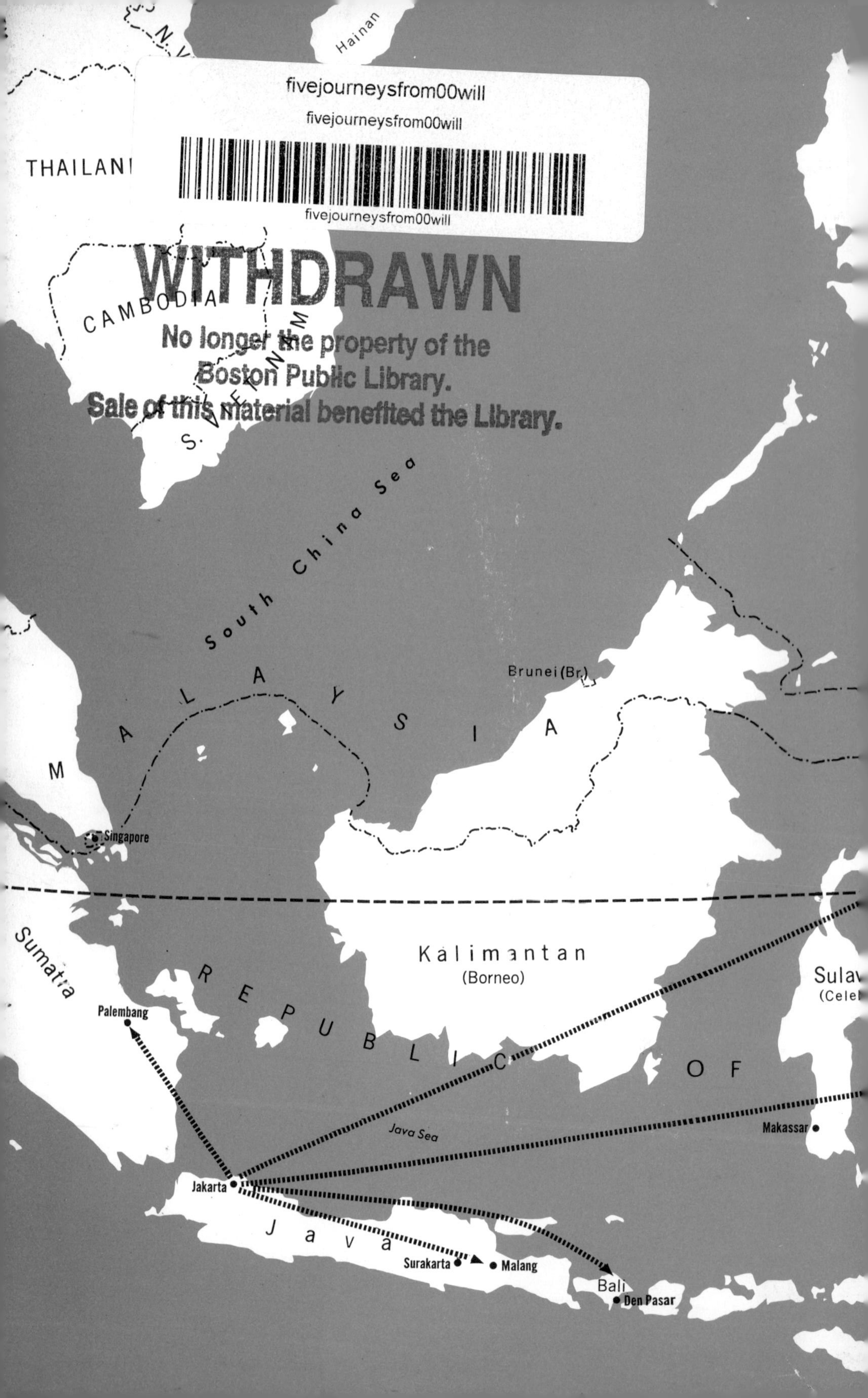
Hainan
THAILAN
CAMBODIA
S. VIETNAM
South China Sea
MALAYSIA
Brunei (Br.)
Singapore
Sumatra
Kalimantan
(Borneo)
Sulaw
(Celel
REPUBLIC OF
Palembang
Java Sea
Makassar
Jakarta
Java
Surakarta
Malang
Bali
Den Pasar